The Reformed Church in China
1842-1951

by
Gerald F. De Jong

The Historical Series of the Reformed Church in America
No. 22

The Reformed Church in China 1842-1951

by

Gerald F. De Jong

Wm. B. Eerdmans Publishing Co.
Grand Rapids, Michigan

Printed in the United States of America

ISBN 0-8028-0661-9

To
Esther, Thomas, Ethel,
and Betty Lou

The Historical Series of the Reformed Church in America

This series has been inaugurated by the General Synod of the Reformed Church in America, acting through its Commission on History, for the purpose of encouraging historical research and providing a medium wherein this knowledge may be shared with the academic community and with the members of the denomination in order that a knowledge of the past may contribute to right action in the present.

General Editor

The Rev. Donald J. Bruggink, Ph.D.
Western Theological Seminary

Commission on History

The Rev. Bernita Babb, M.Div., New York
The Rev. Elton J. Bruins, Ph.D., Hope College
Prof. Bette L. Brunsting, M.A., Central College
The Rev. John Coakley, Th.D., New Brunswick Theological Seminary
The Rev. Douglas Estella, M.Div., Prairie View, Kansas
Prof. Earl Wm. Kennedy, Ph.D., Northwestern College
The Rev. Edwin G. Mulder, D.D., General Secretary,
       Reformed Church in America

Contents

Acknowledgements

I am grateful to the Reformed Church in America for providing me with a modest grant to help defray the travel and other expenses that are naturally associated with researching a book of this kind. I also gratefully acknowledge the help received from a number of individuals. Particular thanks is due my wife, Jeanette, who assisted me in my research and spent countless days in front of a computer typing the manuscript, always realizing there were sure to be additions, deletions, and corrections to follow. I am also grateful to my eldest son, Owen, who graciously took time from his teaching duties to painstakingly read each chapter and make suggestions regarding organization and clarity. Thanks must also go to the following: the Reverend John Hiemstra for the loan of a computer; Russell Gasero, Reformed church archivist, for assistance given me during several visits to New Brunswick Theological Seminary; Arthur Hielkema for graciously allowing me the use of the library facilities at Northwestern College; Professor Donald Bruggink, general editor of the historical series of which this book is a part; and Laurie Baron, copy editor.

Gerald F. De Jong

Introduction

The Reformed Church in America is one of the oldest denominations in the United States, the first congregation having been organized in New Amsterdam (now New York City) in 1628. Like many Protestant denominations, the Reformed church got caught up in the great missionary awakening of the nineteenth century. Within a period of about twenty years, it formally established missions in Borneo (1836), China (1842), India (1853), and Japan (1859). This book is the story of the mission in China.

The Reformed church began work in China February 24, 1842, when one of its ministers, the Reverend David Abeel, arrived in Amoy harbor on the southeast coast of China and began laying the groundwork for a mission that was to last 109 years. Abeel was the first of more than 150 Reformed church missionaries to serve at Amoy.

The term Amoy needs some explanation as there exists both a town, Amoy City (now called Xiamen), and an island by that name. Amoy Island, about thirty miles in circumference, is located a few miles off the coast, and is about 300 miles north of Hong Kong and 550 miles south of Shanghai. Amoy City, whose population was estimated at 150,000 in 1900, is located on the mainland side of the island. Less than a mile southwest of Amoy Island and near the mainland is a much smaller island known as Kulangsu. Although it was little more than a fishing village at the time Abeel arrived, it was destined eventually to become the mission's headquarters.

Amoy Island had a deep water, protected harbor, one of the best in China. Moreover, the estuary and three main rivers gave it easy access to the mainland, including towns like Tong-an, Changchow, and Sio-khe—all of which eventually became important secondary administrative centers for the mission. Because of the ease with which contacts could be made with the hinterland, it became commonplace in the missionary literature of the time to refer to the region as a whole as Amoy and to the mission as the "Amoy mission."

The climate of the Amoy area is subtropical. Bamboo, banyan, and fruit trees predominate, while rice, sweet potatoes, sugar cane, peanuts, hemp, and tobacco make up some of the major crops. Growing two or three consecutive crops a year on the same piece of ground is not uncommon. The terrain is hilly (even mountainous) and often terraced to the very top. Interspersed among the hills are fertile valleys in which are found hundreds of villages of varying sizes.

From the beginning of the mission to its close in 1951, the central purpose was evangelism—that is, spreading the Christian message and winning souls for Christ. At an early date, however, the missionaries also became involved in educational and medical work, both of which can be justified by various passages from Scripture emphasizing the obligation of Christians to perform good works. Interest in education also developed in response to a practical, evangelical need. Because many Chinese were illiterate, teaching them to read enabled them to use their Bibles and understand the religious tracts missionaries distributed.

With each passing decade, these collateral responsibilities—the educational and the medical—received widening attention. Other matters also gradually became increasingly significant, matters that today would likely come under the umbrella of the term "social gospel." These activities included caring for orphans; improving the status of Chinese women; trying to do something about infanticide and arranged marriages; providing relief for opium addicts; and stressing the importance of proper sanitation.

The plan of the book is to begin with an overview of China's political history for those with little or no acquaintance with the country's past. This knowledge is necessary in order to understand how the mission's work fit into, and was frequently influenced by, events taking place in China. Following the political overview, the history of the mission is divided basically into four broad chronological segments as follows: 1842-1863, 1863-1900, 1900-1937, 1937-1951.

The first segment (1842-1863) is concerned primarily with the mission's foundations. The year 1863 was chosen to end this segment because by that date the first churches had been organized and the first Chinese pastors ordained; some work had been done in education; a dispensary had been established; and a union classis or presbytery had been formed with the English Presbyterians. In the second (1863-1900) and third (1900-1937) segments the format is primarily one in which, along with staffing, each of the three aspects of mission work—the evangelical, educational, and medical—is treated in turn. The last segment (1937-1951), containing three chapters, is handled in a more clearly chronological manner. This seemed the best procedure because of the rapidly changing political scene, including war with Japan, reconstruction and civil war, and the triumph of communism—all of which had major repercussions on the mission. The study ends with 1951, the year when the last of the Reformed missionaries left China.

The manner in which the missionaries transposed Chinese characters into Romanized colloquial is discussed in the book. The reader should be aware, however, that Romanization sometimes resulted in differences in the spelling of proper names. Kulangsu, for example, the mission's main administrative center, was often spelled Kolongsu initially. As another example, Iap Han-cheong, the dean of the early Chinese pastors, was sometimes spelled with a "Y" and even occasionally with a "J." For the sake of consistency the spellings that were most commonly used in missionary literature during the closing decades of the mission have been used throughout the book.

The publication of a history of the Amoy mission at this time requires a word of explanation. As an historian who has long been interested in the history of the Reformed Church in America, it seemed appropriate to the writer that 1992, as the 150th anniversary of the founding of the Amoy mission, should not go by unnoticed. What was intended to be a rather brief history, however, gradually developed into something much larger. The reasons for this are twofold: (1) the abundance of research material that was available and (2) the frequent use of quotations, some of them lengthy, which was done to let the missionaries themselves tell the Amoy story so far as possible.

I

An Overview of Chinese Political History to 1951

The achievement of the mission of the Reformed Church in America to China appears all the greater when understood within the context of that country's political history.

Until recent times, the approximately 3,500 years of recorded Chinese history was generally divided along dynastic periods. The oldest of these for which there is recorded evidence was the Shang dynasty (1766?-ca 1100 B.C.) and the last was the Ch'ing (1644-1912). The latter is often referred to as the Manchu period because of the place of origin of its rulers. The Manchus were outsiders of Mongolian background who had earlier established themselves in eastern Manchuria and moved on to seize Peking in 1644. Throughout its long history, China experienced occasional "golden ages" and "dark ages" just as did Western nations. Thus, China enjoyed prosperity and cultural advancement during the first half of the Manchu period, but was declining by the mid-nineteenth century.

Life in China changed very little despite the coming and going of dynasties, even when they were of non-Chinese derivation. Centuries of geographical isolation due to the Pacific Ocean in the east and deserts and mountains in other areas help explain this continuity, but only in part. Other factors contributing to China's cultural insularity included close family ties, the tens of thousands of small communal villages, and the role played among them by the village elders. There was also the rigid examination system required of persons seeking admission into China's civil service. These examinations called for a thorough knowledge of the ancient classics, which had the two-fold effect of emphasizing adherence to China's old way of thinking and stifling creativity. Closely related to all of this was the overriding influence that the Chinese philosopher and teacher Confucius (551-479 B.C.) and his moral code had on the Chinese people.

There were occasional contacts between China and the West in ancient and medieval times, but China was not greatly affected by them. During the Pax Romana, for example, trade in silk was carried on between the Chinese and Roman empires, and during the T'ang period (618-907) the Nestorian brand of Christianity took root in some parts of China. Beginning in the thirteenth century and continuing through the Yuan period (1280-1368), thanks in large part to the more tolerant attitude of the ruling Mongols, some trade was carried on by Venetian merchants such as the Polos. Roman Catholic missionaries, including the Franciscans and Dominicans, also became active. With the appearance of the Ming dynasty in 1368, contacts between China and the West once again came to a virtual standstill. As Immanuel C. Y. Hsu states in his comprehensive *Rise of Modern China*, more lasting contacts "had to wait until one of them could make a sustained drive to reach the other."[1]

The needed "sustained drive" started becoming a reality in the sixteenth century, thanks to Western improvements in navigation techniques and shipbuilding in the late fifteenth and early sixteenth centuries. Other incentives included the desire for economic gain and the winning of souls for Christ. On the economic front, the possibility of trade by sea was opened up with the arrival in 1514 of a Portuguese ship at the mouth of the river leading to Canton. Ships from other nations soon followed. Trade with the West, however, was not extensive at first, as neither the Mings nor the Manchus encouraged it. In truth, there was not much China wanted from the West, while the latter, on the other hand, found a ready market in Europe for Chinese silk, tea, and porcelain.

Interest in mission work was also renewed at this time. Jesuit missionaries, like Matteo Ricci (d. 1610), were welcomed into some of the highest circles of Chinese society because of their scholarship and knowledge of science. This gradually changed, in part due to internecine strife between the Jesuits and other Catholic orders but also because of a growing distrust of the missionaries' motives. A series of imperial edicts finally culminated in the proscription of Christianity in 1742. Meanwhile, China also gradually developed a distrust of Western traders and foreigners in general, with the result that trade eventually had to be confined to the single port of Canton, and then only under strict supervision.

Wars and domestic concerns kept Europe from challenging China's new exclusionist policy, but this began changing by the middle of the nineteenth century. At that time, a combination of factors brought on a surge of European imperialism that drastically affected not only China but South and Southeast Asia and Africa as well. Economics figured prominently among these factors as the so-called Industrial Revolution inspired a world-wide search for new markets and sources for cheap raw materials, as well as places in which to invest surplus capital. In time, the imperialist impulse was also encouraged by a Western desire for naval bases at certain strategic locations.

With specific respect to China, the course of imperialism was heightened by several additional factors. On the economic side, there was Western annoyance at having to channel all trade through the single port of Canton and conduct business through a small monopolistic group of merchants known as the Co-Hong. China also tended to treat foreigners as unequals and refused to follow normal diplomatic procedures in dealing with the West. Differences between China and the West in legal and judicial matters provided additional cause for friction. Because the vast majority of China's trade with the West was in British hands, England was most concerned about these grievances and most determined to change them.

As has been noted, China's main exports were silk and tea, but there was little China needed in the way of imports. As a consequence, the West had to bring in specie to pay for what it imported. It is therefore not surprising that when a substitute for specie put in an appearance, the West seized upon it as a means for redressing the trade imbalance. Unfortunately, the substitute was opium.

Knowledge about opium reached China perhaps as early as the seventh century when its primary use was medicinal. The smoking of opium was introduced to China by Europeans in the early 1600s, creating a demand for the drug that eventually exceeded domestic production. Large scale importation was the result. The British, from their sources in India, became the greatest suppliers, but merchants from other countries, including the United States, were involved. Although the Chinese government had long ago prohibited importation of opium and periodically renewed the bans, traders had little difficulty bringing it in, either through smuggling or by bribing corrupt Chinese officials. As addiction mounted, so too did the demand. The number of chests of opium steadily increased from about 1,000 annually in 1770 to 10,000 by 1820, and 40,000 by 1839. Profits were often as high as $1,000 per chest.[2]

In 1839, because of the addiction problem and the large amount of specie leaving the country to pay for the opium, the Chinese government decided the time had come for strong action. Under the direction of an incorruptible Chinese official, Lin Tse-hsu, more than 20,000 chests of opium were confiscated from British warehouses in Canton and destroyed. This action, together with a few international incidents that followed, led to the outbreak of what is popularly called the First Opium War, also known as the Anglo-Chinese War (1839-1842). While the opium problem was the spark that touched off the war, the combustible situation brought on by restraints on foreign trade and other inconveniences were important background factors.

The Chinese military was no match for the superior British arms, especially those of the navy. Fighting ended with the signing of the Treaty of Nanking, August 29, 1842. Along with the supplementary arrangements that soon followed, the treaty opened five ports to British trade, namely, Canton, Amoy, Foochow, Ningpo, and Shanghai; ceded the island of Hong Kong to England; abolished the Co-Hong system; and introduced the beginning of what became known as the "treaty tariff." By the last mentioned, limitations were placed on Chinese customs duties. Provision was also made for extraterritoriality, meaning that Britishers accused of crimes in China would be tried according to English judicial procedures. Furthermore, the treaty arrangements contained a "most-favored-nation" clause stating that treaty advantages acquired in the future by other countries would automatically accrue to England as well. Finally, China had to pay England an indemnity of $21,000,000. Most of the concessions made to England were quickly acquired by other countries, including the United States. The treaties in their totality, and especially in the light of their general unfairness and most-favored-nation arrangements, make up the beginning of what has become known as the "unequal treaty system."

The outcome of the First Opium War left several questions unanswered, including that of opium (by the 1850s, 60,000 chests of opium were entering China annually) and the matter of establishing normal diplomatic relations. Meanwhile, a new question had arisen, namely, the nefarious coolie trade. The result was, after a series of untoward incidents, the outbreak of the Second Opium War in 1856. The murder of a French missionary in Kwangsi province where he had no authority to be prompted France to join England in the fighting. Once again, China revealed how weak she was in the face of Western armaments. In the end, two more treaties were added to the existing unequal treaty system, namely, the Treaty of Tientsin (June 26, 1858) and the Peking Convention (October 34, 1860). By these arrangements, ten more ports were opened; Kowloon, on the mainland opposite Hong Kong, was ceded to England; more normal diplomatic relations were established; freedom of travel was provided, including that for missionaries; opium was legalized; China was saddled with another indemnity; and privileges with respect to extraterritoriality and treaty tariff were expanded.

Unlike the situation in Southeast Asia or India and Africa, China proper never was annexed by a foreign power or even partitioned during the so-called "New Imperialism" of the last half of the nineteenth century. Portions along the periphery of the Chinese Empire, however, were lost to foreign powers. Burma and Annam, for example, often referred to as tributary states or dependencies of China, were occupied respectively by England and France. Even Russia got into the act by annexing the Trans-Ussuri region and territory along the left bank of the Amur River. Similarly, Taiwan and Korea were lost to Japan.

Although China proper retained its independence, it by no means escaped having to make new concessions to the West. These took various forms. Particularly important were spheres of influence in which China promised several countries preferential treatment with respect to economic development in certain parts of China. Leases were also granted. These frequently allowed a foreign country to build a naval base at a strategic location, which invariably was followed by the right to establish a bank to finance economic enterprises in the region. Rights to build railroads into the interior and to exploit mineral resources along the rights of way were also given. The number of "treaty ports" likewise increased from the five opened by the Treaty of Nanking in 1842 to several dozen by the First World War. The degree of foreign privileges at these port cities varied, but in some instances, as at Amoy, it included governing rights as well as extensive police and judicial powers.

The granting of concessions to foreign countries along with the loss of dependencies has been referred to by some writers as "cutting up the Chinese melon." These developments were naturally resented by the Chinese government, but it became manifestly evident that resorting to armed resistance was not the answer. Various groups of Chinese people, however, occasionally took matters into their own hands. Their resistence took various forms, including protest marches and demonstrations, boycotts against foreign goods, and occasional outbreaks of civilian violence. Humiliation at the hands of the foreigners also led to the formation of new secret societies and the strengthening of old ones. Some of these were directed at both the Chinese government and the West.

The defeats China suffered at the hands of foreigners made it apparent to some Chinese that drastic political and economic reforms were required. Reformers were further animated in their cries for change by having read translations of Western works and, in some instances, by having traveled and even studied abroad. Several reforms were carried out under government direction, including formation of a Western-style army and development of railroads, a telegraph system, and new industries. In 1898, a group of reformers introduced, with the blessing of the emperor, Kuang-hsu, a broad range of reforms. The effort lasted only from June 11 to September 21, 1898 (hence, it is often termed "The Hundred Days") before a reaction set in. Led by the emperor's aunt, Tz'u Hsi, better known as the "Empress Dowager," the emperor was placed under house arrest. She then took over the personal direction of the government. Reform edicts were rescinded and reformers were either arrested or went into hiding or exile.

Among the secret societies opposing Western influences at this time, the best known was the I-ho Ch'uan, or "Society of Righteous and Harmonious Fists," called "Boxers" by the foreigners. Initially, the aim of the Boxers was to overthrow the Manchus, but they later directed their ire primarily at foreigners and Western ideas. In 1899, they resorted to violence and mercilessly murdered over 200 foreigners—mostly missionaries and their families—and several hundred Chinese Christians. The killing and pillaging took place primarily in the northern provinces. To protect the foreigners and Western interests, an international expeditionary army from eight countries, including the United States, was raised and through the use of force put an end to the movement in 1901. The Empress Dowager, having supported the Boxers, was obliged to flee Peking. In the end, the Chinese government had to agree to the Boxer Protocol, which along with other stipulations called for the punishment of those responsible and the payment of an indemnity. [3]

The Empress Dowager, upon her return to Peking, finally saw the need for meaningful change. A reform movement exceeding that of the Hundred Days got officially underway in January 1902. Among other things, education was updated, students were encouraged to study abroad, the centuries-old examination system was abolished, and financial and legal reforms were introduced. The administrative system was revised somewhat and a limited constitutional government was promised in due time. Unfortunately, a new crisis faced China in mid-November 1908, when both the emperor, who was still under house arrest, and the Empress Dowager suddenly died. Pu Yi, a two and one-half year old nephew of the deceased emperor, was placed on the throne—with his father, Prince Chun, serving as regent. Young and inexperienced, Prince Chun fell under the sway of reactionaries, resulting in a slowing down of reform.

With the Manchus becoming discredited once again, movements aimed at overthrowing them soon got underway. The critics were of various backgrounds and held mixed views as to what should be done. Best known among them was Sun Yat-sen (1866-1925). Of humble background but educated in Hawaii and having a medical degree from an English hospital in Hong Kong, Sun was dedicated to reforming China. Following an abortive attempt to overthrow the Manchus in 1895, he fled to London. Thereafter, he spent considerable time traveling and making speeches explaining China's plight and preaching revolution, especially among overseas Chinese. In 1905, he helped cement several like-minded groups, many of whom were Western-oriented, into an organization known as the United League. Its aim was to overthrow the Manchu regime and replace it with a parliamentary democracy.

Plans were being made by Sun and his associates for another attempt to overthrow the Manchus when a rebellion broke out in October, 1911, in the so-called Wuhan cities——three factory cities located near each other about 600 miles up the Yangtze River. The rebellion quickly spread, and several provinces declared their independence of the Manchus. A well-known Chinese general, Yuan Shi-kai, whose advice and support had been sought by the Chinese government after the Boxer uprising, was now invited once again to rescue the Manchus. Prince Chun was asked to resign and Yuan was given the post of chief minister and made commander of all troops.

Meanwhile, Sun Yat-sen and his followers met together in December 1911 and declared China a republic. A government was set up at Nanking with an assembly and Sun as provisional president. Yuan, who had ambitions of his own, thereupon began secretly negotiating with Sun in January and February, 1912. As a result of these talks, Sun agreed to step down as president in favor of Yuan. This was followed soon after by the resignation of the Manchus on February 12, 1912.

Declaring China a republic was one thing; making it work was something else. In truth, the arrangement between Sun and Yuan and their supporters was a "marriage of convenience" with each side hoping to use the other. Yuan had no respect for constitutional government and even had dreams of restoring the monarchy with himself as emperor. Yuan's bargaining power was much greater than that of Sun, who had no experience in government and did not have an army. Yuan moreover had the support of the West. Making the republic work was also hampered by the fact there were ambitious governors in the provinces who had control over local armies.

In preparation for the election of delegates to a National Assembly, Sun and his followers organized the Kuomintang party (really an outgrowth of the old United League) in the summer of 1912. It was successful in the elections, but Yuan refused to accept the results and proceeded to govern by presidential decree. An attempted "Second Revolution" in July, 1913, failed, and Sun went into exile. The Kuomintang was later suppressed, and in January, 1914, the National Assembly was dissolved. Yuan died in June, 1916, leaving a weak and vulnerable "Republic" to his vice-president, Li Yuan-hong, who like Yuan was a military man but lacked competence for governing. Adding to the chaos was the fact that regional strongmen proceeded to govern parts of China to serve their own selfish interests. The period that followed (1916-1927), one of the most confusing in the history of any country, is generally referred to in Chinese history as the "warlord era."[4] Some of the warlords in the north, acting singly or in concert with others, maintained the fiction of a national government at Peking. Meanwhile, Sun Yat-sen, who had fled into exile after the failure of the "Second Revolution," along with his associates established a rival government of their own at Canton in 1917.

Adding to the confusion of the times was the appearance of another disrupting force, namely, communism. It got off to a humble start in July, 1921, when a small group of men, including Mao Tse-tung, met at Shanghai and formally organized the Chinese Communist Party. Although still a small party, Sun, with some misgivings but needing support wherever he could get it (including the Soviet Union), took the Communists into the Kuomintang organization in June, 1923. Soon after this, Russia sent advisors to help reorganize the Kuomintang into a more effective organization and to assist in building an army.

Another power struggle ensued when Sun Yat-sen died in 1925. This one was between the moderate element in the Kuomintang and a more leftist group that included the Communists. In the end, the moderates won out. They were led by Sun's brother-in-law, Chiang Kai-shek (1887-1975). An army officer trained in Japan (and after 1923 in Russia for a brief period), Chiang played a role in the Revolution of 1911 but soon after went into business. Later, upon the urgings of Sun, he agreed to train and take command of the fledgling Kuomintang army. Chiang's winning out in the power struggle was due in part to his popularity with many Chinese for having won several victories over the warlords, but was also due to the support he received from the Chinese middle class and the West.

Although the Communists were expelled from the Kuomintang organization in 1927, Chiang Kai-shek was not without problems. The Communists were still very strong in some parts of China, and there still were warlords to contend with in the north. Campaigns were carried out against both these groups from time to time. In 1928, nationalist armies captured Peking from the warlords, thus placing China, at least nominally, under one government for the first time since 1916. Also facing Chiang was the perennial threat from Japan. No idle threat, this led to a war in 1931 in which China was defeated and had to cede Manchuria to the victor. Finally, among Chiang's problems, there was the overriding need to modernize the country and further Sun's democratic ideas.

The expulsion of the Communists from the Kuomintang in 1927 by no means ended their presence in China. They had numerous rural bases and were particularly strong in south and central China. Military engagements were fought between the two groups from time to time, culminating in Chiang Kai-shek's undertaking a major campaign in 1934. It succeeded in driving the main body of Communists out of the Hunan-Kiangsi area to Shensi province in northwestern China. The drive, appropriately called the "Long March," was a strenuous one involving marching back and forth over 6,000 miles and fighting countless engagements along the way. In the end, only about a fourth of the Communists who started out reached their destination. It was during this time that Mao Tse-tung became the acknowledged leader of the Communist movement.

Kuomintang efforts to dislodge the Communists from Shensi proved unavailing. As the outbreak of another war with Japan seemed almost a certainty, Chiang, under great pressure from members of his own party, agreed in late 1936 to establish a United Front with the Communists in order to deal with the Japanese threat. The anticipated war with Japan broke out in July,

1937, which conflict merged with the Second World War after the Japanese attack on American forces at Pearl Harbor on December 7, 1941.

The fighting started near Peking but quickly spread to other places. Peking fell on August 9, followed soon by the northern provincial capitals. The fall of Nanking on December 13, 1937, was accompanied by one of history's most brutal plunderings. China was no match for Japan's military might, whose troops by mid-1938 had occupied most of China's coastal cities as well as major industrial and railroad centers. Chiang Kai-shek had no choice but to retreat and move his command steadily farther into China's hinterland, finally establishing his wartime capital far to the west at Chungking in Szechuan Province. Here, with Western aid, much of it arriving by plane from India, the Nationalist government remained until the end of the war in August, 1945. Peace feelers were put out by the Japanese occasionally but were rejected. As complete military victory faded away, the Japanese consolidated themselves in the occupied territory and, except for a drive inland in 1944, a military stalemate set in that lasted for the duration.

The United Front of December, 1936, between the Nationalists and Communists proved to be an unnatural alliance. Military campaigns undertaken against the Japanese during the war were not coordinated between the two factions—indeed, hostilities broke out between them on several occasions. In view of the longstanding distrust between them, it is not surprising that when Japan surrendered in August, 1945, Nationalist and Communist forces rushed in to fill the vacuum created by the departing Japanese, and it was not long before clashes broke out. The United States, anxious to have a strong China as a stabilizing influence in East Asia, tried unsuccessfully to mediate a compromise between the two contestants. When efforts failed, full-scale civil war broke out.

In the fighting that ensued, the Nationalists made significant military gains throughout 1946 and early 1947, but they also made some tactical mistakes. Unfortunately, too, corruption, runaway inflation, and failure to introduce meaningful agrarian and other economic reforms gradually caused the Chinese people to lose confidence in Chiang Kai-shek's regime. In late 1947, the military balance began shifting in favor of the Communists and by the beginning of 1949, the Nationalist situation had become desperate. With the Communists pressing the attack, Nanking, the Nationalist capital, fell in April followed by Shanghai in May and Canton, the new capital, in October. Meanwhile, Mao Tse-tung, chairman of the Communist Party, on October 1, 1949, proclaimed in Peking's famous T'ien-an-men Square, the formal establishment of the People's Republic of China.

As the Nationalists retreated inland, Chungking, their World War II headquarters, became the next capital. It capitulated on November 30. Before this occurred, however, Chiang Kai-shek with most of his government and about 50,000 Nationalist troops had fled to Taiwan, where on December 8, 1949, Taipei was declared the new Nationalist capital. Except for some mopping up operations, the mainland was now held by the Communists; only Taiwan, about a hundred miles from the mainland, and a few offshore islands outside Amoy harbor were left to the Nationalists.

With the Communists and Mao Tse-tung in control, their immediate task was two-fold: rehabilitate the economy and consolidate the government's hold on the people. It was primarily the latter chore, which included thought control, that affected the missionaries and their work. This involved attacking "traditional and 'bourgeois' ideas and values through programs of self-evaluation, mutual criticism, and indoctrination."[5] With increasing Communist pressure on the missionaries, especially after the outbreak of the Korean War in 1950 and America's and China's involvement in it on opposing sides, they soon began leaving China. The last to depart was Dr. Theodore Oltman, who left August 18, 1951. The story of the events leading to the departure of the Reformed missionaries is discussed in chapter eighteen, "Closing the Mission."

II
Laying the Foundations

The Reformed church in America began its mission work in China February 24, 1842, when the Reverends David Abeel of the Reformed church and William Boone of the American Episcopal church arrived in Amoy harbor aboard a British warship. Boone remained at Amoy for only a brief period before moving on to Shanghai. The mode of transportation was strange for men who came to preach the Christian gospel, but the First Opium War between England and China was still going on and Amoy had fallen to the British only a few months earlier. Not until August 29, 1842, was the Treaty of Nanking signed by which Amoy and four other Chinese ports were officially opened to foreigners.

Abeel, who graduated from New Brunswick Theological Seminary in 1826, had shown an interest in foreign missions from his youth. It is therefore not surprising that after a short pastorate at the Reformed church in Athens, New York, he accepted a call from the Seamen's Friend Society to serve as chaplain to the sailors at Canton, China, which was open to limited Western trade at this time.[1] He left New York October 14, 1829, and arrived at his destination about four months later. This was still the age of sail, and the common route to China involved a long voyage around the Cape of Good Hope.

On December 20, 1830, after about a year's stay in China, Abeel entered the service of the American Board of Commissioners for Foreign Missions in accord with a prior agreement he had made before leaving the United States. The American Board, as it was commonly called, was organized in 1810 on an interdenominational basis for the purpose of spreading the Christian gospel throughout the world.[2] The Reformed church became a member in 1826 but was unable for some time to play a significant role because of financial and other problems. The situation improved after 1832 when the General Synod, the denomination's highest legislative and judicial body, appointed its own Board of Foreign Missions with responsibility for selecting mission stations, recruiting missionaries, raising funds, and corresponding with missionaries in the field. Because of its lack of experience in these matters, however, the denominational board for many years sought advice from the staff of the American Board and occasionally appealed to it for financial help. In return for these services, the Reformed church was expected to keep the American Board informed of what it was doing and to consult its executive committee before making major decisions.

The arrangement of 1832 continued until 1857, when the General Synod decided that the time had come for its Board of Foreign Missions to take complete charge of the church's foreign missionary program. Although relations between the two boards had always been cordial, the conviction had gradually grown among Reformed circles that termination of the agreement would prompt church members to take their obligations toward missions more seriously. In studying the early history of the Amoy mission, it must therefore be kept in mind that until 1857 the Reformed missionaries had a kind of dual responsibility, namely, to their denomination and to the American Board.[3]

Soon after Abeel entered the service of the American Board in 1830, he undertook at its request an extensive tour throughout Southeast Asia, visiting Thailand, Malaysia, Singapore, and Java. Preaching the gospel became his primary task, but he also distributed religious literature, dispensed medicine, and investigated possible sites for establishing mission stations. Poor health forced Abeel in the late spring of 1833 to return to the United States, where during the next few years he gave numerous addresses to seminary students and church gatherings in an effort to awaken a greater concern for missions. It was in part due to these efforts that the Reformed church took steps in 1836 to establish a mission in Borneo, some of whose missionaries were transferred later to Amoy.[4]

Abeel's interest in China never diminished, and on October 17, 1838, despite warnings from physicians about his delicate health, he again set out for that distant land.[5] The outbreak of the First Opium War in 1839 interfered with these plans and, as a consequence, after spending some time at the Portuguese colony of Macao, he undertook—at the request of the American Board—another missionary tour throughout Southeast Asia, performing about the same tasks as during his previous visit. When the Anglo-Chinese conflict began drawing to a close, Abeel returned to China, arriving at Macao on December 21, 1841. Several weeks later, in the company of the Reverend Boone, he left for Amoy.

Upon arrival in Amoy harbor, Abeel at first confined his activity to Kulangsu, a small island about a mile south of the much larger island of Amoy. It was here that he rented a small house near the water's edge to carry on his work. When an American physician, Dr. William H. Cumming, a native of Georgia, arrived there as a medical missionary in June, 1842, Abeel permitted him the use of a room for a dispensary. Cumming was not associated with any particular missionary society, but supported himself from his own resources and those of friends.

Although handicapped somewhat at first by the language problem, Abeel reported in August, 1842, about a half year after his arrival, that the number of Sunday listeners averaged nearly fifty, some of whom were regular attendants, while others were patients of Dr. Cumming. He also reported that the number of callers at the dispensary was frequently so large that not all could be accommodated in a single day.[6] This problem was alleviated somewhat in November, 1843, with the arrival of another medical missionary, Dr. James C. Hepburn, who had been sent out by the American Presbyterian church. The three men, especially Abeel, soon began making occasional visits to Amoy City, located on the western end of Amoy Island. Amoy City had a population of about 50,000 in 1842. A few trips were also made to the mainland. Although strictly speaking the terms of the treaties that had been signed did not yet permit traveling away from the treaty ports, enforcement of the law depended largely on the local authorities.

In January, 1844, two rooms were rented in Amoy City, one for use as a chapel and the other as a dispensary, enabling the trio of men to introduce preaching and medical work on a regular basis. About a year later, a nearby building was rented to serve as a hospital. Its purpose was to accommodate patients who had undergone surgery and required special care. The general rule that was followed with respect to remuneration was one in which medical care was supplied free of charge, as were rooms for patients requiring hospitalization. Such patients, however, had to provide their own food and any personal attention that might be required.

The introduction of medical facilities was seen to be a valuable adjunct to the task of evangelism. That it could do much more than just relieve pain is clearly shown in the following excerpt from a letter Abeel wrote at about this time to the First Reformed Church of Albany:

> The happy influence of the dispensary is another favorable event....The gratuitous practice [has] made a good impression on all classes of the community. The number of cases treated during the past year has been about 5000; and everywhere we learn how the hearts of the people are opened by the good done to their bodies. They see that foreigners can come with disinterested motives, as well as for the sake of gain. In this way, gratitude is won and confidence gained. The people are induced to respect us as friends, and are prepared to bear more readily the truths that tend to the healing of the soul.[7]

Abeel left Amoy in late 1844, followed by Hepburn in 1845 and Cumming in 1847. The departure of Hepburn and Cumming left the medical facilities without a trained physician until the arrival of Dr. James H. Young of the English Presbyterian Mission in May, 1850. Young remained until August, 1854, when he returned to England because of poor health.[8]

Abeel's departure was due to his steadily deteriorating health. In August, 1844, he went to Hong Kong in the hope that a sea voyage and a slight change in climate would be helpful. This proved of no avail, and he returned to Amoy in September, realizing full well that his enfeebled condition would soon force him to withdraw from China. On December 19, 1844, Abeel embarked for America, arriving at New York April 3 of the following year. His health continued to worsen, and he died September 4, 1846, at Albany, New York, at age forty-two. Thus ended the career of this pioneer missionary to China.[9]

Although Abeel never succeeded in baptizing any converts, he gained the respect of many Chinese through his friendly and dedicated attitude. Moreover, some of his hearers were later baptized by other missionaries. Upon learning of Abeel's death, Rufus Anderson, secretary of the American Board, wrote:

Our brother was not a Paul, nor was he a Peter; he more resembled the beloved John. He was fitted to conciliate, to win....Men could not help reposing confidence in him. His countenance, voice, manner, all tended to disarm prejudice and predisposed men to listen and assent. It was a good thing for the Amoy mission that he was the one who commenced it, and to this, among many other favoring providences, we owe much of the peculiarly tolerant spirit among the leading Chinese of that place.[10]

A few months before Abeel's departure for America, an event occurred that greatly gladdened his heart. On June 22, 1844, he was joined at Amoy by two more Reformed missionaries, the Reverend Elihu and Eleanor Doty and the Reverend William and Theodosia Pohlman, and their families. These missionaries had been laboring among Chinese colonists in Borneo since 1839, and Abeel had for some time been urging their transfer to China. Indeed, already in early 1842, a few weeks before his arrival at Amoy, he wrote the editor of the *Christian Intelligencer*, a weekly periodical issued by the Reformed church:

From a recent visit to Borneo, I can speak from a pretty accurate knowledge of the comparative claims of the [Borneo and China] fields....I have no hesitation in saying that China is far more important and promising in every respect. To this unlimited and opening sphere the majority of our best qualified missionaries ought to come. Here we need not go on long journeys to find a scanty and scattered population. They press upon us, and can scarcely be excluded from our gates. They have minds, too, to appreciate arguments, and habits favorable to reflection....Would it not be well to direct the brethren Doty and Pohlman to join me? They are both devoting themselves to the Chinese, and the few thousands living in different parts of Borneo bear no comparison to the multitudes here.[11]

Upon arrival at their new fields of labor, the Pohlman and Doty families were provided with living quarters on Kulangsu but soon relocated to more comfortable quarters in Amoy City. A trading house was remodeled for their use, with the Dotys occupying the lower floor and the Pohlmans the upper. Worship services continued to be held at first in the rooms Abeel had rented for that purpose, but it soon became necessary to rent a larger building to accommodate the growing number of listeners, who sometimes numbered as many as 200.

After becoming settled in their new home, Pohlman and Doty hired a Chinese teacher to instruct them in the Amoy dialect. This action was essential because the Chinese among whom they had been working in Borneo had their roots in the area around Canton and thus spoke a dialect very different from that of Amoy. As Pohlman explained in a letter written about two weeks after he arrived in China:

> Our tongues are again tied. This strange puzzle of a language has so many dialects, its tones and inflections are so nice, and of such indispensable importance to being fully understood, that in many respects, it is like beginning anew. The dialect we have studied is not spoken at all in this province. Do not understand me that all our labor is lost. Not at all. What we have acquired is of essential service. I am persuaded we shall get this new dialect in half the time it would take a newcomer. My hope is that by the aid of analogical resemblances in words and phrases, by diligence and God's blessing we shall be able to hold forth the Word of Life in one year from the present time, in this great metropolis. I say one year at the extent. Perhaps it may be done in half that time.[12]

Pohlman and Doty naturally profited from Abeel's presence. By listening to his preaching, they became acutely aware of how essential it was to pronounce everything correctly, lest they be greeted with laughter and even contempt by their listeners. Although proper enunciation was important in carrying on a two-way conversation, it was doubly essential when speaking to a group. This is clearly illustrated in a notation made by Pohlman in his journal on October 6, 1844, following a church service in which Abeel delivered the sermon:

Sabbath, October 6. We had about 60 at the Chinese service, and brother Abeel had strength imparted to preach from Matthew 7: 21, 29. The people give good attention, and seem fully to understand. The constant attendants no doubt understand all. Those who come occasionally, perhaps not. The subjects are entirely new, and one tone wrong in a sentence may change its meaning completely. It is only by constant and long continued practice, that in a discourse all tones can be hit, and what we say [can] be clear and intelligible to our hearers. In conversation, it is different. We can repeat again and again, and by inquiry ascertain whether we are understood, and by frequent trials and repetition can make ourselves intelligible.[13]

Pohlman and Doty worked hard at learning the Amoy dialect and progressed rapidly with the help of native teachers. Within a year after his arrival, Pohlman had filled a pocket-sized notebook of 245 pages with important colloquial words and phrases and carried it with him as a ready reference. Unfortunately, he soon began having trouble with his eyes, which made reading and writing difficult. A four-month stay at Canton where he was treated by the noted Dr. Peter Parker failed to give the needed relief. The consequences can be seen in Pohlman's letter of October 24, 1846, to the Reverend Rufus Anderson, chief executive officer of the American Board, and Thomas De Witt, editor of the *Christian Intelligencer*:

I must abandon all ideas of being much of a student. I must be a sort of general agent or overseer engaging in active, outdoor labors, exploring, exhorting, preaching, from house to house; while others devote themselves to the written language, translating, revising, and such work as requires good eyes.[14]

Fortunately, Doty had also busied himself with mastering the Amoy dialect, and his success helped offset Pohlman's affliction. Like Pohlman, Doty began making notes on the local dialect, the result of which was a 212-page manual on the subject. This was

later published at Canton in 1855 and for many years formed the
basis for later manuals not only for Amoy but also for Singapore
and Taiwan, where Amoy was the common Chinese dialect.

From the beginning, the new arrivals suffered the loss of loved
ones. A few weeks after setting foot in China, the Doty's only son,
a boy of six, died. A short time later, the Pohlmans lost two
children. On September 30, 1845, Theodosia Pohlman died at age
thirty-five, and she was followed in death about a week later on
October 5 by Eleanor Doty, age thirty-nine. The grief-stricken
husbands decided that their motherless children (there were two
in each family) should return to America. In November, Doty
therefore left Amoy in the company of his own and Pohlman's
children. He remained in America about a year and a half, during
which time he spoke to various Reformed church audiences,
describing his work in China. He also remarried, and when he
returned to China, his new bride accompanied him. They arrived
at Amoy on August 19, 1847.

A young missionary who had just volunteered for the China
field accompanied the Dotys. His name was John Van Nest
Talmage, who was destined to serve in China for more than forty
years and become one of the mainstays of the mission. Born in
1819, Talmage graduated from Rutgers College in 1842 and from
New Brunswick Seminary in 1845. His primary interest was
missions, and he offered his services to the Board of Foreign
Missions upon completing his theological training. Lack of
funding prevented his being commissioned for two years. He
therefore served for a time as assistant pastor of the Central
Reformed Church of Brooklyn. One of his earliest inspirations to
enter missionary service came as a result of hearing, as a boy of
sixteen, an address by Doty when the latter was making a tour of
various Reformed churches prior to departing for the Dutch East
Indies and Borneo in 1836. Now, eleven years later, young
Talmage found himself in the company of this same Doty enroute
to a mission at the opposite side of the world.

The Amoy missionaries kept up a regular correspondence with
their home churches in the United States as well as with
denominational leaders of the Reformed church and officials of
the American Board. Pohlman, for example, sent lengthy letters
(letters of 3,000 words were not uncommon) at about two month

intervals. Much of the missionary correspondence was published in the *Christian Intelligencer* and in the *Missionary Herald*, which was issued monthly by the American Board. The missionaries also made annual reports to the Board of Foreign Missions, which were published and bound with the General Synod's annual *Acts and Proceedings*.

The "home front," unfortunately, did not reciprocate in keeping the missionaries informed about happenings in America. The extent of this negligence can be seen in this postscript of a letter written by Pohlman in 1846:

> The last letter from the Secretary of the American Board of Commissioners for Foreign Missions is a year old; the last from the Secretary of our own Board, more than two years old; and the last from the church I represent, older still. The effect of such non-intercourse is to diminish all feelings of mutual sympathy. I cannot help feeling deserted and neglected when the ties of relation and common interest are thus forgotten.[15]

As late as 1865, it sometimes happened that three months would go by without the missionaries receiving their copies of the *Christian Intelligencer*, despite its being a weekly publication.

In addition to correspondence, the home front was kept informed through occasional visits by the missionaries. As has been noted, when Doty returned to the United States in 1845 with his and Pohlman's motherless children, he used the opportunity to address various groups interested in missions. Similarly, when Talmage left Amoy in the spring of 1849 to escort Pohlman's sister, Julia Ann, back to America after her brother's tragic death by drowning (to be discussed later), he spoke to several missionary conventions sponsored by Reformed congregations in New York and New Jersey. In 1859, Doty again returned to America, this time to bring his four children there following the death of his second wife, Mary. Before his return to Amoy in 1861, he, too, traveled extensively, addressing Reformed church audiences. The same thing transpired a few years later when Talmage made a second visit (1862-1864), this time to accompany his four motherless children after the death of his wife, Abby Woodruff Talmadge.

It is interesting to note here that despite the many adversities experienced by the missionaries during these early years, their faith in God and a divine providence never wavered. This is clearly evident in the following excerpt from a letter written by Pohlman to the First Reformed Church in Albany soon after his "cluster of afflictions," as he termed the several deaths in his family during a three-month period. The occasion for the letter was the imminent departure of his remaining children who were being sent to America, along with Doty's children, to live with relatives.

> Another sore trial is before us—sending home the two children that remain. This weighs heavily on my spirits, and causes the most intense feeling...This is nature—but grace triumphs. Oh! the comforts of religion—the all-sustaining, soul-supporting, heart-warming, spirit-enlivening grace of God!—fitted for every emergency, bearing up under every trial, upholding in every conflict, and making me conqueror, and more than conqueror, through him that loved me. I see clearly through all. I know my Father is at the helm. It is right-—all right. I bow; I yield; I submit; I kiss the rod; I glory in these crosses and losses, and desire only that Christ may be magnified, God glorified, souls saved, and heaven peopled with thousands from this dark land. [16]

The missionaries discussed a broad range of subjects during their visits home. Of particular interest to their American audiences were descriptions of the daily life and customs of the Chinese people, the physical appearance of their houses and villages, the density of the population, and the physical terrain of the Amoy region. The missionaries gave special attention, of course, to the religious ideas and practices of the people and the efforts being made to convert them to Christianity.[17]

In retrospect, it is surprising how often the missionaries visited America, considering the length of time it took to make the voyage and the inconveniences that were involved. For example, the Reverend Daniel Rapalje, who served the mission from 1858 to 1899, made the China trip six times. On two of these occasions, the drinking water and food became so scarce that they had to be rationed. There was also the possibility of loss of life at sea, as is demonstrated by the experience of the Reverend and

Mrs. John E. Watkins. This young couple sailed from New York for Amoy in 1860 and was never heard of again, their ship having been lost at sea. And Doty, who left Amoy in November, 1864, planning to spend his remaining life in quiet retirement, died at sea only a few days before his ship reached New York after a four-month voyage. Fortunately, the use of steam vessels and the development of ports on the west coast helped make later trips less arduous.

From time to time, missionaries from other religious bodies also arrived at Amoy, but in several instances their stay was brief. As has been mentioned, the Reverend Boone of the American Episcopal church, who had arrived with Abeel in 1842, remained at Amoy for only a few months. The presence of a small band of American Presbyterian missionaries was also brief, as their representatives either died, returned home prematurely due to poor health, or were transferred to other locations without being replaced. In the end, Protestant work in the Amoy region remained largely in the hands of three religious bodies, namely--the Reformed Church in America, the London Missionary Society, and the English Presbyterian church.[18]

The London Missionary Society, which was supported mainly by Congregationalists in England, began its work at Amoy in July 1844 with the arrival of the Reverends William Young and John Stronach. They were joined in 1846 by the latter's brother Alexander. All these men had formerly served among Chinese immigrants in Southeast Asia, many of whom had originally come from the Amoy region. As a consequence, they were already acquainted with the local dialect. This fact, together with the arrival of more recruits from England, soon enabled the London Missionary Society to surpass the other mission groups in the number of indigenous churches and in church membership.[19]

The English Presbyterian church began its work at Amoy in May, 1850, with the arrival of James Young, M.D. He was joined in July of the following year by the Reverend William C. Burns. Both men had earlier served at Hong Kong, which had become a British colony in 1842 by the treaty of Nanking, and at Canton. The Foreign Missions Committee of the Presbyterian Church in England had recommended that they relocate at Amoy on the supposition that its inhabitants were more friendly than those at

Canton. The committee also pointed out that because there were fewer missionaries at Amoy, there would also be less possibility of "overlapping" in their work.[20]

Burns and Young were joined by the Reverend James Johnston in December, 1853, but, as has been mentioned, Young had to return to England in August, 1854, because of poor health. Fortunately, he was replaced in July by the Reverend Carstairs Douglas who, laboring diligently until his death in 1877, became one of the pillars of the English Presbyterian mission. From time to time, Douglas was joined by others of his denomination.

By 1848, the Reformed church and the London Missionary Society were conducting regular services at three locations in Amoy City. Although the places of worship were referred to as chapels by the missionaries, they actually were little more than houses that had been rented for about $100 per year, and thus bore little resemblance to formal church buildings. The Reformed church chapel was located on a street called Boey Koey-hang and held two services each Sunday. The London Missionary Society chapel was located in a section of the city known as Cho-po-blo. The third chapel was really a part of the medical dispensary, where a doctor delivered a sermon on Sunday mornings. The three places of worship were apparently quite near each other. Pohlman reported in December, 1847, that all were located in Ho-hong-po, which was one of eighteen wards.[21] When the English Presbyterians arrived in 1850, they initially left Amoy City to the care of the other two groups (except for assisting with work at the dispensary), preferring instead to concentrate on the mainland.

The Reformed missionaries soon became convinced that although rented houses could serve as chapels, considering the modest numbers of those in attendance, a respectable looking church building was nevertheless a necessity. It would help attract new hearers, especially among the more well-to-do, and could be pointed to with pride by the converts. On December 25, 1846, Pohlman therefore wrote the secretary of the American Board requesting the sum of $100 for the purchase of some land in Amoy City and another $3,000 for the construction of a church. In late July of the following year, the American Board promised to advance the money, with the assumption of seeking reimbursement from the Reformed church. Pohlman was told to go ahead with his plans. The Reformed church did in due time raise the required sum but with difficulty. Most of the donations were in small amounts, but two individuals gave $100, and one gave $500.

Upon receiving the report from the American Board and having obtained permission from the provincial governor to build a church, steps were taken to procure a site in a desirable part of the city.[22] On September 16, 1847, an agreement was reached for leasing a 40 by 100-foot plot of ground in the east central part of the city, upon which stood four ramshackle houses. In his report to the American Board, dated December 13, 1847, Pohlman described as follows the agreement that had been reached:

> It was found to be impossible to rent a suitable place, and foreigners are not allowed to purchase and own property anywhere in the Celestial Empire. The lot was therefore bought by Hok-kui-peyh [one of the first converts] for less than $550, and made over to us by perpetual lease. That sum we have paid him, and no rent is now to be asked, except a small sum, sufficient to pay the taxes. The site is central, yet not in the busy bustle of the city. It is on one of the great thoroughfares, where we may always expect to have good audiences.[23]

Construction of the church began sometime in 1848. When completed, the dimensions were 37 by 68 feet, with a ceiling of about 20 feet. A 10-foot veranda in the front and a tower extending 50 feet completed the structure. It was built of brick, with the front finished in white stucco. An oval slab above the front entablature carried an inscription in Chinese characters, which in translation read as follows: "A Temple for the Worship of the True God, the Great Sovereign Ruler." Underneath was the date "1848."

The building, which provided seating for 350-400 people, had a rear entrance for the women, for whom seats were provided on both sides of the pulpit. The other rows of benches were for the men, who were entirely separated from the women by screens, thereby allowing both sexes to attend without any violation of custom.[24] Because the church was located in a part of Amoy known as Sin-koe-a, which translated means "Little New Street," it became known by that name. It was the first Protestant church building to be erected in China specifically for Chinese worshipers. The lower part of a small two-story building that stood behind the church was used as a parsonage until 1892, when a new parsonage was constructed on the site.

The exact date of completion for the building is not known, but the dedication occurred February 11, 1849. This was indeed a happy occasion but less joyous than had been anticipated because of the tragic death of Pohlman about a month earlier. On December 19, 1848, he left Amoy to take his sister, Julia Ann, who had arrived some time previously, to Hong Kong for her health. While there, he planned to procure some furnishings, including lamps, for the church. Enroute back to Amoy, on January 5, 1849, the schooner *Omega*, on which he was traveling, foundered during a severe storm off Breakers' Point, located about halfway between Hong Kong and Amoy. Nearly all on board perished, including Pohlman.[25] As a consequence, the dedication service, which Pohlman was scheduled to conduct, also became a memorial service for the man who had been primarily responsible for the church's construction. Although the worshipers now had an impressive looking building, it must be borne in mind that they were not yet formally organized as a congregation, complete with a consistory of elders and deacons. This did not take place until 1856.[26]

In 1928, the roof of the Sin-koe-a church fell in and five years passed before a new building took its place. In the meantime, the congregation worshiped in a nearby school. Rebuilt in 1933, its architecture was essentially the same as the first building except that it was enlarged by adding an additional floor, the lower story being designed for Sunday school rooms and offices. The cornerstone of the new building was presented by the General Council of the Church of Christ in China and carries the words: "The First Protestant Church in China."[27]

In 1850, another place of worship was opened in Amoy City. This came about following the return of Talmage on July 16 of that year. As previously explained, he had left Amoy about a year earlier to escort Pohlman's sister back to the United States following her brother's death. Having married while in the States, Talmage returned to China with his bride, Abby Woodruff.

Instead of settling among the other missionaries, the Talmages obtained a house about a mile and a half north of the other Reformed residences. It was ideally located near the water's edge in a densely populated area and along a main thoroughfare, and was to serve as the Talmage's home for nearly twenty years. Originally only one story in height, a second floor was soon added to serve as living quarters. The lower part was then renovated as a hall to accommodate about a hundred worshipers.

In 1859, a formal looking church was constructed near the Talmage site at a cost of $1,300 and dedicated on October 30 of that year.[28] It was sometimes referred to as Amoy's Second Reformed Church, but in most missionary reports it is called the Tek-chhiu-kha Church, after the name of the neighborhood in which it was located. Its attendance soon surpassed that of the First Church. This came about in part because of its proximity to the English Presbyterian hospital, but was also due to the popularity of its first Chinese pastor, the Reverend Iap Han-chiong. Iap was ordained March 29, 1863, and served the Second Church until 1884, when he accepted a call to the newly organized church at Sio-khe, located on the mainland about sixty miles west and south of Amoy.

Attendance at Sunday worship services during these formative years generally averaged between twenty-five and thirty, but sometimes was considerably larger. This was because some business days brought more visitors to the city than other days. In this respect, it must be noted that the Chinese made no special distinction between Sundays and other days of the week. Morning attendance was usually about twice that of the afternoon. The nucleus of the Sunday listeners consisted of the converts, the servants in the employ of the missionaries, and the latter's language teachers. Services at the dispensary would also include, of course, patients who were there under the care of the physician. Sunday services also attracted curious passersby who were disposed to drop in, usually only briefly, as they went about their daily business. This coming and going at will, together with the conversation that went on among the Chinese themselves, caused considerable confusion and noise at times. The Chinese who were attracted to the religious meetings were drawn primarily from the lower class and occasionally from the middle class, but seldom from the upper class.

The tendency for the higher officials and members of the learned class to shun religious gatherings must not be interpreted to mean that they were hostile toward the missionaries. Indeed, relations among them were, on the whole, of a friendly nature—a situation different from the experience of missionaries in some other parts of China at this time, especially at Canton. For example, when in 1846 the viceroy of the province of Fukien made one of his periodic visits to Amoy, he permitted the missionaries to call on him. The interview was friendly, with the viceroy expressing no disfavor toward the presence and work of the missionaries and even indicating a desire to make a visit someday to the United States and England.

Similarly, during a brief visit in 1847 to Tong-an on the mainland about twenty miles north of Amoy, the missionaries were invited to the residence of the highest mandarin of the city for a luncheon of tea and cake. The mandarin himself was not home on this occasion but he had once earlier called on the missionaries during a visit to Amoy and showed himself to be favorably disposed toward them. To cite another example of friendly relations and mutual respect, when two groups of Chinese were threatening to take the law into their own hands in 1848 to settle a dispute that had arisen between them, the highest civil officer in Amoy directed them to see two of the missionaries. The latter, he said, were unacquainted with either of the parties and could therefore, as neutrals, serve as "umpires" in bringing about a peaceful resolution.[29]

In their visits with the missionaries, members of the upper class showed particular interest in the news of the day—especially the troubles at Canton vis-à-vis the foreigners residing there, and the dress and furniture of the missionaries. They were also very interested in Western science. With reference to the latter, an interesting visit took place on December 10, 1847, when Pohlman and Doty were called on by four of the leading officials of Amoy City. These included the mayor, the military commander, the inspector of customs, and the principal civil mandarin. As was always the case, their purpose in coming was not to seek religious enlightenment. As reported by Pohlman:

Their object was to see experiments in electricity, as well

as pay us a visit. After examining daguerreotypes, the microscope, and the telescope, Mr. Doty performed a series of experiments on the electric machine recently received from America. The cause of electricity and the general principles of electrical phenomena were stated to them by teacher U [one of the native evangelists] in the court dialect. At the close, a good charge from the Leyden jar gave them convincing proof of the power of the subtile fluid.[30]

Although the missionaries had virtually no success in discussing religious matters with members of the Chinese upper class, special efforts to cultivate their good graces on that score were made from time to time. For example, whereas ordinary religious tracts (sometimes only one sheet in length) were distributed among the common people, the chief officials and literary men were given, when opportunities arose, materials of better quality, as is explained in this letter by Pohlman dated May 1, 1847:

The following books were sent as a New Year's present to forty or fifty of the literati and men of wealth and influence in Amoy, viz., History of America; copy of the Gospels and Acts, in red morocco, a fine gilt-edged edition bound in London; Christian Almanac for 1847; Life of Christ; and the most important of all our Tracts. These were neatly done up, and a red card attached to the bundle, stating from whom and to whom the books were sent. One object of sending them was to open the way for a personal conversation with each one on the subject of religion. The books being thankfully received, and cards of acceptance sent in return, I proceeded to visit several of the individuals in their homes.[31]

As to how successful these personal visits were for discussing religion, Pohlman further explains:

In all my visits among the wealthy, I have been well received; but the old stereotyped questions of age, name, and a long catalogue of queries about customs, manners, and the most insignificant trifles, all of which must be answered, almost completely nullify the great object a missionary has in...calling on such men. They will talk with you for hours on matters of the most trivial nature, but the moment the gospel is introduced you are made to feel that it is a most unwelcome topic, and every shift and turn seems to say, "Stand by, for I am holier than thou." At the same time they seem to approve of our object, and are lavish in their praise of our self-denying efforts.[32]

The missionaries naturally wished that the upper class would display a more open mind when it came to religion, but they had come to expect this and increasingly accepted the view that they would have to begin their proselytizing with "the lower orders and rise by degrees to the higher." To again quote Pohlman:

We have just the class of hearers here who are generally thought to be the *most* hopeful in all countries. The under ranks are the basis of the community, just as the lowest parts of a wall sustain the higher parts. Religion must *ascend* from the populace to the middle classes, and then again by progressive stages to the higher ranks, to the officers and the Emperor on the throne. We would have much to fear for the genuineness and complete success of Christian efforts in China, were it otherwise. Thus it was in the time of our Saviour, and thus it will ever be.[33]

Pohlman added that although this situation might seem discouraging to some persons in America, they should bear in mind that a similar situation exists among many of their own communities, yet this has not caused "pastors at home [to] shut their churches and cease from preaching."

III

The Modus Operandi
of Evangelism

The Amoy missionaries engaged in various activities in their efforts to win souls for Christ. During the early period their labors centered primarily around religious meetings and distribution of religious literature. With respect to the former, the most conventional meetings were the Sunday services, of which there generally were two. Because, according to the missionaries, the Chinese were "great sticklers" for doing things in a fixed manner, it was considered necessary for Sunday gatherings to take place at set times and be conducted in a routine manner. In view of their own personal experiences in America and their theological training, the missionaries obviously had no difficulty in meeting either of these requirements.

The practice followed by Pohlman was typical, with Sunday services beginning promptly at 9 a.m. and 3 p.m. This, he reported, had the effect of quickly assuming the appearance of Sunday worship in Christian lands, with many of the listeners coming in and taking their accustomed seats "with as much punctuality and regularity as church-goers back home." His order of worship also followed a plan that was reminiscent of Reformed services in the States, the general procedure being as follows: singing, reading a portion of Scripture, prayer, sermon, singing, prayer, and pronouncing the benediction. For those Chinese who were able to read or had committed some things to memory, there occasionally was the recitation in unison of the Ten Commandments or the Apostles' Creed and reading responsively from some of the Psalms.[1]

31

Although the Chinese participated lustily in the singing, it would be some time before congregational singing would win any honors as music. The Reverend Abbe Livingston Warnshuis, after having attended three or four Chinese-language services following his arrival at Amoy in late 1900, reported that the "singing in these Chinese churches is very much like the psalm-singing in our Holland churches, in that everyone sings as well and as loud as he can."[2] Not until after more practice—and especially after the appearance of a few missionaries who had some special training in music—did this situation improve significantly.

The Sunday agenda was only one of several religious activities directed by the missionaries on a regular basis. Among the others, one of the most unique was the so-called "Chinese Monthly Concert." The first of these took place on January 5, 1846, and henceforth was held on the first Monday of each month. As with so many of the religious activities, it was ecumenical in nature, with missionaries from the London Society and later also the English Presbyterians giving support. The meetings involved the reading of papers that had been carefully prepared beforehand and were presented in the Amoy dialect, usually by one of the native language teachers.

The subject matter of the papers varied: one month, it might concern the history of a mission in another part of the world, such as Ceylon or Madagascar; at another time, it might be a biographical account describing a noted missionary or a famous Christian convert; or perhaps it would be a description of another religion, such as Islam or Buddhism, or an event involving religious persecution in some far off land or at some time in the distant past. The Chinese audiences enjoyed these meetings, perhaps because in addition to becoming informed about missions in other lands, they learned something about geography and world history, including contemporary events. It was not uncommon for the sessions to last more than an hour and a half and for interest to be kept high throughout the period. Within a short time, the audiences at the Monthly Concerts increased fourfold, and the meeting place had to be transferred from one of the missionary residences to one of the chapels.

There also were Bible study gatherings that met on a weekly

basis. The first of these was introduced already in March, 1844, by Abeel for studying the New Testament, the next in September, 1846, by Pohlman for studying the Old Testament. Classes were held during the afternoon on Tuesdays for the Old Testament and on Thursdays for the New Testament. At these meetings, particular books of the Bible were selected for careful study--chapter by chapter, verse by verse, and sometimes even phrase by phrase. Classes averaged about twenty members, half of whom generally took an active part in the discussions.

Various other religious gatherings were also held. These included mid-week prayer services, in which native converts played important roles, and special meetings for converts on the Saturday preceding observance of the Lord's Supper. When the missionaries were not occupied with meetings of the kind described above, they usually stayed in their chapels—at least during the early years before they began making regular visits outside Amoy City. In their chapel offices, they received visitors and conducted miscellaneous religious exercises, including Scripture reading, prayer, and singing. They also discussed any topics that might be suggested by those coming to see them.[3]

The missionaries also distributed a considerable amount of religious literature as part of their evangelistic program. In 1846, for example, several thousand single sheet notices were printed describing the chapel meetings and inviting everyone to attend. These were posted throughout Amoy City and scattered among the villages on the island. Visitors at the Sunday services were also provided with literature. As described by Pohlman, this aspect of mission work became a vital means for spreading the gospel outside the immediate Amoy area:

> Not infrequently we will see, seated on the same benches, men from Fuh-chau, from Cheang-chew, from Choan-chew, from Tong-an, and from Cheoh-bey. Visitors to the city on business will come on purpose to seek out our houses; and it is quite common to find men intent on making a visit to the "Sunday Temples," as our chapels are called, before they return to their homes.[4]

The missionaries hoped, of course, that the visitors would later share the tracts with relatives and friends.

Special efforts were made to cultivate the good will of the

Chinese women, and it was not long before regular weekly meetings were held for them. Initially held in the homes of the married missionaries, with the missionary women presiding, these were soon transferred to one of the chapels because of increasing attendance. The deaths of Mrs. Doty and Mrs. Pohlman in the fall of 1845 were serious blows for this aspect of the mission, especially since these women had some acquaintance with the Chinese language before arriving at Amoy. Thereafter, until the arrival of the second Mrs. Doty in 1846 and Mrs. Talmage in 1850, and until these women became acquainted with the language, the male missionaries took turns presiding whenever possible. Married women of the other two missions also helped out.

Chinese women responded favorably to the attention shown them by the missionaries and their wives, as can be seen in this excerpt from a letter of March 15, 1854, written by Doty to the Market Street Reformed Church of New York City:

> That the gospel is drawing out so many of the women, is to us a most cheering fact. One of the darkest features in our prospects, and most soul-saddening a few years past, was the seeming exclusion of the female sex from gospel instruction and influence....It is now usual to meet twenty or thirty, and sometimes as many as fifty or sixty females waiting upon the ministry of the Word in public worship on the Sabbath. Goodly numbers too attend services held by various individuals specifically for women, and the weekly female prayer meeting presents a most cheering aspect.[5]

The Sunday worship services and the other religious activities that have been described were designed primarily for adults. Chinese children, however, were not ignored by the missionaries, although progress among them was slow at first. An elementary school established by the Reverend and Mrs. Doty lasted only a few months due to the untimely death of Mrs. Doty and the increasing responsibilities of her husband. Renewed attempts to establish schools during the next few years, including one for girls, met a similar fate. For a time thereafter, the missionaries followed a less formal approach by holding religion classes for children once or twice a week in cooperation with the

English Presbyterians. Instruction consisted primarily of expounding the Scriptures, singing hymns, and reciting prayers. The number of persons in regular attendance consisted of about a dozen children along with a few adults.

The reasons for the limited concern with formal education of children during the early period were several, including a shortage of personnel and teaching materials as well as a lack of interest among Chinese parents. There also was the fact that the missionaries themselves had mixed opinions at this time about dividing their time between preaching and teaching. This is clearly indicated in the mission's semi-annual report dated December 13, 1847:

> There being no school here ought not to be a matter of regret. The danger is, that where schools and printing and other labors engage the *first attention* of a missionary to the heathen, they are apt to give a turn to his future course, and impress him with the belief that such labors are of paramount importance. Thus it is that operations which in fact are only secondary, may come to occupy the first place, and a mission [may] drag out a poor existence, without ever attaining the great and all-important end, *the oral communication of the gospel of Christ.*[6]

It was not long, however, before the Reformed missionaries began looking upon the education of children in a more traditional light, and by 1856, they had virtually come full circle. This is clearly shown in a letter of January of that year from Talmage to the *Christian Intelligencer*. In it, he declared that although "preaching the gospel" must remain the "first and great work" of the missionaries, it was nevertheless "very important that the children of church members be gathered into a Christian school." He further added that if church members were able, it was "their duty to support such a school" and if unable, the mission "should assist them."[7]

This change of view came about as Talmage and his colleagues realized that the majority of the Chinese were illiterate and thus unable to understand the Scriptures and the religious tracts that were being distributed. Moreover, those few who could read had to be taught the necessary religious vocabulary not found in the Chinese language. As schooling progressed beyond the primary level, it was hoped that education could also be a means for training young men for the ministry as well as for opening up positions of importance in government and business for persons with Christian training. The education of girls could also be a means of emancipating Chinese women.

It thus happened in 1856 that the Reformed missionaries established two elementary schools—the one under the auspices of the First Church of Amoy, the other under the direction of the Second Church. In contrast to previous efforts at establishing schools, these institutions not only survived, but in due time they also flourished. Other than these two instances, however, elementary education did not progress significantly for some time after 1856. This is demonstrated by the fact that a third elementary school was not established until 1869, and a fourth not until 1881.

The documents of the time frequently refer to the schools as "day schools" because the pupils in attendance generally lived nearby and returned to their homes at the end of the school day. They were also termed "parochial schools" because they were intended for children of church members, although other pupils were occasionally admitted. Moreover, they were supported at this time primarily by the mission. Parents were generally too poor to pay for their children's education but were urged to contribute what they could.

A few nonreligious courses, such as geography and arithmetic, were offered, but the curriculum was basically designed to acquaint young minds with "the Scriptures and Christian Truths." Unfortunately, it was not uncommon for pupils to drop out of school when parents thought they were needed at home or when they had to take jobs to help support their families. It was also unfortunate that, because of the traditional Chinese attitude toward females, enrollment was made up mostly of boys. In 1865, for example, of the seventeen students enrolled in the school at First Church, only four were girls; at Second Church's school, the ratio was twenty to three in favor of boys.

The teachers were Chinese with occasional help provided by the missionaries or their wives. Because of the shortage of educated Christians among the Chinese, it was not uncommon to employ non-Christian teachers during the early period. They were expected, however, to adhere strictly to what they were told to teach and were carefully supervised by the missionaries. Later, with the formal organization of Chinese congregations, they were also supervised by the local pastor and his consistory. Fortunately, the founding of the Thomas De Witt Theological Seminary in 1869 and the Boys' Academy (also called the Middle School) in 1881 helped relieve the shortage of Christian teachers.

A major obstacle in combatting Chinese illiteracy among young and old alike was the Chinese writing system, which is radically different from the phonetically based alphabet used in the western world. Chinese writing is made up of thousands of intricate, difficult-to-learn characters that either singly or in combination make up the words in the Chinese language. To be able to read even a few hundred of the numerous Chinese characters and understand their meanings requires a good memory and many months of study.[8]

The hopelessness of the prevailing situation and the desire to facilitate teaching the people how to read soon prompted the missionaries to introduce the use of Roman alphabet letters to represent Chinese words. By choosing eighteen Roman letters and aspirating some of them, an alphabet of twenty-three letters was created. Diacritical marks were inserted when necessary to indicate the fine shades of sound and tone that are so characteristic of Chinese speech. As explained by Talmage in 1851:

> The plan is yet only an experiment, but seems perfectly feasible. We trust that, by some such means as this, much may be done towards the elevation of the great mass of this people. By the use of their present cumbersome characters, the great majority can never become intelligent readers; but by the plan thus adopted, if we can only furnish the requisite number of books, the means of learning to read will be within the reach of almost every individual.[9]

As an illustration of replacing the complicated Chinese characters with the Roman alphabet and the use of diacritical marks, note how the Lord's Prayer appeared in Romanized script:

> Goán ê Pë toà tï thin-nih, goän lí ê miâ tsòe sèng; lí ê kok lîm-kàu, lí ê chí-ì tioh chiân tï töe-nih chhin-chhiün tï

thiⁿ-nih; só tioh·ëng ê bí-niû kin-â-jit hö· goán: goán siá-bián tek-tsöe goán ê lâng, kiû sià-bián goán ê tsöe; boh-tit hö· goán tú-tioh chhì, tioh kiù goán chhut pháiⁿ; in-üi kok, koân-lêng, êng-kng lóng sï lí-ê kàu täi-täi; sim só· goän.[10]

The introduction of Roman letters to represent the sound of Chinese words reduced significantly the amount of time needed to learn to read. The organization of language classes for young and old thus became one of the main features of the mission during its formative years. The process was a laborious one, but significant progress was being made already by the early 1850s. The work was carried out, of course, in the dialect spoken at Amoy.

Romanizing the Amoy dialect was only one part of the problem of teaching the Chinese to read. Closely related to it was the need to translate materials, especially those of a religious nature, into the new script. This task, too, occupied much of the missionaries' time. One of the first translations to appear was the story of Joseph as recorded in the book of Genesis. Its significance was described as follows in an 1851 issue of the *Chinese Repository*:

> This pamphlet [is an attempt] at Romanizing the Chinese language for the purpose of teaching the natives through another medium than their own characters...These nine chapters of Genesis are printed with this object, and the success has been such that the missionaries at Amoy are going to publish the Gospels in the same manner. Their pupils and converts are taught the initials and finals used in that dialect in the Roman character, and the mode of combining and marking them to form all the sounds and tones known to them; they soon learn to read the words, and are pleased—in some instances greatly amazed—to find how readily they understand what they read.[11]

Because of Pohlman's failing eyesight, he was greatly handicapped in compiling translations, but not so with his colleague Doty. In addition to the latter's manual on the Amoy dialect described earlier (which was done in Romanized characters), his translations included *Some Thoughts on the Proper Term of God in the Chinese* (1850); *Translation of Sacramental and Marriage Forms of the Reformed Protestant*

Dutch into Amoy Colloquial (1853); and *Translation and Revision into the Amoy Dialect of Milner's Thirteen Village Sermons, including Milner's Tract on the Strait Gate* (1854).[12]

The most renowned of the Reformed church translators was Talmage, who staked out this type of work as one of his special projects as soon as he arrived at Amoy and pursued it throughout the forty-five years he spent there.[13] Like Doty his early translations consisted of a variety of works, including *A Primer of the Amoy Colloquial* (1852) that went through several editions; *The Book of Ruth* (1853); *Pilgrim's Progress, Part One* (1853); *Liturgical Forms* (1860); and various portions of the New Testament.

Members of other missionary groups were also diligent in translating works into Chinese and advancing the study of the Amoy dialect. By all accounts, the most accomplished lexicographer among the missionaries was the Reverend Carstairs Douglas of the English Presbyterian Mission. A tireless worker, Douglas for about a decade and a half spent every free moment, even while on furlough, working on his magnum opus, *A Chinese-English Dictionary of the Vernacular or Spoken Language of Amoy*, published in 1873.[14] Similarly, the Reverend John Stronach of the London Missionary Society, as a member of a committee charged with cooperating with missionary groups throughout China, labored to bring about a revision of the New Testament. In 1847, he was designated as the Amoy delegate to a conference held at Shanghai to discuss "important questions connected with the new version."[15]

At first, all printing was done from type carved on the face of wooden blocks, but movable type and a printing press were soon introduced. When the Reverend Howard Van Doren arrived in 1865, he was given primary charge of the press. Most printing expenses during the early period were borne by the American Bible Society and the American Tract Society.

The Romanization of the Amoy colloquial was a boon not only for the Chinese people wishing to learn to read, but it also facilitated the learning of the Chinese language by newly arrived missionaries. Thus, the Reverends Alvin Ostrum and Daniel Rapalje, who arrived at Amoy in 1858, were able after ten months to accompany native helpers and engage in some preaching. And a report of 1863 states that the "improved procedures" for learning Chinese enabled newly arrived missionaries, "if they be industrious," to be able to preach "with considerable fluency" within a year after arrival.[16]

The introduction and use of the Romanized colloquial, despite its many advantages, was not readily accepted by everyone. As the Reverend Pitcher remarked, "All innovations of this kind are bound to meet with objection in this country, distinguished for its conservatism."[17] Strongest opposition came, as might be expected, from those who considered themselves members of the literary class. To them, it was boorish and completely lacking in style. Similarly, there were those among the masses who, having been accustomed to look with awe upon the traditional classical language, considered the Romanized colloquial as being fit only for women and children.

Baptizing the Chinese and receiving them into the Christian church as full communicant members was, of course, the ultimate goal of the various evangelistic activities. The first converts to become communicant members under the supervision of the Reformed mission were two elderly men, Lau Un-sia and Hok-kui-peyh, both near seventy years of age. Although they had been ministered to since the arrival of Abeel, they were not admitted as full church members until four years later, April 5, 1846. On that day, a Sunday, they were baptized at the morning service and admitted as confessing church members at the afternoon service. Pohlman was in charge of both services but was assisted by a member of the London Missionary Society.[18] The next event of this kind did not occur until July, 1849, when a widowed mother, age 64, and her two sons, ages 35 and 44, were baptized by the Reverend Doty and admitted as confessing members--again under the supervision of the Reformed mission but with assistance of someone from the London Missionary group.

By 1849, the Reformed mission thus had won only five converts during the seven years since the arrival of the Reverend Abeel in 1842. Possible reasons as to why the Chinese were slow in accepting the Christian gospel will be discussed in a later chapter.[19] It should be noted at this point, however, that the number of "first fruits" being reported by the other two missions was also low during their formative years. The Stronach brothers of the London Missionary Society, for example, after preaching in a rented building in Amoy City since 1844 and having at times as many as 150 listeners, reported their first baptisms—a father and his son—in 1848. Similarly, William Burns, the English Presbyterian who worked at Canton before transferring to Amoy in 1851, is reported to have tearfully told a friend in December, 1853, "I have labored in China for seven years, and I don't know of a single soul brought to Christ by me."[20]

The practice of formally admitting a person as a communicant member on the same Sunday (and sometimes, even at the same service) that he or she was baptized was not uncommon during the early years of the mission. Later, the more common practice was to wait a reasonable period between the two ceremonies. With respect to *baptism*, a letter by Doty gives several hints regarding the procedures that eventually became quite standard. It describes the outcome of a request for baptism by some thirty Chinese. The applicants included persons of both sexes and their ages varied from twenty to seventy. According to Doty, several of them were turned down immediately for not yet being "proper subjects for church membership," but were encouraged to continue their concern about "their souls' salvation." For the others, special sessions were held to instruct them in the meaning of baptism and the responsibilities of church membership. As to the frequency and general nature of these sessions, together with the final results, Doty added:

A part of the time we have held the meetings once in two weeks, generally once a week, though in some instances twice. In these meetings we are usually engaged from three to four hours, during which time we may converse with or examine, as the case may be, three or four individuals in the most searching manner, both as to their experiential knowledge of the Holy Spirit's work in their hearts, and their acquaintance with Chinese doctrine. This brings us into the closest personal contact with their minds, and enables us to give instruction, to correct misconceptions of truth, guide the inquiring, encourage, warn and exhort, so as to meet the difficulties of each individual, and the profit of all. Of those applying, after several examinations, ten were admitted to baptism on the last Sabbath of last month, March 26. Two of these are women, one aged sixty eight, and the other forty-seven; while the males, their ages range from twenty to sixty-four years.[21]

Although the Chinese had only recently been exposed to Christian teachings, their questions at sessions like those described above could be incisive. As explained by the English Presbyterian Johnston who worked closely with the Reformed missionaries:

It was often amusing to hear old difficulties blurted out in Chinese monosyllables: "Teacher, why did God let Adam fall?" "Why was Satan allowed to get into Paradise?" "Why does God not save everyone?" and many such questions, to which only an imperfect answer could be given.[22]

Persons who expressed a desire to be admitted into the church as *full members* met with the missionaries or, after formal church organizations began appearing, with the local pastor and elders. Those wishing to join the church were commonly referred to as "inquirers." An excerpt from a letter of April 20, 1854 written by Talmage to his brother, the Reverend Goyn Talmage, gives a succinct description of what took place at these "inquiry meetings":

We commence by reading and explaining a portion of Scripture, and follow this with prayer. We then engage in conversation with inquirers, and close with a few general remarks, such as the circumstances of the inquirers suggest. In conversation, we endeavor to ascertain how much knowledge they have acquired of Christian doctrine [in order that we may] correct their errors and impart further instruction; also to ascertain as far as possible the state of their hearts, that we may judge whether or not they have really been made new creatures in Christ.[23]

Talmage added that the examinations must be "as searching as we can make them." The fact that considerable instruction as well as questioning took place at these meetings explains why the number of inquirers in attendance at any one time was usually kept small and why a session might last several hours.

The reason for delaying the formal admission to full communicant membership is further described in this excerpt from a letter by Doty to the American Board dated June 25, 1855:

> Our treating with persons just emerging from the darkness of heathenism, as to their soul's condition and their right to church fellowship, is a different thing from what pastors and church-officers [at home] do with those who have been born, and have lived, in the full blaze of gospel light. This deep soul-darkness [in China] can be removed only by much watchful care and diligent instruction. The weak and timid must be strengthened and encouraged. Those who seem to be indulging a hope of salvation on insufficient ground, must have their danger pointed out.[24]

Newcomers to Amoy were impressed by the meticulous care taken by the missionaries before admitting a Chinese to church membership. Note, for example, the following comment made by the Reverend John S. Joralmon in July, 1856, three months after his arrival:

> Just [arriving] from my native land, I have no hesitation in saying that the brethren here are far more careful in the reception of members than are the churches at home. I have learned the principles on which they examine inquirers—their delay in receiving them—their inquiry of those acquainted with them; and even after the most satisfactory examination, they do not admit [anyone] to church membership without the unanimous consent of the elders of the church. Furthermore—and this without any disparagement of our home church members—I have far less doubt of the genuineness of their conversion than I have of the majority of those in church-fellowship at home.[25]

The careful attention given to the admission of new members obviously kept "backsliding" to a minimum, but there were cases from time to time involving the suspension of church members and even an occasional excommunication. Reasons for such actions were various, but the most common was nonobservance of Sunday as a holy day. The temptation to break the Sabbath was particularly pronounced because for most Chinese it was just another business day, and to close a shop on Sundays could mean a loss of needed income. Other reasons for disciplinary action included dealing in drugs, intoxication, sexual immorality, and gambling. The first step in dealing with an errant member was suspension. If after a few months he or she had shown no remorse and was "continuing in sin," excommunication followed.[26]

A discussion of evangelistic activity during the formative years of the Amoy mission would be incomplete without giving some attention to the training of a native Chinese ministry. The important role that such individuals could play was pointedly explained by Talmage in a letter of 1848:

> The Christian in his journey heavenward, seeks companions, and leads others after him to the gates of the celestial city. Thus every true convert becomes in some measure a helper....His example is a "light shining in a dark place." Especially is it true among the heathen, that every disciple of Christ is a city set on a hill, which cannot be hid. . . . Such converts, also, in some respects, may be more efficient than the missionary. They can go where we cannot, and reach those who are entirely beyond our influence. They understand the customs of the people more thoroughly. They remember what were the greatest difficulties and objections and what proved the greatest obstacles to their reception of the Gospel, and they know how these difficulties were removed, and these objections answered.[27]

Until the formal founding of a seminary, theological training took place in the homes of the missionaries. The nature of this irregular kind of education was explained in another letter by Talmage:

> On the thirty-first day of July, I commenced a theological class. It is attended by our colporteurs, when they are in Amoy, and by several other Christian converts, mostly young men of much promise. They meet in my study at 11 o'clock on Tuesdays, Thursdays, and Saturdays. I spend an hour and a half with them each day. On Tuesdays, I instruct them in systematic theology. For the subjects on Thursdays, I am at present taking Edward's

History of Redemption as a guide. On Saturdays, they read
essays, prepared by themselves, on theological topics and
texts of Scripture.[28]

The length of time spent by young men studying theology
varied. For some the training was brief and equipped them to
serve as little more than colporteurs, that is, distributors of
devotional literature. Others who received more extensive
training served as lay ministers with limited duties. In the
literature of the time, they were referred to simply as
"evangelists" or "preachers." Two young men who had received
more than the usual training were ordained in 1863 as
full-fledged ministers. To distinguish them from their
unordained co-workers, they were generally called "pastors." The
London Missionary Society and English Presbyterians also made
a clear distinction between pastors and preachers.[29]

IV
Branching Outward, 1842-1863

The city of Amoy remained the focal point of missionary work during the formative years, but it was by no means the only area of activity. In addition, there were the several dozen villages scattered on Amoy Island and, most challenging of all, there was the mainland. The immensity of the task facing the missionaries can be ascertained from the following communication of September 17, 1845, from Pohlman to the First Reformed Church of Albany:

> It is understood that the prescribed limit for foreigners is anywhere within a full day's travel of the five treaty ports. Taking Amoy as a center, and keeping within this range, we can probably reach as many as 400 villages. The inhabitants are chiefly cultivators of the soil, and combine together for mutual protection. In this way we find the whole country thickly studded with settlements of here several thousands, and there a thousand; here a few hundreds, and there a few fifties.[1]

The five treaty ports referred to by Pohlman consisted of Canton plus the four ports opened by the treaties signed after the First Opium War (1839-1842). These included Amoy, Foochow, Ningpo, and Shanghai, in all of which foreigners were now allowed to reside and trade. By the treaties that followed the Second Opium War (1856-1860), ten more ports were opened, and foreign travel was permitted throughout China. Permission was also granted to lease or buy land and to build houses.

A limited amount of "branching outward" occurred almost

immediately after the arrival of the first missionaries, as was also explained by Pohlman in the letter referred to above:

The first quarter of the year [after becoming settled in Amoy], I went abroad in various directions to view the field in which God had placed me, taking tracts and speaking a word as I could. Besides visiting different parts of the city and suburbs, some of us went about the villages [on the island], teaching in their temples, and preaching the gospel of the kingdom. We went by boat to other islands, and to places on the mainland. These excursions were made in company with our dear brother Abeel.

Pohlman added that the villages of Amoy Island were particularly within easy reach:

Starting after breakfast, we would return in time for tea. Thus, about a dozen villages would be visited. These villages are numerous at every point of the compass, and afford a wide field of itinerary labor. On the island of Amoy alone, 30 miles in circumference, there are said to be 136. All of these are perfectly accessible to the "circuit preacher," and may be reached on foot. [2]

In September 1846, a year after writing the above, Pohlman informed his Albany friends that as a result of "several excursions," all the villages on Amoy Island "have now been visited, supplied with our books, and exhorted to make their peace with God."[3]

Transportation by water via the Amoy estuary and the rivers that flowed into it facilitated visits to some parts of the mainland. This became particularly true after the missionaries acquired their own so-called "gospel boats." The first of these was a somewhat cumbersome affair, but thanks to financial help in 1859 from the Sunday school of the Greenwich Reformed Church of New York City, an improved, sleeker craft was built. Indeed, the funds were sufficient to construct a second, albeit smaller, boat. They were appropriately named the *Greenwich* and the *Thomas C. Strong*. The latter, which was the smaller boat, was named after the pastor of the Greenwich church.[4]

In a letter from Amoy dated August 6, 1863, the Reverend Leonard William Kip, who served in China from 1861 to 1898, described in detail the accommodations of the *Greenwich*:

Our new boat has been completed, and has been in
running order for several weeks. A week ago Saturday I
made my first trip in her up to Chioh-be [located about
fifteen miles from Amoy on the lower estuary]. She is a
good size, about 28 feet long, and sails very well. She is
both safer and much more comfortable than our old boat.
The cabin is comparatively spacious. Though only seven
feet abeam, it is large enough for our purposes. It has two
births, each 2 feet wide, which are so low that they may
also be used to sit on, and a table. Being high enough to
stand upright in, you will see that it is possible to live in
her quite comfortably for a day or two. And since we
cannot always get decent lodgings on shore, this becomes
a great consideration.[5]

At the time Kip wrote the above letter, the financial situation
permitted the hiring of only one permanent crew member for the
Greenwich, but later a second man was added.

Trips to the mainland were often carried out in the company of
another missionary (sometimes from the English Presbyterian
mission) and one or two Chinese converts. Their itineraries
included not only the more populous communities, but also the
villages and hamlets. In explaining their plans on this matter, the
missionaries were wont to liken their responsibility to that of the
prophet Isaiah's injunction to the Israelites (with some slight
paraphrasing), namely, that they "enlarge the place of their tents,
lengthen the cords, and break out on the right and the left."[6] That
is, they hoped to organize churches in the larger places and
establish preaching stations in the smaller surrounding villages.

Thus, in 1847, Pohlman made three trips to Changchow, one of
which lasted three days, and one trip to Tong-an. Both of these
places could be easily reached by boat. Changchow, located about
thirty-five miles to the west of Amoy, was one of the largest cities
in the province of Fukien, while Tong-an, situated about twenty
miles north of Amoy, had a population of about 100,000 and was
the capital of the township in which Amoy was located. Both cities
were within easy reach of dozens of villages.[7]

An idea of what took place during these visits away from Amoy
City can be gathered from the following description of a two-day
boat trip made by the Reverend Joralmon in the spring of 1857.

Joralmon, who served the Reformed mission from 1855 to 1859, was accompanied by the Reverend Carstairs Douglas of the English Presbyterian mission and two Chinese evangelists. The rather lengthy description is given here almost in its entirety because it furnishes an excellent word picture of what the missionaries experienced many times over during the next several decades as they traveled from town to town and from village to village.

At Ko-Kia we divided into two companies, and went into different parts of the town, where we had large and attentive audiences....Our plan of laboring is to have the evangelists commence preaching, continuing say an hour, then I say a few words of exhortation to them, also an invitation to attend our public services....After this, tracts and books are distributed to those who are able to read—which I am sorry to say, is but a small proportion—so that our principal means of reaching this people must be by the oral proclamation of the truth. The only interruption we ever have in these services is a friendly invitation to take a cup of tea or smoke a pipe of tobacco....We distribute freely a broad sheet containing the Ten Commandments, with explanations, etc....

After spending a few hours at Ko-Kia we again embarked and after a sail of an hour and a half reached Lok-go-tiam, on the mainland to the north of [Amoy] island....After ascending a neighboring hill to get a view of the villages on the plain, we returned to our boat, partook of our evening meal, engaged in Chinese worship with the boatmen and evangelists, and then after our own thanksgiving and prayer to God for this people, for our absent loved ones, and for ourselves, well tired-out with the labors of the day, we slept quietly until about 5 A. M., when we again set sail for a little seaport town about five miles distant, called O-thaw, a place where the Word had been preached once before. Here we stopped a few hours until the turning of the tide compelled us to leave. Our preaching-place here was the steps of the principal temple.[8]

Two more places were visited by Joralmon and his party before returning to Amoy City.

In another excerpt from Joralmon's letter we have a good illustration of the important role the Chinese evangelists played on these trips. It also points out one of the advantages of their being accompanied by a missionary:

> I wish you could hear these dear native evangelists plead with their countrymen; often have I been almost affected to tears by their earnest exhortations and untiring labors. On some accounts, their presenting the truth must always be more forceful than that which a foreigner can set before them. The missionary's accompanying them is of great importance, even though he be not able to say a word, as it always assures to them an audience. Even in the smallest fishing villages there are those who are ready to hear, if we accompany them, while sometimes the evangelists have gone alone to a very large village, without being able to collect anyone to hear the truth.[9]

The missionaries were, on the whole, kindly received during their excursions among the villages on Amoy and the surrounding islands. In December, 1845, for example, Pohlman reported that he had recently spent five days visiting them, "sleeping and eating among their inhabitants," who, he added, received him kindly and treated him "as well as people in America."[10]   Receptions were also cordial on the mainland, as explained by Pohlman following his visits to Changchow and Tong-an in March and September, 1847:

> The scenery, the reception, and everything connected with the excursion, rendered them pleasant and long to be remembered. Large and attentive assemblies listened to our exhortations....We found our stock of books not half large enough for furnishing supplies to the readers.[11]

These early visits gave most Chinese people their first opportunity to see a foreigner and they were naturally curious. Not only did they listen attentively, they asked questions on almost every conceivable subject.

A decade later, Joralmon reported receiving similar courtesies during his travels, courtesies he described as quite different from the reception accorded missionaries in the Canton area. A communication of his in 1857 sheds some light on why foreigners at Amoy were viewed differently:

> During our journeys we oft go to places before unvisited by foreigners, and are treated with the greatest kindness. There [at Canton] the most bitter feeling exists between the natives and the foreign community; here everything is pleasant. The people are led to look upon us as very kind to them. At present there is a great scarcity of rice; a number of junks, loaded with this staff of life to this people, had been intercepted by the pirates with which the Chinese coast is infested. Tidings of this were communicated to the British Consul at Amoy, who forthwith dispatched the *Camilla* brig of war stationed here, which vessel was able to bring from the clutches of the pirates two junks with rice. This has occurred several times....A few days since, a number of the merchants of the place made a very fine present to the commander of the brig for his success with the pirates. Within the last week the *Camilla* brought in twenty-five pirates, who were beheaded the following morning.[12]

In the same way that Pohlman contended that systematization and orderliness regarding stated times and places were necessary for preaching in Amoy City,[13] he was similarly convinced that such procedures should be followed in pursuing evangelization programs elsewhere. He therefore expected only limited success in the immediate future from this early "branching out." In describing, for example, his visits to the villages on Amoy Island in 1846, Pohlman wrote: "These itinerary efforts do little more than prepare the way. It is our regular, stated efforts at [Amoy City] that we mainly depend [on] for introducing light and knowledge into these dark minds." He also warned against the missionaries' spreading themselves too thinly, adding that "the more our labors are concentrated on a select few, the more probability is there that the seed will take root, and bring forth fruit."[14]

Pohlman was even more specific on these matters in a letter of the following year:

> Mere curiosity, of course, [draws] hundreds of the rabble to see us, receive our books, and give shouts at hearing a foreigner speak. In general, no impression but that of "the

ridiculous" is left behind. These random efforts are not
only unavoidable, but perhaps important in the first stages
of a mission to this people, but I am fully convinced that as
soon as possible they should give way to more *regular and
stated services*. There should be a *set time and place* for
preaching and teaching. Method is a predominant feature
in the Chinese mind. They have a way of their own—a
form to which everything must be adjusted *just so*, and no
other way will do.[15]

The Reverend John Stronach of the London Missionary Society
agreed that although journeys of the kind described above were a
necessary part of missionary work, only limited success could be
achieved from such "flying visits," as he termed them.[16]

"Regular and stated services," to use Pohlman's words, were, of
course, difficult outside of Amoy City during the early period
because of the shortage of missionary personnel. Before 1855,
there generally were only two ordained Reformed missionaries
in China, and during some years there was only one. Nor did the
situation improve significantly during the next few years. It is
thus not surprising that the missionaries, in their correspondence
to America and in their addresses delivered to religious groups
when they were home on furlough, repeatedly stressed the need
for a larger staff. Typical were the remarks made by Talmage at a
meeting of the American Board of Commissioners for Foreign
Missions in the late summer of 1849. As reported in the *Christian
Intelligencer*, his remarks were delivered in a "language
calculated to arouse attention and cause the ears of every lover of
Zion to tingle."[17] Although speaking before an interdenominational missionary organization, he directed his attention
particularly to the Reformed church:

We do not desire to reprove or find fault. We may, we
must present the facts which we hear and see and feel.
Some of these facts are, that the heathen are perishing
around us, our missionaries are dying off, and the Church
at home has a surplus of ministers....Unless something be
speedily done...the operation of the Reformed Dutch
Church will belong entirely to the history of the past. The
sure process to hasten this consummation will be to leave
those who are now in the field pressed down with their

labors, and without reinforcement.[18]

A similar appeal was made a few years later by Joralmon in a letter to the *Christian Intelligencer*:

> I [must] remind brethren in the ministry, as well as those about to enter the sacred office, that around Amoy, the center of a circle, a little more than sixty miles in diameter, are a million souls waiting for the preached gospel—and only seven to break the bread of life—one minister of the gospel to more than 130,000 souls. Will you stay at home to minister to tens, when here you might have tens of thousands among whom to labor? [This is] a field where seeds are already sown, yea, where the harvest is only waiting for the reaper's sickle. Everything to encourage, everything to stimulate to nobler efforts in this glorious cause. Shall our dear little Zion mourn because the watchmen on her towers are so few?[19]

Responses to appeals like the above fell far short of what was needed. Although twenty-one Reformed men and women served at Amoy during the first twenty-five years of the mission's existence, the number residing there at any one time remained low. In part, this was because of early deaths. Sanitary conditions at Amoy were among the worst in China, and when plagues, such as cholera, broke out, thousands died, members of missionary families included.[20] Among those who died in China during the period were Eleanor Doty, 1845; Theodosia Pohlman, 1845; William Pohlman, 1849; and Abby Talmage, 1862.. All died from disease except Pohlman who, as has been mentioned, met his death by drowning. Several children also died. Nearly all the above were buried in a small cemetery on Kulangsu Island. They were by no means the last to find this hallowed ground as their final resting place.[21]

Several other missionaries remained in China only a few years because of poor health. This was the case with the Reverend and Mrs. John Joralmon, who arrived in 1855 and returned home in 1859; the Reverend and Mrs. Alvin Ostrom, who came in 1858 and left in 1864; and the Reverend and Mrs. August Blauvelt, who served from 1861 to 1864. Early departures like these were doubly discouraging because it took many months of diligent study for a replacement to become adept in the Chinese language. Most male

missionaries who left China earlier than planned, accepted calls to
churches on their return to the States. Sometimes, however, this
had to wait until their health had improved. It took Ostrom, for
example, two years of recuperation before he was able to accept
charge of a Reformed congregation in Nutley, New Jersey.

Fortunately for the success of the mission, there were a few
missionaries during this early period who served for a
considerable length of time. Talmage labored at Amoy for
forty-five years (1847-1892). The Reverends Daniel Rapalje and
Leonard Kip stayed nearly as long. Rapalje went there
immediately after graduation from New Brunswick Seminary in
1858 and was associated with the mission for forty-one years,
retiring in 1899. Kip spent almost as much time in China as
Rapalje, going there in 1861 and returning in 1898.

The missionaries who stayed on (sometimes termed the "Old
China Hands") were naturally disappointed that so many
colleagues remained for only a brief period. Such developments
made it difficult at times for the missionaries to understand God's
will, but, as they did with other disappointments, they accepted
these as having some ultimate good purpose. This attitude shows
clearly in the following letter written by Rapalje on November 25,
1863, when it became apparent that the continued poor health of
Ostrom would soon force him to return home:

> The Lord has been pleased greatly to afflict him, and we
> cannot understand why the affliction has been sent. The
> need for laborers in this field is very great, and why is it
> that another missionary is compelled to leave? This is the
> way in which we, in our ignorance, reason. Still it is true
> that "whom the Lord loveth, He chasteneth." Many things
> that we cannot understand now, will be made plain
> hereafter. Though the laborers are few, the Lord of the
> harvest will in some way, provide for gathering in the
> ripening grain.[22]

The close cooperation existing between the Reformed
missionaries and those of the English Presbyterian church helped
relieve the burdens of the small Reformed staff somewhat.
Indeed, as will be explained in the next chapter, this cordial
relationship eventually led to a formal union. Cooperation was
encouraged not only by the similarities in doctrine and polity of

the Reformed and English Presbyterian churches but also by the disposition of the early English missionaries to look upon administrative responsibilities, even routine pastoral duties, as of limited importance. They preferred instead to move about freely as itinerant preachers and turn over administrative and related matters to the more experienced Reformed missionaries. For example, the Reverend William Burns, who arrived at Amoy in July, 1851, stipulated at the time of his ordination in England as a missionary to China that "he was to be in no way bound to discharge ministerial functions, but to be strictly an Evangelist."[23] His immediate successors also took that position.

Upon Burns's arrival, it was soon agreed that because he was unmarried and interested wholly in evangelism, he would concentrate his work on the mainland while the two Reformed missionaries, Doty and Talmage, would continue for a while longer to confine their activities largely to Amoy City and the villages on both Amoy and the neighboring islands. Because the dialect Burns had learned was Cantonese rather than Amoyese, he delayed almost a year before making his first visit to the mainland in March, 1852. During that year, he gained some valuable experience by visiting, in the company of one or more Chinese converts from the Reformed mission, the various villages surrounding Amoy City.[24]

Intinerant preaching of the kind carried out by Burns on the mainland was not without worthwhile results, but it quickly became evident that permanent mission centers were needed from which the gospel could be spread to the surrounding areas. The city of Changchow was chosen as the location for the first of these centers or "hubs." It was chosen on the basis of the favorable impressions Doty and Talmage received from a visit there in the late 1840s and from a two-week visit made by Burns in April, 1853. A house was rented in the central part of the city to serve as a chapel, and in May, 1853, two native evangelists were sent there to introduce stated preaching on a regular basis. Unfortunately, unforeseen events doomed the project to failure.

One of the men sent to Changchow was U Teng-an, or "Teacher U" as he was frequently called. Born and raised near Canton, U had gone to Thailand at about age twenty-one to seek his fortune. There, through reading some missionary tracts, he became interested in Christianity, and in 1844 was baptized at Bangkok. In 1846, the young convert returned to China, arriving at Amoy in August of that year. In early March of 1847, Pohlman employed him as an evangelist, in which capacity he proved very helpful. One of his responsibilities during the next few months was to conduct informal services at eleven o'clock each morning in one of the vacant houses on the site selected for constructing Pohlman's proposed church. He was also used as a special interpreter when it was deemed expedient to use the court dialect in the presence of high-ranking Chinese officials. U's greatest usefulness, however, was as an itinerant evangelist.

Although the prospects for establishing a mission station at Changchow had appeared favorable when U was sent there, circumstances changed when the Taiping Rebellion moved into that area. The Taiping Rebellion was the most serious of many uprisings that plagued the Chinese government during the nineteenth century. Its leader was Hung Hsiu-ch'uan, who as a young man had become frustrated and seriously ill after repeatedly failing the provincial civil service examinations. For a time he found comfort in religion, having acquired a rudimentary knowledge of Christianity from a few contacts with a Baptist missionary at Canton and from reading some religious tracts. Later, Hung began having visions about being Christ's younger brother and being delegated by God to establish a new dispensation on earth.

In view of the conditions prevailing in China, including political corruption, widespread economic problems, and foreign imperialism, it is not surprising that Hung's "homemade Christianity," which was liberally sprinkled with Confucianism and Taoism, found some appeal. This became especially true when he began advocating the overthrow of the antiquated government at Peking and replacing it with a government based on social justice. In 1851, Hung proclaimed the Taiping, or "Great Peace," Kingdom with himself as the heavenly king. Nanking became the Taiping capital and with the help of several armies the movement spread rapidly. The rebellion reached its height in 1856, although Nanking was not retaken by government troops until 1864. Regional militia units and a foreign volunteer army, together with factional strife within the Taiping ranks, led to its decline and eventual fall—but only after considerable destruction (more than 600 cities and towns were destroyed) and the death of more than 20 million Chinese people.[25]

In the course of the hostilities that broke out between the pro- and anti-Taiping forces at Changchow, U and his associate, being strangers in the city, were suspected by some of the indignant populace of belonging to the insurgents. In events of this kind in which anarchy often prevails, many people frequently are unjustly accused of crimes and summarily tried in a people's court that ignores ordinary rules of justice—and so it happened with U. Although innocent of any wrongdoing, he was found guilty of insurrection and beheaded within a few hours of his capture. His colleague managed, with great difficulty, to escape and make his way back to Amoy to give an account of what had taken place. Needless to say, this turn of events delayed the establishment of a mission station at Changchow, although missionaries and evangelists continued to visit there occasionally.

The reversal experienced at Changchow was partly offset by successes elsewhere on the mainland. The first of these gains took place at Peh-chui-ia. Located about twenty miles southwest of Amoy, Peh-chui-ia was not a large town, having only about 5,000 inhabitants, but it was the commercial center of a valley containing numerous agricultural villages. Its market, which was held every third day, attracted visitors from the surrounding area. Although the Reformed missionaries made occasional journeys there, it was the English Presbyterian Burns who made the first lasting impression. Accompanied by two native converts from the Reformed mission, he visited Peh-chui-ia in the fall of 1853 and again in January of the following year. On the latter occasion, the trio intended to remain only for a few days; instead, they stayed in the area for almost two months. What transpired can be seen in a letter written by Burns:

> I left Amoy on the 9th with two [converts] of the American Church on a missionary tour, and since then we have been in this place, preaching on market days to a few among thousands who then assemble to buy and sell, and on other days going out among the surrounding villages, which are many and populous. We are everywhere very well received, and our message is listened to with

attention, and in some cases we may hope with profit.[26]
The interest shown at Peh-chui-ia prompted Burns to rent a
house, the lower floor of which was converted into a "preaching
hall," while the upper story served as living quarters for Burns
and his associates.

In all these activities, Burns continued to labor primarily as an
evangelist, preferring to turn routine pastoral and financial
responsibilities over to the Reformed missionaries at Amoy City.
This is clearly shown in another excerpt from one of his letters:

> I do not propose, in regard to these people, to act
> differently from what I have always done—viz., confining
> myself to the work of teaching and preaching, and leaving
> the peculiar duties of the pastoral office to others. [To that
> end, I have sent] several persons, eight in all...to Amoy to
> be examined by our American brethren, with a view to
> baptism. With most of these cases, these brethren are most
> interested; and I have told them that I think the time is
> come when, for the good of the Peh-chu-ia people, they
> should take a more special charge of that place as an
> out-station. This they are in a position to do, having native
> agents whom they can employ.[27]

Acting on Burns's suggestion, Doty and Talmage made
occasional visits to Peh-chui-ia to examine any Chinese who
evinced a desire to be baptized and to administer the sacrament to
those who seemed qualified. Like Burns, the Reformed
missionaries were greatly impressed with the spiritual awakening
that seemed to be taking place there. When Doty visited
Peh-chui-ia in March, 1854, he reported that he "found such an
awakening interest and spirit of inquiry" as he "had never before
met with among the Chinese."[28]

When Burns returned to England for a year in August 1854,
his work at Peh-chui-ia was taken over by another English
Presbyterian, the Reverend James Johnston, who had arrived in
Amoy a few months earlier. Although the English Presbyterians
at this time began assuming more financial responsibility for their
work, the Reformed missionaries continued the practice of
examining candidates for baptism, administering the sacraments
when appropriate, and giving further instruction to those needing
additional preparation. On May 17, 1854, a congregation consisting

of five members was formally organized at Peh-chui-ia. Its denominational identity was left in limbo at first, but the congregation later became affiliated with the English Presbyterians.

When Johnston returned to England in 1855 for reasons of health, his place was taken by the Reverend Carstairs Douglas who, in terms of later importance, was to become for the English Presbyterian mission what Talmage was for the Reformed mission. It was under Douglas's direction that the English Presbyterians finally assumed full responsibility, pastoral as well as financial, for the mission work in the Peh-chui-ia area. It was also at about this time that the English Presbyterians became more involved at Amoy City by establishing a station of their own in one of its populous suburbs, E-mng-kang. They, however, continued for some time the policy established earlier of freely using converts of the Reformed mission as helpers in carrying on their work.

Meanwhile, the Reformed missionaries decided to put behind them the unfortunate experience of Changchow, with its martyrdom of their evangelist, and become more directly involved on the mainland. While still cooperating fully as a kind of appendage to the work being done by the English Presbyterians, Doty and Talmage in late 1854 decided to send two of their more literate converts to Chioh-be, where some Chinese Christians from nearby Peh-chui-ia had been carrying on occasional evangelistic work.

The elation over what transpired and the effectiveness of the Chinese evangelists can be seen in this extract from a letter written in late 1854 by Doty to Burns after the latter had returned on furlough to England.

> Again, truly, are we as those that dream. The general features of the work [at Chioh-be] are very similar to what you witnessed at Peh-chui-ia. The instrumentality has been native brethren [from Peh-chui-ia and Amoy] almost entirely....Shortly the desire to hear the Word was so intense, that there would be scarcely any stop day or night; the brethren in turns going, and breaking down from much speaking in the course of three or four days, and coming back to us almost voiceless. An establishment

has been rented in extent nearly equal to that of
Peh-chui-ia. Here daily and almost hourly the Word is
preached, the Scriptures studied, and prayer and praise
offered. There are some fifteen persons who seem to have
been spiritually wrought upon, several of whom give
pleasing evidence of regeneration....Judging from the
visit of last week, I do not see but necessity is laid upon us
to arrange for their being received into the visible
church.[29]

The evangelists at Chioh-be were visited from time to time by
Doty and Talmage, who advised and encouraged them in their
work. Because of the shortage of missionary personnel, however,
these visits had to be brief, as can be seen in this excerpt from a
communication by Talmage:

The missionary arrives by boat...in the evening, is
conducted to the place of worship, and speaks to an
anxious assemblage until eleven or twelve o'clock, then
lies down on a temporary bed (the congregation not
retiring) and is awakened at an early hour to proceed with
his discourse until the time arrives for the boat to return
to Amoy.[30]

The first baptism occurred in January, 1855, when Talmage and
the English Presbyterian Johnston went to Chioh-be to examine
anyone who had evinced an interest in being baptized and who, in
the minds of the missionaries, appeared to be regenerated. By the
end of the year, the number of baptisms had reached
twenty-seven, of whom twenty-two were adults.

The mission station at Chioh-be, like that at Peh-chui-ia, thus
started out as a joint endeavor by the English Presbyterians and
the Reformed, but it quickly became the latter's special project. In
1859, a congregation was formally organized there under the
auspices of the Reformed missionaries, making it the second
Reformed church established in China. The Chioh-be church also
took charge of two outstations.

Soon after the founding of the Chioh-be church, talks got
underway among the Sin-koe-a and Tek-chhiu-kha church-goers
in Amoy City aimed at splitting themselves into two separate
churches, each with its own consistory of elders and deacons. This
division was finally brought about in the late summer of 1860,

thus bringing the number of Reformed churches in China to three. From that time forth, the branching out process occurred more rapidly. By the close of the nineteenth century, there were eleven churches in South Fukien that were under the auspices of the Reformed mission and nearly three dozen outstations.

V

Creating a Partnership in Missions

The Reverend John Fagg, who spent several years in Amoy as a Reformed missionary in the late nineteenth century (1888-1894), described missionaries at work in a new field as being concerned initially with certain basic needs. These, he declared, are shelter, food, a place to preach, a company of believers, and an ability to speak the local language. He added, however, that matters become more complicated as soon as a the number of converts begin to increase. At that point, a variety of questions confront the missionary:

> How shall the company of believers be organized and governed? Shall it be exactly on the model of the church which the missionary represents? If not, what modifications shall be made? Shall the seedling ten thousand miles away be roped to the mother tree or shall it be encouraged to stand alone? What advantages in independence? What perils? What shall be the status of the foreign missionary before the native church just organized? What relation shall he sustain to the home church?[1]

In dealing with questions such as the above, the Reformed church traditionally held the view that any churches and associations of churches, such as classes, organized by her missionaries in foreign lands should resemble those at home in all essential matters. The Reformed missionaries in China, however, held somewhat different views. They believed that self-regulating Chinese associations should be established. They also favored a closer affinity with other Protestant missions than was considered feasible by their overseers in America. For several years, a serious debate ensued over these issues. In the end, the missionary view prevailed and a formal partnership was established between the Reformed and English Presbyterian missions, a partnership that the London Missionary Society joined later.

One of the best examples of early cooperation among the three missions was their agreement to what was known as the "comity of missions." By this arrangement, South Fukien, constituting about 18,000 square miles, was divided into three approximately equal parts. Roughly speaking, the Reformed mission had most of the western area plus a small amount to the north; the English Presbyterians, the southern and part of the eastern; and the London group, the northern and the remainder of the eastern. There was some overlapping in the immediate neighborhood of Changchow between the Reformed and London Society missions.[2] The headquarters of all three missions was initially at Amoy City and moved later to Kulangsu. The "comity" arrangement was designed to avoid duplication of activities and thus unnecessary expenses. It did nothing to interfere with the friendly feeling that had existed among the three groups since the beginning, which prompted the Reverend Johnston of the English Presbyterians to remark later that among the converts, "the name for a denomination was not known among them."[3]

The increase in the number of churches and converts soon prompted discussions about establishing a formal organization among the three missions. The question then quickly arose regarding what form such a body should take. It was at this point that some temporary parting of the ways occurred in the joint activities. As events unfolded, the London Missionary Society established an organization that was compatible with congregationalism and one that gave its missionaries considerable individual latitude in carrying on their work. The Reformed and English Presbyterian missions, however, resolved to establish a common governing organization.

As was previously noted, the close friendship that existed between the Reformed and English Presbyterian missionaries was the outgrowth of several factors, including similarities in the doctrines and polity of the two denominations. There was also the fact that for several years the English Presbyterian missionaries were interested primarily in evangelism and were content to turn over their Chinese listeners to the Reformed missionaries when it came to matters of examining them preparatory to baptism and admitting them as communicant church members.

The spirit of cooperation between the two groups also stemmed from their determination to establish an indigenous Chinese Christian church—one that was neither American nor English nor even a combination of the two. As later explained by Talmage:

We supposed it to be our duty to [organize] the Church in China with reference simply to its own welfare and efficiency in the work of evangelizing the heathen...We did not suppose that we were sent out to build up the *American* Dutch Church in China, but a Church after the same order, a purely Chinese Church....The Church in China is not a colony from Holland, or America. We must not, therefore, entail on her the double evil of both the terms "American" and "Dutch," or the single evil of either of these terms.[4]

In view of the above factors, it is not surprising that when Doty and Talmage began making plans in the spring of 1856 to establish a congregation at Amoy City with its own Chinese consistory of elders and deacons, they asked Douglas of the English Presbyterian church to participate in the new organization. He accepted the offer. In explaining his decision to the corresponding secretary of the Foreign Committee of the Presbyterian Church in England (the equivalent of the Board of Foreign Missions of the Reformed Church in America), Douglas wrote:

I need hardly say that this transaction does not consist in members of one Church joining another, nor in two Churches uniting, but it is an attempt to build up on the soil of China, with the living stones prepared by the great Master-builder, an ecclesiastical body, holding the grand doctrines enunciated at Westminister and Dort, and the principles of Presbyterian polity embraced at the Reformation by the purest churches on the continent and in Britain. It will also be a beautiful point in the history of this infant Church, that the underbuilders employed in shaping and arranging the stones were messengers of two different (though not differing) Churches in the two great nations on either side of the Atlantic.[5]

The decision having been made to organize a church, notices were given on two successive Sundays, April 6 and 13, from the pulpits of the two places of worship in Amoy City (Sin-koe-a and Tek-chhiu-kha) inviting all male members to assemble at the Sin-koe-a church on Monday afternoon, April 14, to consider the feasibility of electing elders and deacons. The two places of worship at this time had a combined membership of 122. On the Sabbath prior to the above meeting, sermons were preached on the subject of church government, including the duties of a church and its officeholders. What then transpired was explained by Talmage in a letter of a few weeks later:

On Monday afternoon, April 14th, the male members assembled according to the previous call. The attendance was full. Rev. Messrs. Doty, Douglas, and Talmage were present, and Mr. Talmage was called to the Chair. The meeting was opened with prayer. After deliberation, it was decided . . . to proceed to the election of four elders and four deacons [and] that Committees be appointed by the Chair to nominate suitable candidates, and that the election be by ballot. The Chair named Rev. Doty, Lim-Tek-choan, and Lo-Tau a Committee to nominate suitable candidates for the eldership. After the Committee retired, the assembly engaged in prayer. The Committee reported the names of six brethren, of whom the [gathering chose four], and they were declared elected. The Chair then named Rev. Doty and the elders-elect as a Committee to nominate candidates for the deaconship, who reported eight names. [Four] were chosen and declared elected.[6]

A set of eight rules for the government of consistory meetings was also adopted.[7]

In accordance with prior agreements, the names of the elected elders and deacons were announced from the pulpits on three successive Sundays to determine if any church members had objections. With none forthcoming, a special service was held in the Sin-koe-a church on the afternoon of May 11, a Sunday, "to set them apart in their respective offices." To quote further from Talamage's letter:

> A sermon was preached by Rev. Doty from Hebrews xiii, 17, on duties of the Church to her office-bearers. The Form for Ordination of elders and deacons was read by Mr. Talmage, [after which] the ministers present gave to them the right hand of fellowship.[8]

Douglas's decision to cooperate with the Reformed missionaries in organizing a church met with the full approval of his church in England. Unfortunately, the plan was less well received in America by the Reformed church's General Synod. In anticipation of criticism from that body, the Reformed missionaries on September 17, 1856, sent a lengthy letter of explanation to the synod's Board of Foreign Missions, along with a request that it be published as soon as possible to enable interested persons to study its contents before their next meeting.[9]

Among the principal arguments used by the Reformed missionaries were the similarities between the two denominations and the extent to which the two missions had cooperated in the past. "We had been laboring," the letter stated, "together in the work of the Lord, were one in sympathy, held the same views in theology, and did not differ in regard to church polity."[10] The letter also stressed the fact that although the Chinese converts realized that the missionaries came from different countries, they nevertheless looked upon themselves as belonging to the same church no matter who preached to them. This, the missionaries declared, was in keeping with the primary purpose for their going to China, namely, to bring the gospel to the Chinese people. If, in carrying out this purpose, it became necessary to organize churches, this should be done solely for the glory of God and the spiritual welfare of the converts without giving any special regard to denominational labels. "Surely," declared the missionaries, "we have acted in this matter according to the leadings of Providence and the spirit and instructions of the Gospel of Christ; for in Christ Jesus there is no distinction of nationalities."[11] A second letter with similar contents was dispatched a few weeks later.[12]

Unfortunately, the letters were not published as had been requested. Instead, they were presented, along with other papers, to the synodical Committee on Foreign Missions for "perusal and recommendations." The committee's report, which was presented to the General Synod at its annual meeting in June, 1857, criticized the action taken by the missionaries:

In reply to...the establishment of individual churches, we must say that while we appreciate the peculiar circumstances of our brethren and sympathize with their perplexities, yet it has always been considered a matter of course that ministers, receiving their commission through our Church and sent forth under the auspices of our Board, would, when they formed converts from the heathen into an ecclesiastical body, mould the organization into a form approaching, as nearly as possible, that of the Reformed Protestant Dutch Churches in our land. Seeing that the converted heathen, when associated together, must have some form of government, and seeing that our form is, in our view, entirely consistent with, if not required by Scripture, we expect that it will in all cases be adopted by our missionaries, subject, of course to such modifications as their peculiar circumstances may for the time render necessary. [13]

In brief, although the report expressed itself in favor of "the formation of churches among the converts from heathenism," it made clear that such churches were to be "organized according to the established usages of our branch of Zion," that is, the Reformed Church in America.

The missionaries raised strong objections to a statement in the report referring to the converts as being "an integral part of our Church." As explained by one of the spokesmen several years later when a similar issue came up:

What made them so? Is it because they were converted through the instrumentality of the preaching of our Missionaries? This is a new doctrine, that a convert as a matter of course belongs to the Church of the preacher through whose instrumentality he has been led unto Christ. Perhaps it was the doctrine of some of the Corinthians, when they said, "I am of Paul, and I of

Apollos," etc., but it was not the doctrine of the Apostle who reproved them. Besides this, how shall we know which of them were converted through our instrumentality? The English Presbyterian brethren and ourselves have preached indiscriminately....If [the converts] be an *integral part* of the Dutch Church of America, they are also an integral part of the Presbyterian Church in England.[14]

The missionaries were greatly disappointed with the General Synod's reaction. They attributed it to a lack of understanding of the situation and expressed disappointment that their recent memorials had not been published as requested—especially since they had no representative at the synod to explain their views.

A temporary respite in the controversy ensued after the exchange of more letters, but it reappeared in the early 1860s over another more serious issue, namely, whether the missionaries had the authority to go ahead with their own plans for establishing a classis (or presbytery, as it was called among Presbyterians). Again, as with the problem of organizing a church, the question was not whether there should be a classis but rather who should belong to it and how much jurisdiction it should have. As early as 1852, the Board of Foreign Missions had suggested the possibility of organizing a classis at Amoy, and the matter was brought up again at the annual meeting of the General Synod in June, 1857. On the latter occasion, it was resolved "that the brethren at Amoy be directed to apply to the Particular Synod of Albany to organize them into a Classis as soon as they shall have formed churches enough to render the permanency of such an organization reasonably certain." This was in keeping with the normal procedure for organizing a new classis, namely, to do so under the aegis of one of the denomination's particular synods.[15]

Obviously, with only one formal church organization in 1857, the "brethren at Amoy" saw little need for a classis, but this view changed as the number of churches increased. A second Reformed church, located at Chioh-be, was formally organized, with the election of elders and deacons, in early 1859. And in the latter part of 1860, the churchgoers at Sin-koe-a and Tek-chhiu-kha in Amoy City decided by popular vote to divide themselves into two separate churches, each with its own consistory.[16] There were also by this time two churches, one at Peh-chui-ia and another at Mapeng, under the special supervision of the English Presbyterians, thus bringing to five the number of churches under the care of the two missions. Each church also had one or more outstations under its care.

Instead of following the General Synod's instructions for working through the Particular Synod of Albany, the missionaries decided to go ahead with plans of their own for organizing a classis. With that in mind, a joint meeting of the five churches was held at Chioh-be in 1861, at which time various matters were discussed, but no decisions were made. The next meeting took place on April 2, 1862, and can be considered the founding of the Classis of Amoy. It was attended by all the Reformed and English Presbyterian missionaries and one elder from each of the five organized churches. Talmage was chosen moderator and one of the Chinese elders was elected clerk. After considerable discussion regarding a name for the new body, it was resolved to call it the Tai-hoey, a Chinese word meaning "Great Meeting of the Elders," the nearest equivalent to the terms classis and presbytery. Minutes were kept in Chinese.

Several problems of church discipline were dealt with at this session—problems that in the past had been settled largely by the churches individually. One of the major difficulties concerned Sabbath observance. A general inquiry was also made concerning the qualifications of two Chinese church elders who had been serving as unordained evangelists and who hoped to be ordained at some time in the future.

The next meeting of the Classis occurred in the autumn of 1862 at Peh-chui-ia. It was at this session that the members decided they had the right to examine and ordain Chinese candidates for the ministry. Authorization was also given for the organization of a sixth church—this one at E-mng-kang, a suburb of Amoy City, to be under the auspices of the English Presbyterians.

Classis met again on February 21, 1863, and proceeded with the examination of two candidates for the ministry, Lo Ka-gu and Iap Han-chiong. Lo was an elder in the church at Chioh-be, and Iap served in the same capacity in the Sin-koe-a church. Both men had for some time also been laboring as unordained evangelists. As

the examinations proved satisfactory, the date of March 29 was set
for their ordination. On that date, Lo was installed as minister for
Amoy's First Church and Iap for Amoy's Second Church. The
mission's annual report of 1864 described their responsibilities as
follows:

> They have full charge of the Churches, whose Pastors
> they are. They preside at the Consistory meetings of their
> respective Churches, and along with the Elders decide
> who are to be received and who not. The Consistories
> thus constituted, exercise discipline also, sometimes after
> consulting with the Missionaries, and sometimes without
> such consultation. These Native Pastors administer the
> Sacraments, using translations of our Church Forms. They
> also perform the marriage ceremony. Their people pay
> them $12 per month as salary, and furnish houses for
> them and their families to live in. [17]

Meanwhile, as might be expected, the growth of the Chinese
churches had prompted the General Synod to take note once again
of the need for a classis at Amoy. Thus, in June, 1862, the
synodical Committee on Foreign Missions recommended to the
synod that the mission in China adopt "more perfect forms of
ecclesiastical organization, according to the wishes and
expectations of General Synod, expressed at its Annual Session in
1857." [18] In the committee's view, a classis in China would be
beneficial because it would enable the "church at home" to see
more clearly the results of her labors abroad and at the same time
would give the Chinese converts a greater sense of being a part of
the "parent church." Such a body would also be advantageous to
the missionaries in carrying out their work, including the
examination and ordination of Chinese candidates for the
ministry. In accepting these recommendations, the synod, of
course, did not realize that the missionaries had already gone
ahead with their own plans for organizing a classis. Upon hearing
the news of what had happened, the General Synod became
deeply annoyed, to say the least.

Before the General Synod met to discuss this new
development, the synod of the English Presbyterian church had
already taken up the matter and had come out solidly in favor of
what the missionaries had done. In its view, the newly created

presbytery (that is, classis) would facilitate the management of local matters in China and make it easier to solve problems that were common to all the churches. The English synod expressed hope that the "brethren in America" would follow suit and likewise approve what had taken place. As explained by the English synod's Foreign Committee:

There are few brethren towards whom we feel closer affinity than the members of that Church, which was represented of old by Gomarus and Witsius, by Voet and Marck, and Bernard de Moore, and whose Synod of Dort preceded in time and pioneered in doctrine our own Westminister Assembly. Like them, we love the Presbyterianism and that Calvinism which we hold in common, and we wish to carry them wherever we go; but we fear that it would not be doing justice to either, and that it might compromise that name which is above every other, if, on the shores of China, we were to unfurl a separate standard.[19]

The attitude of the Reformed church's General Synod was less charitable. Upon learning what the Amoy missionaries had done, the Board of Foreign Missions decided that because it had no *final* jurisdiction in ecclesiastical affairs and had "exhausted all the persuasion which it could command," the entire matter should be placed before the General Synod.[20] With that in mind, the board appointed a special committee of three ministers and two elders to draft a report to be presented to the General Synod at its next annual meeting in June, 1863. The Reverend Elbert Porter, pastor of one of the Brooklyn churches, was named chairman. As he also served as editor of the *Christian Intelligencer*, Porter was a man of considerable influence.

The committee's report strongly denounced what had taken place at Amoy and pointed out the perils of striking out in new directions. It reminded the synod that the past strength of the Reformed church had been due to its "unflinching and unfaltering adherence to our doctrines, our customs, our usages, and our liberal and wise Constitution." Rather than succumb to momentary "flashes of enthusiasm" and to "improvised measures of administration," the Reformed church in the past had steadfastly continued to march "in the old paths" and had remained loyal to the "old traditions, written law, and established doctrine." In brief, the missionaries, instead of going ahead with their own plans, should have applied to the Particular Synod of Albany for assistance in organizing a classis, as they had been instructed to do by the synod's resolution of 1857.

The special committee found several features of the new Classis of Amoy particularly annoying and difficult to understand. Its autonomous and self-regulating nature with reference to ordinations and discipline was especially a source of concern. The committee also found it difficult to understand how missionaries could be members of the Classis of Amoy, exercising full ministerial functions therein, yet retain membership in a classis in America. A similar question was raised with reference to how churches belonging to the Chinese organization could simultaneously be considered "members of the Reformed Dutch Church here [as] they [were] members of the Presbyterian Church of England." Finally, the committee expressed concern that the churches at home might cut down their contributions to missions if what had taken place in China went unchallenged.[21]

Fortunately for the missionaries and those few members of the synod who had supported their actions, the Reverend Talmage was present at the General Synod when the committee's report came up for discussion. He had returned to the United States in the late summer of 1862 to arrange for the proper care and education of his four children following the death of his wife, and did not return to China until 1865. In his address, which lasted almost two hours, Talmage gave a detailed justification of the actions of the missionaries. Rather than give ground to his critics, he took the position that thanks should be given to "the great Head of the Church" for enabling missionaries of different denominations and different countries "through Divine Grace to work together in harmony."[22]

Talmage's remarks were followed by speeches from various members of the synod. It is interesting to note that one of the few persons speaking in defense of the missionaries was the Reverend Gustavus Abeel, cousin of the Reverend David Abeel, who had founded the Amoy mission in 1842. He declared that the synod must be careful about trying to "transfer the Dutch Church, with all its forms and peculiarities, to the heathen world." The main business, he said, was "first, to advance the cause of Christ according to our view of truth; and next, as far as possible, to extend the [Dutch] Church."23 Abeel's remarks struck at the kernel of the main issue in the debate, namely, the extent to which denominational rules and customs should be observed at Amoy.

Most members of the synod agreed that certain nonessential regulations could be left in abeyance at Amoy because of the unique circumstances existing there, but they were adamant in their views that foreign churches had to be kept under the direct supervision of the mother church in most matters of polity. Although the critics expressed personal affection for the missionaries, the discussions became somewhat acrid at times. The strongest remarks were made by elder S. B. Schieffelin, one of the members of the special committee. He declared that if the missionaries "were not willing to respect the action of the General Synod, they deserved rebuke." In a similar vein, the committee chairman, the Reverend Porter, reminded the synod that four of the six missionaries at Amoy had been sent there with specific instructions to carry out the decision of 1857 when deemed feasible; therefore, they knew what was required of them. General Synod, declared Porter, could not let pass unnoticed this annulling of her decisions "at pleasure."24

The president of the General Synod, the Reverend Talbot Wilson Chambers, a pastor of the Collegiate Church of New York, made the concluding remarks. These were lengthy and stirring. Although he promised to do his utmost to see to it that the missionaries would receive the church's "money, sympathy, prayers, and confidence," he declared he could not surrender "the constitution, the policy, the interest of our Church—all of which are involved in this matter." He further explained that "a self-regulating Classis is a thing which had never been heard of in the Dutch Church since the Church had a beginning. It is against every law, principle, canon, example, and precedent in our books." Chambers also warned his listeners to bear in mind that in reaching a decision, the synod was acting for all time:

> It is not this one case that is before us. We are setting a precedent which is to last for generations. Relax your constitutions and laws for this irregularity and you open a

gap through which a coach and four may be driven. Every other mission, under the least pretext, will come and claim the same or a similar modification in their case, and you cannot consistently deny them. The result will be an ecclesiastical chaos throughout our entire missionary field.[25]

In the final vote, after two days of discussion, the great majority of members of synod sided with the views expressed by Chambers and supported the report submitted by the special committee.

In pondering his next move, Talmage concluded that the synod did not fully understand the issues that were at stake. His task therefore became one of trying to explain these once more in the hope of getting the synod to reverse itself at the next annual meeting. Because previous efforts had failed to get the Board of Foreign Missions to publish the views of the missionaries and because of the prejudicial position that the editor of the *Christian Intelligencer* had taken, Talmage decided to prepare a pamphlet and have it privately printed. Totaling seventy-six pages, it contained a detailed analysis and refutation of the arguments that the critics had put forth. To cite an example, Talmage declared as unsound the argument that the action by the missionaries would have an adverse effect on financial support from Reformed members at home. The synod's argument, he declared, implied that the motive for giving was to promote the glorification of the Reformed church. He added: "If our people have not yet learned [it], they should be taught to engage in the work of evangelizing the world, not for the sake of our Church in America, but for the sake of Christ and His Church." He also pointed out that, in his opinion, persons who were most broad-minded in their thoughts were usually the most liberal when it came to giving. Therefore, the adoption of a narrow, sectarian policy in Amoy might dry up more funds than it raised.[26]

In closing, Talmage gave the following cogent summary of his views:

> This is the doctrine: Let all the branches of the great Presbyterian family in the same region in any heathen country, which are sound in the faith, organize themselves, *if convenient*, into one organic whole, allowing liberty to the different parts in things

non-essential. Let those who adopt Dutch customs, as at Amoy, continue, if they see fit, their peculiarities, and those who adopt other Presbyterian customs, as at Ningpo and other places, continue their peculiarities, and yet all unite as one Church.[27]

The editor of the *Christian Intelligencer*, as Talmage anticipated, was less than kind in commenting on the pamphlet. He described it as Talmage's way of seeking support for "his personal and *higher law* theory of the way in which our foreign missionary matters should be managed." In assessing Talmage's argument that the missionaries were subject to the Supreme Authority as well as to the authority of the General Synod, the editor wrote:

Very well. If that claim is well founded, and sustained by right reason, then what is styled "ecclesiastical government" is a simple impertinence or a grand imposture. Pure independency becomes inevitable, and each and every minister or missionary must henceforth walk in the light of his own understanding of the Supreme Authority, and administer government according to his individual notion of what is fit.[28]

Meanwhile, the missionaries at Amoy, upon receiving notice of the synod's decision, lost little time in giving their reaction. They did not berate the synod for its decision, knowing that its members had voted their convictions, but they made it unmistakably clear that they could not comply with it. In a joint communication dated September 16, 1863, they informed the Board of Foreign Missions:

We feel that Synod must have mistaken our position on this question. It is not that we regard the proposed action as merely inexpedient and unwise; if this were all, we would gladly carry out the commands of Synod, transferring to it the responsibility which it offers to assume. But the light in which we regard it admits of no transfer of responsibility. It is not a matter of judgment only, but also of conscience. [By going along with General Synod's decision] we should be doing a positive injury and wrong to the churches of Christ established at Amoy, and that our duty to the Master and His people here forbids this. Therefore, our answer to the action of General Synod must be and is that we cannot be made the instruments of carrying out the wishes of Synod in this report; and further, if Synod is determined that such an organization must be effected, we can see no other way than to recall us and send hither men who see clearly their way to do that which to us seems wrong. [29]

The letter was signed by the five Reformed missionaries who were laboring at Amoy: Augustus Blauvelt, Elihu Doty, Leonard Kip, Alvin Ostrom, and Daniel Rapalje. In addition to the joint communication, each missionary sent a personal letter.

Once again it was up to the General Synod to make the next move. At its June meeting in 1864, it heard another special report from the Board of Foreign Missions on the Amoy question. Also presented were the joint letter and the separate letters from the Amoy missionaries together with Talmage's pamphlet, all of which were referred to another special synodical committee. This committee was split in its views and therefore filed majority and minority reports. In the end, the synod adopted the following resolution:

Resolved, That while the General Synod does not deem it necessary or proper to change the Missionary policy defined and adopted in 1857, yet, in consideration of the peculiar circumstances of the Mission of Amoy, the brethren there are allowed to defer the formation of a Classis of Amoy, until in their judgment, such a measure is required by the wants and desires of the churches gathered by them from among the heathen.[30]

The wording of the resolution implied that the synod's decision was only tentative and that the resolutions of 1857 and 1863 were still valid. This, however, was little more than an exercise in semantics. Nothing was changed at Amoy, and the subject never came up again for debate in the General Synod.

The union classis of the Reformed and English Presbyterian missionaries, as it finally materialized, had the double advantage of allowing each mission to maintain an identity of its own, while permitting them to coordinate their activities. Thus, on the one hand, it allowed for a degree of denominational independence by allowing each mission to keep its financial matters relatively separate and the missionaries to act under commissions from their own denominational boards back home. A degree of separateness was also maintained in that each denomination tended to confine its labors to specified territorial regions. On the other hand, the classical arrangement enabled the missionaries of the two denominations to join forces in such common pursuits as medical and educational work, the publication of books and tracts, and relief for the poor. Moreover, the missionaries, the Chinese pastors and helpers, and the consistories of the various churches could all look upon themselves as belonging to one single Christian church rather than two competing ones and could meet together from time to time to discuss their common problems.[31]

VI

The Missionary and Chinese Staff, 1863-1900

The Reformed missionary staff assigned to Amoy in 1863 included four ordained missionaries, namely, John Van Nest Talmage, Leonard W. Kip, Daniel Rapalje, and Alvin Ostrom. However, only two of these men (Kip and Rapalje) were actually in China when the year began, Talmage and Ostrom being on furlough in America. Although Talmage returned in June of that year, ill health forced Ostrom to resign his commission as missionary. Consequently, he did not return to China. Talmage, whose first wife had died in 1862, remarried while on furlough and brought his new bride, Mary Van Deventer Talmage, with him. Arriving on the ship with the Talmages was Kip's fiancee, Helen Culbertson. The two were married at Amoy on June 2, the day after her arrival. Mary Talmage and Helen Kip both became distinguished missionaries in their own right and between them served nearly 100 years in China.[1]

Thirteen new male recruits, of whom ten were married, were assigned to the Reformed missionary staff during the thirty-seven years from 1863 to 1900. In addition, ten single women were sent out. This brought the number of missionaries recruited during this period to thirty-three.

It is interesting to speculate on the kind of questions that went through the minds of the missionaries as they made preparations for leaving the United States. What would life be like half way around the world where they would be awake while relatives and friends back home were sleeping? What would the Chinese people be like—were many of them really as illiterate and poverty stricken as reported? The missionaries also no doubt speculated on such matters as food and housing conditions and on how soon they would be able to converse in Chinese. And what about the geography—would the topography be mountainous or flat and the climate hot, cold, or mild? Would there be a rainy season? Missionaries with families must have frequently reflected on whether they were doing the right thing in bringing children into a strange environment. [2]

With the appearance of an increasing number of single women among the recruits, it soon ensued that the women outnumbered the men by a significant margin. At times, the ratio was almost two to one. The assistant missionaries, as the women were often referred to at this time, rendered an invaluable service. If there is any truth to the old adage that "a woman's work is never done," it was doubly true of those who served the Reformed mission in China. They engaged in all the major missionary endeavors—evangelistic, educational, and medical. As evangelists, female missionaries made a unique contribution working among Chinese women, especially by visiting in their homes—an entree that was denied their male counterparts. In the area of education it was especially the women who, as teachers and school supervisors, helped lay the groundwork for educating women and children. Their labors in this field also released men from teaching tasks, enabling them to devote more time to preaching tours and other traditional evangelistic programs. In the medical field, the work of the women initially consisted of visiting the sick and suffering. Later, some of them served as nurses and medical doctors.

The importance of new arrivals at Amoy must be evaluated on the basis of more than simply numbers, however. Experience must be taken into account and also their length of stay in China. The significance of the former is clearly brought out by looking at staff losses and gains during the period 1892-1900 when the mission lost five missionaries, mostly veterans, through death or retirement from China: Talmage in 1889, Fagg in 1894, Van Dyck in 1897, Kip in 1898, and Rapalje in 1899. These men served respectively forty, seven, fifteen, thirty-eight, and forty-one years. By 1900 only two men had come in as replacements, namely, the Reverends Hobart Studley in 1896 and Abbe Warnshuis in 1900.

Reviewing the impact of these changes in 1900, Warnhuis noted that, "in numbers the Mission is still lacking three men, and in experience 141 years."[3]

The turnover among new recruits must also be considered. Some of them stayed only a brief period, while others served many years. Among the thirteen new male missionaries, for example, eight stayed seven years or less, including five who remained three years or less. Poor health, either of the missionary or of his wife, remained the primary cause for short terms of service.[4] On the other hand, Alexander Van Dyck, Dr. John Otte, and Philip Pitcher remained for fourteen, twenty-three, and thirty years respectively. The contrast among the ten new single women was even more striking. While half of them stayed only six years or less, the other five—Lily Duryee, Margaret Morrison, Katharine and Mary Talmage, and Nellie Zwemer—remained for a combined total of 227 years!

The problem of turnovers was compounded by the furloughs, some of which were quite lengthy. This is clearly shown in the furloughs of the veterans Talmage, Kip, and Rapalje. Talmage, during his forty-two years of service (1849-1889), was in America during portions of these years: 1849-1850, 1862-1865, 1872-1874, and 1881-1882. Similarly, Kip, during his thirty-seven years as a missionary (1861-1898), had extended furloughs as follows: 1868-1870, 1879-1880, and 1889-1890. And Rapalje, during his career spanning forty-one years (1858-1899), returned to America on five occasions: 1866-1869, 1876-1878, 1884-1885, 1890-1891, and 1894-1895.

Furloughs for missionaries were, of course, necessary. Few critics could find fault with Philip Pitcher's observation that

> missionaries, like all other busy workers, get run down, worn out, and on account of the unvarying daily routine —thinking the same thoughts, doing the same work—become more or less rusty. Physically, mentally, and spiritually the whole life is apt to, and very often does, become sluggish.[5]

In view of the difficult conditions under which Amoy missionaries labored, Pitcher's observations were certainly well-founded.

Unfortunately, the Reformed church at this time had no

systematic schedule for granting furloughs. As a consequence, the number of missionaries actually present in China varied significantly from year to year. The resulting difficulties can be inferred from an excerpt from the mission's annual report for 1891:

> In 1888, we numbered fifteen members, thirteen on the field. But our bow did not long abide in its strength. In July 1889, Dr. and Mrs. Talmage were compelled to embark for the United States owing to Dr. Talmage's much enfeebled condition. Mr. and Mrs. Van Dyck took ship in December 1889, Mr. and Mrs. Pitcher set sail in April 1890. Mr. and Mrs. Rapalje and family, and the Misses Talmage were ticketed for home in May of the same year. During the greater part of 1890 the field was held by three missionaries and their wives.[6]

Furloughs among women caused no less a hardship for the mission than did those among the men, as can be seen in these remarks by Mary Talmage in 1898:

> Our work for women has been sadly crippled by four of our active workers (Misses Duryee, Zwemer, Morrison, and Capon) being obliged to return to the United States during the year. This necessitated the closing, in the autumn, of the Tang-oa women's class, and the Changchow girls' school with its twenty-two pupils; and country work everywhere has greatly suffered.[7]

The absence of clear-cut rules for the Reformed missionaries regarding the number and length of furloughs was in contrast to the policy being followed by their English Presbyterian colleagues, as is shown in this report for 1871:

> For the last five years we have only averaged two effective workers on the ground, while [the English Presbyterians] have averaged nearly twice that number. Their policy is, "Visits home once in seven years, but let them be short." Thus, they preserve their health, and lose but little time. Our practice has been, visits home more rare, except when ill health compels, and much longer continued.[8]

As early as 1865 Rapalje suggested, but to no avail, that the Board of Foreign Missions draft specific rules concerning the frequency and length of missionary furloughs.[9]

For the same reasons that furloughs were important for the physical and mental well-being of missionaries, occasional vacations were equally relevant during the long time span between furloughs. Initially, missionaries working inland often spent a few weeks during the hot, humid summer months at Kulangsu, where at least nights were cool—thanks to the ocean breezes. Northern China was also a favorite vacation spot. Occasional visits were also made to Japan and Southeast Asia, and in 1885, John and Mary Talmage went to Australia "for a needed change and rest."[10]

Beginning in the 1890s, it became increasingly commonplace for missionaries to spend their vacations at Kuling, a small community in the Ku-liang mountains. Trips there were made in stages, beginning with a night journey by steamer along the coast to Foochow (the capital of Fukien Province), followed by a thirty mile boat trip up the scenic Min River, and ending with a three- or four-hour "chair ride." Kuling's moderately cool climate during the summer months and its beautiful scenery soon made it a favorite retreat for missionaries from other denominations as well as foreign diplomats and merchants. The *Chinese Recorder* reported in 1896, for example, that Kuling boasted of "forty or more houses for sanitariums built by the missionaries and foreign merchants."[11]

As more missionaries from other denominations found Kuling to be an excellent place for rest and relaxation, it quickly became a pleasant and natural site for missionary conferences. Note, in this respect, the comment made in 1897 by a member of the London Missionary Society who wrote that "apart from the rest and coolness" of the retreat, there was

> the additional charm of meeting with many kindred spirits, representatives of many other societies; for dotted about on the hills are other little cottages. And how delightful the conversation, the Sunday and daily services, the joy of meeting with and getting to know so many busy at the same work in different parts of South China, and to learn and profit by their experiences.[12]

Land could be leased at Kuling for a period of twenty-five years for the small sum of sixty dollars with an option of renewal for three dollars per year, and houses could be built for six hundred dollars. As described by Pitcher, the Reformed "sanitarium" was "a modest little dwelling, comprising a central room and three bedrooms (with lofts) at the sides, and kitchen in the rear," all of which was paid for by donations from friends of the missionaries and involved no payments from mission funds.[13]

In view of the turnover rate among the missionaries, it is not surprising that numerous articles appeared in the *Christian Intelligencer* stressing the need for reinforcements. In these articles, as in much of the missionary writing coming out of Amoy at this time, missionaries were ingenious at using just the right words and phrases to get their message across. Typical was this appeal by Pitcher, in which he asserts that "soldiers of the Cross" who fight for the liberation of "soul bondage" were as important as soldiers who fight for the liberation of "physical bondage." Pitcher enriched his request for help by calling the attention of his readers to two recent events in American history and making an analogy between them and the needs of Amoy:

> The preservation of the Union and the emancipation of 3,000,000 slaves was magnificent and the liberation of Cuba [from Spain] enlisted the admiration of the whole world; but what shall be said of that work which has in mind the freedom, enlightenment and eternal salvation of China's 400,000,000 souls—nearly a third of the habitable world? And if the appeal for the liberation of the colored people of the South and the subjects of Spain in Cuba so appealed to our young men, how much more should this appeal from Amoy fire the zeal, *love for souls, and love for Christ's kingdom*, in the hearts of the young men of the ministry in our churches.[14]

Appeals also came occasionally from Chinese Christian leaders themselves. Thus, in 1886, several Chinese pastors sent a lengthy letter to that effect to the General Synod. The letter noted that the combined communicant membership of the sixteen congregations under the care of the Reformed and English Presbyterian missions totaled 1,800. The pastors expressed thanks for what the two missionary groups had done to achieve that figure, but added

> when compared with the multitudes of heathen around, the Church is but small. In Chin-chew City, for example, there are more than 250,000 inhabitants and only one

church; while in the prefectures of Chang-chew, and
Ting-chew there are still many cities and towns each with
several tens of thousands of inhabitants in which there is
yet no place of worship, and large districts of country in
which there is not a Christian. Truly the harvest is
plenteous and the laborers few!

The letter closed with a plea for help in "rescuing" those who
were still

sunk in superstition and sin....Very pitiable is their
condition! Without the Gospel they must finally perish.
We therefore beseech the Synod to continue to manifest
sympathy for the people of China by sending, in still
greater numbers, faithful servants of the Lord to do His
work in this land.[15]

The problem that the Reformed church had in sending
additional "faithful servants" was due in part to a shortage of
volunteers, but there also were occasions when the church was
prevented from doing so because of lack of funds. In fact, because
of adverse economic conditions in the United States and a decline
in church giving, it occasionally happened that the Board of
Foreign Missions directed the Amoy missionaries "to retrench, to
abandon hopeful fields, and to draw their work into a narrower
compass."[16] The effect this had on the morale of the missionaries
can be seen in this notation of 1897 by Dr. Otte: "Our greatest
burden, one which at times threatens to make us spiritless, is to
see open doors not entered, opportunities lost, the effort of years
wasted, simply from the want of sufficient force to carry out the
work."[17]

Problems resulting from the generally small size of the
American missionary staff were offset somewhat by the significant
growth of the Chinese staff after 1865. By 1900, the number of
Chinese pastors had increased gradually from two to eleven, and
the number of preachers from twelve to twenty-seven. The
training of these men was facilitated by the establishment of a
theological seminary in 1869 and a boys' academy in 1881.

The main difference between pastors and preachers remained
as it was before—the former were ordained and the latter
unordained. As a consequence, pastors continued to have charge
of churches, whereas most preachers worked at outstations. A few

preachers also served in miscellaneous capacities. For example, among the twelve Chinese labeled as preachers in 1865, four actually had no fixed appointments, but labored in different parts of the field as necessities of the situation might demand. Such persons, often simply termed "native helpers" in the statistics, frequently worked as colporteurs, that is, as distributors of religious literature.

The responsibilities of pastors increased steadily during this period. As congregations grew in size, more and more of a pastor's time involved calling on church families. It is interesting to note that "family visitations" conformed closely to those carried on by Reformed ministers in the States, with such pat questions being asked of family members as "How long have you worshiped?"; "Do you read the Bible regularly?"; and "Do you have family prayers?" Perhaps the only question put to the Chinese that would sound unusual to American church members was "Can you read?" As the number of outstations increased, they created a heavier burden on pastors who were required to visit them periodically to administer the sacraments and admit and discipline members. Finally, pastors had to devote an increasing amount of time teaching inquirers who were interested in becoming communicant church members.

The foremost pastor of this period was the Reverend Iap Han-cheong, who served Second Amoy from 1863 to 1884 and the Sio-khe church from 1884 to 1880. After meeting Iap, Secretary Henry Cobb of the Board of Foreign Missions had this to say about him:

> Pastor Iap is a fine specimen of a Chinese Christian and preacher. Tall, somewhat venerable in appearance, with an air of natural grace and spiritual refinement, he is much respected by all classes, and is a useful minister. He has a large family, and their home, which we visited in the course of the day, is a model—scrupulously neat and clean, and thus quite an exception to the rule. His wife is a gentle, lady-like woman, and seemed a worthy companion and helper to her excellent husband.[18]

With respect to Mrs. Iap's having been a helpmate to her husband and highly respected in her own right, John Fagg filed this report following her death in 1896:

Last summer, when Mrs. Iap...died, so genuine and widespread was the appreciation of that exceptionally noble woman's character, that...on the day of her burial in the lone cemetery on the hillside in the Sio-khe Valley, thirty women, many of them with bound feet, and upwards of two hundred men, many of whom had walked from neighboring villages eight and twelve miles away, followed in quiet, mournful procession to the place where they laid her away.[19]

Sunday services at the outstations were less substantive than those of the churches—unless presided over by a visiting pastor or missionary. When the local preacher was in charge, there was generally only one service. This practice was followed in part because preachers sometimes looked after more than one outstation and thus had a rigid schedule to follow on Sundays. It was also done because preachers were less well trained than pastors, and had difficulty preparing two or three different services for a single day. Because of difficulty in composing new sermons, some preachers were transferred periodically. On the other hand, those who showed promise were encouraged to return to school "to increase [their] stock of Scripture knowledge" and maybe even to prepare themselves for ordination someday.

It happened occasionally that a preacher was dismissed from his office. The usual reasons included immoral behavior, engaging in business on the side, and preaching false doctrine. With respect to the last, note this excerpt from the mission's annual report of 1873:

With our reduced Missionary force, our supply of helpers is altogether too small for meeting the demands of the work. At the same time we feel that *quality* is more important than quantity, and accordingly, at the close of the year, we dismissed one of our assistants whom we could no longer trust, and who, we had reason to believe, preached too much from the standpoint of heathen morality, and too little from that of the Gospel.[20]

Everything considered, however, dismissals of preachers were rare, and it was from their ranks that most pastors were recruited when vacancies occurred in the churches.

Street preaching on week days in the local community and

neighboring villages became a regular part of the responsibility of pastors, as well as of preachers who had the necessary experience and training. This kind of activity might involve a day or two, and even the better part of a week. If more than one person were engaged in "working" the streets, it went on with few pauses. When one man ceased preaching another would begin, and whoever was free would likely occupy himself by distributing and selling tracts and Bibles. In some areas, it was not uncommon for the pastors and preachers to meet together in one of the larger towns on a monthly basis for two or three days. At these gatherings, the first day would be devoted to discussing common problems or special points of theology. During the rest of the time, the men would break up into groups of two or three and move about the town or visit neighboring villages preaching in the streets. Both pastors and preachers generally reported being well received by the people during these visits, as is evident in this communication of 1889 by Fagg:

> Another feature of encouragement has been the increased willingness to hear the gospel. Native preachers have frequently remarked recently, that the past year was the best in their experience. Years ago they were scolded, abused, stoned. Today they go into villages where chairs are brought out to rest them. They are entertained to tea and sweet-meats. They are invited to come again.[21]

The spirit of ecumenism that prevailed during the early period between the staffs of the Reformed and English Presbyterian missions continued after 1865. One of the best examples of cooperation concerned the new Douglas Memorial Chapel at Kulangsu, named in honor of the Reverend Carstairs Douglas, who had labored with great diligence on behalf of the English Presbyterians for twenty-two years until his death in 1877. Most of the costs for construction were provided by his estate in Scotland.[22] With the two missionary groups taking responsibility for the worship services on alternate Sundays, the new chapel was attended by both Reformed and English Presbyterian churchgoers. It also became a common place of worship for students from the Middle School and theological seminary, both of which were union institutions.

Ecumenism was also clearly in evidence when in 1885 Leonard

Kip and a Chinese pastor of one of the Reformed churches were invited to attend a session of the Swatow Presbytery in nearby Kwantung province. Swatow had for many years been the scene of considerable English Presbyterian activity paralleling that of their English brethren to the north. Its presbytery dated from about the same time as the founding of the Tai-hoey at Amoy. Later, the Reformed mission, after working for a number of years among some people known as the Hakka, turned that field over to the Swatow Presbytery.[23]

Cooperation between the two missions continued in other ways too. Sharing duties when a missionary became ill or was on furlough went on as before, and in 1893, the English Presbyterians transferred one of their preachers to the Reformed mission when the latter was in need of someone to serve the Changchow area. The transfer took place despite the fact that the preacher had been educated at the expense of the Presbyterians and could have been put to good use at one of their chapels. It was also at about this time that a Reformed outstation in the Sio-khe district united with two English Presbyterian stations in calling a common pastor, enabling them to organize the union church known as Chi-lam. In writing to the Board of Foreign Missions in 1894, Daniel Rapalje described this cooperation with the English Presbyterians as "additional proof, were any needed, that their work and ours are regarded as one."[24]

There was also occasional cooperation with the London Missionary Society during this period. In accordance with the comity of missions and the desire to eliminate unnecessary overlapping, the three Protestant missions agreed not to establish chapels in close proximity to one another. When it was discovered in the late 1890s that the Reformed mission had unwittingly located an outstation in the Hong-san area rather close to a station of the London Missionary Society, the latter amiably agreed to withdraw. The Reformed mission, however, felt it had been the one that had erred and therefore graciously turned its station over to the London group. Early in the twentieth century, this kind of cooperation eventually prompted the London group to join the Tai-hoey and to participate in some of the union schools that had been established by the Reformed and English Presbyterians.[25]

The ecumenical spirit existing among the three Protestant

missions in South Fukien did not extend, however, to Roman Catholics, who were viewed with great suspicion at this time. They were variously described by the Reformed missionaries as being "antagonistic," "quarrelsome," and "irreconcilable," and of trying to draw followers away from the Protestants by constructing majestic churches in close proximity to the more simple-looking Reformed chapels, which in many cases were little more than rented houses. On some occasions, even stronger accusations were made. Thus, in 1886, Kip wrote the Board of Foreign Missions that in addition to "heathen oppressors" hindering missionary work, there were the Roman Catholics, who "by means of lying accusations...can certainly equal the heathen, from whom they differ but little in character."[26]

One of the most biting criticisms of the Catholic methods of proselytizing was this report from Sio-khe filed by Fagg on March 6, 1890:

> They institute rites and ceremonies which are only a shadow removed from those performed in Buddhist temples. They baptize freely. They are careless as to Sabbath observance. They exercise no discipline. They never excommunicate. To advance their cause they proselyte; they adopt rejected girl babies and bring them up to give to heathen men on condition that they will become Roman Catholics. This appeals to the Chinaman's mercenary spirit. For he has ordinarily to pay from $100 to $800 for the woman he marries. Ceremonialism is prominent, preaching quite secondary.[27]

Fagg added that the foreign priests were Portuguese and Spanish and thus "naturally represent Roman Catholicism in some of its widest departures."

The Roman Catholic missionaries were also criticized for being too quick to intervene with the public authorities when a Chinese Christian got in trouble with the law. For example, in 1898, the Reverend Hobart Studley, who served as a Reformed missionary in China from 1896 to 1903, accused the "Romanists," as he called them, of bringing grievances, "good, bad, and indifferent," to the attention of the public authorities in behalf of the Chinese in return for a "consideration." Many of the Chinese populace thought Protestant missionaries should follow the same procedure, but, according to Studley, when the Chinese found out differently, they no longer showed interest in the work of the American and English missionaries. In justifying the Protestant criticisms, Studley added: "While there is no doubt that the truth can find lodgment within hearts actuated by low motives, yet we feel that a few seekers after truth are better than a multitude who are seeking 'the loaves and the fishes.'"[28] Fortunately, the animosity between the staffs of the Reformed and Roman Catholic missions did not last forever, but its alleviation was slow.

In reviewing what happened with respect to the missionary and Chinese staff during the period 1863-1900, it is obvious that there was progress—but not as much as was needed. Despite repeated appeals to the Board of Foreign Missions for more recruits, the increase was minimal. The thirty-three new missionaries who were sent out represented an average of less than one per year. Moreover, there still remained the high attrition rate resulting from early returns to America for reasons of health. There was one bright spot, however, namely, the increase in the number of women missionaries. This was especially significant because of the success they had in working among Chinese women and because of their help in establishing mission schools and nursing programs. The increase of the Chinese staff was another important development of this period, although here, too, the number remained small in comparison to what was needed. Moreover, as has been described, not all Chinese clergymen were equally qualified.

VII
New Churches and Stations, 1863-1900

In accordance with the comity of missions, the area assigned to the Reformed church extended about eighty miles east to west and fifty miles north to south, encompassing about 3 million people. Within these bounds, the Reformed missionaries had three churches under their care in 1863. Two of these were located in Amoy City, namely, First Amoy, or Sin-Koe-a, founded in 1856, and Second Amoy, or Tek-Chhiu-kha, founded in 1860. The third church, established in 1859, was located at Chioh-be, a large town of 60,000 inhabitants about twenty miles west of Amoy. There were also five preaching stations, of which Kang-thau and O-pi, both located on Amoy Island, were under the supervision of First Amoy; The-soa and Ang-tung-thau, both on the mainland, were under the care of Second Amoy; and Changchow, also on the mainland, was under the supervision of the church at Chioh-be.

Of the three churches, the Second Church of Amoy was the most prosperous, having 165 members in 1900, which was more than double what it had in 1863. As mentioned previously, the reasons for the increase were primarily two: first, it enjoyed the services of a very popular native Chinese pastor, the Reverend Iap Han-cheong, for twenty years (1863-1884); and second, it had the advantage of being located in close proximity to the English Presbyterian hospital. The other two churches meanwhile experienced more limited growth, with each having slightly less than 100 members in 1900. The problems of Chioh-be were particularly difficult. Setbacks were brought on by the reappearance for a time of Taiping rebels in the area, and later by having to contend with the shortcomings of its pastor, the Reverend Tiong Lu-li (1872-1882), and the long pastorless hiatus that followed his deposition in 1882.

Measured in terms of the number of new churches, the evangelization program of the period 1863-1900 would have to be judged moderately successful, the number having increased from three to eleven. The names of the new churches and dates of their organization were as follows: O-Kang (1868), Hong-san (1870), Tong-an (1871), Changchow (1871), Sio-khe (1881), Thian-san (1891), Lam-sin (1892), and Poa-a (1894).[1] The communicant membership of the eleven churches in 1900 was 1,133, distributed as follows:

First Amoy	98	Chang-chou	114
Second Amoy	165	Sio-khe	176
Chioh-be	88	Thian-san	117
O-Kang	109	Lam-sin	72
Hong-san	88	Poa-a	107
Tong-an	199		

Of the new churches, the Sio-khe church showed significant growth from the beginning and became one of the principal mission centers on the mainland. Although the town itself had only about 8,000 inhabitants, there were more than 350 villages scattered throughout the surrounding plain, bringing the church in touch with tens of thousands of souls. It was also an important commercial center where various staple products of the valley, such as sugar cane, rice, tobacco, figs, and garlic, were bartered and sold. The construction of a missionary residence in 1886 and the hard work of its first occupants, Leonard and Helen Kip, contributed further to the church's success. So too did the labors of their successors, Alexander and Alice Van Dyck and John and Margaret Fagg. Finally, the importance and success of the Sio-khe church was enhanced by the decision to make educational and medical work a vital part of its evangelical program.[2]

Two other churches that eventually did well were those at Changchow and Tong-an. Expectations for early success were high at both places. In addition to their being important commercial centers, they had large populations (Changchow had over 200,000 inhabitants) and relatively easy access to surrounding towns and villages (200 in the case of Changchow).

Secretary Henry Cobb of the Board of Foreign Missions reported in 1892, following a visit to both cities, that more inviting and promising fields could hardly be found anywhere.[3] Yet, it was not until the late 1890s that they showed significant growth. The reasons for their slow start were several, including local opposition,[4] shortage of funds and clerical personnel, membership reduction due to upgrading some outstations to the status of churches, and the mission's paying greater attention to other churches.[5]

All the new churches began as outstations. In several cases, a change in status came about through a kind of collegiate arrangement between two or three outstations that were located near each other. In such instances, a union consistory of elders and deacons was elected from among the members of the outstations, and steps were taken to call a common pastor. The first of these arrangements occurred in 1868 with the formation of the O-Kang church consisting of worshipers from two villages, O-pi and Kang-thau, both of whose outstations had been founded by First Amoy and were located about four miles apart on Amoy Island. In similar fashion, the church known as Hong-san was organized in 1870 through a collegiate agreement among the worshipers at the Te-soa and Ang-tung-thau outstations. Both of these were on the mainland and had been under the supervision of Second Amoy.[6] The formation of new churches in this manner did not by any means decrease the number of outstations. Rather, it often had the opposite effect, as new churches gradually established outstations of their own.

The number of outstations increased from five in 1863 to forty-one by 1900. A request to establish an outstation frequently had its roots in the urging of a small number of Chinese among the local populace. Such a genesis group initially became acquainted with Christianity by such means as attending worship services in a neighboring community, spending time in one of the mission hospitals, or reading religious tracts. A proposal to establish an outstation was referred to the Tai-hoey, which in turn appointed a committee to investigate the matter. The final decision rested on such factors as the sincerity of the persons making the request, their willingness to assist in meeting some of the financial needs for maintaining the new station, and, above all, the possibilities for future growth. The last factor included such considerations as the number of people living in the community and whether it was a market town that would attract visitors from the outside. The views of the local literati and mandarins were also taken into consideration. Naturally, too, the decision would rest on whether the mission had someone available to staff the station.

When a decision was made to go ahead with plans for establishing an outstation, rooms or a house were invariably rented until there was greater certainty about its future success. As explained by Fagg in 1890, following a three-week visit to four "country towns," most places of worship at the outset were

> not marked by anything very churchly, either interior or exterior. You would not be likely to recognize them as you do a country church in New York or New Jersey. They are usually rented Chinese houses or shops....The furnishings too are not likely to come under the ban of extravagance. They consist of the plainest wooden pulpit or table, backless, unupholstered benches, two or three cheap hanging lamps, and a brass gong to announce the hour for worship.[7]

Even on Amoy Island as late as 1900 it was possible to find a place of worship that was not very "churchly" in appearance. This is obvious from the scene described by the Reverend Abbe Livingston Warnshuis following a Sabbath day visit to a village outstation a few weeks after his arrival in China in October, 1900. Warnshuis's observations are also interesting for the unique manner in which the worship service was conducted.

> One side of the chapel was entirely open to the street, which was one of the more important roads leading to Amoy City. For this reason the stream of passers-by was almost continuous, and many of these would stop at the open side of the chapel to listen for a longer or shorter time. I did not learn how many women there were behind the screen, but there were about ten men present, who were indeed very attentive. Each one took some part in the meeting, all read a verse of Scripture in turn, one read the Commandments, several led in prayer, and others read the hymns. Of course, no one paid any attention to

the pig wallowing in a mud-hole ten feet from the door, or to the dirty dogs which came in and went out as they pleased, nor were they disturbed by the curious crowd in the street.[8]

In cases where it was apparent that a new outstation was not making satisfactory progress and there seemed little hope for its future, the Tai-hoey did not hesitate to close it. Such closings were surprisingly frequent, although in some instances it simply involved relocating them in a neighboring town or village.

When an outstation was doing well, and if funds were available, consideration was given to constructing a permanent place of worship. Certain criteria were kept in mind in choosing a specific building site. In addition to good drainage and a lot large enough to permit future expansion, attempts were made to locate near a main thoroughfare. This had the advantage not only of convenience for the local populace, it was important for attracting transients as well. Consideration was also given to the reaction of the people living in the vicinity of the new station. It happened occasionally that some Chinese opposed to having a "Bible temple" in their neighborhood would cause trouble for the workmen during the construction period or would damage the building after it had been finished.

Lack of funding became a primary reason for delaying the construction of a new place of worship. Even organized congregations sometimes had to wait a long time before such construction could begin. As late as 1888, for example, four of the eight organized churches were meeting in rented rooms or houses. In this respect, it must be noted that church buildings were costing more than formerly—sometimes two and three times more by 1900—because of rising construction costs and because in some instances more elaborate structures were being built.

Construction costs obviously became one of the major items in the mission's annual budget. A glance at an appeal for $4,080 that Fagg made in 1891 to the Board of Foreign Missions gives a clear indication of the variegated building projects. His list included a church kitchen, parsonage, and rooms for visiting missionaries at Tong-an; a chapel for the outstation at To-kio; remodeling the church at Chioh-be; a parsonage at Thian-san; a church building at Lam-sin; and a new building for the boys' school at Sio-khe. Fagg

made it abundantly clear that the amount being requested was not
sufficient by itself to complete these projects, but that the "native
brethren" were pledging to contribute money and labor. He added
that if it were not for their substantial cooperation, "the amount
appealed for would be quite inadequate."[9] In a letter a few years
later, describing the newly completed church at Lam-sin, Fagg
gives some specific information on the type of contributions made
by the "native brethren":

> The brethren, besides buying the site and paying for
> various furnishings, have put five thousand days of work
> on the church building. Some brethren worked fifty or
> sixty days, taking this time from their farms and business
> affairs. They carried stones and tiles and bricks. They
> drew water. They mixed and carried mortar. They helped
> in the "house raising."[10]

From the beginning, Chinese Christians were urged to
contribute part of their income to help pay the salaries of pastors
and preachers. Although the two Chinese pastors at First and
Second Amoy were being supported entirely by their respective
congregations, this was the exception for many years despite the
low salary schedule. Top salaries for pastors were about twelve
dollars a month, and they started at about one-half that amount.
The allowance gradually increased according to competence and
experience, but very few reached the twelve dollar bracket.
Preachers were paid even less. A report of 1880 suggests that the
mission made a conscious effort to avoid paying high salaries lest
some individuals seek church offices from "improper motives."[11]

In fairness to the Chinese congregations who found it
impossible to come up with more than half of the amount due
their pastors, it must be noted that even four or five dollars a
month was no meager sum, considering the low wage scale of
most laborers. As late as 1891, the mission reported that the
average monthly income of most Chinese was only four or six
dollars, and some received considerably less.[12] As Talmage
pointed out in 1868, Chinese contributions were actually quite
commensurate to their incomes:

> In the matter of contributions, it is still a day of small
> things, but I know of no Churches, whether in Christian
> or heathen lands, more benevolent, according to their

ability, than those under our care at Amoy. They are very
far in advance of most of the Missionary Churches.[13]

Secretary Cobb later echoed this observation when he wrote in
1906 that "In nothing are [Chinese communicants] more
remarkable than in their liberality."[14]

The missionaries were determined that the churches in due
time become self-supporting. They used the same arguments put
forth in the early 1860s during the crisis with the General Synod
over the classis question. Talmage, for example, in 1872 warned
that great care must be taken not to establish

a beneficiary Church, dependent on the Churches of
other lands instead of on themselves for the support of
their own institutions. The native Churches ought to be
trained as fast as possible, not only to support themselves,
but to become benefactors to others, learning the luxury
of bestowing instead of receiving benefactions. When in
Mission Reports, except in those describing new Mission
fields, we read [about] a large proportion of the native
members of the Churches as being in the employ of the
Mission [and] supported by mission funds, and the
Churches not self-sustaining, we regard it as evidence of
an unhealthy native church.[15]

The need to avoid the impression of establishing a foreign
institution in China became increasingly valid as the tide of
Chinese nationalism rose in response to the West's steadily
expanding the terms of the "unequal treaties" forced upon China
after the Opium Wars of the 1840s and 1850s. Anti-foreign
sentiment was further inflamed by America's restricting Chinese
immigration during the latter part of the nineteenth century.

By 1900, definite progress was being made toward achieving
self-supporting churches, as shown by a few excerpts from the
annual reports of the late 1800s: "We have eight organized
churches, five of which are self-supporting," (1888); "This Church
[at Hong-san] supports its pastor, pays all running expenses, a
quarter of the school teacher's salary, and contributed thirteen
dollars toward Domestic Missions," (1898); and "The church [at
Tong-an], in the way of self-support, pays the salary of the pastor,
all current expenses, nearly half of the teacher's salary, and
contributed forty dollars toward Domestic Missions," (1898). At

both Hong-san and Tong-an, however, the mission paid the
salaries of the preachers who were assisting the outstations and
also the remainder of the teachers' salaries.[16]

Some Chinese churches contributed more than others, of
course. In 1901, for example, First Amoy with 108 members
contributed an average of $8.88 per member, which was "equal to
at least forty-four dollars in an ordinary home church." Second
Amoy, with 179 members, did even better—about $13 per
member. Overall, the average giving for each of the 1,400 communicant members for the year 1901 was approximately $5.85.[17]

To help meet the mission's financial needs, there was, besides
the contributions from the Chinese Christians, the annual budget
provided by the denominational Board of Foreign Missions. This,
however, was seldom sufficient. Moreover, the amount varied
from year to year, depending on the state of the American
economy. During times of economic stress, fewer funds flowed
into the board's coffers, on which occasions the missionaries were
called upon to limit and sometimes even to cut back on their
operations. Such circumstances left the missionaries
understandably bitter, as can be judged by the following notation
sent in from Amoy by Philip Pitcher on Christmas Day, 1888:

> Before the Church here stands a gigantic evil. The
> Church must make gigantic efforts if she expects to
> remove it. Does her faith waver? Alas! There comes no
> message across the water telling us of such effort. Quite
> different the message. One-fifth of the required
> appropriations for the year raised, and half of the year
> gone. From this time until the close of the year will we
> again be served with "In extremis," "How to clear the
> debt," and "How to raise money" articles?
>
> Progress! There ought to be progress in this field;
> there ought to be more of the Lord's money used here.
> We truly are only playing at Mission here. What are we
> and our sixteen thousand dollars [among] this
> host—these three million idolators? Is this to be our
> Church's standing army in China? Are these...the only
> funds that are to be entrusted to the little band to save
> these three million? With years and strength it might be
> done, but in the meantime millions must have passed

down to an *endless doom*![18]

Fortunately, special groups among the Reformed churches in the States occasionally provided funds for particular mission projects. Thus, an imposing church building and a parsonage were erected at Sio-khe in 1884, in part from contributions that came from various Sunday school groups throughout America. Later, several Sunday schools in New York City joined forces in raising money for beds for the mission hospital at Sio-khe. In the early 1890s several special gifts from the Woman's Board of Foreign Missions provided for the construction of a girls' school at Sio-khe, the alteration of the church at Chioh-be, and the building of a new church at Kio-tan on Amoy Island. And in 1893, when rented rooms were needed at Hai-teng to serve as an outstation for the Chioh-be church, an organization known as the "King's Daughters" of the Second Reformed Church at Poughkeepsie, New York, paid the costs.

There were also private benefactors. For example, a servant woman who had been in the employ of Kip's parents in America for many years left a large legacy to be used by the Amoy mission in whatever way Kip saw fit. From these funds, the church at Tong-an was renovated in 1890 at a cost of $900; a new chapel and parsonage were constructed to serve the Thian-san congregation; and a chapel, parsonage, and rooms for visiting missionaries, all built of brick and surrounded by a high wall, were constructed on the mission premises at Soa-sia. In like manner, a "generous friend" from New Jersey provided funds in 1893 to assist in the construction of a "commodious building" for the worshipers at Lam-sin, and through the kindness of a Mr. P. Semelink, a "nice chapel 35x26 with a porch seven feet wide" was erected at Te-thau in 1899.

By the close of the century, the Chinese congregations, as they increased in size and number, were able not only to assist more in paying the salaries of their pastors and preachers, but also in paying some of the building costs. Thus, in 1891, the worshipers at Poa-a contributed over $300 toward the construction of their new outstation. And in 1895, when the church at Sio-khe had to be enlarged, the congregation purchased a lot at the rear of the building for $200 and contributed $150 for the remodeling.

From time to time, Chinese churches and stations also

contributed funds for other projects. For example, in 1888, the church at Changchow raised $30 in a two-week period for famine sufferers in North China. In 1891, the Chinese churches, acting in concert, raised over $600 for famine relief in the northern province of Shantung, and in the following year they gave several hundred dollars for flood sufferers near Tientsin. Similarly, in 1892, Sio-khe and its two stations, Soa-pi and Toa-lo-teng, contributed $18 for flood victims in the Tientsin area and $25 for a new bridge. In explaining the latter contribution, Fagg, the resident missionary at Sio-khe, declared its purpose was not only to give financial assistance for a much needed neighborhood improvement, but also

> to show the heathen that while there were many public demonstrations in honor of the [local] gods, in which Christians could not join, still they had not lost their public spirit, but were quite as ready as the heathen to contribute to a worthy public enterprise.[19]

By 1900, several of the churches had formed benevolent organizations composed of women and known as Dorcas societies. These groups held regular meetings devoted to the sewing of clothing, with the mission generally supplying the materials. The finished products were either distributed among the poor or sold, with the proceeds being given to worthy causes.

As in the past, delegates from the Reformed and English Presbyterian churches continued to meet together, usually on a semiannual basis, as a classis or Tai-hoey. Prompted in part by the increase in the number of churches, but primarily by their scattered nature and poor travel accommodations, the Tai-hoey was divided in two in 1893. By the new arrangement, nine churches formed the Choan, or Northern Classis, and ten made up the Chiang, or Southern Classis.[20] Plans were also made for organizing a synod made up of delegates from both classes. Known as the Synod of South Fukien, it held its first regular session in April, 1894, in the Douglas Memorial Chapel at Kulangsu. Present were sixteen ordained pastors, nineteen elders, and eight missionaries representing the two missions. As reported by an English Presbyterian historian, the formation of a synod "was a natural spontaneous development derived from that day in 1862 when a few far-sighted missionaries and Chinese elders had sat down on equal terms and united in Christian fellowship."[21]

The synod was convened annually, usually within a few days after the classes had met. Until about 1910, it met at Kulangsu; thereafter, it generally rotated among several cities. Sessions lasted about five days and, as might be expected, involved routine reports on such matters as new churches and outstations, membership growth, and finances. Persons in attendance also learned about the status of the mission schools and hospitals. There also were the so-called "overtures." These were matters that had been brought up in the classes and considered important enough to be called to the attention of the synod.

Most overtures were of a serious nature. Some of them dealt with problems that were not new but had taken on greater importance than in the past. Among other matters, overtures included questions about how best to limit the cultivation of opium; objections about the undue influence of missionary delegates as compared to Chinese delegates at ecclesiastical gatherings; concerns as to the propriety of ordaining women as elders; complaints about consistory members being consistently re-elected because of their wealth or social influence rather than their "Christian worth"; and criticism of infanticide and arranged marriages. Some matters, such as the opium question, came up frequently. Another problem discussed frequently concerned polygamy on the part of men who wished to become church members. The usual ruling was a denial, unless the man could put away his second wife without wronging her or the children—obviously not an easy solution, which explains why the matter came up so often for discussion.[22]

In the late 1800s, the Reformed missionaries resolved for administrative purposes to divide the territory under their special jurisdiction into districts, of which there were four by 1900. Each was named after a particular community in its district as follows: Amoy, Changchow, Tong-an, and Sio-khe. Plans called for a resident missionary to serve as supervisor for each district. The purpose of the arrangement was in keeping with a recommendation made in 1880 by a special three-man committee acting in behalf of the Board of Foreign Missions. The recommendation called for the mission

to allow a part of its force to reside at some points inland, at least for a large portion of each year, as the missionaries could thus be brought into a more close and continual contact with the interior life of the thickly-settled country, instead of sallying out on occasional Gospel campaigns.[23]

In time, the inland headquarters evolved into rather elaborate mission compounds. Secretary Cobb gave a good description of one of these, namely Sio-khe, following his visit there in the spring of 1892. As described by Cobb, the mission hospital, located between the river and the main road, was the largest building and planned in such a way that additions could be made easily. It was surrounded by a large courtyard around which was a high wall with a gateway. The large house of John Otte, the mission's physician, was located nearby. It faced the river and afforded a fine view of the mountains in the distance. Another house, smaller than Otte's but also two stories high, was about 225 yards from the doctor's dwelling. This was the house of the district missionary. Both houses were constructed of brick and had neatly shaded courtyards. Also nearby was the home of the local Chinese pastor. Although smaller than the other two houses, it was described by Cobb as being "a good specimen of the better class of Chinese dwellings." Next to the pastor's house was the church. Built of brick, it was the largest place of worship that the Reformed mission had outside of Amoy City. Connected to it by a narrow passageway was the so-called street chapel. The original place of worship at Sio-khe, it was kept open daily with someone in attendance "to receive and answer inquirers." The upstairs of the street chapel housed a girls' school at the time of Cobb's visit, but later a separate building was erected for the girls and another was built for the boys.[24]

Alexander Van Dyck described the immense task facing a district missionary and his staff in his report of 1889 to the Board of Foreign Missions regarding the Sio-khe district. As explained by him, the area under his supervision included the Sio-khe valley, containing at least 300 villages and towns, along with 200 more in an adjoining valley to the south, and another 250 in a valley to the southwest—750 in all. Surrounding these valleys were numerous mountain villages, a few of them 1,400 feet above sea level. Although some of the communities contained only a few tens of inhabitants, others contained tens of thousands. Scattered throughout the region were one church (Sio-khe) and four outstations, Lam-sin, Poa-a, Po-a-hi, and Toa-khe. To assist Van Dyck in ministering to the needs of his district, there were, in addition to Dr. Otte, two assistant missionaries—Alice Van Dyck and Frances Otte; one Chinese pastor; four Chinese preachers; and one Chinese teacher. In view of the amount of territory involved and the limited staff, Van Dyck's concluding remarks in the 1889 report are not surprising: "During the past year we have preached in hundreds of the hamlets and villages in the surrounding valleys, but it will take more than one, two, or three years to visit every place."[25]

Van Dyck's situation at Sio-khe was not unique. For example, Pitcher, in addition to serving as principal of the Middle School at Kulangsu (a full-time job in itself), acted for several years as supervisor of the Tong-an district. This territory, located north of Amoy, was about forty-five miles long, twenty-five wide, and had a population of 600,000. Scattered throughout the region were two churches and six outstations under the care of two Chinese pastors and seven preachers. As Pitcher remarked to his overseers on the Board of Foreign Missions in America, "Where at home will you find so large an area, with an equal population, so undermanned?" No wonder he called it his "diocese"![26]

The increase in the number of churches from three to eleven and outstations from five to forty-one during the period 1863-1900 is rather remarkable considering the limited size of the missionary and Chinese staff. The increase obviously placed a great responsibility on the upcountry mission staff, as has been described in the case of Van Dyck. The rise in the number of places of worship is likewise remarkable in view of the financial problems that regularly faced the mission. Credit for dealing with this matter must be shared by several groups, including congregations and private donors in the States and the Chinese Christians themselves. Help received from the latter as they struggled to achieve the mission's goal of establishing a self-supporting Chinese church is particularly significant in view of the low wage scale that prevailed in China.

VIII
Missionary Tours and Visitations, 1863-1900

New churches and outstations were placed in the hands of the Chinese as soon as possible, with the missionary staff continuing to visit them whenever it was workable. Places of worship near the home base of a missionary were visited quite frequently and required a journey of only a day or two, but the shortage of personnel caused more distant places to be visited less often—sometimes only once or twice a year. An itinerary involving several places frequently resembled that of a circuit minister, that is, it ran along a kind of circular route with the end being relatively close to the beginning. Tours of that kind could last as long as four weeks and were often made in the company of another missionary. Because the means of travel were limited, no activity occupied more of a missionary's time than preaching tours and visits to the churches and outstations.

In some instances, especially when the heat was excessive and the distance to be traveled relatively short, missionary visits were simply made by walking with a staff in one hand and an umbrella in the other. A "burden bearer" frequently followed close behind, carrying provisions, religious literature, and, if the journey included an overnight stay, some extra clothing and a mattress. Travel by horseback was also resorted to, as the Reverend John Fagg pointed out in this communication of 1891:

> Sometimes I go out on our pony, with a rubber cloth wallet, containing lunch and a few books and papers, slung over my shoulder. If it rains, I mount our ranger clad in a rubber coat, rubber boots, and sun hat which serves as an

umbrella to shield my head and face from the spring downpour.[1]

The common means for land travel, however, was a kind of portable chair, frequently covered, for carrying a single person and borne on poles by two men. Sedan chairs, as these means of conveyance were commonly called, were about the only type of "vehicle" that could be used for land travel, considering the narrowness of the roads, which often were little more than footpaths. Sedan chairs, however, left a few things to be desired. In the event of numerous ridges or steep mountain paths, passengers generally had to walk, and in the summer months the sedan chair could become uncomfortably warm. To deal with the latter problem, the Reverend Leonard Kip recommended that travelers take two special pieces of "equipage" along: a wet sheet to throw over the top of the chair, which could otherwise become too hot to even touch, and a wet sponge "to cool the head...to escape sunstroke."[2]

Passengers rode at the mercy of their chair bearers if the latter's qualifications were unknown to the traveler. In addition to running the risk of the bearers being opium addicts, there was the problem that while some bearers carried their load in an easy and smooth manner, others moved along in a jerky fashion. Those of the latter type were an especial bane to the inexperienced traveler, as Secretary Henry Cobb pointed out when he visited Amoy in the summer of 1892 for the Board of Foreign Missions:

> At the best it is not easy to keep from sliding forward in a heap. For this, the feet and knees must be kept constantly braced, which becomes wearisome after a while. Unless one leans back, his head bobs back and forth like one of the curious nodding mandarins the Chinese make, and if he does lean back, it is likely to beat a perpetual tattoo on the headrest behind him.[3]

Making one's way by sedan chair could also be boring, which, when traveling with companions, was another reason why missionaries sometimes preferred traveling by foot. Sedan travel was also slow. To quote from another communication by Fagg:

> The majestic slowness of sedan chair travel may be judged from a journey undertaken ten days ago from Changchow to Soa-sia, a distance of twenty miles over a fairly level

road. I started at 5:30 Monday morning and arrived at Soa-sia an hour after the sun had set, fifteen hours enroute. Excepting an hour for an examination of the school at Tian-po, all the time was spent jogging along on a hot summer road. The excessive heat forbade walking, or we should have tried our own marching equipment, with the hope of scoring a somewhat higher record. [4]

There was also, according to Fagg, this problem: "Chair bearers are usually a loud-mouthed and vulgar people, and do not form very worthy [traveling companions] when one is going to preach the true God and exhort men to repentance and salvation."[5]

Travel by foot or sedan chair, although slow and not without headaches, did provide travelers with ample opportunity to view the beautiful scenery in that part of China. John Otte recorded the following remarks after completing a trip in 1891 from Sio-khe, his home base, to Koah-tek, a small village twenty miles distant and about 2,300 feet above the Sio-khe plain:

Our road often lay along the side of precipitous mountains. High above us the evergreen foliage, interspersed with the beautiful feathery, golden bamboo, and set off by a beautiful blue sky, made us forget the rough road and stimulated us to renewed effort to gain sight of still finer scenery, of which we could catch glimpses in the mountain rifts. Hundreds of feet below us ran a mountain stream, whose beautiful blue waters, collected in deep rocky basins, we could often see through the bamboos. As it leaped over the rocks, its music, coming to us from distant depths, would induce a feeling of loneliness, which in turn was relieved by the sight of human habitations perched upon the very tops of the precipitous mountains across the stream. [6]

Fortunately, in view of the discomfort and other shortcomings associated with travel by sedan chair, another and often better means of transportation was available, namely, by boat. In truth, it may be said that rivers at this time in China's history were her great highways. Because of the importance of travel by water and the differences in the depths of the rivers and strengths of their currents, it is not surprising that the mission's "gospel fleet" included several types of vessels, each suited to a particular need or problem. As described by Fagg in a letter of June 1893, these craft included

> the Harbor Boat, for communication between Kulangsu island, Amoy City, and two of the nearer stations on Amoy island; the Gospel Boat, for voyages up and down the channels and arms of the sea reaching out to Chioh-be and Hai-ten on the west, and Te-soa, Te-tan, Ang-tug-tan, and Tong-an on the north; the River Boat, sailing up and down the West river between Chioh-be and Changchow; [and] the Sio-khe House Boat, cruising up and down the same West river beyond Changchow to Tian-po, Soa-sia, and Sio-khe.[7]

Of these, the oldest was the Gospel Boat. It was a large sloop of about ten tons, with a cabin that could accommodate up to four people. The River Boat was smaller, of lighter draft, and could, at best, carry three adult passengers. It was equipped with a rectangular sail made of grass matting, but because of the strength of the current, oars and poles had to be used frequently by the Chinese crew.

The Sio-khe Houseboat was the most colorful and most typically Chinese of the various craft comprising the gospel fleet. It was a long, flat-bottom affair with a blunt stern and bow, but having curved sides tapered somewhat toward the front. Over it was a bamboo frame about four feet in height that could be covered with palm leaves as protection from the rain and hot sun. It was also equipped with a tall mast and square-cut sail that could be raised when the river was wide enough to catch a good breeze. Secretary Cobb, who traveled aboard the Houseboat during his visit to Amoy in 1892, has painted a vivid word-picture of some of its other features:

> The boat was commanded by a vigorous old woman, seventy-two years of age, as she informed us! For crew, there were her daughter, son-in-law, and a hired hand. The daughter's children, four in number, composed part of the company, for this was their only home. All the conveniences of home were also there, including a little furnace for cooking, the smoke from which, drifting sternward, almost blinded us when the family meals were being prepared, [as well as] sundry pots and kettles,

baskets and beds. Nor was this all, for lifting up one of the deck planks forward disclosed a litter of rabbits, and still another, the inevitable family pig! Every Chinese house has one or more—why not the house boat? There he lay under the deck, from daylight till dark, scarcely uttering a sound, and only rising when the plank was lifted that he might be fed. That the home might not lack adornment, two or three pieces of red paper, printed in Chinese character, were pasted against palm-leaf walls, and two or three potted plants reposed securely on a shelf in the bow. The Chinese are great lovers of flowers, and of the numerous boats we passed, scarcely one lacked the pots and plants.[8]

As was true of the River Boat, the crew of the Sio-khe Houseboat was hard put at times to keep the craft moving. To again quote from one of Cobb's letters:

Then began the old toil of poling up against the current and over the shallows, the wind this time drawing ahead and making our sail useless. As we went on, the shallows became more frequent and the toil increased. The boatmen struggled mightily with their poles. One in particular would brace his feet against a stiff plank lying athwart the boat, throw his whole weight upon the pole, and push until he lay almost flat on his back upon the deck, at the same time uttering a prolonged and dismal groan that would have done credit to a case of bilious colic or a guilty conscience.[9]

In view of the arduous work involved in propelling the larger crafts, Cobb raised the question of why the missionaries did not make use of a steam engine. The explanation, along with some personal observations by Cobb, follows:

To my surprise, I found that the use of steam launches is forbidden to foreigners. Some years ago the E. P. Mission had a steam launch, and were using it to great advantage, no Chinese questioning their right to do so. But there happened to be a foreign gentleman (?) residing here who had an antipathy to missionaries. He complained to the authorities that these missionaries were violating the treaty in making use of steam. It proved to be a fact that steam was not allowed by treaty. He professed to show, and the authorities to see, that its use by foreigners was a menace either to the trade or the safety of the Empire, and the result was the suppression of the harmless little craft and an interdict on all others. By a sort of poetical justice the interdict was probably made more comprehensive than the originator designed, and made to apply to all foreigners, consuls, merchants and others, as well as missionaries. The restriction is felt to be burdensome, but there seems no possibility of its removal without a change in the treaties. So much harm one evil-disposed person has it in his power sometimes to do. We did not bless him.[10]

Travel by boat was more relaxing than that by foot or sedan chair, and likewise afforded ample opportunity to view the countryside. The following excerpts are from accounts written by Cobb describing a boat trip of several days that he made in April, 1892, from Amoy to Sio-khe, with stops along the way. The first account gives some of his observations on the leg of the journey from Chioh-be to Changchow.

I was not at all prepared to find the scenery in this part of China so beautiful. The plains stretching away on either side were clothed with flourishing crops of rice and other vegetation. The banks were dotted, and sometimes lined, with clumps of graceful, feathery bamboos or spreading banyans. At short intervals we passed village after village, their white walls gleaming through the thick shade of trees, many of them in most attractive locations, and, at a little distance, inviting in appearance. On either hand rose hills, wooded, or terraced and cultivated to the very summit, and still beyond them, blue and hazy in the distance, ranges of glorious mountains, with pyramids and jagged peaks.

The second account describes scenes along the route from Changchow to Soa-sia:

The scenery through which we passed was not less interesting and charming than the day before. High mountain ranges appeared on either hand, sometimes at a distance, and sometimes closing in upon the river which wound its way between them. Peculiar low hills appeared, conical or pyramidal, terraced to the very top affording space for cultivation. Here and there a temple, nestling among shady groves, was perched on the hillsides. Large and square towers, with strong walls, refuges of different clans in troublous times, stood half-ruined and falling to decay. A changing but ever beautiful panorama of villages and verdure unrolled itself on either side.[11]

A few quotations from letters and other communications written by missionaries can further illustrate the peculiarities of travel in the Amoy area at this time. The first two excerpts are typical of the shorter tours. Both were written by John Fagg from Sio-khe, the first on April 2, 1891:

Last Saturday in company with Pastor Iap, I went to our most southern station, Toa-ke. We had to cross two or three mountain passes, a thousand to fifteen hundred feet high; we had one sedan chair between us, so changed off, riding over the levels, and trusting to our canes and muscle to climb the heights. This station is a market town, thirty miles from Sio-khe.[12]

The second excerpt was written on April 29, about four weeks after the above:

I went to Lamsin last Saturday; it is about twelve miles southeast [of Sio-khe]. I had arranged the evening before to take a sedan chair, but on Saturday noon the men were so intoxicated with opium that they could not go. So I walked, getting there about 6 that evening. On Sunday we observed the Lord's Supper. The church was full.[13]

Before returning to Sio-khe, Fagg spent a couple days at Lam-sin "reconnoitering" for a site to build a new place of worship, the old one having become too small for the growing congregation.

For journeys involving overnight stays, some churches and chapels were provided with a special room to accommodate visitors. Often dubbed the "prophet's room," these facilities occasionally left something to be desired, as Fagg observed during an extended tour in 1890:

We left Chin-chew to visit chapels at four country towns, 12, 16, 20 miles away.... At two places the "prophet's upper room" was so dingy and suspicious that we made the preaching hall our sleeping apartment. We put two or three church benches side by side, spread our matting and small portable mattress on them, and managed to pass the night quite comfortably.[14]

Leonard Kip did more "touring" than any of the other missionaries during this period. Each year at the time of the Chinese New Year (which generally occurred around the first of February) he made an extensive journey, bringing the Christian message to places where the mission had as yet no regularly established work and visiting churches and stations along the way. He chose that season of the year for such a trip because for about two weeks it was a "time of leisure" for the Chinese people and therefore easier to get a "hearing" among them. As part of this practice, he customarily took with him a missionary who had recently arrived from America. What follows are excerpts from an account by Dr. Otte describing a tour he made with Kip in the early part of 1891. Because of the approaching Chinese New Year, work at Otte's hospital at Sio-khe was lax and could be handled by one of the doctor's Chinese assistants. The trip, which lasted almost a month, was to be the doctor's first prolonged acquaintance with Chinese village life. When possible, the two men spent their nights in the home of a native preacher or in the facilities found at an outstation. When such accommodations were not available, the usual recourse was to stay at a Chinese inn. Thus it happened that on the first night of the tour Otte and Kip stayed at an inn in the small mountain village of Koah-tek, located about twelve miles from Sio-khe.

Otte, after a long, hard day of travel, was looking forward to a comfortable night's rest and was obviously taken aback when Kip stopped in front of a low, one-story adobe building and informed his traveling companion that this was where they would be spending the night. In a letter of March 6, 1891, to a friend in America, Otte gives a detailed description of the inn. In understanding his dismay with the accommodations, it must be borne in mind that this was Otte's first real acquaintance with this kind of a situation.

> I had expected little but I saw less. The building was about thirty-five or forty feet square, and consisted of a series of low structures built around a small open court.

On entering the doorway, we stepped into the kitchen. Its furniture consisted of a low hearth made of mud, without chimney; a black, dirty, greasy table set on some old stools; and some mangy dogs. These served as scavengers, and made brooms almost an unnecessary luxury. From the kitchen we stepped into the open court. Here one had to be careful for fear of stepping into the numerous small pools of filth. On the right of the court, and directly in front of it, were some guest chambers (guest pens, rather). On the left was a large cesspool, and back of this a pigsty. This, by the way, was possibly the cleanest part of the hotel. Facing cesspool, pigsty, and another unmentionable abomination, at a distance of about three feet, was our guest pen. Our host introduced us into this, his best apartment, with a delightful smile and a wave of his hand worthy of a Fifth Avenue hotel clerk. There was nothing to be gained by objecting to the dirty black mud walls, for there was no better room to offer us....

After becoming accustomed to the gloom, we surveyed the situation, and found ourselves in a room ten by fifteen feet, having a doorway but no door. (We borrowed the kitchen table after a little while, and this served us as a door.) There also was a small window, but this was fortunately stuffed with straw to keep the cold out. I say fortunately, for in this way at least some of the fearful odors from the different abominations directly under this window were kept out. A wide bench occupied the largest part of the room, and this served as a bed for eleven persons. As the bed was only fifteen feet by six, we objected to so many, and by paying for eleven men (twenty-two cents) only two men were put in the room with us, and these were Christians in our employ.

Otte and Kip spent two days at Koah-tek, going about preaching the gospel and dispensing medicine. During the remainder of the trip, the two stayed in six other inns, only one of which had the luxury of a door. In the cleanest of the seven, Otte asked the proprietor how frequently he swept out the corners of his establishment, to which question the latter replied laughingly, "Not in seven years."[15]

The missionaries carried out a variety of functions during their visits to churches and outstations. These included consulting with the local pastors and preachers, meeting with consistories when deemed advisable, holding "inquiry" meetings with any Chinese seeking to become communicant members, administering the sacraments when needed, visiting the local mission schools, and assisting in the organization of Sunday schools and catechism classes. Upon arising in the morning from whatever accommodations were provided, the visitor or visitors would finish whatever work might remain, and then journeyed on to the next church or outstation where the process would be repeated.

Outstations along a tour route were generally given the greatest attention, with churches being visited only briefly. This procedure was followed not only because the missionary's time was limited but also because the pastors, as ordained ministers, would have had more training and were presumably better able to carry out their tasks than were the preachers at the outstations. Also, the missionaries thought it wise not to "meddle" too much in the work of the pastors, as is clearly shown in this excerpt from the mission's report of 1873:

> As there is now a native pastor at Chioh-be, we do not visit the place as often as we formerly did. It is desirable that the native churches should learn to take care of themselves as soon as possible. The tendency is to lean too much on the missionary, and so while visiting Chioh-be occasionally to confer with the pastor, and encourage him and his people, we feel that most of our time should now be given to the regions beyond.[16]

While enroute from one station to another, the missionaries took advantage of any opportunities that arose along the way for proclaiming the Christian message. Note, in this respect, an account given by the Reverend Hobart Studley who, in early 1897, in order to gain some firsthand experience (having arrived in China only a month earlier), accompanied the veteran Kip on a mission tour that lasted about three weeks and covered nearly 250 miles:

> In all of these places, Kip preached the Gospel to a good many people, and in the inns where we stayed he explained the truth to any individuals who came to talk, to

buy our literature, or [were] attracted by mere curiosity.
In addition to his proclamation of the Gospel, we trust
that much good seed was sown in the large amount of
literature which we disposed.[17]

Street preaching—as impromptu, open-air type of evangelizing
was often called—took place wherever people congregated to carry
on business. Shopkeepers generally did not mind this activity
because it could be a means for attracting customers. Indeed, it
was not uncommon for a shopkeeper to bring out a bench for the
convenience of the speaker and even to serve him tea. During hot
days, however, the shade of a wide-spreading banyan tree was
often sought or, better yet, the eaves of an ancestral temple. As
explained by Alexander Van Dyck in a letter of January 6, 1889,
"It is there that those congregate who have the most leisure, and
there is almost always a large space for an audience."[18] By
standing a little apart from the main crowd, the playing of an
accordion or small portable organ was always a sure means of
attracting listeners.

The missionary women also went out occasionally on tours to
call on churches and outstations. Because of family
responsibilities, the married women usually limited their visits
to a day's journey from their homes. Exceptions to this practice
were made, however, when traveling in the company of their
missionary husbands. Helen Kip, for example, frequently made
extended journeys into the interior with her husband as he
visited churches and outstations. So, too, did Margaret Fagg.[19]
When an unmarried woman went on a tour involving more than a
day's journey, she usually traveled in the company of another
missionary woman. As can be seen in the following
communication, it was not uncommon for her companion to be
someone from the English Presbyterian mission:

Miss K. M. Talmage returned yesterday morning from a
tour of nearly three weeks' duration among the
outstations. She went with Miss Maclagan of the English
mission. Today Miss M. E. Talmage and Miss Johnston
[also of the English mission] have started on a similar
tour and expect to be away about a fortnight.[20]

If a visit extended over a Sabbath, missionaries would instruct
the Chinese women after worship services. On other days, they

were taught at some prearranged central location or in their homes. With respect to home visits, the women missionaries had an entree that the male missionaries did not have. In addition to instructing the Chinese women in the Bible, they took these opportunities to acquaint mothers with the advantage of sending their children to one of the mission schools.

On these tours, the missionaries occasionally came into areas where foreigners were seldom seen, and in some cases had never been seen. It naturally happened that the inhabitants of such places were curious and came out as much to get a good look at the foreigners as to hear the gospel message. According to missionary accounts, such an occasion often became one not only of curiosity but also of merriment, with plenty of generally good-natured witticism exchanged at the expense of the visitors. Note, for example, Fagg's comments of December, 1888, following a tour of some distance inland:

> People flock out of their little villages to see the strange faces and to them ridiculously queer clothing of the "barbarian." We hear "foreigner," "barbarian," every few rods from somebody. We never imagined we were very peculiar, but we must be, if appearances are true. How seldom do we see ourselves as others see us. We are gazed at with much astonishment. We are laughed at. A few times we hear "foreign dog" from some naughty boy. At one village, we are called "savages," literally "green barbarians."... All this is not malicious, however; it is simply curiosity. Many of these people, I imagine, have never been out of their village. We are a veritable little circus to them. They have heard of us, now they actually see us.[21]

If the missionary men were viewed with curiosity in the outlying regions, this was even more true of the missionary women—especially when it was discovered that they could converse in Chinese. This is clearly evident from some remarks by Margaret Fagg, following a visit she made with her husband to several villages in late 1896:

> When a lady missionary goes to a country village the women crowd about laughing at her strange costume and

asking all sorts of questions. "Are you a man or a woman?"
"Why do you wear such a long shirt?" "Why are your
sleeves so tight?" "How much did those buttons cost?"
"Why have you got such big feet?" Perhaps they invite her
to some nearby house to drink tea. The neighbors press
into the courtyard, jostling and pushing to get a close view
of the queer-looking foreigner. When their curiosity has
been somewhat satisfied, the missionary begins to tell her
message. Then the word goes round—"she speaks our
words!" The gospel story is told in simple language; the
hearers are invited to attend service at the nearest
Christian chapel.... Women and girls are exhorted to
come to the mission schools where they will be taught to
read and write and learn under more favorable conditions
what Christianity is.[22]

With occasional exceptions, missionaries were well received by
the local populace on these tours. Typical of their receptions was
this one accorded Fagg and his native Chinese helper in early
1889 during a visit to Chang-chin and some surrounding villages:

Everywhere we are received with great kindness. We
are treated to tea sweetened with Chinese rock-candy. A
bowl of sweet potatoes is set before us, and the hostess is
evidently pleased as we munch away at a few of them. We
are handed an orange or two to eat on our way to the next
village.[23]

Missionary women were equally well received on their tours.
Katherine Talmage reported in 1896, for example, of the kind
treatment she and her traveling companion, Elizabeth Cappon,
experienced during a trip about fifty miles northwest of
Changchow, during which they visited several outstations as well
as other places. They reported being hospitably received even
when staying in "heathen villages." As Talmage explained it:

We found the people very quiet everywhere. Nothing
like trouble in this part of the country. The people were
very civil. When the chair bearers stopped to rest at the
different towns along the way, we found many men and
women who were glad to have us read hymns to them and
were grateful for the books we distributed. We feel as safe

as ever in traveling about this country. In fact, these last few years, the people have not made as many rude remarks as in former times.[24]

IX

Elementary Education and Education for Women, 1863-1900

The history of the Amoy mission during the period 1863-1900 was one of consolidation and expansion. As has been described, this involved the founding of more than forty places of worship and frequent missionary tours into the outlying areas. Concomitant with these developments, the mission gradually became a more multifaceted enterprise through the establishment of schools and hospitals.

With respect to education, the concern was mainly one in which the missionaries and their overseers at home became increasingly convinced that more had to be done in that field if evangelization were to achieve significant results. As John Talmage explained in the mission's annual report of 1872: "The development of the good order of the church, and its future efficiency, will depend much on the care taken of its children and their proper education."[1] Philip Pitcher expressed it in similar terms in the 1889 report: "The school is the necessary result of evangelization. To evangelize and leave the people ignorant is to do only half our duty."[2] Remarks by the General Synod's Committee on Foreign Missions in 1870 indicates that Reformed church leaders at home shared these views: "We cannot but regard the establishment and expansion of schools as of primary importance to success and to the assimilation of the Gospel leaven."[3]

To be more specific concerning the growing interest in education, it was becoming increasingly clear by 1863 that the problem of illiteracy had to be dealt with if the distribution of

Bibles and religious tracts were to have any significant impact. Similarly and particularly at the higher levels, education could be an instrument for dealing with the mission's shortage of Chinese teachers and preachers as well as for providing businesses and the government with persons of Christian training. In view of the great respect shown for learning in China, education could likewise be a means, perhaps the most important means, for reaching the upper classes. Finally, education could be of great influence in making life more bearable and meaningful for China's down-trodden women.

The increasing importance attached to education must by no means be interpreted, however, to indicate a lessening interest in preaching and evangelization. This was made abundantly clear in the prefatory remarks to a lengthy article by Pitcher entitled "Christian Education a Factor in Evangelization":

> That I may be perfectly understood let me say right here that with others I agree nothing should be more prominent, no department of mission work should be so prominent as preaching. Let me not be understood anywhere in this paper as being an advocate of ever desiring to make this agency [of preaching] subordinate to any other.[4]

An observation made by the veteran Mary Talmage in 1922 indicates this view did not change in later years:

> I am a firm believer in educational work on the Mission field, otherwise I would not have given nearly fifty years to it. But education on the field, to my mind, is only worth while so far as the Bible is made the chief textbook in our Mission schools.[5]

Pitcher's and Talmage's views were also those of the Woman's Board of Foreign Missions. Established in 1875, it can be said that no organization in the Reformed church did more for the support of education of women and children in China. In carrying out its work, however, the Woman's Board never saw education as an end in itself but rather as "a handmaiden to evangelization," that is, as a means of converting pupils, young and old alike, to Christianity.[6]

Education at the elementary level was naturally given the greatest attention. As Pitcher expressed it, that age level comprised "the most plastic period of life," making it the ideal time to "infuse minds" with the gospel message:

It is the law of the human mind...that in its beginning it is soft like wax, susceptible to all kinds of impressions, joyous to receive new ideas, but as it grows it hardens and becomes like adamant, retaining what it has received, like the stone slabs in our museums retain the footprints of birds or animals that have walked across the beach "in old, old times."[7]

Plans called for establishing an elementary day school for each church, but growth was slow at first. To the two schools established in the 1850s, a third was not added until 1869 and a fourth not until 1881. By 1900, however, ten day schools had been established among the eleven churches then in existence, and enrollment stood at 194. As a rule of thumb, a school was not started until it could be assured of having a minimum of ten pupils. It thus happened occasionally that a school had to be closed temporarily because of lack of interest. One of the most successful was the primary school associated with the Second Church at Amoy. It usually had forty or more pupils.

An innovative development of this period was the founding of schools designed specifically for girls. Although girls were invited to attend the mission's regular day schools, few did so. This was due in part to the traditional Chinese attitude toward female education. It was also the result of the general aversion of parents toward letting girls mingle too closely with boys. Some parents likewise hesitated to allow their daughters to walk the streets unattended on their way to school. To remedy these problems, a girls' school was established in 1870 providing accommodations for both day and boarding scholars. Known by the Chinese name for "Character-Developing-School," it was located in a house near the Second Amoy Church. Helen Van Doren was placed in charge. When poor health forced her to return to America in 1876, she was replaced by Mary Talmage, who served as its head for nearly forty years.

The school began instruction with twelve students: eight day scholars and four boarders. The need for an institution of this kind was quickly demonstrated when enrollment increased in the following year to twenty-three, fifteen day students and eight boarders, and in 1872 to thirty, about evenly divided between day and boarding students. The increase in the number of boarders was due primarily to the attendance of girls from the country churches and outstations. The mission assisted in supporting most of the students, especially with respect to board, while part of the other expenses, generally between fifteen and twenty dollars a year, was met by parents.

Van Doren described the significance of the school as follows in the mission's report of 1875:

> The school is not simply the only girls' school in the city of Amoy, a city of 200,000 inhabitants, but also the only girls' school in all the region, inhabited by millions of souls, and the graduates of this institution are the only educated Chinese women in all this vast population. [8]

The report also pointed out several unique bonuses of the school, including the fact that upon their graduation, the girls were in a position to demonstrate the advantages of literacy to their families and friends. In addition, the experience demonstrated that females could do as well in school as males. Providing young preachers and pastors with the prospect of educated wives was another bonus.

In 1879, for reasons of convenience and health, the girls' boarding school was transferred to Kulangsu where, with help from the Woman's Board, a small building was erected. It continued to prosper. In 1899, for example, seventy-six pupils were enrolled in the fall term. Their ages ranged from eight to twenty-one, the average being fourteen. Various missionary wives and single women assisted in the teaching. As enrollment increased, a strain was placed on the school's accommodations, especially with respect to sleeping provisions. A much-needed new building was thereupon constructed in 1900, again with funds contributed by the Woman's Board. The former building was then remodeled for use as a boys' elementary school.

The success of the girls' boarding school at Kulangsu prompted similar ventures on the mainland. These included institutions at Sio-khe in 1888, Changchow in 1895, and Tong-an in 1896. Missionary women played important roles in starting them—Alice Van Dyke at Sio-khe, Elizabeth Cappon at Changchow, and Nellie Zwemer and Lily Duryee at Tong-an. Each of these schools began operations in rented houses and, as at Kulangsu, it was the Woman's Board of Foreign Missions that made possible the construction of appropriate buildings to replace them. The Woman's Board also contributed regularly to the running expenses of the schools.

The poor facilities that existed in some schools prior to the generous help furnished by the Woman's Board are described in this report by Secretary Cobb on the situation at Sio-khe. His remarks were made following a four-day visit in the spring of 1892.

> Over the chapel is the girls' school. Here up a narrow and steep flight of steps, we found eighteen smiling, happy girls with their teacher, who gave us a cordial welcome with salutations, recitations, songs, and tea. It is a pity they have not better quarters. The whole upper story—about 12 or 15 feet by 25—is divided into two departments, the front for sleeping and the rear for school and living room. The windows are small, the rooms dark and dingy looking, and wearing an aspect not at all inviting to our eyes.[9]

Even under such cramped conditions, there was always a waiting list of girls seeking admission. Facilities were initially bad at other schools too, and continued to be for some time after 1900. In 1905, for example, in a school at Kulangsu, five and six boys had to share desks designed for three, and as late as 1916, a girls' boarding school at Changchow was sleeping three and four to a bed. At some places the aisles were too narrow to walk through comfortably and were so light and airy as to be called "fresh-air schools."[10]

The curriculum in the elementary schools became increasingly standardized during the period 1865-1900, regardless whether they were boys' or girls' schools, day or boarding schools. As with the two day schools established before 1863, the study of Scripture and Bible history was the main *raison d'être* for their existence, but courses of a secular nature were by no means overlooked. These included geography, arithmetic, Chinese literature, language study, a smattering of art and music, and the sciences. Arithmetic at this time gave pupils the most trouble, especially the multiplication tables. Also difficult to comprehend was the use of zero since, as the students put it, "It stood for nothing, and yet if omitted throws everything out." In the girls' boarding schools, attention was also given to home economics, about which most girls were ignorant at the time of enrollment.

Although there was some variation, the norm was to devote mornings to the "common" branches of learning and the Bible, and the afternoons to language study. The latter included both the traditional Chinese characters and the Romanized colloquial. Because the Bible was used as a basic reader, language study became a vital adjunct to the mission's evangelistic program. Students were expected to commit various parts of the Bible to memory, including the parables and miracles of Jesus, the Sermon on the Mount, and many of the Psalms. Advanced students also read *Pilgrim's Progress* and attended "inquiry sessions" from time to time centering around the Heidelberg Catechism. All instruction was in Chinese, and Chinese teachers directed most of the classwork, except in the girls' schools, where missionary women took over some of the supervision.

John Talmage once observed that the girls' schools appeared to be more efficient than those of the boys, a situation he attributed to the missionary women having more time to supervise the girls' schools than did the missionary men with respect to the boys' schools.[11] Perhaps so, but the women in their work could be just as busy as the men in theirs, as can be judged by the schedule of Helen Kip during the 1882-1883 school year. In addition to being in charge of the girls' school at Kulangsu while Mary Talmage was on furlough in America, Kip, according to the mission's report of 1883:

> has been able to keep up the Women's Meetings in connection with the two Amoy Churches. This has not been without risk to her health; but the women who attend have so few opportunities for instruction, that Mrs. Kip decided to continue both meetings in Mrs. Talmage's absence [while she was also on furlough]. The instruction given during the year has been principally in Scripture History and in Pilgrim's Progress. Mrs. Kip has also visited the Amoy Boys' Schools, and has given lessons to the lads in geography.[12]

When the schools were not in session, it was not uncommon for the "indispensable Mrs. Kip" (Pitcher's description of her) to accompany her husband on his preaching tours.

The elementary schools were graded and designed for a study program covering six years. An academic year consisted of two terms divided as follows: mid-September to mid-January, and mid-February to mid-June. Pupils underwent a series of rigorous examinations at the close of each school term to determine the extent of what they had learned.

Although the missionaries were on the whole pleased with the progress being made in the elementary schools, they did have a few misgivings. Some of their concern centered around the emphasis that the Chinese teachers placed on the classics, whereas the missionaries preferred giving more attention to such courses as geography, mathematics, science, and, of course the Scriptures. The missionaries were similarly upset about the teachers placing so much emphasis on rote learning.[13] Unfortunately, advice and instructions on these matters were not well received by the Chinese teachers.

The missionaries were particularly annoyed by the difficulty of introducing a system of classes in which pupils were grouped together according to the level of their progress. On this vexing problem we have an interesting comment by Pitcher in a report of 1900:

> We have made them all graded schools, but it is about as difficult to get these teachers to...uphold the schedule, as it would be for the iron horse to keep on the post road. They would rather have a different schedule for each boy, and each boy would be delighted to have a teacher and to be a class by himself. They seem to have no idea of school order or class division. However, there must be beginnings in everything, and though they make a bad start, yet we hope they will make a grand finish.[14]

Annoyances like the above were bound to remedy themselves after more Chinese Christians who had attended the mission's lower schools entered the teaching profession. Until that time, however, the missionaries had no choice but to employ teachers who were products of the traditional Chinese system of education. As Pitcher expressed it in late 1888, after having just completed a tour of all the schools: "If we cannot get wood to burn, we must do as the Chinese do, burn grass. At present it will not do to vex ourselves because we have not better material, for we must use what we have or go without."[15]

There were other problems, too, over which the missionaries had little or no control, such as those associated with the prolonged illness or death of a teacher or the outbreak of a contagious disease. Any of these events could bring about the closing of a school for a period of time. For example, at the beginning of the 1890 school term, enrollment in the eight elementary schools stood at 174; at the close of the term, it had dwindled to only 84. This was due to the closing of two schools for lack of teachers—one having died and the other having been forced to resign because of a mental breakdown. In addition, instruction at three other schools had to be suspended for several weeks (one of them for ten weeks) because of the outbreak of typhoid fever.

Everything considered, the future was looking brighter for the elementary schools by 1900. As noted, their number had increased significantly and included several boarding schools for boys and girls who otherwise would have been unable to receive an education. The Chinese churches were also contributing more financial support. Of the ten day schools, three were entirely self-supporting and the others were partially supported at the local level. Indeed, the opinion was expressed occasionally in the 1890s that if nothing unforeseen developed, education at the elementary level would soon be entirely self-supporting.

The problem of inadequate and insufficient textbooks was also less acute by 1900. As might be expected, Pitcher, as chief administrator for educational matters during most of his years in China, was particularly active in this endeavor. Among other works, he wrote several texts on geography and history. Because education became one of the main fortes of the missionary women, it is not surprising that they turned out a variety of textbooks. Helen Kip, for example, wrote books on astronomy, physiology, and child rearing, and the two Talmage sisters wrote several books for young children.

Although parental indifference toward education was still a problem in 1900, the situation was gradually improving. The changing attitude stemmed in part from the realization that traditional Chinese schools lacked certain advantages compared with mission schools. The latter, for example, were cleaner, had better lighting, and maintained stricter order. Western-style classrooms were also appreciated for such furnishings as wall maps, tripods holding several large sheets of informative material that could be folded back over one another, pictures on the walls, blackboards, and clocks. Even more appreciated was the fact that although the Chinese classics were not ignored in the curriculum, attention was also given to practical subjects like mathematics and science.

The number of qualified teachers was also rising by 1900, due in part to the founding of the Middle School and the seminary. With respect to the latter, it was not uncommon for seminary students to drop out of school for a year or two to serve as teachers in one of the mission's lower schools. This practice was encouraged because it gave students practical experience in dealing with people. The quality of teaching was also improving thanks to the arrival of an increasing number of missionary women, especially single women who did not have family responsibilities.

Although not usually considered a part of education in the traditional sense, notice must be taken of the mission's efforts to do something for young orphans and unwanted baby girls. The basis for this concern can be readily seen in the following excerpt from the mission's annual report of 1888.

> Infanticide is still prevalent in China. That horrid monster is not yet destroyed. Little baby girls are, in these days, being drowned, smothered, stamped to death, and in other cruel ways deprived of life. Or if parents are not willing to kill them, they will sell them, which is a fate often no better than slavery. [16]

In response to situations like the above, women of the Reformed and English Presbyterian missions joined forces in 1887 to establish a foster home for children. It was supported entirely by private funds from friends in Amoy and the home countries of the missionaries. Chinese women were employed as matrons.

The home began in a rented house in Amoy City, but was soon moved to a two-story brick building in Kulangsu. A literal translation of the Chinese name placed over the entrance read "Mercy upon the Children Institution," but it was popularly and simply called the "Children's Home." There also was a plaque with the inscription, "Suffer the little children to come unto me." Within two years, fifteen children had been admitted: a figure that had reached forty-three in 1900, by which time a large wing had been added to the original structure. Because of the precarious condition of the children when they were received at the home, the death rate was quite high. Some children were adopted by Christian parents, while others, when old enough, were placed in one of the girls' boarding schools.

The Children's Home was obviously a great improvement over what the Chinese themselves provided. As described by a member of the London Missionary Society:

> Sometimes in China you meet with a foundling house for gathering in these unhappy outcasts. We went to see the one established at Amoy. It was a most awful sight—filled with babies, all like little old women. Their appearances showed a distressing want of nourishment and clean-liness. We have never forgotten the sight, and can only think of it with a feeling of sickness. It would have been much better for the poor children to have passed away to God, instead of existing in such a state of living death; especially in view of the fact that if they live to grow up they are gladly got rid of to any who apply for them, although often for the worst of purposes. Even the nurses look wretched.[17]

Because of the increasing number of children entering the home, it was divided in 1917 and housed in two buildings, one under the control of the Reformed mission and the other under that of the English Presbyterians.

One of the most unique activities in the field of education during this period was the effort the mission gave to raising the status of Chinese women. References to their plight are frequent in the correspondence of the missionaries. Typical is this comment made in 1893 by Pitcher:

> Of the two sexes, women's minds are the most neglected, as they have no opportunity to learn. Men may learn, women not. Whilst the Chinese boast of a

civilization, yet the treatment of their women has been
little better than barbarian.... The Chinese woman has no
business to know anything, and few do. She is little more
than a slave of her husband and her mother-in-law.
However much mothers-in-law may be abused in our own
land, it is a painful truth that in China they are perfect
terrors. Under her dominion, the young wife's
epitomized history is recorded in these few words: "Rise,
run, work; eat little, spend little, be silent, obey, bear."[18]

Pitcher's views were shared by the Reverend James Sadler, who
served the London Missionary Society for forty-five years
(1866-1911):

In nothing is the ignorance, sin, and misery of
heathenism more manifest than in the condition of
women in China, and in nothing, therefore, does
Christianity appear to more advantage than in the work of
instructing, reforming, and blessing them.[19]

In their efforts to make life more bearable for Chinese women,
the missionaries were prompted not only by humanitarian
considerations, but also because Chinese women, despite their
downtrodden existence, were not without influence in the
homes. Winning them for Christ could thus be a means for
winning over members of their households as well.

One of the major steps taken to improve the lot of Chinese
women occurred in 1874 when the three Protestant missions at
Amoy sponsored an organization for the suppression of foot
binding.[20] Known as the "Anti-Foot Binding Society," it was one
of the first such organizations to be established in China. A pledge
was drawn up against the practice and signed by over forty
women. To add support to the movement, the missions later made
unbound feet a pre-condition for entrance to the girls' schools,
along with a promise that the parents would continue to abide by
the mandate.

Ministering to the spiritual needs of Chinese women consisted
initially of holding weekly prayer meetings, a practice started by
the wives of the Reverends Pohlman and Doty in the 1840s, and
continued by the missionary women who followed them. These
meetings soon made it apparent that the widespread illiteracy
among Chinese women would have to be dealt with if

Christianity were to be advanced among them and, through them, among their children. As expressed in a report of 1869:

> Imagine, if you can, what would be the efficiency of a Church in the United States if none of the female members could read. What could you expect of families with such wives and mothers? What of the children trained by them?[21]

The problem of female illiteracy would, of course, eventually improve as more girls attended the day and boarding schools, but what about the girls who did not attend? And what about the women, who obviously would feel uncomfortable in a girls' school? There were also those who could not spare the time away from their families to attend school on a regular basis.

Attempts by missionary women during the early period to teach adult women to read Chinese characters met with very limited success. After several years' effort, most women had progressed sufficiently to enable them to find passages in the Bible and follow the pastor as he read from the pulpit on Sundays, but very few were able to go further than that. Not until the complicated and numerous Chinese characters were replaced by the Romanized script was creditable progress made. The initiative in this approach was taken by Helen Kip, who in 1866 began devoting a half-hour after her weekly prayer meetings on Thursday afternoons at Amoy's Second Church to teaching the Romanized colloquial. The experiment worked so well that Mrs. Mary Talmage commenced a similar program at the First Church on Friday afternoons. Within a matter of months, nearly forty women in the two churches could read the colloquial Scriptures with some degree of fluency and could recite answers from a religious question book. By 1871, an additional class had been started at Second Amoy, and a class for new nonreaders had been organized at the union church at Kulangsu.

In 1884, thanks to financial help from the Reformed church's Woman's Board of Foreign Missions, a building was erected at Kulangsu at a cost of $1,300 for the specific purpose of giving Christian instruction to women and teaching them to read. The building was equipped with a kitchen, dormitory rooms, and a classroom. Initially called the "Bible Readers' Home," its name was changed in 1886 to the "Charlotte W. Duryee Bible School for

Women." This was done in memory of the woman who had died the previous year after having served as a corresponding secretary of the Woman's Board since its inception in 1875. Mary Talmage, who had primary supervision over the institution until her retirement in 1909, devoted the hours from 9:30 to 1:00 to instruction at the school each day except Fridays, when she visited hospital patients. A Chinese matron took primary charge in the afternoons. Ladies from the English Presbyterian and London missions also rendered assistance from time to time.

The daily routine consisted of Bible study and learning to read in the Romanized colloquial. For the latter, a four-page primer was used for new enrollees. After mastering it, they were taught the Lord's Prayer, the Ten Commandments, and a few hymns. Upon satisfactory completion of this part of the curriculum, a learner was "promoted" to the Scriptures. Particularly popular with Chinese women were the Psalms, the Gospel of Luke, and the Epistles of Paul. A Romanized colloquial version of the Heidelberg Catechism was also used as a text. A common learning procedure used by teachers was for everyone to read together a few times from an assigned lesson, and then for the instructor to question the women on what had been read. Work in arithmetic was also available for those who were interested and had the time. Although the women remained in the school varying lengths of time, about three-fourths of those who attended were able to read upon leaving. And though many of the women were not churchgoers (at least not in the usual sense) when they enrolled, it was not uncommon for them to become members before leaving.[22]

The school quickly became a success. It opened its doors in 1884 with five women in attendance; five years later, in 1889, twenty-four women were enrolled. Of these, ten belonged to the Reformed mission, while the English Presbyterian and London missions each enrolled seven. On their arrival at the school, two things especially impressed the women: first, the cleanliness of the rooms as compared to those of their own homes, particularly the neat cubicles with their plank bed-steads and spotless kitchen; and second, the mingling of younger and older women. The women came from places in the immediate Amoy region and ranged in age from fifteen to seventy, although most were between twenty-five and fifty. At the time that Mrs. Talmage retired as supervisor in 1909, more than 700 women had attended the school. The length of their stay varied from a few weeks to several months. Family responsibilities and illnesses accounted for most of the variation in the length of their stays. Enrollment was lowest in the autumn, when women were needed at home to help with the rice harvest.

Meanwhile, in 1875, three single missionary women at Amoy—Katherine and Mary Talmage (daughters of the above mentioned Mary Talmage) and Helen Van Doren—resolved that the literacy problem should also be dealt with among women residing on the mainland. The three therefore began making Sunday visits, traveling sometimes singly and sometimes as a group, to the country places near Amoy. Their efforts met with only limited success. The main opportunity for language instruction was during the two-hour break between worship services, but the Chinese needed much of that time for cooking and eating their noon meal of rice. To meet with the women after the second service was not the answer either because many of them had to leave early to get home before dark. It must be borne in mind that the cruel custom of footbinding among females was still being practiced at this time, which made walking a trying experience even for short distances.

The practice of having the missionaries meet with Chinese women on weekdays at centralized locations was also tried, but this too had serious drawbacks. Because of the scattered nature of the country congregations, the distance that some Chinese women had to travel proved to be a problem. Moreover, the struggle for subsistence was such that another day, along with Sundays, away from their labors made attendance difficult. Finally, the missionary women themselves found it very difficult to visit the distant country places on a regular basis.

In view of these difficulties, it soon became apparent that the task of instructing "country women" in the Romanized colloquial had to be approached in some other way. One of the most successful new procedures involved employing Chinese Christian women who had been taught by the missionaries and were capable of teaching others. The first of these appointments on a full-time basis occurred in 1879. It met with considerable success, and other appointments soon followed. By 1900, their number had reached eleven. These "Bible women," as they were called, went from house to house, spending a few days in each village, and living for a time with those whom they could teach.

Miss Mary Talmage assumed chief responsibility for supervising the program. Her frequent visits to the villages had given her considerable familiarity with the problems of Chinese women. The significant role Bible women came to play in the work of the mission can be seen in the following excerpt from a pamphlet of 1907:

> They keep in constant touch with their sisters, making frequent visits to their homes, teaching them to read, encouraging them to come to church or school, exhorting the delinquents, visiting and ministering to the sick, in home and hospital—all in all, a field unlimited in a land where women are still regarded as an inferior class of beings, and often totally neglected even by many of our Christians.... These Bible women who supplement the work of the preachers and pastors are gleaners of no small importance.[23]

The question may well be asked at this point why the missionary women, especially those who were single, did not follow the same procedure as the Bible women. John Talmage has given an explanation in a report to the Board of Foreign Missions in 1876:

> In consequence of the discomforts in which the masses of this people live and the want of cleanliness in their streets and houses, such a course cannot be entered on by any foreign ladies. It would very soon cost them their lives. It often takes some time for the head and stomach to rally from the effects, even of walking through the streets and making short visits in the houses.[24]

Another approach that was eventually followed for meeting the educational needs of Chinese women on the mainland involved the establishment of Duryee-type schools at key locations. The first of these was established in 1893 at Sio-khe. It was placed under the supervision of the resourceful Helen Kip, whose husband served as administrative missionary for the Sio-khe district. Eight boarders enrolled when the school opened and stayed for varying lengths of time. Several women also came in as day scholars when they could spare the time, and visitors dropped in occasionally out of curiosity. A few years later, in 1896, another school was opened, this one at Tong-an under the direction of Nellie Zwemer.

In summary, it is apparent that the missionaries took seriously the remarks expressed earlier concerning the need to give greater attention to education. The number of elementary day schools, for example, increased from two in 1863 to ten by 1900; and as the need arose to accommodate pupils living some distance from the day schools, boarding schools at the elementary level were also established. By 1900, there were two such institutions for boys and five for girls. A home for young orphans and unwanted children was also established that included facilities at the preschool level. Steps were likewise taken to deal with the widespread illiteracy prevailing among adult women. Last, but by no means least, attention was given to education beyond the elementary level, culminating, as will be described in the next chapter, in the founding of a theological seminary in 1869 and an academy or middle school in 1881.

X

The Seminary and Middle School, 1863-1900

The training of Chinese preachers and pastors was initially carried on in the homes of the missionaries. Although a house was eventually fitted out so that students could live together, instruction continued to take place in missionary homes. This situation improved in 1869 when, thanks to a grant of $300 from the denominational Board of Foreign Missions, a building specifically designed for theological instruction was erected at Kulangsu. The two-story brick structure measured thirty by forty feet and provided one lecture room, which was also used as the dining room, eleven bedrooms, and a kitchen. It was constructed so that it could be enlarged if necessary. On the recommendation of the board, it was called the "Thomas De Witt Theological Hall" in recognition of the Reverend Thomas De Witt's long-standing interest in foreign missions.

A three-year program of study was introduced that included Old and New Testament Exegeses, Systematic Theology, Genuineness and Authenticity of the Scriptures, Homiletics, Church History, and Chinese Language and Literature. The last mentioned concentrated especially on the Chinese classics. Initially, the curriculum also included a course in mathematics, the purpose of which was to provide "mental training," something that, according to the missionaries, was sorely lacking among the students at this time. It was discontinued later when the Middle School was established, as students were expected to have had some background in mathematics before enrolling in the theological school. The offerings in Chinese classics were also

134

later cut down for the same reason.

The missionaries, with assistance from the pastor of First Amoy Church, did all the teaching, except for courses in Chinese language and literature, which were placed in the hands of two Chinese tutors. A "preaching hall," opened in 1892, gave students an opportunity to gain practical experience in composing and delivering sermons. They also received useful training by occasionally taking charge of worship services at the outstations on Amoy Island.

Young men entering the seminary were not always accepted as bona fide theological students who would someday become ordained pastors. This is clearly seen in an excerpt from the mission's report of 1881 describing the nine students who were enrolled at that time:

> Perhaps only three of the nine should be called theological students. To three others we only hold out the prospect of being fitted for school teachers. But if, hereafter, they manifest proper qualifications, they may become preachers. Two others may be employed as chapel keepers to assist the preachers at some of the more important outstations. One other since the close of the year we have recommended to return to his former employment.[1]

Because of the great need for evangelists and teachers, even students who showed great promise were sometimes encouraged to drop out of school temporarily after their first or second year to meet those needs. This was done with the understanding they would complete their theological studies later.

About the same time the Reformed mission established De Witt Theological Hall in 1869, the English Presbyterians and the London Missionary Society established similar institutions. Relations among the three seminaries were close from the start, and especially so between the Reformed and English Presbyterians. For example, a report of 1871 states that besides the instruction given by the Reformed and English Presbyterians to their own students, they met together from time to time to listen to lectures given under the supervision of the Tai-hoey. A few years later, the two missions instituted a common system of graded examinations for each of the three school years. By 1878, the London Missionary Society had also become a party to the united examination system, followed soon after by its participation in the joint lecture program. As reported by the Reformed missionaries, this kind of cooperation represented yet "another illustration of the essential unity of the various branches of the one Church of Christ."[2]

The Reformed missionaries became convinced soon after the establishment of the theological school that another level of instruction was needed—something comparable to a secondary school in America. Such a school, it was argued, would provide an opportunity for Chinese boys who excelled at the elementary level to obtain additional education. More importantly, it would help supply the need for teachers in the elementary schools and serve as an intermediate step for preparing young men for theological school. Discussions on this matter with the English Presbyterian missionaries revealed they too felt the need for such an institution. The result was a pooling of resources by the two missions and the founding of a union school.

The school opened in January, 1881, in a recently remodeled Chinese house belonging to the English Presbyterians, located near their seminary and missionary residences at Kulangsu. The new school was officially called the "Boys' Academy," but became popularly known as the "Middle School" because its curriculum was between that of the elementary schools and the seminaries. It was also given the Chinese name of Sim Goan Tiong, meaning "Seeking the Origin of Truth." Alexander Van Dyck was placed in charge until 1887, when Philip Pitcher began his twenty-eight years of work with the institution. Acting independently of the other two missions, the London Missionary Society likewise established a type of middle school at this time.

Limited accommodations restricted enrollment during the first year to fourteen students. Each mission paid a proportion of the teacher salaries and running expenses based on the number of pupils it had in attendance. It was assumed that before long, all students would pay their way in part or in whole. This unfortunately did not happen, and for many years very little was paid by the students or by their parents. Indeed, as late as 1889, with annual expenses per student at about twenty-four dollars a year, a few paid eight dollars, some three dollars, and many nothing at all.

In order to have regular hours and to accommodate students coming from the country churches and outstations, the school functioned as a boarding school with all students required to reside in the building during term time. Because of its nearness to their compound, the English Presbyterians were given primary administrative responsibility. Missionaries from both groups shared teaching responsibilities equally, however, and were assisted by a Chinese tutor. Applicants had to pass entrance examinations, and the standards for admittance were raised from time to time. As stipulated in a report of 1888:

> Any boy of Christian parents, or parent, fifteen years old, who can read and write the Romanized colloquial, also read six books of the Foochow Chinese character lessons, two books of the classics, the four Gospels in characters, elementary geography, including China proper, and understands the first four rules of arithmetic, may enter the school. [3]

During its first decade of operation, the curriculum involved three years of study, which included geography, astronomy, physiology, arithmetic, reading composition, the Chinese classics, the Heidelberg Catechism, and the Bible. All instruction was in Chinese. In 1889, the Chinese teacher who taught in the seminary was added to the Middle School staff in order to give additional instruction in Chinese character composition. Arithmetic was the most difficult subject for the students. As explained in a report of 1890:

> The bane of a Chinese lad is arithmetic. If there is any stumbling block in the way of his progress in education, it is the foreign method of computation. Yet it is not all "love's labor lost." Some do master the science, and show that they understand what they are doing. And many, as they become familiar with it, are learning to grasp the science and solve the problems of the mysterious symbols. [4]

A fourth year was added in 1890, making the school more comparable to secondary schools in America. An examination of the fourth year curriculum illustrates further the kind of education that graduates of the school received: Holy Scriptures

(Job, Proverbs to Malachi), advanced Chinese classics, advanced algebra, physics, history (American, Russian, and Spanish), reading and writing the Amoy Romanized colloquial, composition, drawing, and music.[5] Women members of the missionary staff, when available, taught courses in drawing and music.

The considerable emphasis the curriculum placed on Chinese classics was justified on the basis that graduates should be thoroughly versed in their own literature if they were to command genuine respect among the people, especially the literati. The same was true for a knowledge of western science. As the John Fagg expressed it, "A first-class training in their own sages...along with a thorough course of scientific studies" would enable Christian young men to acquire "other positions of honor and usefulness" in China besides that of the ministry.[6] As explained by an English Presbyterian historian, requiring students to study Confucius and other Chinese sages would also help seminaries avoid criticism that they were "more anxious to Westernize their students than to Christianize them."[7]

In 1897, the study of Mandarin Chinese was introduced by popular demand for third- and fourth-year students. This later had to be suspended for a time because limited funds made it difficult to retain a qualified teacher. Demand for this course was strong among students because it was *the* language proper of China. Although there were many local dialects, some of them distinct enough to be looked upon as languages, Mandarin was the main language spoken in eleven of China's eighteen provinces. It was also the "polite" speech of China as well as the official tongue. It is thus not surprising that students were eager to become acquainted with it.[8]

The demand for courses in English also steadily increased and was rapidly becoming a vexing problem among Christian educators throughout China. As Pitcher, who labeled the issue a "bugbear," remarked in 1890: "Some undoubtedly wish the question were buried deeper than the ruins of Pompeii, so that no novice could even dig it up and ask: 'Will you please...give your opinion about teaching English in mission schools?'"[9]

Several considerations made the English question a thorny problem for the Middle School. According to some critics, courses in English might secularize education too much at the expense of the school's primary purpose, namely, evangelization. Also raised was the question of whether church funds should be used for such a purpose. It was similarly argued that because the desire to learn English was so great among young Chinese, its introduction might attract students for that reason only. Finally, fear was expressed that some young men who entered the school with the intention of becoming teachers or pastors might later change their minds and take employment with business firms seeking persons having a knowledge of English. [10]

Not all missionaries held these views, however. Even Pitcher eventually came out in favor of it, declaring that if Christian educational standards were kept "pure and aggressive," there should be nothing to fear about the introduction of English. Other supporters pointed out that such a course could provide an opportunity for "raising up" Christian-minded business leaders and public servants. Proponents also noted that the course's absence from the curriculum might cut down enrollment. As events turned out, English was finally introduced into the curriculum in 1904.

Despite the variety of course offerings at the Middle School, it must be emphasized that they were ancillary to meeting the spiritual needs of the students. To quote from the mission's annual report of 1890:

> We have sought first, and above all, to lead these lads to the fountain of all truth, and to know that the beginning of wisdom is "the fear of the Lord." ...So, as opportunity offered, we have endeavored to impress the great truth of Christianity upon these young minds that there can be no successful life, no complete education, unless concentrated to the service of the Lord. [11]

The primary goal of the Middle School is further amplified in "The Aim of the School" as stated in the 1895 *Catalogue and Special Report of the Boys Academy*:

> The development of the Spiritual part of the boy is held to be of first importance, hence the Bible is the foremost of textbooks in the school. The Bible is taught and studied more hours a day, and more hours a week, than any [other] one book. [12]

There were also regular religious exercises in which all students had to participate. An hour was given each morning at 9:00 and each evening at 7:30 to devotional exercises consisting of songs, Scripture, a short sermon, and prayer. There were also special religious services on Friday evenings in which students took an active part. On Sundays, all students were expected to be present at divine services in the mornings and afternoons at Douglas Memorial Chapel. They were also required to attend a discussion class on the Heidelberg Catechism.[13] Neither the emphasis placed on religion nor the rather rigid entrance requirements and demanding curriculum had an adverse impact on enrollment, which increased steadily from fourteen when the school was organized in 1881 to forty-three in 1895.

A look at the Middle School's student body in 1889 provides some indication of the school's composition and goals. The ages of the twenty-five enrollees ranged from fifteen to twenty-two. All the students were members of Christian families and two thirds were classified as "professing Christians." Five did not finish the academic year—one left to teach school, three withdrew because of poor health, and one died. Of the seven who finished the program that year, four entered the seminary, two began studying medicine under Dr. John Otte of the mission hospital at Sio-khe, and one became a teacher. Further light on the composition of the student body is provided in this analysis of the 200 students who had enrolled up to 1901:

> From this number, 59 are in the distinctive employ of the church as preachers, teachers, and seminary students; 24 are either medical students or are practicing medicine; 31 are still enrolled; 10 have died. Total 124. 67 have either entered business or English speaking schools, while 9 have been dismissed.[14]

Along with imparting knowledge, the Middle School tried to impress students with the need for cleanliness and orderliness. As reported in the *Mission Field* of November, 1897, Chinese boys "are in many respects like American boys, in love with fun and full of the same kind of mischief, but when it comes to the questions of cleanliness and order we have a different class to deal with."[15] As a consequence, all student rooms were inspected once a week, and each boy was graded according to the condition in which his room was found. Increasing attention was also given to physical exercises in the 1890s, a practice already being followed in the elementary schools, where students were put through a half hour of gymnastics early every morning. As Hobard Studley explained in 1897, such activity "not only ensured bodily exercise, which is absolutely necessary [for good health], but inculcates habits of early rising and united action."[16]

In the late 1890s, the local British consul and other "gentlemen" presented the Middle School and the boys' elementary school at Kulangsu with sets of cricket gear and footballs to further encourage physical development as well as sports. Judging by the following report by one of the school's staff members, the physical education instructor obviously had his work cut out for him:

> I cannot say that the boys are crack cricket players, or even football kickers, but I am sure they get an immense amount of fun out of these sports—especially football—and at the same time afford much amusement to the spectators. When a vigorous kick (the whole *sole* in it) is made at the "pesky sphere," the shoe of the kicker is more apt to go soaring toward the celestial heights than the ball, for you must remember that the shoes of the Chinese are unadorned with strings as ours are.[17]

A puzzling question facing Philip Pitcher as principal of the Middle School and chief supervisor of the mission's elementary system was that of knowing how fast and to what degree western pedagogical methods should be introduced. Particularly difficult was the matter of dealing with the lack of self-control among the students—a problem that according to Pitcher was one that faced China as a whole. His explanation of the situation follows:

> In a majority of cases, when a lad enters our school he comes for the first time under real restraint and discipline. It is a lamentable fact that Chinese parents either do not possess the power, or having it, do not exercise the power of control over their children. In the child we find the nation, and everywhere over this vast Empire no defect is more real in the national life than the lack of discipline, restraint, and order.... The Emperor posts up his high-sounding edicts and proclamations, and

the people have no more idea of obedience than of flying. In fact, the people do not believe the Emperor means what he says—merely scolding *in loco parentis* and nothing more. When a lad, therefore enters our school, if he has met with such [practice] at home, and comes in touch with a few well-defined rules and regulations, he has arrived at that stage of intelligence where he says: "Surely I am not expected to observe them—neither does the teacher expect me to." But he soon finds that he is mistaken, and that rules are not ornamental but useful, and that the teacher does expect due observance.[18]

It is at this point, declared Pitcher, that the teacher's work really begins—work that before many months have elapsed often leaves the teacher exhausted in both body and spirit. Only the "determination of a Columbus and the patience of a Job" will change for the better this "bedlamian way of acquiring lessons." He added this caveat, "Here, too, one finds a wide field for the exercise of the law of forgiveness: until seventy times seven."

In view of these problems, it is not surprising that the missionaries sent requests almost annually to their home offices in the United States and England asking for a young man who was thoroughly trained in pedagogy to serve as principal for the Middle School. It was hoped that whoever came out would also supervise the elementary schools. Unfortunately, no candidates presented themselves for the position and the missionaries had to make do with what they had. Alexander Van Dyck helped direct the work until 1887, when he was appointed administrator of the Sio-khe district, which was too far from Kulangsu for him also to continue his responsibilities at the Middle School. Following his departure, Pitcher assumed the joint responsibility of principal of the Middle School and overseer of the primary schools. Because he also served as mission supervisor for the Tong-an district, he obviously was able to give only limited attention to his pedagogical duties. In 1891, for example, he made only one visit to the more distant elementary schools.

In 1893, John Fagg drafted for the Board of Foreign Missions what was certainly the clearest statement yet of the need for a man to take over Pitcher's pedagogical responsibilities, and the kind of a person the mission was looking for. In itemizing the necessary qualifications, Fagg explained that the candidate need not be an ordained minister but someone who would be "right" in other ways. Needed was

> a Divinely called, thoroughly qualified man, a lover of youth, an enthusiast as a teacher, a man whose life and work, expanding as he turns up the fallow soil and sows and reaps, shall be its own magnet to draw young men and boys of various conditions and classes to himself. [He must get] as a clear a call from his laboratory, or academy, or Normal school as Amos got from the pastures of Bethlehem, or Moses from the shadow of Sinai.[19]

Fagg's request, like others before it, brought no reinforcements, but it must be noted that the economic depression of the early 1890s in the United States and England added to the difficulties of the "home offices" in providing relief. Along with periodic requests for someone trained in pedagogy, the missionaries also made frequent appeals for a teacher of the "higher sciences," but these too went unheeded, although various scientific apparatuses were received from time to time. A course in physics was not introduced until 1904.

While these developments were going on regarding the Middle School, an important event had meanwhile taken place with respect to the seminary. The joint effort of the Reformed and English Presbyterians in providing for a union academy had worked so well that after a series of discussions, they decided also to merge their seminaries into a single institution. This took place in 1885. As part of the agreement, it was decided that the theological students would be housed and taught in the building of the English Presbyterian seminary, and the Middle School activities would take place in the building of the Reformed seminary, that is, the Thomas De Witt Theological Hall.

Administrative supervision of the seminary was placed in the hands of the English Presbyterians, but the two missions shared equally the work of instruction. Among the Reformed missionaries who participated at one time or another as instructors, were John Talmage, Daniel Rapalje, Leonard Kip, John Fagg, and Alexander Van Dyck. Important English participants included the Reverends William McGregor, Henry Thompson, and John Watson. Instructors taught one or two courses two or three times a week, but it must be kept in mind that teaching was considered a matter of extra duty. Visiting country churches and other obligations involved many hours of their time and took precedence over teaching responsibilities. Moreover, furloughs to the United States or England occasionally left the missions so shorthanded that the seminary was forced to close temporarily.

Enrollment stood at only eight, four from each mission, when the two seminaries joined forces in 1885. This low figure was not particularly surprising, since enrollment had never been high in either of the seminaries and was one of the considerations that led to unification. Enrollments improved later but never reached significantly higher figures. They also fluctuated from year to year. With few exceptions, the number in attendance was divided about evenly between the two missions.

The reasons for low and fluctuating enrollments were several. Admission requirements were high, and unless there was a very good reason for granting a waiver, applicants were expected to have completed a prescribed course of study in the Middle School. In justifying the high admission requirements and rigid course of study demanded of theological students, the missionaries were determined that the Chinese clergy be an educated one. As Pitcher explained it in the Reformed mission's annual report for 1889:

> Above all, we desire men who are thoroughly consecrated body, soul, and spirit, and we desire them to be decidedly in earnest, but, in addition, we think it of little less importance that they should have a proportionate amount of knowledge. We cannot afford to place an ignorant ministry in the midst of an already ignorant and perverse people.
>
> Our ministry is weak as it is, [therefore] let every effort that is put forth to strengthen it, be upheld and encouraged. Quality, not quantity, we consider best for the speedy success of the cause.[20]

Another reason seminary enrollments tended to be low was the need for teachers and lay evangelists. As earlier noted, it was not uncommon for students to drop out of school for a year or two in order to serve in one of those capacities. To quote again from the annual reports, note the following with respect to the enrollment for 1890:

> Pupils connected with the E. P. Mission, eleven; connected with our Mission, nine; total twenty. Of the nine connected with us, two spent the greater part of the year in evangelistic work, and three were most of the time engaged in teaching. This arrangement becomes necessary because of the small supply of preachers and teachers. At the same time, it is found that the practical work of preaching and teaching develops the powers of the students so employed, and in most cases, enables them to study to better advantage when they return to the school.[21]

In many instances, students were admitted with the specific understanding that their stay at the seminary would be interrupted for a time while they served as teachers at the mission schools or lay preachers at the outstations. Students temporarily leaving the seminary for either of these reasons were encouraged to keep up with their studies as best they could on their own, but under the guidance of a local Chinese pastor or with help from an occasional visit by one of the missionaries.

In 1889, the two missions entered into another agreement, this one aimed at providing enlarged facilities for both the Middle School and the seminary. By this arrangement, the Reformed missionaries assumed responsibility for securing funds for a new Middle School building and the English Presbyterians did the same for the seminary.

The Middle School was especially in need of either remodeling or a new structure. As can be seen in this series of comments made by Pitcher in late 1888, the building had several shortcomings in addition to overcrowding:

> Whatever I have previously said about the school building I wish to reiterate. I feel that any description of it will convey but a vague idea of its true condition. It is not comparable to the school buildings of your other missions: a common school-house, board benches, with only a four-inch board for a desk, cheerless rooms, and uncomfortable beds.

With more than a hint of an appeal to the vanity of potential donors, Pitcher declared the present structure did not do proper honor to the denomination, and added:

> Has it not always been an acknowledged fact that the Reformed Church has ever been among the standard bearers in this department of mission work? The recently endowed seminary in India, Van Schaick Hall, and Ferris Seminary in Yokohama, Sandham Hall in Tokyo and the other school buildings scattered among these heathen nations, testify to her praiseworthy efforts in this direction. Is the Church to fall behind in this work in China?

In seeking financial help, Pitcher also duly noted the internal changes taking place in China and the challenges these presented to traditional Chinese education:

> There is no doubt in my mind that there is to be as great a desire for Western education in China as there is now in Japan. We must keep pace with this spirit of development and encourage it in every way. China's massive walls of superstition are crumbling, the electric wire connects Peking with Canton, and soon the iron rail will bind her four quarters. The egotistical ignorance of her so-called educated classes is becoming more and more plainly evident to be ignorance only, and to be educated means something more than being able to read or commit to memory, parrot-fashion, the wise sayings of Confucious, or to rattle off two thousand characters without knowing the meaning of ten in the context.[22]

In 1890-1891, Pitcher, while on furlough in the United States, campaigned diligently among churches, Sunday schools, and private individuals for funds to construct a new Middle School building. He succeeded in raising $5,868. Upon his return to China, the Reformed mission staff, after long and careful deliberations, resolved to use $4,500 of the amount to purchase some property that had just come up for sale and was considered an ideal site for the Middle School. Although the purchase involved a large amount of money, the site was considered too good to pass up. Consisting of several hundred square feet, and located on a high ridge near other mission buildings, it commanded on one side a view of Amoy Island, the harbor, and the region beyond, and on the other side the ocean and the range of mountains along the coast. All the missionaries agreed that rather than purchase a cheaper, less desirable piece of land and build immediately, it would be better to buy this property now and wait with building until later. As Pitcher informed the Board of Foreign Mission: "Rather than be a fire-fly in the damp, unhealthy lowland, you will pardon us if we aspire to be the beacon on the hill-top."[23]

A few years later in 1895, thanks to donations acquired in the United States from another fund-raising campaign, a building costing about $4,000 was constructed on the recently acquired property. The two-story brick building, designed by Corydon Wheeler, an architect from Poughkeepsie, New York, had a frontage of seventy-five feet and a width of thirty-six feet, except for one wing which extended back an additional forty feet. In the central section of the front, two rows of arcades supported wide, spacious porches for both floors and added greatly to the structure's beauty. Twenty-eight comfortable sleeping rooms provided accommodations for sixty students, a figure that could be increased to eighty with a little crowding. In addition, there were three classrooms, a large study room, a chapel, a dining room and kitchen, and an exercise room for gymnastics. To provide for better oversight of the students, a room was also provided for one of the Chinese instructors.[24]

The new Middle School building was appropriately named "Talmage Memorial Hall" in memory of John Van Nest Talmage and his forty-five years of tireless service to the Amoy mission. The school's name was inscribed in large letters above the upper arcade. Above the lower arcade were placed two inscriptions, both in Chinese, which in translation read "Seeking the Fountain of Truth" and "Hall of Learning."

Meanwhile, the English Presbyterians had fulfilled their part of the 1889 agreement and constructed a new building for the seminary. Because a suitable place could not be found for the new building, it was finally decided to tear down the old structure and build on its site. Completed in 1892, and constructed of brick and cream colored stucco, all with neat trimmings, the building contained two classrooms and thirty-five single bedrooms for the students. The cost was $3,000. In the same manner that Pitcher helped make possible the new Middle School building by soliciting funds among Reformed people in the United States, William McGregor of the English Presbyterian mission made the new seminary building possible by soliciting funds among Presbyterians in Scotland and England.

XI
Developments in Medicine, 1863-1900

Medical work, like education, became an important means for disseminating the gospel message during the period 1863-1900. As Philip Pitcher expressed it in 1890, two hands are better than one in any kind of work, and in the missionary enterprise, "medical work is the right hand...and educational is the left." By "a judicious and systematic mixture" of evangelism with the dispensing of medicine and the founding of hospitals, he added, "the age-old primary purpose of the missionary endeavor would not suffer."[1] The mission also soon realized that caring for the ills of the body helped greatly in promoting good feeling. To quote from another work by Pitcher, no other activity of the foreign missionaries was "more thoroughly appreciated by all classes, literati officials, merchants, shopkeepers, farmers, than medical work."[2]

The Reformed church became involved in medical work soon after David Abeel's arrival at Amoy. On June 7, 1842, an American physician, Dr. William H. Cumming, opened a dispensary in one of the rooms of the house occupied by Abeel at Kulangsu. Cumming was not associated with any particular denomination but was supported by his own funds and those of friends. In 1843, he was joined by Dr. J. C. Hepburn of the American Presbyterian church. When the Reverends Doty and Pohlman arrived from Borneo in 1844 and, along with Abeel, located at Amoy City, Cumming and Hepburn moved their dispensary into one of the rooms the Reformed missionaries had rented for religious services.

Hepburn left in 1845 and Cumming in 1847, after which medical work by the mission was limited for many years to visiting the sick in their homes and in hospitals maintained by various groups. These included a makeshift facility established by Dr. James Young of the English Presbyterian mission soon after his arrival in 1850. This hospital closed in 1854 when Young left China because of poor health. Later, in 1865, a small community hospital that was open to Chinese was built from funds contributed by merchants and other foreign residents; and in 1871, a marine hospital for foreign sailors was established by the American government. In 1883, the English Presbyterians entered the medical field once again when a Dr. A. L. Macleish opened a hospital in two small buildings the Reformed mission had been renting near the Tek Chhiu Kha Church (Second Amoy). The English mission assumed the rental costs, but the Reformed mission shared other costs and also took its turn looking after the hospital's evangelistic program. This hospital was closed in 1893 when Macleish retired and returned to Scotland.

In the meantime, after numerous appeals from the Reformed missionaries, the Board of Foreign Missions finally resolved to send out a trained physician. Through financial assistance from the Woman's Board of Foreign Missions, Dr. Y. May King was commissioned for the field by the General Synod in 1887. Dr. King was a Chinese woman in her early twenties who, at the age of two, had been adopted by Dr. MacCartee and trained for a medical career. Acquiring a woman doctor who could work among the Chinese women exceeded the fondest hopes of the Amoy missionaries. Unfortunately, Dr. King remained only a few months. Poor health prompted her in October, 1888, to relocate at Kobe, Japan, where her foster parents had gone earlier to do mission work.[3]

Sustained medical work by the Reformed church thus really did not begin in China until the arrival of Dr. John Abraham Otte in early 1888. Otte, only twenty-seven when he set foot in China, had emigrated from the Netherlands in 1867 at age six with his parents, and had grown up in Grand Rapids, Michigan. From an early date, his Christian upbringing had prompted him to consider preaching as a career. However, a voice problem, brought on by several bouts with diphtheria, and his discovery that he was more interested in science courses than those associated with a preseminary program, brought about a change of mind. Instead of becoming a minister, Otte resolved to become a medical missionary. To that end, upon graduation from college, he enrolled in a medical program at the University of Michigan and relayed his plans to the Reformed church's Board of Foreign Missions. The latter encouraged him in this endeavor and informed him that upon completing his studies he would be sent to the Amoy mission, which had been requesting a medical doctor for some time. Unfortunately, when the time came to send him, the board lacked the necessary funds.[4]

Unable to go to China immediately, Otte decided to spend a year in the Netherlands doing post-graduate work at the Universities of Utrecht and Amsterdam, both of which had more to offer in terms of medical training than did Michigan at the time. As events turned out, his stay in the Netherlands not only provided him with additional medical training, but also with funds from Dutch people who had learned of his desire to serve as a medical missionary. Returning to the United States, Otte was overjoyed to learn that the Reformed church now had sufficient funds to enable him to embark on his chosen career.

Otte sailed from New York November 5, 1887. He was accompanied by his wife, Frances Phelps Otte, and the Reverend John Fagg, who had just been commissioned for the China field. Their being routed by way of the Netherlands proved a fortuitous development. While the ship laid over at Rotterdam for a few days, Otte was able to pick up additional funds for his work in China.

Otte arrived at Amoy January 13, 1888, and was forthwith assigned to do medical work at Sio-khe. The assignment was part of a careful plan by the Reformed missionaries to make Sio-khe into a mission center. Although not a city (it had less than 4,000 people), its importance lay in its being located in a very fertile valley of more than 300,000 people. Communities were relatively easy to reach, thanks to a good road that ran the length of the valley. Sio-khe also had the advantage of being located along a waterway that gave it access to Amoy in one direction and the interior of China in the other. By the time of Otte's arrival, Sio-khe already had one of the mission's most thriving churches, several promising outstations, and a flourishing girls' school. Sio-khe was also fortunate in having one of the most highly respected Chinese pastors, the Reverend Iap Han-cheong, and a capable young resident missionary, the Reverend Alexander Van Dyck.

Otte was somewhat disappointed about being assigned to Sio-khe instead of Amoy City or Kulangsu, but he set about his work with diligence. With $1,200 at his disposal from donations in America and the Netherlands, he quickly began constructing a hospital. Problems were numerous, not the least of which was the need to transport building materials some distance up the winding Sio-khe River. There also was some opposition from the local populace, but this soon subsided. Indeed, it was not long before some of the local mandarins and well-to-do citizens contributed to the hospital's construction. Being an amateur architect who enjoyed working with his hands, Otte personally designed the hospital and assisted from time to time in its construction. According to his own account, careful supervision of the workers was necessary to prevent the walls from being out of plumb and clay being substituted for mortar. Unable to find a skilled carpenter, Otte himself made much of the wooden furniture.

When all was finished, Otte was obviously pleased with the end result. He later wrote his friends in America: "It would fill your heart with gratitude to an almighty God to see what a neat hospital, nice house, and comfortable surroundings we have at Sio-khe."[5] Completed at a cost of $1,800, the exterior was of brick with a tiled roof and was two stories tall. The lower floor included a dispensary, consultation room, woman's ward, chapel, storeroom, and kitchen. On the upper floor was a general ward for men, eye ward, surgical ward, and two small rooms for students. The upper floor also had a wide verandah, and the ground floor had two open courts—one for men and the other for women. With provision for only thirty beds, conditions obviously were crowded.

The hospital was officially opened March 5, 1889. As described by Otte, the dedication exercises were simple:

> At about 8 o'clock [in the morning] our native pastor of the church at Sio-khe in the presence of Mr. Van Dyck, my students, a number of patients and myself, stepped upon

an improvised platform in the hospital chapel (the pulpit was not built at the time), and announced a hymn. As there were but few native Christians present, and Mr. Van Dyck and myself not possessed of any musical abilities, you can readily imagine that the discordant notes of the natives did not remind us very vividly of home music, but though the melody of music was wanting, there was no want of grateful hearts. After singing the hymn, Pastor Iap offered prayer, and then read and explained a portion of scripture. These were all the opening exercises we had.[6]

On Otte's insistence, the new hospital was appropriately named "Neerbosch Hospital" in recognition of the first financial help he received for his work in China. This was in the form of some small sums of money given him by Dutch children at a large orphanage at Neerbosch, the Netherlands. The donations were a token of gratitude for Otte's looking after the children for several weeks during a severe epidemic of measles while he was doing post-graduate work at the University of Utrecht.

Eighty Chinese were treated on the opening day, and their number increased steadily thereafter. It soon became necessary to limit the number of patients by closing the hospital gates at eight-thirty and refusing admittance to any who arrived after that time. The Chinese thereupon started assembling as early as 2 a.m. waiting for the gates to open at 5 a.m. As reported by Otte:

All classes came: the well-to-do and the beggar; the proud scholar; the attache of the Mandarin as well as the untutored toiler of the soil.... In the first three months of operation, 1,500 different patients visited the hospital and received treatment 7,000 times.[7]

They came in such numbers that Otte had to bring in medicine from Amoy and elsewhere. Fortunately, Alexander Van Dyck was available to help in compounding prescriptions. "But for his help," the doctor reported, "I fear I could not have stood the strain."[8] Otte also soon had the service of a medical assistant—the son of the Sio-khe pastor and a former pupil of Dr. Macleish of the Presbyterian hospital at Amoy.

The Chinese, according to Otte, were on the whole unaccustomed to cleanliness, and particularly so when it involved food and cooking. He therefore departed from the practice he had observed during his visits to the hospitals at Amoy, where the in-patients provided their own food and did their own cooking. For a few cents a day to cover costs, the hospital furnished food. Although this practice cut down somewhat on the number of patients who would otherwise stay at the hospital for treatment, Otte felt that the end result of maintaining cleanliness and preventing disease was worth the loss.[9]

The months of traveling between Sio-khe and Amoy, where Otte's family first stayed on arrival in China, and superintending the construction projects at Sio-khe and the subsequent overwork when the hospital finally opened, proved too much for the doctor's health. On the insistence of his fellow missionaries, the hospital was therefore closed for part of July and much of August, 1889, while Otte took a much needed vacation to Amoy and Kulangsu. He continued this practice during his remaining years at Sio-khe. These months were a time of extreme heat in the interior of China, and Otte simply followed a custom that other inland missionaries were following. As many of the Chinese were busy in the fields at this time anyway, it was a somewhat lax period at the hospital.

The hospital was enlarged from time to time during the seven years Otte served at Sio-khe. By the time of his departure in January, 1895, on a furlough to the United States, the bed capacity of the hospital wards had increased from thirty to forty-five, and the overall space of the hospital had more than doubled in size. The most interesting additions were perhaps two small rooms designed especially for wealthy patients who would not consider staying in the general wards, and who were able to pay for better accommodations. The rooms were of a size enabling patients to take their wives with them. Also among the additions was a room for a Chinese nurse who had meanwhile become a part of the hospital staff.

Funds for enlarging the hospital came primarily from the Chinese people, both Christian and non-Christian. There also were occasional donations in kind from the Chinese. The most common was labor, an example being the high wall that volunteers built around the hospital compound. Special gifts were also received from time to time, including a good quality microscope from a Chinese physician from Changchow whose son had been treated by Otte. The mission staff too made donations in kind. Leonard Kip, for example, gave a plaster of Paris manikin, valued at $300, that became extremely helpful as a teaching aid for Otte and his students.

Contributions in the form of money came from donors in the United States and the Netherlands. To help defray costs of operating the hospital, Otte came up with the novel idea of placing notices in Reformed church papers urging readers to subscribe $35 (or 100 Dutch guilders) for the maintenance of a bed and its occupants for one year. The money could be sent directly to Otte or to the Board of Foreign Missions in New York or to a Mr. Lindenhout at Neerbosch in the Netherlands.

In view of the opium scourge plaguing China, it was only natural that Otte would do what he could for addicts who came to his hospital for help. Giving assistance was particularly difficult at first because there were no facilities to house and isolate addicts—something highly necessary for proper treatment. But he did what he could. Fortunately, the local civil mandarin was also concerned about the problem, and in the summer of 1891 agreed to head a campaign to collect the necessary funds for constructing a special facility. The equivalent of nearly $200 was collected, and Otte was soon able to add another ward to the hospital. Appropriately named the "Opium Refuge," it was large enough to accommodate five patients.

Upon admission to the hospital, an opium patient was required to deposit the equivalent of two dollars and agree to remain at least three weeks and up to five if necessary. If he left before the prescribed time, he forfeited the money. The patient was then locked up and generally not allowed to leave the Refuge for at least three days. After this, he was permitted a daily walk, under supervision, within the hospital grounds. When the worst of the treatment was over, he was allowed to walk about the grounds at will, but could not go outside the gate until dismissed. Upon dismissal, the cost of his food was deducted from the two dollars he had deposited and the remainder of the money was returned. [10]

Of the struggles and agonies addicts had to endure during the treatment, Otte has given us the following graphic description in the mission's annual report of 1893 to the Board of Foreign Missions:

For the first five days these patients are considered and treated as maniacs. They are locked up, and their food is handed them through a barred window. It is only in this way that they can be kept in the hospital.

At one time during the winter, five men came a distance of ninety miles to be cured of the opium habit. After each had paid the two dollars, they were locked in the Refuge. They were told beforehand of what suffering they would have to undergo, and they consented to the treatment, being intensely desired to be cured. The first day all went well, but the next day they became raving maniacs. Night and day they did nothing but crawl on the ground and howl like wild beasts; their room became filthy, and, when the coolie went in to clean it, four men [were needed] at times to watch the room to keep the patients from escaping. Often it was necessary to use physical force to prevent their escape. For four nights the students and patients in the adjoining rooms were kept awake with the noise. Whenever the physician or assistant appeared, they would beg on their knees to be let out, if only for a few minutes. When reasoned with, they said they were doing their best to keep quiet, but they seemed to have lost all self-control. Knowing this, they were patiently and kindly treated. When left alone, they made strenuous efforts to escape, and finally succeeded in wrenching off a foreign lock from the door. This was discovered in time, and heavy iron staples were clenched on the inside, and the door secured on the outside with a padlock. But on the fifth night they bent the staples with their fingers, so as to open the door. They then jumped down from a verandah twelve feet high and made their escape.[11]

Otte portrayed as "indescribable" the sufferings that opium addicts endured in their efforts to kick the habit. "If ever," he wrote, "I have been able to conceive what the sufferings of hell must be," it has been laboring with these addicts. Opium as a medicine, he added, has been one of the best of God's gifts to mankind, but when used where it is not called for, it is one of the greatest curses that mankind suffers. There was little doubt in

Otte's mind as to where the primary responsibility lay for the excessive use of opium in China: "England *forced* opium upon China. Not a single intelligent native doubts this from Li Hung Chang down. This is England's sin for which all the thousands poured into the coffers of the various missionary societies cannot atone."[12]

In 1894, Otte reported that on the basis of having treated seventy-four opium patients that year, the "agonies" that they suffered were in no way due to the manner of their treatment, as every known method was tried with no difference in the amount of suffering—with one exception. That occurred in instances where opium was given out in gradually reduced amounts. In these cases, he noted, "the sufferings were not appreciably less, while they were greatly prolonged."[13]

Some idea of how effective the efforts were in the long run can be gathered from a report covering the period from July, 1891, to July, 1892. During that twelve-.nonth time, sixty-six opium patients were admitted. All of them stayed for as long as was considered necessary, except seven who managed to run away. Otte reported he had no way of determining how many of the fifty-nine "remained firm" after they left, but he considered the effort had been more than worthwhile if even one-fourth of them did so. In a notation of two years later, Otte reported sixty-four patients as having been "cured" during the previous year. How large a proportion of them would later return to the habit he again could not give any precise data, but he did add the following interesting bit of information:

> The largest number of these will continue to suffer from the effects of their former habit as long as they live. These effects are indigestion, neurasthenia, atony of the bowels, and, in the worst cases, impotency. It is among these that a danger of a return to the habit is greatest. They feel so miserable most of the time, that they naturally resort to the drug that once afforded them momentary relief. Still, many (how large a proportion it is impossible to state) never return to the habit, and it is one of our sources of pleasure to see these, after a time, coming back to the hospital, bringing their friends to be relieved of what they consider the curse of their life.[14]

Among the various extra duties that Otte took upon himself, one of the most rewarding was the training of students for careers in medicine. Their number varied from year to year but reached as high as seven on one occasion. Those who stayed on were initially trained for a four-year period, but this was extended to five years in 1894. The first graduation took place in 1893 and involved three students. As to the kind of training he offered, Otte gives a good description in a communication of 1894:

> Though they had not completed all the studies offered in a good university course, still they have studied as faithfully as their time and opportunities have permitted, and they now posses a fair knowledge of Anatomy, Physiology, Therapeutics, Pharmacy, General, Analytical, and Physiological Chemistry, Minor Surgery and a more limited knowledge of General Surgery, Diseases of the Skin, Ophthalmology, Obstetrics, Diseases of Women. These later studies, however, still engage their attention, and we expect to give them in addition, a practical course in Histology and Pathology.[15]

Examinations, which Otte reported "were in all cases very severe," were given students from time to time in all the various branches of medicine. In addition, advanced students were given special responsibilities in order to gain practical experience. These included consulting with patients, dispensing medicine, performing minor surgery, and assisting Otte when major surgery was called for. They also assisted in looking after the dispensaries located in neighboring communities and, except for serious and midwifery cases, occasionally called on patients in their homes. Students who graduated were quickly replaced by others, of whom there was always a waiting list.

The practice of looking after "the diseases of the spirit as well as those of the body" (Otte's words) was not lost sight of. From the beginning, the hospital employed a Chinese evangelist—a young man who Otte described as one "who would be an honor to any home church"—to assist in bringing the gospel message to the patients. The Reverend Iap also did what he could to help with evangelization, as did Van Dyck when he was not calling on outstations in the Sio-khe district. The missionary women too played an important role in looking after the "diseases of the spirit," especially among women patients. The extent of the hospital's evangelistic program can be seen in this report of 1891 to the Board of Foreign Missions:

The "Neerbosch Hospital" at Sio-khe is an evangelizing agency second to none in importance. A preaching service is held on every out-patient's day at nine in the morning. All who wish to consult the physician are expected to attend. No patients are examined and no medicine dispensed until after this service. After the regular preaching service, while the patients are waiting their turn to enter the consulting-room they are approached individually and in a kind, familiar way shown the duty and privilege of worshipping the true God. In-patients have the monotony of the long day broken up by being taught hymns and portions of the Scriptures. The entire hymn-book of fifty-nine hymns will sometimes be memorized by a patient tarrying several months.[16]

In early 1894, a colporteur was added to the staff whose duty it was to distribute and sell religious tracts and Bibles. What was particularly needed though was a full-time, trained evangelist to do follow-up work after the patients returned to their homes. But such an individual was not easy to come by. As Otte wrote in 1894:

Thousands have heard the gospel in the hospital during the past six years, and hundreds have been visibly touched, but all these need still to be labored with in order to preserve the seed sown in their hearts. Some of these are being brought into the fold, but many more could be saved if only we had a larger foreign and native force to gather in the harvest. It is sad to allow so much seed to go to waste. Oh, that the Lord of Harvest would send us more laborers! At present we need this more than anything else.[17]

Otte's workload continued to increase from year to year. Along with the growing number of in-patients who needed regular attention, he made occasional housecalls when necessary in and around Sio-khe. There also were regular visits to three small dispensaries he had helped establish in nearby villages. From the time Neerbosch Hospital opened in March, 1889, until early January, 1895, when Otte and his family left on a well-earned furlough to the United States, the hospital treated about 50,000 out-patients, more than 2,400 in-patients, and performed over 1,500 operations. [18] Upon his leaving, the hospital was placed under the direction of Dr. I. S. F. Dodd, an appointment made financially possible by a kind donor in the States. Unfortunately, Dodd was able to remain in China only for a few months due to poor health. Thereafter, Neerbosch was closed until the arrival of Dr. C. Otto Stumpf in 1900.

When Otte returned to China in 1897, it was with the understanding that he would oversee the establishment of a new hospital in Amoy City. Realizing this, it is not surprising that he spent much of his furlough time soliciting funds for the proposed institution. Consideration was first given to remodeling the English Presbyterian hospital which had been closed since the departure of Dr. Macleish in 1894. This possibility was soon discarded because of the extensive repairs that were needed. Attention was next given to constructing a new building on this site, since the property already belonged to the Reformed mission and was simply being rented by the English Presbyterians. Locating the new hospital there would also be advantageous because it was close to the Tek-chhiu-kha (Amoy Second) Church. This possibility too was quickly eliminated when it was discovered that costly pilings would have to be driven into the ground to obtain a good foundation for the size of the hospital under contemplation. The unsanitary conditions of the Tek-chhiu-kha area, one of the most unsanitary in the city, also discouraged building there. It was therefore decided to use the old hospital building for a dispensary and look elsewhere for a suitable site.

On the suggestion of the local American Consul General, Otte selected a hospital site on the island of Kulangsu. As happened at Sio-khe, there was some initial opposition, but on this occasion it came not from the general Chinese populace but primarily from foreigners. Kulangsu by this time had become a kind of international settlement of foreign businessmen and consular officials, and they were fearful the hospital would bring in contagious diseases. The opponents appealed their case to Peking and even to Washington, but to no avail. Acceptance was no doubt made easier when critics were informed there would be special rooms for foreign patients and wealthy Chinese. Tension was further eased when it was learned that male patients who were "not clean enough" for the Kulangsu hospital would be admitted to one of the small wards attached to the Tek-chhiu-kha dispensary. As explained by Otte, "In this way we are able to separate the desirable patients from those less so."[19]

Construction of the new hospital, called Hope Hospital, had progressed sufficiently far by October, 1897, to begin accepting a few patients. The dedication ceremonies, however, did not take place until April, 1898. Otte's report for that year to the Board of Foreign Missions gives the following description of the new facility:

> Hope Hospital is a substantial two story brick structure, situated on the water's edge, and at high tide, surrounded on three sides by water. It contains a chapel, dining room, kitchen, two servants' rooms, office, dispensary, dark room for eye work, two storerooms, bathrooms, operating room, school room, four students' rooms, and seven wards, in which are forty-five beds.[20]

In reference to the chapel, Frances Otte described it as "a large, bright, airy room, and with its rows of stiff stools, minus backs, high narrow pulpit and small platform is well adapted for a Chinese audience—the omnipresent screen is there too."[21] The latter, of course, was for separating the men and women worshipers. Medicine, dressing, and bedding were furnished free, but the patients had to pay a small sum (the daily equivalent of 2 ½ cents U.S. currency) for their rice. Any other food that they might desire had to be provided by the patients themselves.

On the same day that Hope Hospital was dedicated, the cornerstone was laid for another hospital. Situated behind and slightly to one side of the Hope building, it was specifically designed for female patients and small children. It thus became popularly known as the "Women's Hospital," and Hope was henceforth often termed the "Men's Hospital." Officially, however, the former was called the "Wihelmina Women's Hospital." It was built in the same general style as the Men's Hospital and had virtually identical facilities, except for the operating room and chapel which were located in Hope. Also, it had at the outset only twenty-five beds as compared to forty-five at

Hope.

Naming the second hospital after the beloved queen of the Netherlands was very appropriate because the necessary funds for its construction came entirely from generous groups and private donors in the Netherlands who had become interested in Otte's work. This explains why it was also sometimes referred to as the "Netherlands Women's Hospital." To correlate this support, an organization was created known as the "Netherlands Society for Building and Maintaining Missionary Hospitals in China." By agreement with the Board of Foreign Missions, the society furnished the initial funds of $2,518 for constructing the hospital, and $800 for its maintenance, leaving the board to use the money "in accordance with its own rules."

Support did not end with these initial funds, as Netherlanders continued to show an interest in this beneficent enterprise. Several nurses from the Netherlands, for example, volunteered their services from time to time. In view of this kind of help, it is not surprising that Otte wrote in 1899: "If every branch of Mission work was so well and heartily supported, as is the Women's Hospital by the friends in the Netherlands, many of the anxious moments spent by so many of us would be changed to times of joy."[22]

As was true with Neerbosch Hospital at Sio-hke, Otte personally drew up the architectural plans for the two hospitals at Kulangsu and occasionally assisted in the construction. He did this in part because he enjoyed working with his hands, but also because he did not have much respect for Chinese workmanship. Note, for example, this excerpt from one of his letters:

> You can hardly appreciate what it means to put up a good building here in China. The workmen are such inveterate liars and cheats that if I am prevented from going on a tour of inspection even for one day, I am sure to find something wrong. Sometimes it is absolutely impossible to get them to budge. I bought the roofing material for the hospital in the Netherlands. It is a composition of asphalt, etc. When I gave this to the contractor to put on the roof, he persisted that he did not know how to put it on. I then proceeded to show him, but every time he began he would do it in just the way I did not want it done. So in sheer

desperation, I proceeded to put it on myself. It took me two weeks of hard work, but finally it was all done and then I simply crowed. You ought to have seen me when at work. I was covered from head to foot with sticky asphalt. Even my baby, when she came with her mother one day to the hospital said, "This is not my papa."[23]

Otte's active participation in construction projects was not without its problems when a patient came in who needed immediate attention, as can be seen in the following addendum to the above letter:

Sometimes right in the midst of my work I would be called out on a serious case. Then I would hurriedly wash my hands in kerosene, change my clothes, and go to the case. Think of having to operate on the eye under such circumstances.[24]

Both hospitals were enlarged from time to time through gifts from the United States and the Netherlands as well as from former patients and students. In 1899, for example, thanks to gifts totaling nearly $2,000, the number of in-patients that the Women's Hospital could accommodate increased from twenty-five to forty. Despite enlargements and additional beds, the hospitals at times were so full that patients were sleeping on the floors and on benches. Even then, some had to be turned away.

The procedure that was generally followed in receiving and handling patients was carefully described by Helen Kip who, as the wife of Leonard Kip, repeatedly assisted the mission in whatever ways possible. This included helping out at the hospitals.

In most hospitals certain days, two or three times a week, are set apart for seeing out-patients, who come from far and near to be treated by the wonder-working foreign doctor.

Each one on entering the door receives a slip of bamboo on which is a number, which settles the order in which they are seen by the physician. As it is "first come first served," all are anxious to be on hand when the doors are opened so as to be attended to early in the day. Then, too, as there is a limit to the number who can be treated in a day, if there is a big crowd, there comes a time when the slips are exhausted, and those who are so unfortunate as to come late must wait for another day. For these reasons, I have known cases in which patients have spent the night in the street to make sure of being on hand in time.[25]

When the hospital doors opened, usually at about 9:00, the patients, after receiving their bamboo slips, were all ushered into the chapel, where someone—a missionary, native pastor or preacher, a student, or even the doctor himself—delivered a brief religious message. After the service was over, the patients, while waiting for their appointment with the doctor, met in small groups for further Christian enlightenment. Religious tracts were also distributed among those who could read. Helen Kip describes what transpired next:

> When the doctor is ready to see the out-patients, he takes his place at a desk with his students about him, each with his appointed work. A large book is opened in which is recorded the name, age, occupation, residence, disease, and other items of information about each man, woman, and child who comes to the hospital.
>
> A man who sits at the door now calls out the numbers in regular order, and the patients with the corresponding tally are admitted one by one into the doctor's presence to have their ills attended to. Some are disposed of in a few minutes, and receiving a ticket and prescription, go to take their places in the line waiting at the dispensary window for their medicine to be passed out. Others may be advised to come as in-patients for an operation, or course of treatment in the wards of the hospital. But some must be told they have waited too long, and nothing can be done to help them, or that their disease is an incurable one, and that no skill can save them.[26]

In-patients were, of course, exposed more fully to the Christian message. In addition to being required to attend daily worship services, they were approached on an individual and small group basis. A common procedure, especially among the women, involved teaching them one or more of the hymns or psalms, set to meter, that contained the essential beliefs of the Christian faith. As the patients committed the words to memory, the contents were explained. It was hoped that the patients would, upon leaving the hospital, sing and explain the songs to their relatives and friends. Much of this type of work was carried on by the missionary women, including those of the English Presbyterian mission.[27]

Dr. Otte himself was one of the most indefatigable evangelists. When possible, he took his preaching turn in the chapel and did whatever evangelistic work he could do when visiting local dispensaries in neighboring villages or when accompanying missionaries on their tours. It is thus not surprising that when Otte was on furlough in 1896, the General Synod granted him the privilege of becoming ordained. The ordinance was formally administered by the Classis of Michigan in the First Reformed Church of Grand Rapids on July 7 of that year.

The practice that Otte had introduced at Sio-khe of training Chinese medical students was continued at the Kulangsu hospitals. In 1898, he reported having nine male and four female students under his direction. Because of his own deep convictions, he chose only students who were committed to Christianity and made it clear that they were expected during their time of training to play an active role in the mission's evangelistic program. Those unwilling to do this were dismissed with little hesitation. As part of these responsibilities, the students taught in the Sabbath schools, took their turns at preaching in the hospital chapel, and went to neighboring communities to preach from time to time. Regular twenty-minute evening prayer sessions were also held in the student quarters. Students served without pay, but were given board and room.

Some indication of the busy schedule Otte set for himself can be seen from these statistics for the year 1900: over 10,200 patient visits (many of which, however, were repeats by the same persons) were made to the two hospitals at Kulangsu and Tek-chhiu-kha; 1,206 in-patients were treated; 631 operations were performed; and 155 teeth were extracted. In-patients remained for an average of sixteen days. The patients came from far and near, some having traveled over 100 miles.[28]

XII

Staffing, Funding, and Ecumenism, 1900-1937

The number of Reformed missionaries assigned to the Amoy mission in 1900 totaled twenty-two, comprising six men and sixteen women. The latter included, besides spouses of the men, nine single women and the widow of the Reverend Talmage. Increase was gradual during the next two decades. The all-time high during the period 1900-1937 was fifty-one (twenty men and thirty-one women), reached in 1922, after which there was a slow but steady decline. In 1937, the number of missionaries totaled thirty-six, comprising thirteen men and twenty-three women. Among the men, four were unordained—three of them medical doctors and the other an educator. The women were about evenly divided between married and single.[1]

The territorial size of the Reformed mission increased significantly during this period when in 1919 the London Missionary Society, for financial reasons, transferred responsibility for the rugged North River area to the American body. Comprising 2,000 square miles and 1 million Chinese, the transaction increased the scope of the mission's responsibility from 6,000 to 8,000 square miles and from 3 million to 4 million people. Scattered throughout the new territory were five churches and twenty-one outstations. These figures compared with the other four Reformed districts as follows: Amoy, four churches and eight outstations; Changchow, four churches and eleven outstations; Sio-khe, four churches and eight outstations; and Tong-an, three churches and eleven outstations. To assist the mission in the North River district, there was one ordained

Chinese pastor and about twenty preachers, most of whom had little or no theological training. Visiting the various churches and stations meant traveling some 300 miles over cobblestone roads and mountain ridges that sometimes were 3,000 feet high, thus compelling one to walk much of the distance.

As in the past, Kulangsu continued to receive the greatest attention as a place for missionary residences, with one-third to one-half of the missionaries usually residing there. In 1910, for example, the thirty mission staff members were distributed by districts as follows: Amoy, thirteen; Tong-an, seven; Changchow, six; and Sio-khe, four. Similarly, in 1918, twenty of the thirty-eight missionaries lived on Kulangsu. In understanding this situation, it must be borne in mind that several mission schools (including two of the highest grade level) were located there, as were the best hospitals. Kulangsu's unique importance to the mission as a whole is clearly shown in the way its twenty missionaries were classified in 1918: one was teaching in the seminary; one (a new arrival) was engaged in language study; three were connected with the hospitals and another three with boys' educational work; two were associated with the girls' school and two with the women's Bible school; one was in charge of the women's evangelistic work and another was serving as part-time secretary and part-time womens' evangelist; and six were classified as associate members (meaning perhaps spouses).[2]

There were several special reasons, too, why Kulangsu became an attractive missionary center. Amoy City, which had a population of 150,000 and the mission's two largest churches, was separated from Kulangsu by only a half mile of water. It was thus easily accessible. The presence of English Presbyterian and London Missionary Society staff members at Kulangsu also made for easy contacts among the three missionary groups. Similarly, the deep harbor, one of China's best, facilitated contacts with the outside world. Finally, Kulangsu had a special attraction because its foreign settlement enjoyed certain self-governing privileges guaranteed by international treaties.

Despite the continued dominance of Kulangsu, the mission after 1900 began diversifying its administration somewhat. Ideally, the policy, as explained in the annual report of 1909, was

to have and to maintain in each of the districts [of Amoy,

Changchow, Sio-khe, and Tong-an] at least two ordained
men and two single ladies besides those in charge of
institutions, in order that both the evangelistic and
educational work among men, women, and children may
be successfully prosecuted and given much needed
supervision.[3]

When the mission took over the North River area in 1919 as
another district, a committee from the mission, after a careful
survey, chose Leng-na as its chief center.

The turnover rate among missionaries continued to be a
problem after 1900. As a consequence, even when a significant
number of new missionaries arrived, it did not automatically
mean that the foreign staff increased by that amount. This is
clearly indicated by what transpired in 1908. In that year, six new
missionaries joined the staff (the largest addition in sixty-six
years) and four returned from furloughs, yet the mission ended
up having only two more persons in the field in 1908 than in 1900.
It is also interesting to note, in respect to turnovers, that more
than one-half of the missionaries serving the Amoy field in 1921
arrived after 1915.

Despite better missionary homes and improved medical
facilities, matters of health remained the primary reason for early
departures from China. An article entitled "Why Missionaries
Break Down," written in 1922 by Francis Potter, a distinguished
member of the Board of Foreign Missions, sheds some light on
why the health problem continued to exist. As might be expected,
Potter singled out unsanitary conditions and the change in
climate as major factors, but he also gave considerable attention to
mental strain brought on by the growing complexity of mission
work:

The missionary heroes of the early days of our missionary
enterprise wrought wonders in their attempts to carry the
Gospel to the non-Christian world, but their mode of life
was governed largely by themselves; they were able more
or less to plan the wise expenditure of their time, giving
due regard to the importance of safeguarding health.
Today a work which has grown to great proportions, which
has developed a business organization that includes
institutions of various types with set hours and crowded

schedules, makes its demand upon our missionaries and threatens to control and almost overwhelm them. It is no uncommon thing for a man to be manager of several important institutions, to be solely responsible for the administration of many thousands of dollars each year, and in addition to be required to tour a large district and act as guide, counsellor and friend to the preachers and teachers in its borders. And to be driven by such a work, to burn the midnight oil and rise soon after dawn, to work without surcease…these are demands to which the tired body of the missionary cannot respond indefinitely without overdrawing his slender reserve of strength.[4]

As in the past, requests for reinforcements and replacements were sent almost annually to the Board of Foreign Missions. The situation was particularly critical in the early 1900s. Thus, following a meeting of about a dozen missionaries at the home of Mrs. Talmage, Dr. Otte on May 30, 1901, wrote Henry Cobb, secretary of the Board of Foreign Missions:

The position of this Mission is desperate, no other word will express it. Things cannot go on as they are doing…. I have pleaded with you in the past, so I need not plead again. Every member of the Mission, male and female, old and young, feels that it would be wrong to leave us any longer so undermanned as we are.[5]

Requests were also sent by Chinese brethren. One of these, received February 2, 1902, from the pastors of the Changchow district, pointed out that there were only two ordained missionaries, the Reverends Hobard Studley and Abbe Warnshuis, to "superintend" the entire Reformed mission. Although there were "12 native pastors and about 20 native evangelists to assist them in their work," the request described them as

like little children just learning to walk and talk. How can they understand the deep things of the Gospel? How can they arrange in order and care for the government of the churches? It grieves us to think of this state of things, and so with one heart we earnestly request your honorable Board to graciously appoint several more ordained missionaries for this field, that they may earnestly engage in the work of bringing this people to Christ, that the body of Christ may be enlarged and the affairs of the Church arranged in an orderly manner.[6]

As an indication to the churches at home of how shorthanded the mission was, the Reverend Henry De Pree made the following interesting comparison in 1911 between the situation at Changchow, where he was stationed, and the situation among the Reformed churches in America:

Only to think of the population of this city alone makes it seem like a stupendous task. Our Reformed Church at home has a membership of about 120,000. There are over 700 ministers who are concerned with their spiritual needs. In the city of Changchow, we have a population just as great, 120,000, and in all there are but three foreign and three native ministers; and these foreigners have schools and evangelistic work for tens of thousands in the inland districts to take their time as well.[7]

The shortage of missionaries meant that staff members had to be shifted occasionally from one location to another as vacancies occurred. It also meant they often had to perform several distinct duties, including those of evangelist, educator, and administrator. This dividing of a missionary's time obviously resulted in slighting some of his or her tasks. As explained in the mission's report of 1901:

God can work where and how He will, but the history of the Church in every age shows that He has elected to work through men, and if the work is to prosper the man must be forthcoming, not half, or a third, or a quarter of a man, as [happened] in recent years, but a whole man.[8]

The need for women volunteers was just as imperative as that for men, if not more so. This is not surprising in view of the increasing variety of duties they were called upon to perform—primary and Sunday school work, calling on Chinese families in their homes, nursing, visiting hospital patients, and calling on churches and outstations. The need for single women was especially acute at times. In a letter of early 1930, the Reverend Henry De Pree, as secretary of the mission, informed the board that the retirement of Nellie Zwemer and the furlough of Ruth Broekema meant the mission currently had six fewer women than was the case six years earlier. He further noted that the Tong-an and North River districts had no single women workers, and the Sio-khe district had only one (Elizabeth Bruce) as did the Changchow district (Leona Vander Linden). De Pree also reminded the board that the three inland hospitals at this time had no missionary nurses to help in their work.[9]

Requests for additions were sometimes very specific and inclusive. Thus, in 1917, the mission asked for sixteen new people distributed as follows: three men for the district boys' schools and one for Talmage College, all preferably with some theological training; two men for evangelistic work; three doctors; one pharmacist; three trained nurses; and three single ladies, one of whom should have kindergarten training.[10]

Fortunately, as in the pre-1900 period, there always were some missionaries who served a significant number of years. The careers of a few of these veterans predated 1900, including those of the Reverend Philip and Anna Pitcher, who arrived in 1885 and served until 1915, and those of the widows Mary Talmage and Helen Kip, who served respectively from 1865 to 1912 and 1865 to 1918. Similarly, the two Talmage sisters, Katherine and Mary, whose missionary careers began in 1874, served until 1927—for a combined total of 106 years. Also helping give continuity to the mission was the fact that of the seventy-nine new missionaries who arrived during this period, about two dozen served twenty or more years and would have served longer had it not been for the outbreak of war.[11]

A gradual but steady increase in the size of the Chinese staff also helped give the mission a greater degree of permanence. In 1900, the statistics for the Chinese staff were as follows: ordained pastors, 11; native helpers, 30. At the close of 1932, the figures were respectively 13 and 252. The "native workers" were divided as follows: preachers, 50; teachers, 134; hospital workers, 40; and Bible women, 28. In terms of gender, the workers were about evenly divided between men (123) and women (119). In 1937, the Chinese staff consisted of 19 pastors and 281 workers.[12]

Despite such increases, the size of the Chinese staff remained far short of what was needed. As to how large it should be in the minds of the mission, the following excerpt from a pamphlet of 1907 provides a clue:

We have not yet even nominally occupied that small part of Fukien province which has been wholly given to us for evangelization. Before it is thoroughly occupied, there should be chapels and churches located throughout all this region so that no one would need to go more than five miles to attend Christian worship. In order that there may be at least one preacher to every 5,000 of the population, the church in our districts will need to have 600 men where it now has fifty.[13]

On the basis of the above ratio, when the mission later added the North River territory in 1919, that district alone would need 200 preachers. In view of these estimates, it is little wonder that the mission reported in 1921 that "to marshall [our] scanty force so that their impact on heathenism may be most effective [will take] much careful thought and wise planning."[14]

Finding qualified preachers constituted the crux of the problem. Although many of them had the benefit of some training in the theological school, their number was far from sufficient. The mission thus often had to rely on "earnest Christian brethren" chosen from among the congregations to fill the need. This was done with regret, but there was no choice. As explained in its report of 1904, "The taking of a short cut to the ministry in this land is probably more to be deplored than elsewhere, but also more difficult to prevent because the supply of Chinese preachers is so limited." The report also noted some of the results of the problem:

The greatness of this need for more and better trained and more spirit-filled men is realized only by those who at close range see the work in the outstations where these men reside. If Hoe-khe, E-lang, Toa-pi, Peng-ho, Am-an, Ang-tung-than had men of more training, of deeper spiritual life, who can say what progress might not have been made? And what of E-che, Tiu-ka, Chun-tin, E-go, To-kio, where the Mission could send no one because there was no one to be sent?[15]

The difficulty of not having enough "spirit-filled" preachers was not easily solved. It was still manifestly present a decade after the above was written, as can be seen in these excerpts from the report of 1913 concerning the situation in the Sio-khe district:

"We are sometimes inclined to think that many of the preachers are interested only in their salary and position"; "Little deep spirituality, concern for souls, [and] zeal as servants of the Lord are in evidence"; The preacher at Hong-thau-poa is at home "more than at his post, and when at it, doing little in the way for Christians or heathen"; "We are thankful that the preacher [at Taw-kio] has resigned."[16]

There were, of course, some dedicated preachers whose zeal made up for some of their lack of education and training. The mission's report for 1923 gives a good example of such a person:

> The Poa-nia preacher [in the Tong-an district] has not very much education but lots of religion, plenty of enthusiasm and bubbling vivacity. Where most of his congregation walk at least an hour over paths that do not deserve the name, tending more toward the perpendicular than the horizontal, he has his church filled every Sunday and often overflowing. He has kept up a good mid-week prayer meeting and made heroic efforts at securing laymen's work to carry out his programs. Each new hearer is listed in a class and taught progressively, so that the [ordained] pastor always has a class of inquirers ready for baptism to examine on his visits. This man is musical and carries an accordion as he goes about preaching.[17]

The union synod of the Reformed and English Presbyterian missions and their classes frequently discussed the need for more and better qualified preachers. Much of their discussion revolved around salaries. Although pastor salaries by 1900 were being paid by their respective churches, most preacher salaries were still being paid in part, if not in full, by the two missions. In 1915, the synod therefore put into operation a plan that divided its territory into five regions, each headed by a section board made up of representatives from the churches in that region and the mission responsible for it. Each section board, in turn, chose delegates to a general board whose responsibility was

> to receive all money for the maintenance of the unordained preachers, evangelists and colporteurs, and disburse it [among the section boards] according to a budget previously presented; to appoint preachers each year; fix their salaries; and arrange for their examination

and graduation.

The pay a preacher received was to be based on such factors as educational qualifications and number of dependents, but provision was also made for merit. It was hoped that as the amount raised for preacher salaries increased and the amount the missions had to put with it decreased, the missions could use more of their foreign budgets for "pioneer work" in the "countryside." It was also hoped that these measures would further along the ultimate goal of establishing a self-supporting, self-governing, indigenous Chinese church. [18]

Soon after the above plan was inaugurated, the synod took steps for convening annual conferences for preachers and pastors. These were usually held in July or August, lasted about a week, and were well attended—there frequently being over a hundred Chinese present as well as several missionaries. Sessions consisted of inspirational addresses (usually by speakers brought in from the outside), Bible study, prayer meetings, and discussion groups on church problems. The younger men found the group discussions led by older and more experienced pastors to be of great help. This was particularly true of preachers who labored in isolated areas and who seldom had an opportunity to seek answers to their problems. To help remedy this matter further, it later became commonplace to hold district meetings of a similar nature on a quarterly basis.

Although fewer Bible women than preachers were required, here too, there was the problem of finding enough suitable workers to meet the need. Recruitment had become more critical than formerly because of the increasingly itinerant nature of their work—going out every day, traveling from place to place (sometimes spending several days at a village), and living with Chinese families. Therefore, not all women were suitable for serving as Bible women. Those with household and family responsibilities, for example, obviously had to be ruled out. As a consequence, more and more Bible women after 1900 were drawn from among older women, especially widows. The success and popularity of the preacher/pastor conferences soon prompted the convening of similar annual institutes for Bible women. These were held during the summer at one of the Kulangsu schools. Lasting about ten days, they were attended by women from all three missions, including the London group. The conferences primarily featured workshops along with addresses by missionaries and well-known Chinese workers. [19]

Along with a general shortage of missionary and Chinese staff members, the mission, as in the past, had to contend with a shortage of funds. This became particularly serious whenever economic recessions at home caused a decline in church giving. Because of economic straits in 1900, for example, the Board of Foreign Missions reduced more than half of the mission's estimates by 43 percent, which was followed by a 31 percent cut in 1901. Reductions like the above were especially discouraging because they fell not upon the salaries of the missionaries but upon the work they were doing. The missionaries therefore not only had to refrain from advancing their work but had to retrench in some instances. As they explained in their report for 1900, after having "carefully scrutinized every item of work and reduced every expense to the minimum...we felt a good deal like a ship in distress, with every stitch of canvass close-reefed and all the hatches sealed." Not until 1902 did the board grant an increase, although it was very slight. Funding also declined for a few years after the First World War, forcing the mission once again to carry on a work that was expanding—but with appropriations that remained virtually stationary. [20]

As might be expected, appropriations from the board were likewise cut drastically during the economic depression of the 1930s. In dealing with this, the Chinese Christians themselves did what they could. In many instances, teachers and preachers took a voluntary cut in salary—teachers at Kulangsu Primary School, for example, took a 30 percent cut in 1935. Although enrollment in the schools was increasing and some buildings were in serious need of repair, everyone was told to try and make do with what they had. However, in situations where something obviously had to be done, it was usually carried out. Thus, when enrollment in the Girls' Middle School at Kulangsu increased from 150 to 225 in a two-year period, approval was given in 1933 to add a three-story wing. This was done with no solicitation of funds from the States. As reported by the mission, these sacrifices are "a striking evidence of Chinese support of the missionary program." [21]

In addition to requiring the normal operating appropriations from the home board, the mission was in chronic need of money to meet various special demands. These were anything but small, as can be seen in the following list of "gifts" requested in 1912, all of which were described as "immediately urgent." [22]

For the purchase of the new residence on
Kulangsu $8,000
For a residence in Changchow 3,850
For another Ladies'House and additional rooms for
the girls' School on Kulangsu 5,000
For more land for schools in Changchow 1,650
For our share in the new church on Kulangsu 3,500
For a boys' school building in Tong-an 3,500
For the Changchow Boys' Higher Primary School
building 2,500
For the Changchow Kindergarten building 1,200
For assistance to the Sin-koe-a Church in building
a parsonage 400
For a third residence in Changchow for the teacher
in the Bible School to be opened in 1913 4,000
For a new recitation hall for the Middle School ... 1,650
For a new chapel for the Middle School 1,100
For a new dormitory for the Middle School 2,750
For the Kulangsu Higher Primary School building 5,000
For school laboratory apparatus 1,500
For the Haiteng Chapel 400

In noting requests like $8,000 for a missionary residence (number one in the above list), and in looking at photographs of missionary homes and seeing the contrast between some of their dwellings and those of the masses of the Chinese people, it is understandable why missionaries were sometimes reproached for undue extravagance. In fairness to them, however, a case can be made justifying the costly and rather lavish homes some missionaries enjoyed. Such was the conclusion at least of the Reverend John Fagg, secretary of the Board of Foreign Missions, in his support of a 1910 request for $3,500 to build a new residence at Tong-an for the Reverend Frank Eckerson. Because Fagg himself had served several years (1888-1894) in China, he had firsthand acquaintance with the inconveniences and concerns that went with living there—an experience that obviously strengthened his argument as to why missionaries deserved comfortable homes:

> To a man and his family in the midst of the peaked roofs and crowded and narrow streets of a Chinese city, home is everything. It is a shelter from the intense and protracted sub-tropical heat. It is their fortress against prowling thieves and possible riotous mobs. They must find their recreation almost solely at home. The streets are utterly uninviting, badly paved, lined with dilapidated and malodorous shops, beset with vicious and mangy dogs, and filthy, grunting swine and foul-mouthed men and boys. There are no parks or bicycle courses. There are no entertainments or concerts or lectures. The monotony of life in a Chinese city is one of its seldom-mentioned, but real, trials. Does not our appreciation of our own homes prompt us to give the men and women who devote themselves to live in the midst of the degradation and disease and filth and ostracism and unnameable abominations of heathenism, at least a secure and inviting home?[23]

As in the past, funds from the States came not only from what was budgeted by the Board of Foreign Missions, but also from contributions made by churches, societies, and individuals. Contributions from such sources were generally designated by their donors for specific causes, many of which involved construction projects. Thus, in 1908, members of the Collegiate Church of New York City provided $3,500 to be used for a missionary residence at Sio-khe, and a contribution from a Mr. Lansing of Albany was designated for building a church at Ho-sang. In similar fashion, in 1911, members of the West End Collegiate Church in New York City provided several generous gifts to be used for remodeling Neerbosch Hospital at Sio-khe. One of the most unique gifts was one of $1,500 given in 1909 by a Mrs. Cornelius Low Wells of Flatbush in honor of her husband, a medical doctor. The money was to be used for a mountain retreat near Amoy which, hopefully, according to the bequest, would contribute to the health of the missionaries. Nor did the Middle West shirk its obligations. A committee of church members in

Sioux County, Iowa, for example, collected $3,000 in 1909 for a new boys' school at Sio-khe.[24]

It also was not uncommon for churches to underwrite salaries of missionaries. Thus, the Clinton Avenue Church in Newark, New Jersey, took responsibility for Eckerson's salary, as did several churches in Whiteside County, Illinois, for Frederick Weersing's salary when he was sent to Amoy in 1915 as a kind of superintendent for the mission's primary schools. Similarly, the Bergen Reformed Church of Jersey City took care of Dr. Matthijs Vandweg's salary when he agreed in 1919 to take charge of the mission hospital at Tong-an; and the Park Hill Church of Yonkers, New York, assisted in meeting Elizabeth Bruce's financial needs when she went to China in 1921.

A surprising number of gifts were received from members and families of members who served on the mission staff. Looking at just the decade beginning in 1907, for example, these included: a gift from a Mrs. Havilaar (who as Miss M. Van B. Calkoen had served in China 1896-1899) for constructing a chapel at Pos-thau-chhi; a gift in 1910 from Alice Duryee for a new missionary residence at Tong-an where she and her sister had worked; a bequest in 1910 from Elizabeth Cappon for a new chapel for the Neerbosch Hospital where she had faithfully served for fourteen years; financial help in 1914 from the family of the late Elizabeth Blauvelt for the Elizabeth Blauvelt Memorial Hospital at Tong-an where Elizabeth had worked; money in 1915 from the Talmage sisters for a principal's residence at Tong-an, given in memory of their mother; and a gift of $4,000 in 1918 presented by Helen Kip following her departure from China after fifty-one years of service, to be used for "direct evangelistic work."

Gifts in kind were also given. Organs from America were particularly appreciated by the Chinese congregations, as were gramophones. When one of the latter was given by the Heidelburg Guild of the Clinton Avenue Church of Newark, New Jersey, to the Tong-an church, the pastor reported back in 1913 that its "versatility" was proving especially useful as he

> went one night each week to preach to a heathen audience
> out of doors...and on Sundays to get people to come to
> church earlier, and to keep them from gossip at the noon
> intermission, and [to introduce] some new hymns which

form good texts for little "preachments."[25]
The Clinton Avenue Church responded in kind again when it gave the Reverend Frank Eckerson, before his return to China in 1913 after a furlough, a gift of church bells—one for each chapel in the Tong-an district where he was laboring. These were given in gratitude for having received several ideographed scrolls and banners from the Tong-an church.

In the same manner that contributions from churches and individuals in America increased, so, too, the Chinese Christians grew "in the grace of giving." Indeed, Chinese giving increased almost annually during this period, and sometimes did so significantly. In 1912, for example, the mission reported a gain of about $2,500 in Chinese benevolences—an increase of nearly 30 percent over the previous year. In equating benevolent giving with real wages at this time, the mission reported in 1912 that the average annual gift per communicant member was equal to "the sum total of a working-man's wages for a month, constituting a notable achievement when reached even in the most forward lands."[26] In the recently annexed North River district, the Christians at Chung-chau in the early 1920s gave over a thousand days of labor for the enlargement of their church, and both the preacher and teacher gave several months of their salaries.

The Chinese churches were also increasingly providing some, and in a few cases all, of the funding for constructing new churches and chapels. In the spring of 1930, for example, when Francis Potter, assistant secretary of the Board of Foreign Missions, spent several days at Amoy City and the surrounding area, he came away pleasantly surprised at what he observed. Not only had the First and Second Amoy churches (both of which had been started by the Reformed mission) become self-supporting and self-propagating, but some of their "offspring" had gone through similar metamorphoses and were themselves now self-supporting and self-propagating. Potter also took note of a church in the "country" at Kio-thau, for which the mission had been primarily responsible during its early stage and was now not only self-supporting but helping maintain two chapels in the vicinity.[27]

In many instances, new construction involved replacing a crude-looking and woefully inadequate church with one more substantial and eye-appealing. That some of the old places of worship left much to be desired is evident from this 1907 description by Warnshuis of the chapel at Hong-thau-poe in the Sio-khe district:

> The building now occupied consists of three rooms, one occupied by the preacher and his wife and child, the other by the school teacher and by some of his pupils by day-time, and the middle room, ten feet square, open on one side, used as a chapel, in which, together with the adjoining court, more than forty inquirers meet each Sunday, and half that number each evening. In the rear is another small room, also open on one side, which serves as an additional school room. The bare ground is the only floor in all these rooms. It is time that more suitable building accommodations were secured for all this work.[28]

According to Warnshuis, the five men who were baptized in this makeshift, crowded chapel on October 21, 1906, were "the first fruits after three and a half years of preaching."

The mission reports are silent as to whether the Hong-thau-poe congregation ever got a new church, but there are several cases on record in which the old adage that "patience has its own reward" was given some credence. For fourteen years, for example, the Sin-tng congregation in the Sio-khe district had to put up with preaching conditions described as "totally inadequate," but all this changed when their new chapel was dedicated on Sunday, January 23, 1910. A letter from the Reverend Harry Boot describes their new place of worship and the adjoining parsonage, all built in the Chinese style of architecture:

> The new chapel is a neat structure, and is built entirely of hard brick. The windows are sufficient in number to make of this church the most airy and the best lighted in this whole region. Window and door frames are of dark red, while all woodwork within is painted a pale blue. Walls are hard finished and pure white. The pulpit, though small, is neat and durable. When crowded, the church will seat 200 people.
>
> Kitchen and residence are spick and span, and durably built. The parsonage has a verandah on both floors. All woodwork is neatly painted. Part of the kitchen is walled

off and fitted up as a consistory room, and can be used as a guest chamber.

The two structures were surrounded by a solid but picturesque wall. It was built at a cost of about $1,000 gold, of which nearly one-fourth came from the congregation. The latter also provided the site itself as well as 300 days of manual labor. As Boot remarked, "All in all, we have an admirable piece of property, of which the church here, the donors at home, as also the Board, may well be proud."[29]

The Reverend Boot gave a similar account of what happened at Phaw-ah (also in the Sio-khe district) a year later. For ten years, its congregation had been meeting in small, dark, unsuitable rented quarters. As described by Boot, it "had its ups and downs, now closed, now open; now well attended, now almost forsaken; now attracted by the Truth, now by the hope of present gain." But the congregation persevered and in 1911, a year after Sin-tng received its new chapel, Phaw-ah received one of similar appearance.[30]

A few churches built during this period were by no means small. One of these was for the congregation at Second Amoy (Tek-chhiu-kha) whose church, along with the parsonage and school and about a hundred houses, was destroyed in early October 1903 by one of the city's worst fires.[31] Thanks to kind friends in America and the liberality of some wealthy Chinese Christians at Amoy, a commodious new church was erected at a cost of $7,000, with each group defraying about half of the expense. Other buildings were constructed later, along with a jetty to provide better access by water. When Secretary Potter visited the church in the spring of 1930, he was pleasantly surprised by what he saw:

> In addition to the church auditorium itself, there was a comfortable parsonage, reception and social rooms, and most of the conveniences which we accept quite naturally at home. There was also a large building where the church conducts an Elementary School with an enrollment of 190 scholars and in another building a Kindergarten is carried on, some 180 children being enrolled.[32]

Like Amoy City, the Changchow church also had some wealthy patrons, as was exemplified in 1922 by the considerable enlargement of the boys' school, thanks to funds contributed by one of the church elders. This was soon followed by the construction, without any outside help, of a new church building capable of seating 1,200 people.

Staff shortages and concerns about funding in no way prevented efforts to further the ecumenical movement—something that had been very dear to the hearts of the missionaries since the early days of the great John Van Nest Talmage. At the provincial level, the Reformed and English Presbyterian missions in 1920 finally succeeded in persuading the London Missionary Society to join them and become a full member of the South Fukien Synod. Several earlier instances of cooperation among the three helped prepare the way for this enlarged union. In the summer of 1907, for example, a five-day teachers' conference was held at Amoy City attended by 112 representatives from all three missions. And in the following year, the three cooperated in forming the South Fukien Religious Tract Society for the publication and distribution of Bibles and devotional literature.

Quiet discussions among delegates from the three missions resulted in the appointment of several committees in 1918 to study the various problems still hindering the proposed union. Fortunately, these problems revolved primarily around matters of church government rather than doctrine, thus making concessions easier. Major differences in polity included the propriety of having deaconesses; the relationship between elders and deacons; how much authority should be given to regional organizations such as classes and presbyteries; and whether local churches should have the authority to excommunicate members, as was the case with the London group.[33]

Difficulties were finally worked out and an agreement consummated January 6, 1920. The result was the formation of the South Fukien United Church under the direction of a combined synod and six classes. Because of overlapping territories in some instances, two of the classes included delegates from all three participating missions. The annual report of the Reformed mission for 1921 described the makeup of the new organization as follows:

> The pastors, 40; unordained preachers, 183; school teachers, 472; communicants, 9,352; baptized non-

communicants, 5,944; catechumens, 8,021; total Christian community, 23,317. Church schools, 226; scholars, 9,582. There were contributed for pastors' salaries, $5,045; evangelists', $6,886; congregational expenses, $4,671; benevolences, $2,239; for all other purposes, $44,855. This represents an average per communicant of $4.80.[34]

A look at the mission's annual report for 1927 regarding the meeting of the South Fukien United Synod gives a good indication of the type of matters brought before that body. The session lasted eight days and was preceded by two days of committee meetings. Some attention was given to the Domestic Mission Society, particularly with respect to finances and new work that should be undertaken. Considerable regard was likewise given to improved salary schedules for pastors and preachers and the current lack of funding for those offices. The union theological seminary came under discussion regarding the need to increase its budget and raise entrance requirements. The synod also admonished the seminary to be careful when inducting new instructors by "securing their promise to teach in harmony with the doctrines held by the South Fukien Church of Christ."[35]

Several classical overtures were also discussed, the most important of which were: first, whether to have the mission schools observe ceremonies every Monday in honor of Sun-yat-sen, as requested by the Chinese government (this was voted down "lest they be interpreted as worship"); second, that consideration be given to having delegates from the hospitals and middle schools attend synodical meetings; and third, that the synod deal with the so-called New Theology, including the denial of the Virgin Birth and "other cardinal doctrines." With respect to this last overture, the synodical delegates, with particularly strong support from the Chinese,

> insisted in no uncertain words that teaching and preaching by both foreigners and Chinese, whether in pulpit or seminary, must be in harmony with the Bible and the standards held by the South Fukien Church of Christ, and that those who cannot give an unqualified affirmative to the gospel of Redemption in Christ Jesus our Lord should withdraw or go home. There can be no compromise here.[36]

While the three Fukien missions were gradually drawing closer together, ecumenism on a wider scale affecting virtually all of China was also attracting the mission's attention. This broader ecumenism was inspired by several factors, including the summer vacation gatherings of missionaries from various denominations at resort places like Kuliang and the interdenominational activities of worldwide Christian organizations, such as the World's Evangelical Alliance and the World's Sunday School Union. The movement was further encouraged by several organizations specifically designed to serve the entire missionary body in China. These included the Educational Association of China and the China Medical Missionary Association, as well as an interdenominational journal, the monthly *Chinese Recorder*. Finally, the gradual closing of ranks among many of the Chinese churches was furthered by the growth of Chinese nationalism and the country's improved transportation facilities.[37]

The first major example of this expanded ecumenism was the convening of the Centenary Conference at Shanghi in 1907. This was held in commemoration of 100 years of Protestant missionary work in China since the arrival of Robert Morrison of England in 1807. Delegates from over fifty societies attended, including six from the Reformed mission. Common problems were discussed and remedies sought, but the dominant theme centered around unity, that is, how best to further the creation of one single Christian church for all China. Plans called for creating a national organization, but these never developed. Instead, a new body, known as the China Continuation Conference, was formed in 1913.[38]

The China Continuation Conference was an outgrowth of discussions at the World Missionary Conference held at Edinburgh, Scotland, in 1910. Basic to these plans was the goal of greater cooperation among missionary forces throughout the world. To achieve this and related goals, Continuation Conferences were organized in various parts of Asia and Africa to do follow up work on what was discussed at Edinburgh. The first meeting of the China Continuation Conference, made up of missionaries and Chinese Christian leaders alike from throughout China, was convened at Shanghi in 1913. It urged giving priority to such matters as uniting missions of similar ecclesiastical makeup, expanding educational and medical facilities, improving standards for the training of missionaries, placing greater responsibility on the Chinese themselves, and pushing evangelism in those areas of China where little or nothing was currently being done.[39]

To assist the conference in realizing its priorities, the China Continuation Committee was created to meet on a regularly scheduled basis. In 1922, the Continuation Conference gave way to the National Christian Conference, and the Continuation Committee in turn was replaced by the National Christian Council. As described by one mission authority: "There is an immense difference between a conference—which meets, discusses, passes resolutions, and then disperses—and a council, which has a continuing existence, a permanent staff, and regular activities."[40]

The Reformed mission participated fully in all the above proceedings and in special committees that were established from time to time. The Reverend Abbe Warnshuis played an especially vital and commanding role in the first China Continuation Conference and in the several preparatory meetings that preceded it. So impressed were others with him that, in 1914, when the Conference resolved that a special National Evangelistic Secretary should be appointed, the position was offered to him. The appointment required that Warnshuis relocate at Shanghi, although he retained his membership in the Amoy mission. A generous member of the Board of Foreign Missions, the Reverend William Bancroft Hill, volunteered to become responsible for his salary.[41]

In 1919, after several years of discussion, an organization of a somewhat different kind evolved when representatives from the Reformed, English Presbyterian, other Presbyterian, London Missionary Society, American Board of Commissioners, United Brethren, and a few other missions joined in drafting a preliminary plan for establishing some type of broad union organization. Other meetings followed, leading to the convening from October 1 to 11, 1927, of the first General Assembly of the Church of Christ in China, as the new organization was called. A constitution and statement of faith were adopted and various committees established. The new organization represented a church membership of 113,000 from thirteen of China's eighteen provinces.[42] Subjects that received major consideration at this and the next session (held in 1929) included mission schools, theological education, use of literature in evangelization, medical work, church property, and the role churches should play in China's present restless political situation. In matters of doctrine, it was agreed that mission members should be permitted to retain their own creedal statements. Henceforth, General Assembly sessions were held every three or four years.[43]

Indicative of the increasing role the Chinese themselves were playing in ecclesiastical matters by this time is the fact that three-fourths of the delegates at the first General Assembly were Chinese, as were the moderator and vice-moderator. This development was in contrast to the earlier ecumenical gatherings, where only about one-third of those in attendance were Chinese. The transformation obviously pleased the Reformed mission in view of its long-standing interest in establishing a self-governing, indigenous Chinese church. As was the case with the several ecumenical gatherings following the Shanghai Conference of 1907, and so, too, with the discussions leading to the founding of the Church of Christ in China, tribute was frequently paid to the Church of South Fukian and its missions for having helped set the pattern for the China-wide ecumenical movement.

According to Kenneth Scott Latourette, one of the leading authorities on Christan missions in China, most churches in the new organization at this time were "Calvinistic in background and Congregational and Presbyterian in polity." Latourette also made the interesting observation that it was "more inclusive than any ecclesiastical union ever formed in any country." However, in indicating it was still a rather loose union, he added the caveat that the Church of Christ in China "was a name which as yet expressed a hope rather than a reality."[44]

More reassuring were the remarks by a delegate from the London Missionary Society following the third General Assembly meeting of October 1933:

> We came from different denominational origins...but from the first felt our essential unity as one Church. There were differences of background and points of view which were enrichments to the Church as a whole. There

is gradual progress to still closer union, especially in Spirit, yet no desire for rigid uniformity. There is freedom for each synod and church within its own sphere, yet the guidance of the Church as a whole and the common fellowship is a strength to all.[45]

XIII

Evangelism, 1900-1937

The task of spreading the Christian gospel and winning converts remained preeminent in the thinking and planning of the mission throughout the period 1900-1937. As Warnshuis wrote in 1901: "We must remember that evangelization is our first duty. To this, all medical and educational work must be subordinate."[1] This was reiterated in the report of 1921 declaring it was the mission's clear opinion "that our only warrant for being in China is the blood of Christ shed unto the remission of sins of those who appropriate His sacrifice through faith; and that our aim in all our institutional work is the upbuilding of the Chinese Church."[2]

With the winning of souls for Christ as the mission's primary purpose, it was natural that several new approaches to evangelism would be tried during this period. One of these involved placing greater emphasis on Sunday schools, which in the past had been considered rather impractical because of the peculiar conditions existing in China. But in response to numerous inquiries, including some from the Board of Foreign Missions, in 1910 Sunday school classes were introduced in the Amoy City churches. Their success quickly prompted repetition at Sio-khe, Tong-an, and elsewhere, with the result that within a few years the number of Sunday school scholars reached several hundred, and the practice had become a recognized part of mission activities.

Although Sunday schools were intended principally for children, the larger churches had classes for older churchgoers as well. For the latter, classes had to be based on their reading ability and understanding of the Christian message. At about the same time the Sunday school movement was taking form, daily kindergarten classes began appearing in the churches. Still later, vacation Bible schools were introduced. All of these developments received their initial start in the Amoy City churches.[3]

In some communities, book rooms were established where reading material was available on the premises and devotional literature could be purchased. The book room at Changchow became a particularly important center of evangelistic activity. It reported in 1913 as follows:

> The sales of Bibles netted more than double the amount received in 1912; and amounts taken in the Sunday School literature and Hymn Books (a very good evangelistic agency) were almost doubled. 657 Bibles or portions [and] 529 hymn books passed into buyers' hands. In addition to these, there were 88 evangelistic books, 1,936 tracts, and 1,744 sheet tracts. Nothing is given away, for we find that things paid for are appreciated more, and more sure to be read. The Book Room has not only been a granary from which this seed has been sent broadcast, but it is most encouraging that many are glad to talk with the Manager about spiritual things. Many who do not attend the church continue to come and present a good field for personal evangelistic effort.[4]

With the outbreak of the Revolution in 1911-1912 and the chaotic situation that followed, large numbers of Chinese visited the book rooms daily to find out what was taking place on the political scene. A report of 1918 regarding its use at Changchow, for example, states that "more than a hundred [users] a day have been counted."[5]

Toward the close of the period 1900-1937, book rooms in some cases were also becoming youth centers. One of the first of these was at the Tek-chhiu-kha Church, in Amoy City described here by Katherine Green:

> At the Tek-chhiu-kha Church we are decorating three good-sized rooms which are to be used for social intercourse. One room is to be fitted up with good books and magazines, one to be supplied with games (halma, skittles, etc.), and the third, which is on the ground floor,

is to be a general recreation room. This is especially to make the church home attractive to the young folks so that their friendships will be formed among their fellow Christians, and their amusements and reading be supplied by the church. It is a very vital step in attaching the young folks to the church.[6]

As in the past, members of the Reformed mission continued to publish religious literature, much of which found its way into the book rooms. A major step forward was taken in 1908 when the mission joined with the English Presbyterian and London missionary groups in creating the South Fukien Religious Tract Society. As to the work of this organization, note the following from the annual report for 1925:

The South Fukien Religious Tract Society of Amoy reports an increase of publications, 878 in Romanized and 1,101 in character. One of the newly revised and reprinted books in the Romanized is the second part of the Pilgrim's Progress, out of stock for a number of years. The Church Hymnal has also been edited and soon a new and somewhat larger book will be available.[7]

The society also assisted in issuing the bimonthly Romanized *Church Messenger* which was usually under the joint editorship of the missionary women. It sold for only a few pennies, with any deficit being made up by the society. As described in 1919, "No material of a controversial nature is printed. The news of the churches, the schools and the country, Romanized book reviews, articles on hygiene, short stories and an occasional serial comprise the twenty-six issues of the year."[8] By 1920, circulation of the eight-page paper was reaching more than a thousand readers.

Revival meetings, frequently labeled "evangelistic campaigns," became another popular means of evangelization after 1900. Some of these were carried on by local missionaries. The Reverend C. Campbell Brown of the English Presbyterian Mission, for example, directed five days of meetings (two sessions each day) at Amoy and Kulangsu in mid-February, 1905. Audiences frequently exceeded 800. Brown also directed meetings at Changchow and Sio-khe. Similarly, in the early fall of 1929 the Reverend William Angus joined with the Sio-khe pastor in an evangelistic campaign of several days in the Lam-sin area. And following the ordination of a new pastor, also in 1929, at Hoa-hong in the North River district, the Reverends Henry Poppen and Michael Veenschoten, along with some Chinese pastors attending the ordination ceremony, participated in several days of revival meetings at the church. Veenschoten, in commenting on the ordination ceremony, remarked that there was present "an apostolic fervor" which was often missing at such events in America.[9]

From time to time, outside speakers would direct the revival meetings. Among the most outstanding was George Sherwood Eddy, YMCA secretary for Asia. No less than 15,000 attended a series of his addresses at Amoy during a four-day period in early November, 1914. Other popular revivals included those given in 1915 and in later years by the Reverend Ding Li-mei, a Chinese evangelist who served as traveling secretary for the Chinese Student Volunteer Movement for the Ministry. David Yui, a graduate of Yale and employed by the Lecture Department of the YMCA, also directed meetings at Amoy and Changchow on a few occasions. One of the most popular revival leaders was Dr. John Sung, a native son of Fukien Province who had studied six years in America. His theatrical antics and realistic illustrations, along with his occasional singing, held the attention of his overflowing audiences for literally hours on end.[10]

Preparations for revivals were made long in advance in order to build up the "proper" frame of mind among the people. Care was also taken in the matter of follow-up work after the meetings had come to a close. Typical in both these respects were the activities associated with the special evangelistic services held at several locations in late 1922 by Eli Stanley Jones, a Methodist missionary serving in India, and Brewer Eddy, a brother of George Sherwood Eddy:

> The aim was to reach two classes—students and business men. Groups of volunteer workers were gathered in the churches and aroused to a sense of their own responsibility for bringing audiences to the main meetings. Each worker was made responsible for not more than five men. He was, first of all, to bring them to the meetings, and then do the necessary follow-up work until his men became members of the church; this might be within a month or five years. These workers had weekly

meetings in their churches for Bible study and
consultation, under leaders of their own choosing.[11]

By all accounts, revivals provided a spiritual uplift for many
Chinese who attended them and inspired churches to conduct
follow-up work after the leaders had moved on. Primary themes
were the importance of prayer, Bible study, and Christian service.
China's desperate needs were sometimes pointed out, with stress
being placed, of course, on the acceptance of the Christian gospel
as the only sure way of meeting those needs. That the public
authorities offered no objections to meetings like the above was
demonstrated at a luncheon given for the Reverend George Eddy
at Amoy in 1914. To quote from Eddy's report in the *Mission
Field*:

> At this luncheon, addresses of welcome were given by the
> Lieutenant Governor, the Minister of Foreign Affairs, the
> representatives of the gentry, the officials of the Chamber
> of Commerce, the educators of the city and the American
> Consul. Following this luncheon, a special meeting of the
> officials of the city was held at which I was able to present
> Christianity as the only solution for China's desperate
> need.[12]

Along with the revivals involving one or two inspiring leaders,
there were evangelistic movements of other kinds, especially
during the latter half of this period. For example, a campaign to
raise the standard of literacy using the Romanized vernacular got
underway in 1918. In the early 1920s, there was the "Forward
Movement," also termed the "Five Years Evangelistic Campaign,"
which had as its aim the preaching of the gospel within five years
to every village within a specified distance from Kulangsu.
Another movement, this one in the early 1930s and called the
"Five Year Advance," sought to double church membership within
five years. In most of these campaigns, cities and rural areas were
divided into sections, with "bands" of volunteers assigned to each.

To sustain these movements, and at the same time to provide
advice regarding follow-up work for revival campaigns, short term
"leadership training institutes" for lay persons were introduced.
Participants ranged in age from their middle teens to over fifty,
but the majority were young volunteers. The institutes lasted two
to four weeks. Some classwork was informational in nature, such

as Bible study (the Book of Acts and Paul's Epistle to the Romans were popular), church history, and fundamental church doctrines. Much of the training, however, was practical, including methods for house-to-house visitation and street preaching, suggestions for working with children, and plans for chairing meetings and leading classes in singing.[13]

Several unique forms of evangelism were also introduced late in this period. Two of Amoy's leading hotels, for example, were persuaded to place Gideon Society Bibles in some of their rooms. In the early 1930s, under direction of the Student Department of the Y.M.C.A., one of Amoy City's daily papers began carrying a brief religious message at regular intervals. Similarly, with improved roads and more bus traffic, religious tracts were distributed in the "motor stations." Following a custom used in other enterprises in China, one of the most novel forms of evangelism involved placing bulletin boards in conspicuous places on which were tacked religious posters that were changed every few weeks.

Believing that members of church consistories could play significant roles in evangelistic work, several three-day sectional conferences were held in 1936 for elders and deacons. Their purpose was "to help them better understand what the Church is and what its program in the building of the Kingdom of God is, and at the same time give them a clearer understanding of their place as office bearers in the program." The first conference, representing nineteen congregations, was held in Changchow. Present were seventy enrollees, fifty-three of whom were men and seventeen women. As reported in the *Intelligencer Leader*, "the ladies were not wives of the elders and deacons...but were all honest-to-goodness elders and deacons."[14] Meetings elsewhere had even better ratios of women to men. Reactions to the conferences were favorable. As further reported in the *Intelligencer Leader*:

> Many attending the conferences confessed that they had never before realized the sacredness of the office they were holding and had they known they would not so carelessly have assumed the office. Others confessed that they had never realized just what their relation to the minister was. Many of them said, "Why did we have to

wait all these years for an opportunity like this, how much better we could have done our work had we only known what we now know."[15]

Although revivals and other new forms of evangelism were important after 1900, much of the evangelistic activity continued to be pursued in the traditional manner, that is, with the missionaries calling on churches and stations, meeting with Chinese pastors and preachers, and visiting villages that as yet had no regular preaching. Until transportation facilities improved, evangelistic tours on the mainland proceeded much the same as in the past with some involving only a day or two, and others lasting a few weeks.

The following notations of a visit in 1902 by the Reverend Douwe Ruigh to several stations in the Sio-khe district can serve as an example of one of the more lengthy tours of this period. Starting from Sio-khe, Soa-sia was the first station Ruigh visited. The "outlook here is quite encouraging," he wrote. He went to Leng-soa next, noting that its church was "filled to overflowing each sabbath." Ruigh then journeyed to Hoe-khe, writing that "the situation is not at all encouraging, there are only four or five members and very few hearers." Next came E-lang, about which no remarks were made. This was followed by a return to Leng-soa and a trip to Chun-tiu, which he noted "almost rivals Hoe-khe in its rottenness [but] our work here is a bit more helpful." At Chich-kio and Tng-hu, the last places visited before returning to Sio-khe, he wrote that he was "very favorably impressed."[16]

Tours like Ruigh's involved, of course, much more than just calling on mission stations. Some conception of events that took place on such travels may be gathered through noting several excerpts from a lengthy letter by the Reverend Frank Eckerson. This letter describes three days' happenings that were part of a late 1916 tour in the Tong-an district. Regarding the first of the three days, he wrote:

> I have moved my spots like a perambulating leopard and am now at Sai-fo, making use of the few minutes before dark, while I rest my legs and voice from the day's walk. I think we [Eckerson does not mention the name of his companion] made about eighteen miles, and I stopped to preach five times, made three pastoral calls, and sold 53

coppers' worth of literature...and had some good and
some discouraging conversations with fellow travelers
along the way.

Eckerson describes stopping for lunch under a large banyan tree
where he purchased from two women something called "salt rice,"
or rice plus whatever may be cooked with it. It was, he noted, "one
of the biggest mixtures I've had in some time," containing, among
other things, garlic, celery, and dried shrimp. He finally yielded
to "temptation," as he put it, and opened a tin of sardines he had
been carrying and mixed it with the "concoction." Eckerson and
his companion likely spent that night in one of the mission's
chapels that lay along their route of travel. The account continues
as he describes some events of the next day:

We put in about three hours in the market, preaching and
selling literature. It was a good day for preaching, but
selling was slow. At noon we ate in the church, packed up
the baggage, and at 2:45 started the burden [i.e., burden
bearers] off. I talked business with the preacher for about
a half hour and then trailed after it. At the midway place I
struck a good crowd of men. To gather so many men in a
few minutes is unusual, and, what is more unusual, they
at once bought all the literature I had with me. They also
listened to about a fifteen minute sermon. Then I had to
hurry on, and finally caught up with my [burden bearers]
at dusk, just as they got to the Poa-nia church. That night
it was cold, and the next day it was colder...The preacher
wasn't there—had gone home to get over his malaria—so I
had evening prayers with the people, and then shortly
went to bed.

The following day being Sunday, Eckerson explains how he
spent the Sabbath:

I had to run up and down a hill a couple of times to get
warm enough to preach, but I got to a state where I could
conduct the service. I would have given a week's wages
for a streak of sunshine to stand in while I
preached....Then I went down the hill to see why a
brother hadn't been on hand; back again and had my
lunch; looked over my notes for the afternoon; talked with
a lot of the brethren who dropped in to chat; and then

conducted the afternoon service. There were two babies to be baptized.... I inquired the names and the [one] man said he hadn't thought of any yet, and asked me what I thought. It may be rather dangerous to provide names for other's children, but I didn't want any delay in the service, so I said, "Would you like a Bible name?" "Very much! Fine!" "Why not call her Sat-Liap? That is a good name, used by all nations, and has a fine meaning. Moreover, it was the name of Abraham's wife." "First rate! Fine!" So I baptized her. At that service we celebrated the Lord's Supper, too, and there were seven of us to partake.[17]

This ends Eckerson's communication, but the next day he and his companion went on to another village and to other villages after that, having, no doubt, similar experiences and perhaps a few new ones as well.

Even during this period there were, within the territory assigned to the mission, hundreds of villages visited only occasionally and others not at all. Note, for example, the experience of two missionaries who made a tour to three distant outstations in the Sio-khe district in 1919:

We were impressed anew with the sad fact that there are still many neglected fields in this province.... Riding in sedan chairs along the mountain sides, we saw many large villages in the valleys and many small hamlets nestling among the hills, where no seed, which is The Word, has ever been sown, and as we thought of the [small number of] workers and the distance of these benighted places from any church, we wondered how they would ever hear of The Light of the World.[18]

Newcomers on tour and visiting these places for the first time must have found it difficult to be optimistic about some of them—their surroundings and problems having changed very little from what they had been during the earliest years of the mission. Note in this respect a comment from the annual report of 1914:

The first visit into [such] a village shows the indescribable difficulty of interesting those who have never read a book, never seen a newspaper, know nothing

of the world fifty miles beyond them, live in dread terror
of a thousand superstitions, hope for nothing beyond
appeased appetites, know of God, at most only that His
worship is a mark of "the foreign barbarians."[19]

Chinese preachers serving in these situations merit special
sympathy when it is realized how their isolation provided few
opportunities to discuss their problems with others. They
obviously looked forward with anticipation to those few occasions
when an itinerating missionary called on them. In addition to
engaging in some preaching, these visitations called for such
things as administering the sacraments, receiving new members,
presiding at consistory meetings, and accompanying the preacher
on his "rounds" among other villages. Despite the burdens
associated with these visits, missionaries seemed to derive an
inner satisfaction from this kind of ministerial work. As explained
by the writer of the mission report of 1914, "It is a joy to spend
occasional days...in such bayoneted charges right into the enemy's
trenches."[20]

Several single missionary women also did considerable
evangelistic perambulating. Their visits, often involving a
hundred miles or more of travel, included calling on the homes of
Christian women and anyone else who showed an interest in the
"doctrine," preaching along the way to whoever would listen,
holding Bible study classes, and assisting groups of women who
were learning to read. This kind of work, of course, was generally
carried on as a corollary to other responsibilities—teaching,
visiting hospitals, and carrying on administrative duties.

Typical of such women was Nellie Zwemer, who served in
China from 1891 to 1930, spending most of the first part of those
forty years at Tong-an and the latter at Sio-khe. At both places, her
primary task was that of a teacher. At Tong-an, for example, she
was responsible for looking after the girls' and women's schools
and supervising several elementary schools in the district.[21] But
like two of her brothers, Samuel in the Arab world and Frederick
James as a classical missionary in the Dakotas, she did more than
her share of "itinerating." Indeed, in a tribute to Zwemer
following her death in 1945, a colleague and close friend wrote
that Nellie's "greatest contribution to the establishment of the
Kingdom was her work of visitation both in the towns in which

she was living and far afield among the villages in the mountains and on the plains."[22] At Tong-an, her travels were generally made alone, but at Sio-khe they were often made in the company of Leona Van der Linden, who served in China from 1909 to 1947. When touring, the two women would share their breakfasts and suppers and the same crude sleeping arrangements at night, but would go their separate ways during the day in order to cover more territory.

Katherine Green, who served in China from 1907 to 1950 (except for the period of the Second World War), replaced Nellie Zwemer at Tong-an. Like her predecessor, Green, too, literally "worked her heart out." In a letter to the *Mission Field* of August 1917, she informed readers that the women's school, which was under her charge, was "as full as can be." She also assisted at other schools, including the girls' school, which was likewise "very full," and the boys' school in which about 200 were enrolled. Green was likewise busy when it came to preaching tours. To quote further from her letter:

> As usual, our fall weather was beautiful and I limited my school work so that I might seize the opportunity thus offered for the outside preaching. In December, I made a twelve-day trip up into our beautiful An-khoe mountains, and visited my old friends at those three mountain chapels.... At Poa-nia I was royally entertained by the Mrs. Preacher and the Mrs. Teacher, both of whom were ex-Tong-an pupils.... During that twelve day trip, I walked over ninety miles and still live to tell the tale. At first I was afraid that I had gotten "soft" with so much car and auto riding while on [my recent] furlough, but it seems as if I need not worry about that.

It is interesting to note that although Green made the above tour on foot, she was one of the few missionaries who made use of a horse for traveling. To quote once more from her letter:

> We have a new horse, a more than worthy successor to my friend Brownie, and I have made some trips on him. [Brownie died while Miss Green was on furlough.] He is a lively little beastie and I am constantly expecting to find myself precipitated upon the ground, but thus far he has not thrown me. May he choose a moderately soft (not

slushy) rice field in which to deposit me when he decides
to assert his authority.[23]

Katherine Green later showed that women could be the equal
of male evangelists in the performance of other tasks too. In 1929,
she asked for a transfer to a place with less vegetation because the
pollen at Tong-an was steadily worsening her hay fever. Her
choice fell on Amoy City, which had been without resident
Reformed missionaries since their relocation seventy years
earlier at Kulangsu. Green's variegated activities at her new
location, as described in a report of 1929, would seem to indicate
that the mission had been neglectful in not stationing someone
there before on a permanent basis:

> Miss Green has organized girls' clubs, children's
> meetings, Bible classes, has got entrance into schools and
> homes and circles of society that Christians were not
> touching; has become the trusted assistant of each pastor
> and preacher in the city; has originated plans for
> house-to-house visitations, selling Gospels and street
> preaching, in whose realization all the churches have
> worked together; has put new spirit into the Bible Women
> and given wise direction to their work; was the energy
> that led to opening a library and reading room; has been
> taken into the regular monthly Preachers' Meeting of
> Amoy; has helped all the regular church meetings by her
> attendance and participation; has been training people to
> carry on what she begins.[24]

Transportation improvements gradually made evangelistic
excursions easier during this period. Because travel by boat
remained one of the most important means for covering long
distances, some of the earliest advances occurred in this mode. As
to the need for such improvements, the Reverend Harry Boot
remarked in 1904 that the trip from Amoy to Changchow "was
noted mainly for its duration, thirteen hours to go thirty miles."[25]
The introduction of steam-powered launches, which earlier had
been prohibited by treaty,[26] cut this time somewhat, but the
launches could go only as far as Chioh-be. After that, because of
the shallowness of the river, travelers had to transfer to slower
man-powered craft to complete the trip.

Thanks in large part to the efforts and foresight of Dr. John

Snoke, the mission acquired a gasoline-powered motor boat in the summer of 1913. Snoke described it as follows: "The boat is 35 feet long, has a 7 foot beam, seats 40 people, and with 40 people on board draws 10 inches of water and makes 9 to 10 miles per hour. It is fitted with a 17-horsepower Ferro 3-cylinder engine and a 20 inch screw." In a trial run made with Snoke and about a dozen passengers and considerable baggage, it made the trip to Changchow in less time than a steam launch, but the real test came in continuing the trip to Sio-khe. Here, it fared even better. To quote further from Snoke's report:

> We had high flood water and a very strong current, but we made the trip in ten and one-half hours, as against three and a half days for the native boats under these flood conditions.... A few days later the boat [returned] to Changchow down river in five hours. It usually takes a day and a half.

Travel by this means also cut expenses by more than half.[27]

Road building programs also gradually altered some of the old ways of travel. The future significance of this is clearly brought out in an excerpt from a report of 1923: "Journeys which now occupy days of strenuous walking or uncomfortable chair-riding [will soon] be accomplished in a few hours by auto, and more time and energy [can] then be invested in the actual work of preaching, teaching, and home visiting." As missionaries were wont to do, the writer of the report could not pass up the opportunity to draw a parallel between what was taking place in China and the travels of the early missionaries: "May the new roads," he wrote, "be to China what the Roman roads were in the early days of the Church—highways for the more rapid spread of the glorious gospel of salvation."[28]

By 1930, there was considerable evidence indicating that roads were indeed making the missionary's task much easier. Thus, in 1929, the Reverend Edwin Koepe, who had been serving in China since 1919, wrote from Tong-an:

> Many roads are being opened and cars are already running in five directions. The greatest progress has been made on our An-khoe road. With autos already running on each end of it and [with] only six miles through the mountains in the middle yet to be built, we have a reasonable hope

that within the coming year our work in that section will
be greatly facilitated.

Koeppe added that "several of our outstations can now be reached
by auto-bus."[29]

Better transportation facilities were also appearing elsewhere.
For example, the Reverend H. Michael Veenschoten in his report
of 1930 concerning the Changchow district, called attention to
"the constantly increasing use" being made by the missionaries
"of the available public motor service." He also took note of the
new railroad lines being opened up—one of about eight miles to
Soa-sia, where the mission had a church, and another of thirty-two
miles to Amoy.[30] Improved roads were even putting in an
appearance in the rugged North River district. To quote from
another mission report, this one of 1928:

> A wide motor road was laid through the city [of Leng-na],
> running out into the country fifteen miles to the East and
> West of the city. The first motor made its appearance in
> February. Since then a regular service has been
> established. Plans are underway to connect Leng-na with
> Chow-chow-fu, in Canton Province, and also with
> Changchow.[31]

Until macadamized "dressings" were placed on these new
roads, however, the combination of wet weather and soft clay
sometimes left the roads virtually impassable. There was another
problem also awaiting solution, as Dr. Harold Veldman, writing
from Tong-an, pointed out in 1929: "The increased motor traffic
has introduced another type of work into our surgical wards. The
people have not yet learned to gauge the speed of an auto, or how
to step off a moving car."[32]

As in the past, missionary recruits spent several weeks among
the various districts getting practical field experience by being
"farmed out" in turn to more experienced missionaries. Thus, the
Reverend William Giebel, in a letter of 1910 to the *Mission Field*,
describes how he initially spent some time during his first year in
China with Snoke at Sio-khe, then with De Pree at Changchow,
followed by Eckerson at Tong-an, and finally with Warnshuis at
Kulangsu.[33] The value of such experience was succinctly pointed
out by Harry Boot in early 1904 (he had arrived the previous
year) after having made an eight-day trip with Warnshuis that

covered more than a hundred miles: "I really enjoyed that trip very much; it gave me an insight into the nature of the work, and how to go at it, that is not obtained from books; and I might have sat in Amoy all year and not learned that practical application."[34]

Going on these tours was something of an eye-opener for new arrivals. Frederick Weersing, for example, who had been sent out in 1915 to oversee the mission's education program, was surprised at how Chinese reacted to hearing the gospel message for the first time. He described his feelings in a letter written a few months after his arrival in China, and after having accompanied Eckerson on a preaching tour:

> Again and again on the trip I listened to the telling of the, to us, old and perfectly familiar stories of Christ's work and of Bible characters and incidents to people who had never heard of them before and who stood in open-mouthed amazement as they listened. "What is that you say? He could see? The blind man could see? He spit on his eyes and then he could see? Well, well! How long is this ago? Where was it? What was his name? And you have come to tell us? You want no money then? No? Peace? No, we have no peace. We always have trouble and work and sadness. Saved from sin? I don't know what you say. Wait till my man comes home. We women can't understand." And so on, and on. All through the conversation they put in, "Sit down." "Come in and sit down." "Come in and have some tea." "But do sit down now." "Yes, I hear what you say, but won't you sit down now?" And so on until you leave.[35]

The beauty of the mountains and the pastoral appearance of the countryside excited newcomers on these tours in the same manner they had impressed veteran missionaries upon their own arrival in China. The following was written by a new arrival after accompanying Eckerson on a tour in the Tong-an district:

> After staying over Sunday here, we again took up our way over the mountains and through the valleys and passes. I could not if I had space tell you of the beauty of the scenery, the wonders of nature and the things of interest it offered along the way. For this reason we enjoyed

walking a large part of the way—enjoying mountains and valleys, trees and flowers and ferns, rivers, ravines, and waterfalls. Besides these there was the interest lent by the observation of the people, their modes of life and work and the study of the colloquial.... Everywhere the farmers were harvesting their crops—digging sweet potatoes and taking them to market. The rice harvest we saw in all its stages: cutting, binding, threshing, drying the grain, and in some places the harvest had been already received. The one harvest reminded me of the great need of another, which, let us pray, shall soon be ours—or better, His.[36]

There were, of course, occasional cheerless moments on these tours. For the novice traveler, there was certain to be some fatigue at the end of the day. There also was inclement weather to contend with. The Reverend Lyman Talman, for example, in describing his initiation to Chinese modes of travel soon after his arrival in 1917, began his account of "My First Walking Trip" with this memoranda: "Duration of trip, 13 days; distance covered, about 120 miles, of which I walked about 100; good weather, 3 days; rain, 10 days."[37]

Like other newcomers before him, Talman was impressed by the friendliness of the Chinese he met and was enamored of the scenery; but he was less than complimentary about some other matters. He noted the narrow, slippery clay paths that had to be traversed; the netting that had to be used at night to keep from being eaten by myriads of buzzing mosquitoes; the steepness of many of the mountain trails; the rivers that had to be waded because floods had washed away bridges; the tea offered by friendly Chinese in cups that were never washed (Talman explained that the Chinese considered it a waste of good tea to keep the insides of the cups clean); and the uncomfortable Chinese beds consisting of boards with a piece of matting for a mattress.

New missionaries coming to China also continued to express surprise at the nature of the Chinese church services. This is clearly shown in a short article "Worship in a Chinese Church," written in 1916 by Dr. Taeke Bosch a few months after his arrival at Amoy:

Could you worship in a Chinese Church? Suppose you
enter a large hall with a ten feet high screen dissecting
the church into two parts, a part for all the men and a part
for the women, for men and women would better not see
one another while worshipping—a little of this would
better not hurt even in our enlightened countries. From
the screens and snifflings, you make out that women take
all the children along to church and do not provide them
adequately with handkerchiefs. Sometimes a more or less
dirty dog wanders about to the great hilarity of the
youngsters; sometimes this dog is met by a friendly
neighbor dog, to the great hilarity of both dogs and
youngsters; sometimes this dog meets a hostile dog, to the
great disturbance of the foreign visitor, but the Chinese
themselves keep on listening.

There is nothing of the style we find in some of our
American Churches. The organ is poorly played, the songs
are poorly sung, but everyone sings. There is something
emphatic about the Chinese preacher, something of
having found the solution of a century-old problem
lingers about him, something of joy of having seen the
light experienced by the man formerly blind who has his
sight restored. And his people do worship, though as a
rule his sermons are not deep, for his audience requires a
simple presentation of God's word. After the sermon, the
collection is taken up, a form of worship in which again
everyone partakes, even the youngest toddler. The
congregation having been exhorted to walk the heavenly
way, and having received the benediction, is dismissed. [38]

Getting accustomed to chairing a Chinese consistory meeting,
especially with respect to the outward appearance of the members,
also took some mental adjustment for new arrivals. The Reverend
Harvey Todd describes in 1920 one of the first such meetings he
attended:

Not one of them as he entered the room removed his hat,
for the reason that none of them wore hats. They had not
blackened their shoes before coming to church, but this
was not due to personal untidiness so much as to the fact
they were barefooted and wore on their feet only wooden

soles which were kept on to the bottoms of their feet by
straps which passed over their toes. Their coats and
trousers being blue but not blue-serge had never been
pressed up neatly because the Chinese do not consider
that as essential to good dress. Furthermore not one of
them wore a white shirt or collar because the Chinese
only launder those belonging to Western people. [39]

Despite the variety of forms that evangelism took during this
period and the enthusiasm of the participants, evangelism could
not be considered a great success in terms of increases in church
membership, as demonstrated by these statistics:[40]

Date	Number of Communicants	Received on Confession
1900	1374	99
1905	1509	159
1910	1756	121
1915	2069	124
1920	2945	148
1925	3617	210°
1930	3432	157
1931	3489	138
1932	3370	96
1933	3289	89
1934	3348	158
1935	3551	392
1936	3850	318
1937	3850	230
1938	3916	145
1939	3707	184

(°The comparatively large increase between 1915 and 1925
resulted from the annexation of the North River district
in 1919.)

Scattered political disturbances and bandit activities obviously
interfered with normal church growth, especially in the 1920s and
early 1930s. So too did the increasingly tense international
situation, which finally culminated in war with Japan in 1937.
There also were the usual impediments discussed previously that
kept church membership down.[41]

Although this period closed without too much visible evidence
of winning large numbers of new souls, there were, of course,

gains in related matters. For example, although the number of communicants increased by only slightly more than a hundred (from 3,432 to 3,551) during the "Five Year Movement" of 1930-1934, the mission, always looking at the bright side, reported that "the work accomplished during the five years was eminently worthwhile. The deepening of the spiritual life, the sense of need, and the longing for spiritual quickening, are showing their results in the churches."[42] For future growth, there was also the fact that the number of outstations and preaching places increased from 65 to 84 between 1930 and 1934.

A positive development in church growth during this period was the gradual increase in the percentage of women members, especially after ca. 1920. Whereas in the past, women constituted a third or less of the church membership, by 1925 it was about equally divided between men and women.[43] As to why women's membership had been significantly lower, an excerpt from the mission's report of 1909 concerning the Sio-khe district gives several interesting reasons:

> [First], the lack of foreign workers and the consequent lack of regularity in visiting the stations; second, that this district has no Bible women; third, that so many of the preachers have married wives who are not Christians, or who are not themselves qualified to teach others; fourth, that the men who are counted Christians have not Christianity enough to feel responsible for the salvation of their wives and children.[44]

But changes for the better were taking place with respect to Chinese women. The Reverend Henry Beltman, in an article published in the *Christian Intelligencer*, wrote in 1926, "One becomes fairly depressed when one sees the subjection to which Chinese women have been held. But one's heart leaps with joy when we see here and there the breaking of the dawn of a new day."[45] One of the earliest examples of change was the gradual removal of the screens that had traditionally separated the women from the men during worship services. But the most important step forward in behalf of women churchgoers was taken in December, 1916, when the South Fukien Synod upheld the right of churches to appoint women as deacons.[46] It was not the Reformed mission, however, that helped set the pattern for this development, but rather some London Missionary Society churches, which as early as the 1890s were already using deaconesses.[47] The extent to which the Reformed mission eventually followed the practice is clearly evident in the makeup of the district conferences that were held for consistory members in 1936. As many as a third of those in attendance were women, including not only deaconesses but also several elders.[48]

XIV

Developments in Education, 1900-1937

In the usual trio of missionary operations—evangelistic, educational, and medical—the educational field undoubtedly showed the greatest advance during this period. Not only did the number of schools and enrollments increase significantly, but education became more self-supporting as the Chinese churches enlarged their contributions and school fees steadily increased. There also was greater cooperation among the Reformed, English Presbyterian, and London Society missions in matters of education. Last, but by no means least, schools introduced more Western learning into their curriculums in response to China's so-called "awakening."

The primary aim remained what it had always been—namely, to acquaint the students with the Christian message. As the Reverend Philip Pitcher, principal of the Middle School for almost thirty years, wrote in 1908:

> We should never lose sight of what these schools stand for, viz., a Christian education, the *raison d'être* for our existence. Other schools there may be of the very highest excellence [but] ours have a special mission, i.e., to lead these benighted souls to the beginning of wisdom. Not that it is my idea to transform our schools into churches and chapels, but into sanctuaries where truth and light shine in mid-day brightness, and where the pupils realize in fullest measure that only an education that builds for eternity is worth having.[1]

Despite the importance of education, it was not to be pursued at the expense of more traditional avenues of evangelization. A statement made in 1921 by Frederick Weersing, who served as overseer of primary education from 1915 to 1922, indicates that the missionaries were emphatic on this point:

> Christian education...should never be allowed to sap the strength of organized church work, either by taking up an undue share of the available funds, or by usurping the time of the missionaries and pastors. That would be parallel to harvesting a large crop and afterwards letting it be destroyed by the weather for lack of barns and granaries to store it in. Each has its proper sphere and place, and each has a claim on the support of all ardent Christians.[2]

By 1930, the gamut of the mission schools extended from the primary departments, through middle schools, and on to the theological seminary. Primary schools continued to be the most essential of the various levels of instruction. As described previously, the mission considered a student's mind at this level to be most susceptible to new ideas like Christianity.[3] Moreover, it was still a truism in China during the early 1900s that primary schooling was the only education the vast majority of young people would ever receive. Writing in 1906, Philip Pitcher noted that pupils entered school from ages seven to eleven and remained only from one to five years. In one district, he noted that 50 percent remained only one year and only 33 percent stayed two years. These statistics, Pitcher reported, probably represented a fair estimate of the situation among all the other districts. Of the pupils finishing the program, only a very small percentage entered higher schools of learning.[4]

The mission's goal continued to be the establishment of a day school wherever there was an organized church, and a boarding school at every district headquarters. Day schools were also founded at some outstations when there were assurances that ten pupils would enroll and a certain amount of funding would be subscribed locally. Schools continued to vary in size and efficiency. The norm was four to six grades for day schools and eight grades for boarding schools. Because of their locations at district headquarters, boarding schools had more foreign supervision and better facilities. Most of the increase in the number of primary schools occurred during the early 1900s. Day schools, for example, more than doubled between 1900 and 1910. Thereafter, the increase continued at a slower pace and in some years actually declined, due primarily to the rise in the number of government schools.

Compared with standards of previous years, primary schools steadily improved after 1900, although at times they still had to put up with teachers addicted to traditional Chinese methods. This situation gradually changed for the better as more teachers were drawn from the middle schools—where they became exposed to the "new learning" and had an opportunity to take one or two teacher training courses. Demands among Chinese parents that their children receive more Western learning also had a wholesome effect on discarding antiquated teaching methods. Helpful, too, was the practice of some church consistories to appoint special committees to visit the schools and submit reports regarding their standards.

Despite what the Amoy Girls' School and the boys' Middle School were doing in the area of teacher training, the shortages continued. This was due in part to a growing demand for teachers in government schools, and in part to low salaries. An indication of what was considered a fair salary for primary school teachers is provided by Pitcher in an article written in 1906 based on a salary schedule approved that year by the South Fukien Synod:

> Those who have been through the Middle School and Theological School receive $6 per month; others, $5.50. If married, the teacher receives an increase of 50 cents a month. Each child receives an additional allowance of 50 cents a month. Length of service and proficiency are always rewarded. The Mission pays the larger share of the salaries, but every school is required to pay a proportion.[5]

Unfortunately, as with preachers' salaries, it was not always possible to honor what the synod suggested. The teacher shortage was especially acute among girls' schools. This was due in part to the old custom of girls marrying young and remaining in their homes after marriage. There also was a growing tendency for girls to continue their studies beyond the usual time when they would begin teaching.

Various efforts were made in the early 1900s to coordinate the work of primary schools. These included attempts by the synod to introduce a common program of study, but these efforts did not fare too well until late in the period. Attempts were also made to introduce uniform examinations in hopes such measures would bring an end to irregularities currently existing in the schools, while indicating those that were weak. Such a measure could also encourage teachers to put forth greater effort to avoid embarrassment when the results of the examinations became known. These efforts had mixed results, at least initially, although they were quite well received in the better schools.

In explaining why some schools failed to improve, Pitcher concluded it was partly due to the whims of teachers but also to local officials and parents having their own views about doing things or being indifferent to what was happening.[6] Superintendent Weersing in 1920 explained the root of the problem this way: "The Chinese have no idea of strictness and accuracy such as we have, and it has often been said that the greatest curse of China is *chha-put-to*, a common expression current everywhere in China, meaning 'approximately.'"[7]

A major step forward was taken in 1918 when, after more than three years of discussion, the mission created a Boys' Primary School Committee as a permanent department of missionary activity. With an annual budget of $600, its main purpose was to develop greater uniformity among elementary schools. As described by the committee's "superintendent" in the mission's annual report for 1920:

> To accomplish our aim we have divided each semester's work into four parts and print monthly test questions for every subject in each grade which every teacher is obliged to use. It is manifestly impossible for a central office to look over the returns for all monthly tests from every school, but we take occasion to look at them when we visit the school and have found them of great value in showing teachers not only how to ask questions and what kind of questions to ask, but also what points to emphasize in their teaching and what is expected in the way of standard accomplishment for pupils in every grade and subject.
>
> In addition to the work involved in the preparation of tests and examinations, our routine work includes the

inspection of schools, assignment of teachers, division of appropriations, selecting text-books, revision of the curriculum, keeping records and statistics, and a considerable volume of correspondence with principals and teachers concerning almost every phase of school work.[8]

The committee also concerned itself with raising funds for buildings and current expenses, recruiting boys for the Middle School and seminary, and stressing the essential reason for Christian schools. With respect to the last mentioned, the superintendent made this observation:

I am very much afraid that in our boys' schools too much is made of educational and material problems and not enough of Jesus Christ. In many places education is put before religion, with a resulting stagnation of the spiritual life of teachers and pupils alike.[9]

To assist in the committee's paperwork, a full-time Chinese secretary was employed. This became increasingly necessary when it was decided to issue a monthly *Education Newsletter* as a means of keeping teachers informed of important educational developments elsewhere in China. The *Newsletter* attracted widespread attention with numerous requests for copies coming from teachers outside the mission, even from as far away as Shanghai and Peking.

Accommodations at some primary schools in the early 1900s still left a great deal to be desired. Note for example, a communication by the Reverend David Ruigh written in 1904 describing the school at Changchow:

The room is dark and dingy. Even on Sunny days the light is insufficient. How pupils manage to study on dark and cloudy days is beyond my comprehension. With but one door and three and a half windows, and almost surrounded by other buildings, it is exceedingly hot, close and unsanitary in summer time. In short, the place is so unattractive and unsatisfactory in every way that it is surprising we can secure even the small number now attending. As for furniture, suffice it to say that the pupils supply their own desks and chairs! No maps, charts, globes or any of the furnishings which in ordinary circumstances are deemed indispensable.[10]

Fortunately, financial support for schools gradually improved during this period, although assistance from the home Board of Foreign Missions was generally minimal and declined in times of economic hardship. The big contributor was the Woman's Board of Foreign Missions. Thanks to it, each of the four district headquarters by 1906 had a modern boarding school for girls. Moreover, whenever any facilities proved inadequate, the Woman's Board, as soon as it was able, provided funds to either enlarge them or construct new ones in their place. Although it tended to concentrate on the needs of women and girls, the Woman's Board contributed to the education of boys from time to time as well. Thus, in 1906, it provided $3,000 for the boys' primary school at Kulangsu and promised a similar amount in the near future.

In some instances, donations came from several sources, as was the case in 1915 at Tong-an when a new boys' school was needed. In the past, the old school had to share space in the small mission compound not only with the church and parsonage but with residencies for the teacher, the Bible woman, the Reverend Eckerson, and the sexton. Moreover, the compound was situated on a piece of ground lower than the street, so that, as Eckerson reported, "We live in a stagnant drain in rainy weather."[11] Gifts for building a new school came from Lily Duryee (given in memory of her sister Alice who had served at Tong-an) and from the Talmage sisters (given in honor of their mother). Help also came from Americans who had visited Tong-an. But the bulk of the money came from Sunday school contributions in America during the 1913 Easter season, which also happened to be the time that the centenary of the great David Livingstone was being observed. It was thus appropriate that the new school was called the Livingstone Easter School.

What happened with respect to gifts for education at Tong-an was repeated many times elsewhere. Donations in the mid-1920s from the Reformed churches in Sioux County, Iowa, for example, helped meet construction costs for a new primary school for boys at Sio-khe. Similarly, in 1926, a generous gift from the Young Men's Bible Class of the Fifth Reformed Church of Grand Rapids, Michigan, made possible the purchase of seats and desks, laboratory apparatus, and bugles and drums for the boys' primary school at Leng-na. Some churches also helped out with salaries. Thus when Frederick Weersing was sent out in 1915 to undertake the oversight of the mission's educational work, four Reformed churches in Whiteside County, Illinois (Fulton, Morrison, Ustick, and Newton), took it upon themselves to pay his salary of approximately $1,200 as well as his and Mrs. Weering's travel expenses.

The most impressive source of help for education during this period came from the Chinese themselves. In the matter of new construction, they assisted especially by furnishing building sites and donating their labor. For maintaining the schools once they were built, both Chinese churches and students were expected to contribute their fair share. The growing importance of student fees is clearly seen in what occurred at the Kulangsu boarding school for girls in 1912:

> The year was a record year in number of pupils, and also in fees, which amounted to $1,552, which covered more than half the running expenses of the school, including all the salaries of all the Chinese teachers, the repairs, new furniture, taxes, and all other expenses. Five years ago the fees amounted to $584, just one third of the year's expenses, and ten years ago they were only one-ninth of the expenses. [12]

The Kulangsu girls' school set the pace for girls' institutions. Beginning its work in 1870 with twelve students in a small rented house in Amoy City, it moved to Kulangsu in 1880. At the time of the move, the school had about thirty pupils and a total expense of $345, with the pupils paying a fee of about one dollar each per term. In 1899, thanks to the Woman's Board of Foreign Missions, the school moved to a new home not far from the old. The school grew steadily during the early 1900s in terms of both facilities and enrollment. By the time of its fiftieth anniversary in 1920, it comprised a five-building complex and 338 students, of whom about two-thirds were day students. Expenses were slightly more than $5,000, of which about three-fifths were covered by fees. Even more impressive was its educational program comprising a first rate primary department and the first two years of middle school work. To handle all of this, the staff in 1920 consisted of the foreign principal and fourteen Chinese women (all former pupils of the school) and four Chinese men (three of whom were part-time). The men taught Mandarin and Chinese classics. Occasional help was also provided by various missionary women residing at Kulangsu.[13]

Nearly 1,500 girls had enrolled in the school by the time of its fiftieth anniversary in 1920. A look at what some of its graduates were doing, as reported in 1918, gives a clear indication of the school's success and its wide influence:

> One is studying in Northfield, Mass., one is in Peking, one is in Ginling College, Nanking, and two others in a high school in the same city. Two are studying in Shanghai, one in Foochow, four in the Hackett Medical College, Canton, one teaching and two studying in the Philippine Islands. Four are teaching in Singapore and two in Rangoon. Many are married and living in these and other places equally distant, such as Penang, Java, and other islands. A rough estimation gives 40 as scattered in these various places, besides nearly 50 others who this year have been teaching either in our own schools or in other schools in the Amoy region.[14]

In contrast to the Kulangsu school, enrollment at the other girls' schools showed only limited increase at first. This was due in part to the lingering view in the "countryside" that education for girls was a waste of time. Enrollment was also hampered by poor accommodations and limited curriculums. As these conditions improved, so too did enrollments. Also helpful in attracting more students were the house visitations by the local Chinese clerical staff, especially those of the Bible women, as they encouraged education for girls. Another stimulus was the fact that more educated young men, especially Christian young men, were preferring educated wives—a development that no doubt helps explain why more applications were coming in from parents who wished to enroll their daughters in a mission school. Finally, the mission itself increasingly stressed the importance of educating women. Note, for example, the comments on this matter in the annual report of 1913:

> From the ranks of their studentry must come the future school mistresses of China. Thence must come the future

Bible women, matrons of schools, hospitals, and orphanages. There are being formed the characters of wives and mothers of a nation. The day will soon come, when in this Republic, also, the family will be considered the unit, and the hand that rocks the cradle will rule the State. And these, our Girls' Boarding Schools may be called upon to serve as an important factor in shaping the destiny of Church and State here. [15]

Although girls were not provided with an education beyond the primary grades until after 1900, boys had had that advantage since 1881, when the Reformed and English Presbyterians cooperated in founding the union Middle School, later called Talmage College. The school's aims in 1900 were the same as when it was founded, namely, to provide young men with professional training, especially as teachers and ministers, and to serve as an evangelizing agency for exposing non-Christian students to the gospel message. A look at a report of 1903 indicates that to achieve these aims, the work of the school had changed very little over the years:

The students have done faithful work along the lines mapped out, and with rare exceptions all have passed creditable examinations on the following subjects: the Old and New Testaments; the "Classics," both historical and poetical; composition; reading and writing the Romanized Colloquial; History (China and England); Geography; Physiology; Elements of Astronomy; Arithmetic; Algebra; and Physical Geography. Under the instruction of Mrs. Pitcher, the boys have produced some excellent work in map drawing and free hand drawing, and also in penmanship, or more correctly, brushmanship, as the boys use a brush for writing, not a pen. [16]

Although the basic curriculum remained the same, a few new courses were added during the early 1900s, including English, nineteenth century history, advanced mathematics, biology, physics, and additional work in the classics. [17]

A landmark in the history of the Middle School was reached in 1909 when a fifth year was added, followed soon by a sixth year. These developments prompted the institution on January 2, 1914, to assume the name of "Talmage College," taken in grateful memory of the Reverend John Van Nest Talmage who had devoted forty years of his life to the Amoy mission. In celebration of the school's improved status, about forty of its alumni met a few days later for a happy reunion and organized the "Students' and Alumni Association."

Adding post-secondary years was in keeping with what was long considered a deficiency of the Middle School. As explained by Warnshuis in 1907:

> The Church must have better trained men than it can now get. Just as twenty years ago the Middle School was established to meet that demand, in order that the ministry in this Amoy Church might be leaders in the new China that was believed to be coming, so now the demand is for still higher education in order that they may continue to have as good an education as any in the community in which they are working. *For the sake of the Church* a college is demanded.[18]

Warnshuis also pointed out that if Middle School graduates were sent elsewhere to college, they might encounter some difficulty because of their need to adjust to a new dialect.

The additional two years of course work were dropped after a short time. This was done partly because of insufficient funds and lack of foreign instructors but also because, as explained in the annual report of 1919, "the Mission now has a share in the Fukien University at Foochow where we can send our students at less expense to ourselves and at a greater benefit to the pupils."[19] The school continued to use the name Talmage College, however.

A review of the period 1900-1920 reveals that 473 students enrolled at Talmage. Of these, only 112 completed the prescribed program. This small percentage (slightly more than one in four) was due in part to the school's high academic standards. The high esteem in which these standards were held can be seen in the extent its graduates were accepted by other institutions. In 1921, for example, two students were accepted for entrance to the pre-medical department at Peking Union Medical School and a third was placed on the waiting list with assurance of admission later. Considering that the entering class was limited to twenty-five students and less than 30 percent of the candidates from throughout China were accepted, Talmage had reason to feel proud. Similarly, in 1924, five of its graduates were accepted by Amoy University, two by Fukien Christian University, two by Canton Christian College, and six by the mission's own theological seminary.

The size of the teaching staff was enlarged during this period, although not proportionately to the rising enrollment. By 1921, the staff numbered thirteen Chinese and four foreign instructors. The enlarged staff obviously increased the school's expenses, but, as with other aspects of mission work, these were being increasingly met by the Chinese themselves. In 1921, for example, the three missions were responsible for less than one-third of Talmage's annual budget, and the boarding department, which had been a major item in the past, was entirely self-supporting.

Responsibility for overseeing the principal and his staff was for many years in the hands of a Board of Management made up entirely of foreigners. In 1917, in order to give Chinese a greater voice in running the school, a new organization was created known as the Board of Trustees. It consisted of twelve persons, with equal representation of Chinese and foreigners. The board was reorganized again in 1931 and once more in 1934. After 1934, it was composed of the principal of the school, two members appointed by the South Fukien Synod, four by the Alumni Association, two by the Reformed mission, and four others elected by these nine.[20] Meanwhile, in 1929, through efforts of the principal, Herman Renskers, the day-to-day administration was placed in the hands of three men—Renskers and two Chinese. One of the latter, Mr. K. G. Chen, was appointed chairman. As an alumnus of Talmage and the holder of an M. A. from Columbia University Teachers' College (which was also Rensker's alma mater), Chen was well qualified for the position. Bringing more Chinese into the administration at Talmage was in keeping with the trend taking place among the operations of the South Fukien Church.

In the early 1920s, Talmage College, prompted by lack of space for campus expansion and the inflated land prices at Kulangsu, began making plans for relocating at Changchow. The need for expanding the school's facilities is demonstrated by the steady growth of the student body from 60 in 1915 to 112 in 1917, 135 in

1919, and 245 in 1922. The choice of Changchow as a site was a good one. It had a population at this time variously estimated at between 100,000 and 200,000, and until recent years had surpassed Amoy City in size. The mission's district "headquarters" that was located there had five churches and more than a dozen outstations under its care. Because Changchow lay athwart the line dividing the territories assigned (in accordance with the comity of missions) to the Reformed church and the London Missionary Society, the latter was also strongly entrenched in the area—a fact that could help student enrollment at Talmage. In addition to a hospital and missionary residences, the London group had several places of worship in the vicinity.

The mission acquired an eighteen-acre tract of land in Changchow, and an architect, a Mr. Kale from Shanghai, prepared a general scheme for the new campus. The mission gave its approval at a meeting in July, 1923, and construction soon began on a combination classroom/administration building, a dormitory, and faculty residences. School opened at the new location in the spring of 1925 with an enrollment of 203. Since this was only twenty less than the previous year, any fears that the move would result in the loss of a large number of students was alleviated. Work on new buildings continued during the spring term, and by fall a second classroom building was ready, bringing the total number of classrooms to fifteen. Much of the credit for the rapid completion of the buildings must go to the Reverend Henry Beltman, who served as construction supervisor.[21]

Along with expanding academic programs, extracurricular activities gradually became an important feature of all the schools. Athletics for the upper grades became especially popular and were encouraged by the foreign staff and further stimulated by contests with other schools. The extent to which physical education became a part of Talmage's activities is clearly evident in this excerpt from the school's 1935 catalogue:

> In addition to military drill, all boys are required to take at least three hours of athletic exercises a week. A complete schedule is arranged so that each boy has a chance to learn the rudiments of the different track and field events as well as the more popular games such as basketball, football, volleyball and tennis. Two basketball

courts, two volleyball courts, a tennis court, jumping pits,
a football field and a running track supply our athletic
needs.[22]

Practice in military drill received an impetus when Dr. Taeke
Bosch kindly consented to drill the students three times a week.
Dr. Bosch, who served on the mission hospital staff from 1915 to
1931, had once been a sergeant in the Dutch army.

In time, physical education was also introduced in the girls'
schools. As described by one of the missionaries in 1926, this was
just one more example of the gradual emancipation of Chinese
women:

> Seven years ago, a large athletic meet was held in this city
> [of Amoy], and there was not one girl student who took
> part in the meet. Last fall a similar athletic meet was held
> and about one out of every four participants was from
> some girls' school.[23]

Music, too, became a popular extracurricular activity in the
schools, and often served as a unique means for presenting the
gospel message. A cantata, "The Star of Light," put on in 1916 by
thirty-three students and accompanied by a small orchestra, was a
completely new venture for the Chinese community. The
performance packed one of the churches, including "the aisles,
windows, and entrances." Taking his cue from the popularity of
the school's string orchestra, the Reverend George Kots, one of
the instructors at Talmage College who served in China from
1923 to 1926, organized a twenty-piece band in 1925 which was
soon in great demand at various church functions and for concerts
in city parks. A particularly different kind of entertainment for
Chinese was the Christmas musical put on in 1921 involving a
mixed chorus of twenty young women from the Amoy Girls'
School and fifteen young men from Talmage College. The
following account indicates that social changes were obviously
taking place in China with respect to mixing the sexes:

> Though a [similar] attempt was made five years ago, public
> sentiment was still too strongly opposed to it. This time it
> found such favorable response that it was not even
> considered out of place to have a flashlight picture taken at
> the close of the program.[24]

By the mid-1930s, the curriculum of the Girls' Middle School was devoting considerable attention to developing music teachers for primary schools and choir directors for churches.

A major figure in music education during this period was Stella Veenschoten, who came to China with her husband in 1917 and, except for the period of the Second World War, labored at the mission until 1951. As an accomplished pianist, she was in great demand as an accompanist at various musical events and played a major role in founding glee clubs in the mission schools. She also assisted in starting an orchestra at the Girls' Middle School using only Chinese instruments.

One of the challenges facing mission schools after 1900 was the competition from the Chinese government as it began founding more public schools. There was even talk in missionary circles that the Chinese government was planning to establish "within ten years, primary schools to the number of one for every two hundred families...and higher schools in proportioned number."[25] This did not cause much concern at first because of the low regard in which government schools were held. But their situation gradually improved. In 1908, for example, Pitcher reported, after visiting three government elementary schools and two government middle schools: "If we in our Mission primary schools expect to keep up with the procession we will have to keep moving too, or we will all fall behind in that race in which we had such a splendid start."[26] A report of 1915 also indicates that the government schools were making significant strides:

> The government schools are doing better work than before and better methods are used. A class in arithmetic is no longer taught by a teacher putting two problems on the board, working them out and leaving the class to copy them while he goes away to spend the hour smoking. The schools open early in the term and close late.[27]

Despite continued improvements in public education, the mission still did not become overly alarmed. Thus, when the government began prescribing certain curricula that all schools should follow, the mission thought it would have little trouble adhering to them as long as it could retain Bible study. Indeed, as late as 1921, according to Weersing, mission schools were adhering more closely to the government's school program than were government schools themselves. He ascribed this to "the

Christian schools' being better managed, and better taught, and staffed by more faithful and earnest teachers than...the Government schools." Weersing especially singled out mathematics, science, and English as being invariably better taught in the mission schools.[28]

The mission's rather sanguine feeling gave way to one of apprehension, however, when the government in the mid-1920s began considering a set of regulations requiring mission schools to register with public authorities and to abide with whatever standards that might entail. As described in the mission's report of 1926, such a requirement posed not only a threat to the Christian character of the mission schools but also ran counter to their evangelistic purpose:

> Registration, among other questions, involves property control, government supervision and inspection, nationality of [the] principal and religious education. Religion is not permitted to be given as a required subject, nor is religious propaganda allowed in class instruction. Compulsory chapel is also banned.[29]

The regulations, it should be noted, applied to all religions in China, not just Christianity.

Meanwhile, as described in a letter by Tena Holkeboer, who had been laboring in China since 1920, the government presented the schools with a problem of a different kind:

> Another difficulty has been in regard to the Sun Yat-sen Memorial Ceremony which the Kuomintang insists all schools shall observe weekly. This included the reading of that portion of his will urging the completion of the republican revolution, three minutes of silent meditation, and three bows before the picture of the departed hero. To many this service has no significance except as a memorial, but to some it partakes of the nature of worship; and in order to avoid such an interpretation we have deemed it wiser not to hold it in our schools.[30]

The regulations were, at first, quite different in various parts of the country, but in April, 1929, the government took steps to unify and enforce them. To deal with this, the mission held a special meeting in May to discuss the matter. After two days of talks, it was decided by a substantial majority that the policy of required chapel attendance and Bible study must be continued as a part of the curriculum.[31] Later, various religious bodies, including the Church of Christ in China, of which the Reformed mission was a part, sent a petition to the Ministry of Education at Nanking urging the government to reconsider. A reply was soon forthcoming. It stated that the government's objection was not to a school's teaching religions *plural* but to confining it to just one religion:

> If we allow only one religion to inculcate exclusively its own principles in non-adults of junior middle school grade and below, this will preempt their minds and deprive them later on when they have reached years of maturity of the ability to exercise freedom in the choice of their religion. This is really the placing of shackles upon their liberty of thought.

The closing remark of the Ministry's denial of the petition indicated the government's view was firm: "Let this be considered final and not subject to further review." The ruling was to take effect in mid-1931.[32]

In the end, the mission schools decided to conform to the government's ruling that participation in religious courses should be voluntary and not take place during regular school hours. The request regarding the Sun Yat-sen ceremony, however, was turned down on the grounds it might be interpreted as worship.[33] It was further resolved to transfer the schools to local boards of management made up of Chinese Christians. Mission property would then be leased to these bodies on condition it be used for educational purposes and that no anti-Christian teaching be allowed. As noted in the mission's report for 1930, "At least these schools will be far better than the government or other private schools where there is often anti-Christian teaching."[34] It was hoped that bringing more Chinese into the administration of the schools would prompt local authorities to be somewhat lenient in enforcing the full letter of the law with respect to registration.

Looking further at the positive side, it was expected that by having Chinese Christian teachers, a strong Christian atmosphere could still be maintained in the schools. It was similarly anticipated that pupils from Christian homes, who at this time constituted an average of about a third of the student body, would also have a salutary effect.[35] Finally, there was general agreement throughout the mission that by strenuous efforts many of the younger generation could be reached through Sunday schools and other church-centered activities.

The school registration question was closely related to the increasing anti-foreign, even anti-Christian, nationalism taking place in China in the late 1920s. Although undercurrents of opposition were nothing new for the area, the momentum was more severe than usual. On the recommendation of their consuls, foreigners left their inland posts twice in the 1920s to find safety in the coastal cities. In the case of the Reformed missionaries and their families, this meant going to the International Settlement at Kulangsu.

Except for Leng-na and the North River district, political conditions began returning to normal by 1930. In examining the situation at Talmage College, for example, the mission had several reasons to feel good about the way things were turning out. As described in the mission report for 1930, dangers from the outside seemed in the end to draw faculty and students into a closer bond than had existed for some time. Even the dismissal of two staff members for spreading anti-Christian views and trying to indoctrinate the students with communist principles had only a ripple effect. As a specific example of renewed local support for the school, it can be noted that when, because of reduced enrollment, the year 1929 ended with a deficit, the school was able with little difficulty to raise $500 quickly among Chinese friends. An excerpt from the 1930 report describing the work of the school band also indicates a change of attitude by the community:

> The school band has had a very successful year. On many occasions it has taken part in programs at the city park and in the local churches. Twice it was invited to play in places out of town. In the autumn, a banquet was given the boys by the local authorities in recognition of what they had done.[36]

Although the primary and secondary schools, on the whole, flourished during this period, the theological school had its ups and downs. As has been discussed previously, a theological class was started in one of the missionary homes in Amoy City in 1855, and a seminary was formally organized at Kulangsu about a decade later in 1866. It met at first in a rented house, but in 1870 the Thomas De Witt Theological Hall was constructed. Here, the work was carried on for fifteen years until 1885 when the Reformed and English Presbyterian missions joined in establishing a union institution known as the South Fukien Theological Seminary. By 1900, it had enrolled approximately eighty students. [37]

The seminary program in 1900 was similar to what it had been since its inception, namely, a three year course involving the following subjects: exegesis, homiletics, dogmatics, apologetics, pastoral theology, sermonizing, church history, music, mathematics, and Chinese classics. Generally, only about one-half of the students finished the complete program, many of them dropping out to become teachers or preachers rather than ordained pastors.

One of the problems facing the seminary in 1900 and, according to the mission, the hardest to solve, was the shortage of qualified young men presenting themselves for the ministry. Admission standards therefore had to be kept quite low to attract students. A few enrollees were graduates of Talmage College, but most entered by preliminary examination. In 1907, for example, the majority of the thirteen entering students (seven from the Reformed mission and six from the English Presbyterian mission) were described as being "without previous education." The report added, however, that some of those who "have not had the advantage of preliminary training, [nevertheless] show good ability and give promise of being useful preachers." [38]

The seminary frequently had to contend with a shortage of foreign instructors. Indeed, for several years (1904-1908) even the Reformed mission was too shorthanded to help out, except for an occasional "mini-course." This shortage obviously placed a burden on the English Presbyterian missionaries as well as on the Chinese tutors, of which there usually were two—one for Chinese classical literature and the other for Mandarin. Fortunately, local Chinese pastors helped out with instruction from time to time.

The close ties that the Reformed and English Presbyterians had with the London Missionary Society eventually led to talks aimed at bringing the latter in as a full-time member of the seminary. These talks bore fruit, and in 1908 the London group became an integral part of the union arrangement. This naturally had a complimentary effect on enrollments. In 1908, the number of students totaled thirty-three, distributed as follows: Reformed mission, eight; English Presbyterian mission, ten; and London Missionary Society, fifteen.[39]

In 1910, a special commission made up of delegates from three missions was appointed to discuss plans for better management of the school. As finally agreed upon, the commission's recommendations called for two levels of schooling involving a two-year junior program at Choan-chiu (where a Bible school had long been maintained by the English Presbyterians) and a two-year senior program at Kulangsu. As described by an English Presbyterian missionary at the Choan-chiu school, "The [Kulangsu institution] will send out men to man the city pulpits and the more developed country stations; the Bible School will give pioneers for the unevangelized districts and preachers for our smaller country stations."[40] A second junior level school was planned for Changchow to be under the Reformed mission.

Admittance to one of the Bible schools required only a "common school" preparation, whereas admittance to the higher school required, at least ideally, graduation from a middle school or its equivalent. The curriculum, as agreed upon by the three missions, consisted of twenty-four hours of classroom work that included Old and New Testament exegeses, church history, homiletics, Bible readings, Chinese character, and music. Two afternoons per week were devoted to street preaching. In addition, the students did considerable Sunday preaching in the neighboring churches and outstations. When the Changchow Bible school opened its doors in February 1914, it had an enrollment of eleven students, of whom six belonged to the Reformed mission, one to the English Presbyterian mission, and four to the London Society.

As events turned out, the senior level of theological training at Kulangsu was placed on hold after a few years due to a shortage of foreign staff and lack of students. Thus it happened in 1918 that five students from the lower grades were sent to Union Theological College at Nanking where, as described in the mission report for that year, "we hope the students may receive great benefit, since the teachers [there] are not so much hampered by other work as is the case here."[41] Students were also encouraged to take advanced work at Fukien Christian University at Foochow, where each of the three missions had a representative on the Board of Managers.

The seminary classes at Kulangsu resumed in September, 1921, in rented quarters, but in a slightly different form than the special commission had envisioned. Work gradually returned to normal, and optimism was high with enrollments near twenty. As reported in 1922:

> The Seminary's future is bright with hope, both in the applicants for entrance and in the demand for high standards. The rigid enforcement of entrance requirements and the turning down of unqualified applicants at the beginning of the year has had a salutary effect, and has considerably raised the Seminary in the esteem of the student body. [42]

Unfortunately, the high hopes were not soundly based. By the mid 1920s, it had become largely an operation of the Reformed mission. In 1924, for example, the staff consisted of three men—two from the Reformed mission and one Chinese. In addition, one of the Reformed missionary wives devoted some time each week to music lessons, and Katherine Talmage and one of the local Reformed Chinese pastors each contributed two hours per week to religious education and Sunday school work.

In 1925, the seminary joined Talmage College in relocating at Changchow. Here, a hall was rented that housed rows of 400 wooden ancestral tablets supposedly containing the spirits of various members of a clan extending back seventeen generations. The hall was intended to be a temporary measure as the South Fukien Synod planned to reunite the two levels of theological education in one place, but had trouble deciding on a suitable location. Meanwhile, judging by the following rather humorous report sent to the *Christian Intelligencer* by one of the instructors, the staff tried making the best of the situation:

> Our school is not beautiful, but where is the theological school which can boast of an attendance of over four hundred? Our Seminary alone has that distinction, I

think. Although most of these four hundred students do not take any part in the classroom recitations, they at least afford us subjects for lively discussions. Each morning as I teach my class in Romans, I look at the four hundred ancestral tablets ranged along the side wall, in which reside the spirits of the deceased of the clan called Chng. If "silence gives consent," they are acquiescing to and approving of all I say.[43]

In 1926, the synod decided the time had come to rejoin the two levels of instruction. It also took steps to put into operation more of the recommendations put forth by the special commission. These included a theological board of twelve men, evenly divided between foreigners and Chinese, and among the three missions. It was answerable directly to the synod, which took full responsibility for selecting and publicly installing all seminary instructors and accepted responsibility for financing the school. The institution was henceforth commonly referred to as the South Fukien Theological Seminary.

Temporary quarters for the rejuvenated school were established in a small village on Amoy Island where a large house had been rented. Classes under the new arrangement began in February, 1927, with instruction being carried on by three foreigners—one from each mission—and three Chinese. The location had its pros and cons. To the school's advantage, it was removed from much of the political turmoil affecting China at this time. On the other hand, student quarters were cramped, and faculty members living at Kulangsu had to spend time each day crossing the harbor by sail or motor boat. The location also caused some inconveniences for students engaged in evangelistic work. Finding a better site, however, was not easy. During the next few years it moved from place to place until the London Missionary Society finally made part of its compound at Changchow available.[44]

No matter at what level or at what location students found themselves during this period, practical experience in Christian work was provided as in the past. This included helping as teachers in Sunday schools, going out on Sundays to conduct religious services, and calling on the sick in the hospitals. But there were some new developments, too, such as giving assistance at vacation Bible schools for children and visiting inmates in the local prisons. On some occasions, small groups of students banded together on week-end preaching tours, leaving on Fridays and returning on Mondays. Students were also urged to spend their summers getting practical experience by supplying the pulpits at vacant churches and outstations. As to the value of their summertime "on-the-job-training," note the experience that a number of students had in the summer of 1924:

> Eight of the boys were out serving churches during the summer, others had new and trying experiences in difficult travel, lonely fields, discouraging church problems through lack of efficient lay leadership, disciplined church members, and the like; but all these things have been a very useful training for them. [45]

Enrollment remained relatively constant throughout the 1920s despite the various moves the school had made. Eight students graduated in 1928, seven of whom accepted calls to churches under the jurisdiction of the Synod of South Fukien. Significantly, all but one of the churches were "country" stations. The eighth graduate, having developed views on church government and the sacraments at variance to those of the synod, chose to work independently as a Christian minister. A major landmark was reached in 1929 when among the new students for that year were four young women. As explained in the Reformed mission's annual report for that year:

> They take the same classes as the men, and in Bible knowledge or eagerness to learn are not a bit behind them. While the men go out to do street preaching, their practical work is done visiting in the hospitals or in homes under the direction of one of the missionary ladies. Many of the Chinese leaders have been keen on our receiving women students as our work needs better trained Chinese women; but undoubtedly we have not yet reached the ideal course they should have. There will have to be more adaptation to the special requirements of women's work. [46]

In the final analysis regarding the education of ministers, the question must be asked, "How effective were the Chinese as preachers?" The Reverend Henry De Pree, who worked closely with them for many years, gave the following answer in 1916:

> The truth...is that Chinese preachers in general have the
> ability to present the gospel very forcibly and clearly.
> They follow very much the example of Jesus when he
> taught the people in parables, and many foreigners are
> ready to acknowledge the superior ability of Chinese in
> the art of illustration.... It is a most hopeful feature that
> they learn so readily the art of effective public speaking.
> Sometimes, perhaps, they are a bit too fond of finding
> allegories in everything. I remember one student in our
> Bible School who preached a sermon on "Nimrod was a
> mighty hunter before the Lord." By drawing several
> allegories it was surprising how much good teaching he
> found in his text. But even when taking the more
> common texts of Scripture it is surprising how much light
> they can throw on them by illustration.[47]

XV
Developments in Medicine, 1900-1937

The Reformed mission in China had three hospitals under its care in 1900. The oldest, known as Neerbosch, was established inland at Sio-khe in 1889. The other two, both located at Kulangsu, were Hope, opened in 1897 and designed primarily for men, and Wilhelmina, established in the following year and designed primarily for women. Neerbosch had been closed for a few years in the 1890s due to the lack of a physician, but was reopened in late 1900 with the arrival of Dr. C. Otto Stumpf. The Kulangsu hospitals were under the direction of Dr. John Abraham Otte, who came to China in 1888 and initially served at Neerbosch. Assisting Otte at Kulangsu was Dr. Angie Myers, who arrived in 1899 and served primarily at Wilhelmina. The importance of the Kulangsu hospitals was shown in 1900 when they treated over 10,000 cases, and performed 631 surgical operations. Similarly, Neerbosch, which did not reopen until December 2, 1900, handled nearly 900 cases, and performed 25 operations before the end of the year.[1]

The number of patients increased almost annually. To handle this growth, the hospitals underwent considerable renovation and enlargement from time to time after 1900. For example, Dr. Otte reported in 1906 that when current plans were finished for Wilhelmina, it would be twice as large.[2] As to the specific kind of changes being made, note the following excerpt from the mission's annual report for 1916:

> The building contracts let in 1914 for the Woman's
> Hospital, the additions to the administration building and

men's hospital, and the rebuilding of the chapel have been completed at a cost of $18,000 Mex. In addition, necessary changes, not included in these contracts, have been made at a cost of over $3,000. A contract let in November 1915 for building a kitchen, boiler room, and laundry has also been completed at a cost of $1,500. Machinery consisting of a boiler, water heater, engine, washing machine, steam pump and steam cookers, ordered August 1915, has been received and installed. The contract for electric wiring has been let and the work is nearing completion. This will enable us to care for any night emergency work.[3]

When the above alterations and additions were completed, the Kulangsu hospital complex consisted of several buildings, including the men's building; the women's building; a chapel, located in the center; the administration building, known as the "Otte Memorial Building," which contained offices, two operating rooms, sterilizing room, two laboratories, two pharmacies (one for men, the other for women), examining rooms for patients, and storerooms; and a miscellany that included the kitchen and the engine room and machine shop. The men and women's buildings and the administration building were three stories high. Scattered on the top floors were maternity wards and living quarters for the foreign nurse, the Chinese students, and the Chinese assistant doctor. As a general rule, charity cases were housed on the first floor and more well-to-do patients on the second. Patients with contagious diseases were usually located on the first floor.[4]

At the same time that the Kulangsu hospitals were being reconstructed, the Neerbosch Hospital at Sio-khe was also being enlarged and provided with better facilities. Although Sio-khe itself had only a few thousand inhabitants, the hospital was important because the town was the geographical center of missionary work to the west and south of Amoy. Unfortunately, because of lack of staff, the hospital was closed in the late 1890s and again in 1904-1905. Neglect during those years left it in need of considerable repair—indeed, portions of it had to be entirely rebuilt. Accommodations for women had particularly deteriorated. An indication of the crowded conditions can be seen in this report written by Dr. Stumpf in 1905, the year before he left China:

It has been almost impossible to supply sleeping room for patients. There are 45 beds and an average of 70 or 80 patients. Except for very important cases, I have set the beds together and crowd as many in as the patients will allow, then [I] have a ping-pong table on the floor on which four men may sleep. The remainder have to manage on the floor with mats and straw.[5]

Under the direction first of Dr. Elizabeth Blauvelt, who served at Neerbosch from 1905 to 1908, and then under Dr. Snoke who followed her, a virtually new hospital was constructed. When completed, it consisted of three buildings, ranged side by side two stories high, and presenting a front of 177 feet to the street. The central structure, which was primarily for administration and medical examinations, separated the men's building from that for women. More specifically, as described in a report for 1911, the facilities were as follows:

In the middle building: downstairs are the chapel, consulting room, eye room, and the dispensary; upstairs: the operating room, sterilizing room, lecture room for students, laboratory, and physicians study. In the men's building are four large wards, two upstairs and two down, each ward containing fourteen beds and fourteen small cupboards, one for the use of each patient. The white walls, the large windows, and the twelve foot high ceilings make the wards light and airy. An eight foot veranda, extending all along the back or south side of this building, adds to its beauty and general usefulness.... An extension to the men's building contains rooms and bath for students upstairs, for coolies and contagious diseases downstairs. Two separate small buildings serve as kitchen and dining room for patients and students.

The women's building contains two large wards upstairs, each containing fourteen beds and cupboards, while downstairs it has the women's chapel, hospital storeroom, rooms for women students, and two private rooms for patients. This building also has an eight foot veranda along the south side.[6]

In the same manner that Dr. Otte had to supervise personally virtually every bit of construction of the Kulangsu hospitals in the mid-1890s to avoid slipshod workmanship,[7] so, too, did Dr. Snoke at Neerbosch a decade and a half later. Although contracts were let, Snoke wrote in late 1910 that in reality he was the contractor:

> I furnished all material and was responsible for everything. I had to lay out the lines, see that they were at the right place, and that the corners were square; that the walls were built to the lines, and perpendicular; that they were built to the required height and level; that the foundation ditches were dug according to the lines and were deep enough; that there was enough mortar used, and that it was of the right proportions; that the stones were properly wedged, etc., etc. Several times I was called away and on returning found that they had not finished the work they were doing when I left, but had started something else, had used the wrong lines and of course it would have to be torn out. In short, I had to watch everything they did. But you say, are they not able to make things straight? No, they are not. They don't "mean to be so bad," but they just can not do it; even the contracting mason on the upper buildings is always making them crooked. [8]

Construction projects were frequently of such an extensive nature that a hospital or segment of it had to be closed temporarily—sometimes for several months. These inconveniences affected primarily in-patients. The dispensaries, or clinics, as they were commonly called, where out-patients were seen and treated, generally remained open.

The improvements at Neerbosch and Kulangsu were made at little expense to the mission. In addition to patient fees, there were donations (some financial and some in kind) from Chinese friends and from churches and societies in America. Financial gifts from the Chinese were frequently substantial. Thus, a group of four Chinese patrons subscribed $5,000 for repairs at Hope and for the construction of a sanitarium for male consumptives, another group gave a gift of nearly $3,000 for an X-ray machine, and a third group contributed money for a new electrical plant. At Sio-khe, a Chinese official, after having made several visits to observe the work at Neerbosch, donated $1,000 as an expression of goodwill. He specified that $400 be kept as a fund to defray expenses of poor patients who were unable to pay the required few cents per day for food, and that the remaining $600 be used as the hospital saw fit.

One of the most unique "gifts in kind" was a horse that Hope received from a wealthy Chinese friend. Because the medical staff was responsible for looking after the health of the mission's three schools on Kulangsu Island and occasionally had to visit patients in their homes, the horse no doubt was put to good use. It came with no upkeep expense to the hospital, since the donor furnished the feed and provided a groom.

Another unique gift was a motorboat given in 1910 by the American consulate. To understand the background of this gift, it must be noted that the doctor in charge at Hope served as chief physician for the American consul and his staff and supervised the work of the United States Public Health Service in Amoy. The latter responsibility included examining Chinese emigrants departing from the port of Amoy for America or the Philippines, which was an American colony at the time. In 1911, for example, the head doctor, as consular surgeon, issued bills of health to forty-three steamers that left for the Philippines and inspected 4,863 passengers. As noted in the mission's annual report for that year, "Not only does this service yield a liberal remuneration to the hospital treasury but it also affords us the opportunity of distributing religious tracts to the passengers."[9]

In view of the many Chinese who emigrated to the Philippines, it is not surprising that contributions for the mission frequently came from that quarter. One such group sent $12,350 silver ($6,000 gold) to be used for alterations at Hope. Similarly, when the boiler for the Kulangsu hospitals needed repair in 1919, new flues were purchased in Manila, where the bill for $500 was paid by a prominent Chinese lumber merchant formerly from Amoy.

Reformed churches in America, along with their women's societies, mission bands, and Sunday schools, did what they could to help the medical program in China. Some churches contributed generously. The West End Collegiate Church of New York, for example, gave financial help on a regular basis for the reconstruction of Neerbosch, and when Dr. Snoke returned to Sio-khe after a furlough in 1915, it sent back with him an entire electrical plant. When this plant broke down in 1927, the Bethany Reformed Church of Chicago sent a replacement that was larger and better than the old one. Other churches and groups sent such basic hospital supplies as bandages, bed sheets, towels, and gowns.

In the same way that the Woman's Board of Foreign Missions gave significant sums for education, it did likewise for medical work. Upon learning, for example, of Neerbosch's need for better accommodations, it responded with its characteristic liberality by providing $2,000 in 1908 for constructing a women's wing. Similarly, in 1927, it provided Neerbosch with $1,000 for a building to be used as a nurses' home and for holding clinicals.

Legacies, too, were an important source of funds. Thus, a generous legacy provided by Elizabeth Cappon, who served in China from 1891 to 1909, was designated for the reconstruction of Neerbosch. Similarly, as a memorial to the mother of Dr. Andrew Bontius, who served the mission from 1909 to 1914, the family made provision for a new chapel to serve the Kulangsu hospitals. Like the building it replaced, it served the three-fold purpose of chapel, reading room, and hall for lectures. The former chapel was then converted into a large hospital ward.

In 1925, Hope and Wilhelmina hospitals, which formerly led a largely separate existence, were amalgamated. Their staffs henceforth acted as a single body under the direction of an American superintendent and a board of trustees made up of both Chinese and foreigners. Less distinction was also made regarding separate wards for men and women. As reported later, this seemed to make sense because of "the freer association of men and women" taking place throughout China.[10] The change was also designed to bring about greater cooperation among staff members and to deal with the problem of space. Under the old arrangement, male patients had approximately 100 beds available, while female patients had only half that number.

When the Tek-chhiu-kha hospital in Amoy City burned down in 1909, a small but serviceable building—intended primarily for women and children—was built as a replacement at a cost of $1,800. Except for $200, it was paid for from fees charged wealthier patients at Kulangsu. On the urging of Dr. Taeke Bosch in 1926, some relief from overcrowding at the Kulangsu hospitals was achieved by enlarging the Tek-chhiu-kha hospital. In its new form, completed in the summer of 1927, it could house between forty and fifty patients in two public wards and ten private rooms, and had the usual operating room, drug room, kitchen, and store-rooms. It was equipped with electricity and running water. Costs for enlargement and alterations came to over $10,000, but the task was carried out at no expense to the mission—all costs being met from patient fees at the two Kulangsu hospitals and by donations. When the alterations were completed, it was placed under the same general overall management that governed the mission's medical work at Kulangsu. [11]

Reopened in August, 1927, the Tek-chhiu-kha hospital treated more than 2,000 out-patients by the end of the year as well as a "goodly number" of in-patients. Like the hospitals at Kulangsu, it, too, quickly became self-supporting. Because it was designed primarily to handle patients who did not require a long stay, it was sometimes called the "Lying-In Hospital." Short stays by patients and the absence of a student training program explain why the staff consisted of only nine people, all Chinese: two physicians (a man who had fifteen years experience in various mission hospitals and a woman who received her training at the Hackett Medical College in Canton), three graduate nurses, three orderlies or servants, and one Bible woman. By contrast, the Kulangsu hospitals with their 150-bed capacity and equipped to handle more serious cases was reported in 1930 as having one foreign doctor and general superintendent; one foreign nurse and nursing superintendent; three Chinese doctors; four Chinese graduate nurses; fifteen student nurses; nine medical students; one preacher and one Bible Woman; and twenty-eight cooks, "coolies," and washermen. [12]

According to the 1928 mission report, the hospital complex on Kulangsu had receipts of $42,618.87 Mex. and the hospital on the Amoy City side had $8,350.45 Mex. In the case of the former, this involved 19,907 out-patients and 1,948 in-patients; for the latter, the figures were 5,924 and 300, respectively. The report further noted that the poorer people, constituting about 90 percent of the patients, received special consideration regarding their fees, while the other 10 percent were charged extra to help the less fortunate. In explaining this, the report stated: "We have no intention at all to help the well-to-do financially; contrary-wise, every rich patient is brought face to face with our problem, his problem, to help the poor."[13]

For a patient to be considered rich did not mean that he or she had to live in palatial surroundings, as is strikingly brought out in this excerpt from a letter written by Dr. Otte in late 1907:

I have just returned from my visits to the out-patients. The first one I visited this morning was a nice little boy of four years old, suffering from fever. I am sure if you could have visited that home with me you would wonder at the mildness of the fever, fully expecting that disease and death were near neighbors to such a filthy home. The entrance was through a narrow alley some two feet and a half wide, serving as a drain to the dozens of houses abutting on it. A very narrow door led from this alley into a small court, paved with filth, the home of a large black pig. Opening on this court was the kitchen, viler and dirtier even than a pig-stye. A narrow, steep stairway led to the living rooms above. All were stuffy and hot, and much too small for the large number occupying them. The floor of the principal room had never been washed. It was being swept, however, when I entered it. The main furniture consisted of the family altar, with its idols, candlesticks, and incense pot. A small table and two really fine chairs stood on either side of the room. Two rather nice looking young women received me, while the old grandmother brought in the sick child from the adjoining bedroom. Now you will say that these were probably very poor people. Far from it. They paid me five dollars for my visit, the equivalent of twenty dollars at home. They paid me gladly. They have done it a number of times before. That is my regular charge to outside patients who can afford to pay so much. It is in this way that a large proportion of the cost of maintaining Hope Hospital is met.[14]

Meanwhile, as these developments were taking place among the mission's older hospitals, two new hospitals were established during this period—one at Tong-an, the other at Leng-na. Both were completed in the early 1920s. Initial construction of the former was made possible by a gift from the Blauvelt family. It was given in remembrance of a daughter and sister, Dr. Elizabeth Blauvelt, whose work at Neerbosch Hospital was cut short by a serious illness, followed by death soon after her return to America. Additional memorials came from Dr. Blauvelt's college classmates at Bryn Mawr. The new institution at Tong-an was therefore appropriately called the Elizabeth Blauvelt Memorial Hospital.

Plans for erecting a hospital at Leng-na took root almost as soon as the Reformed mission took over the North River region from the London Missionary Society in 1917. The people of Leng-na were anxious to have a hospital and quickly raised $2,000 to be used toward the purchase of a site. Much of the funding for construction was provided by the Collegiate Church of New York City as a tribute to the Reverend John Fagg who had served the mission from 1887 to 1894 and later served as pastor of one of the Collegiate churches (the Middle Dutch Church) for twenty-two years. It is thus understandable that the Leng-na hospital was named the John Gerardus Fagg Memorial Hospital.

Construction of the two hospitals remained in the planning stage for some time because of the absence in each case of a physician to oversee the work. This problem was alleviated in 1919 with the arrival of Dr. Matthijs Vandeweg at Tong-an and Dr. Clarence Holleman at Leng-na. Both men began their healing labors at their assigned places even before the hospitals were completed. Holleman, in particular, lost no time in getting to his destination—arriving at Leng-na only twelve days after setting foot in China. A limited amount of medical supplies were kindly provided by Hope Hospital. With these supplies and "bars of soap and plenty of hot water," as Holleman put it, he began his work. Since he was still unacquainted with the language, he had to work through an interpreter. In 1920, Dr. Bosch, then serving at Neerbosch, dispatched one of his Chinese assistants to help him.

Until the Leng-na hospital was completed in early 1922, biweekly dispensary days were held in an old Chinese ancestral hall. Here Holleman treated about 3,000 patients in 1920 and slightly more than 4,000 in 1921. Two small rooms and a hall were fitted out with boards and saw horses and used as beds to accommodate patients whose conditions were too severe to be sent home. In 1921, he reported carrying out 300 minor and eight major operations. The latter, all of which were successful, included the removal of an eye, two operations on the bladder, and one on the kidneys. Holleman obviously looked forward to the time when the hospital would be finished, but as he wrote in his report of 1921, "that pleasant anticipation is not unmixed with misgivings." As he further added:

> To look after about six thousand dispensary cases and in addition have charge of a fifty to seventy bed hospital is about all one man and one reliable assistant can properly take care of. How happy shall be the time when the Board sends us news of the appointment of a nurse.[15]

Dr. Holleman's concern about overwork was not unfounded, as the number of out-patients increased from 5,943 in 1922 to 9,620 in 1929, in-patients from 145 to 533, and *major* operations from 9 to 25. Some patients came from as far as a hundred miles, which, as the doctor explained, was "equivalent to the distance of New York from Chicago if we figure the number of days and expense required to reach one's destination."[16]

The situation at Tong-an was similar to that at Leng-na, as Dr. Vandeweg, too, had to put up with makeshift facilities until his hospital was ready. Until the kitchen was finished, for example, patients had to bring their own small charcoal stoves and do the cooking themselves outdoors against the compound wall. Those who were too sick to do this brought a relative or friend to help. Similarly, until an electrical plant was installed, lighting consisted of kerosene lanterns. Unfortunately, because of the abnormal rise in the monetary exchange rate, the funds given by relatives and friends of the late Dr. Blauvelt were insufficient to complete construction. To meet the crisis, Dr. Vandeweg received permission in 1920 to seek help from Chinese of Amoy extraction residing in the British and Dutch colonial settlements in southeast Asia. Vandeweg's trip, which lasted about five months, raised about $20,000 (Mex.)—a sum sufficient to complete the building and to provide the necessary equipment. As a specific example of giving, a Mr. Chan Kuang Pi of Rangoon gave 20,000 rupees, an amount that was enough to pay for the cost and installation of an electrical plant.[17]

When completed, the Tong-an hospital facilities and staff were utilized to their fullest capacity. In the first eight months of operation, the hospital handled 6,492 out-patients, an average of 811 per month. An encouraging circumstance (one that was also true at Leng-na) was the fact that some of the first patients were men of influence, which obviously helped promote the hospital.

In the same manner that Bethany Reformed Church of Chicago helped sustain Neerbosch, and the Middle Dutch Church of New York helped support Fagg, so too Blauvelt had a special benefactor in the Bergen Reformed Church of Jersey City. Even before Vandeweg began his work, the consistory voted to pay his salary. The women did their part by holding periodic "sewing meetings" at which times "they prepared gauze compresses, roller bandages, hospital towels and other items needed in surgical work and forwarded some eleven shipments" to the hospital.[18] The young people likewise contributed their share. For example, upon learning that Vandeweg pounded on a hollow log with a heavy stick to summon worshipers to the hospital chapel, the Sunday school helped raise $300 for a bell. An inscription, in raised moulded letters, read:

FOR THE GLORY OF GOD

PRESENTED TO

THE ELIZABETH BLAUVELT MEMORIAL HOSPITAL

TONG-AN CHINA

BY THE

BERGEN REFORMED CHURCH

JERSEY CITY, N.J.

In the 1930s, the Reformed mission became involved in yet another hospital venture in China, this one at Changchow. Missionary hospital work in that city was by no means a new thing. Indeed, it dated back to 1888 with the arrival of Dr. Achmed Fahmy, a Christian of Egyptian background laboring in the service of the London Missionary Society. Although Fahmy's hospital was a rather crude looking row of connected buildings located in an area that frequently flooded, it was invariably overcrowded with patients. Fahmy, exhausted after more than thirty years of work, retired in 1920 and returned to England. When a replacement could not be found, the hospital was closed.[19]

In 1928, the London Missionary Society sent Dr. Wilfred Busby to Changchow to take charge of a new hospital that was being planned. After its construction was delayed several times due to lack of money and internal controversies, Fahmy's old hospital, after undergoing some renovation, was reopened. When Busby returned to England, the society sent Dr. Douglas Harmon to replace him. Meanwhile, the Reformed mission, having been invited to assist in broadening the medical work at Changchow, assigned the task to Dr. Richard Hofstra. A veteran of several years work in China, serving first at Neerbosch in 1922 and then at Hope-Wilhelmina, Hofstra was named superintendent of what became known as Changchow Union Hospital. Plans for a new hospital building remained in the offing but were laid aside when war broke out with Japan in 1937.

Health problems, along with a few deaths, resulted in a significant turnover among mission doctors. Thus, Dr. Angie Myers, who had come in 1899 primarily to help Dr. Otte, resigned for reasons of health in 1904. Early in the following year, Dr. Stumpf was given a brief furlough from Neerbosch because of family illness. Upon his return to China, he stayed only a few months. Dr. Elizabeth Blauvelt, who arrived at Amoy in 1905, replaced Stumpf at Sio-khe. She remained until 1908, when poor health forced her to return to America. Her early departure was doubly regrettable as she had been especially designated to oversee the new women's wing at Neerbosch.

The mission suffered a grievous loss in 1910 with the unexpected death at age forty-eight of Dr. Otte from the plague, which he had contracted while attending a young Chinese patient.[20] It was providential that a year before his death, Dr. Andrew Bontius had arrived to assist him in his work. Unfortunately, he and his wife Nellie remained only until 1914. Meanwhile, in 1911, Dr. Edward Strick arrived, who with his wife Edith remained until 1924, and in 1915, a year after Bontius's departure, Dr. Taeke Bosch and his wife Margaret arrived, remaining until 1931. When Strick had to leave China temporarily in 1915 because of his wife's illness, Dr. George Dunlap took his place until 1917. Dunlap at one time had been a student of Strick in Chicago. The arrivals of doctors Vandeweg and Holleman at Tong-an and Leng-na in 1919 and Hofstra at Neerbosch in 1922 have already been noted.

In view of Dr. Vandeweg's indispensability at Blauvelt Hospital, it was a serious loss and shock when he died unexpectedly on November 5, 1926, after an illness (influenza) of only four days.[21] A Chinese physician and Maria Vandeweg, a registered nurse, carried on as best they could until the arrival of a replacement, Dr. Harold Veldman. He remained for only four years, returning to America for health reasons in 1930. He, in turn, was replaced by Dr. Theodore Oltman, who remained until the Second World War and returned to China soon after the war.

Fortunately, a few native Chinese doctors began appearing on the scene in the early 1900s to assist the foreign medical staff. To help out at Neerbosch, for example, there was Dr. Chu who "graduated" under Stumpf and later served as an assistant to Snoke. Later, Chu's wife also became an accredited doctor after completing the necessary five-year training program. And at Hope, there was a former student of Otte, Dr. David Huang, who became a certified doctor in 1897 and worked alongside Otte until the latter's death in 1910 and continued his service for many years after that.

In explaining the presence of Chinese doctors, it must be noted that their training remained an important part of the work of the mission hospitals during the early 1900s. The program of study was similar to what it had been in the past and involved a minimum of five years. Unfortunately, as the number of patients increased, the doctors had less time to engage in teaching, and the students in turn became increasingly critical of not receiving enough instruction and having to perform menial tasks. As noted by the doctors in 1911, "It is a problem to manage a hospital successfully and at the same time have a good medical school."[22]

The problem of training doctors was alleviated somewhat by the mid-1920s as a larger number of Chinese doctors were graduating from more legitimate medical schools. Thus, the two Kulangsu hospitals in 1925 reported having, in addition to Dr. Bosch, five Chinese doctors, all of whom were graduates of accredited medical schools. These included a graduate of the University of Texas Medical School, another from a medical school in Shanghai, and three from the Hackett Medical School at Canton. Other hospitals, too, were boasting about the quality of their Chinese doctors.[23]

The appearance of more Chinese doctors was greeted with delight by the foreign medical staff. As described in the mission's report for 1928:

> It is a great pleasure...to welcome *colleagues* to our
> hospitals instead of *assistants*, to have people who can
> carry on almost any kind of work in the medical line and
> do that work well. They constitute a staff of efficient and
> faithful workers, who are in many ways better than the
> foreigners, since language, customs, and knowledge of
> peculiar conditions need not be acquired by them as is the
> case with foreigners.[24]

The growing number of trained Chinese doctors also gave
"encouragement to the view that eventually all missionary
institutions [would] be placed under the direction of the Chinese
themselves, with the missionaries willing to serve in a secondary
capacity, if necessary."[25]

An overview of the hospitals would be incomplete without
taking note of the increasing attention being given to the nursing
profession. The Kulangsu hospitals in 1925, for example, had four
registered nurses—one of United States registry, another of
Danish registry,[26] and two of Chinese registry. With fewer
medical students available for such tasks as changing patients'
dressings, dispensing medicine, and helping with surgical
operations, it was imperative that the nursing program be
strengthened. In response to this need, a three-year training
school for nurses was started in 1924 at Kulangsu under the
direction of Jean Nienhuis, whose nursing career in China began
in 1920. The school opened with fourteen students. By 1937,
forty-four young women and four young men had graduated from
the program. Nurses' training programs by this time had also been
introduced at the other hospitals. All were encouraged to upgrade
their nursing programs in order to meet the more stringent
regulations and training curriculum prescribed by the Chinese
Nursing Association. This organization required all prospective
nurses to engage in three years of strenuous study and practice
and take national examinations comparable to those required of
registered nurses in the United States.

Health care in the 1920s was also improved by the fact that the
wives of four of the five foreign doctors who arrived 1919-1930
were trained nurses. It also happened occasionally that wives of
missionary pastors were registered nurses and could assist in the

hospitals. Nellie Westmas, wife of the Reverend Adam Westmaas, for example, was able to help out as a registered nurse at Fagg Hospital in Leng-na where her husband served for a time in the 1920s.

The diseases that were treated in the hospitals differed little from those of the pre-1900 period. Malaria generally headed the list. Tuberculosis and typhus, as well as nutritional ailments, also ranked high, and in the event of extensive flooding, so did cholera. The treatment of tuberculosis created a special problem because of its contagious nature. Sanitariums were eventually built on the hospital compounds, but they were small and could accommodate only a few patients at a time.

Operations and special examinations also differed little from before, but their numbers increased significantly, as can be ascertained from these statistics for 1913 at the Neerbosch Hospital: "Operations performed, under chloroform, 212; under local anesthesia, 20; for cataracts, 8. Examinations made of sputum, 127; urine, 16; blood, 14; pus, 8. Teeth extracted, 162."[27] For more specific statistics on the type of operations performed, note these figures for 1914 at Hope-Wilhelmina: eye, 99; gynecological and obstetrical, 19; dental, 196; and general, 302—for a total of 616.[28]

The statistics cited above for Neerbosch in 1913 also list "inoculations against plague, 129; vaccinations against smallpox 33." Figures such as these rose significantly, of course, when serious epidemics of one kind or another broke out. Thus, in 1924 when a severe smallpox epidemic struck Amoy City and Kulangsu, Hope Hospital immediately opened a free vaccination clinic. Over 4,000 Chinese responded and were vaccinated. This was done in cooperation with the Kulangsu Municipal Council, which contributed over $400 to help meet expenses.[29] Space was nearly always at a premium in the hospitals and was especially taxed when a plague broke out. Note Dr. Otte's remarks regarding such an occasion in 1907:

> The hospitals are very full of patients. They are sleeping all over the place, even on the benches in the chapel. We ought to add another ward. Now we often have to put communicable eye-cases in the same bed with an ulcer case. This is hardly right.[30]

In-patients were favorably impressed by some aspects of their hospital stay and annoyed by others. The cleanliness of the rooms impressed the patients very much, especially those who came from the country villages where mud houses were common fare. With the introduction of improved water systems, all in-patients were obliged to take baths at the time of admission. Not everyone, however, took kindly to this, especially the women. Nor did everyone appreciate the general quietness that the hospital attendants tried to maintain in the halls and wards. On the other hand, patients had some privileges that would have been frowned upon in an American hospital. For example, as described in the mission's report of 1908, many of them,

> after they have been attended to and the morning service is finished...go out until midday. Then they are allowed to make tea and cook as much as they like, though...three times a day they do get a meal from the hospital cook.[31]

The staff drew the line, however, when it came to patients cooking and making tea late at night.

Everything considered, the Chinese became increasingly more trustful of the mission hospitals and the foreign doctors, as is shown in this excerpt from the mission's report for 1914: "One is surprised at the confidence the Chinese seem to have in Western surgery, and still more surprised at the new willingness of women to undergo examinations."[32] The Chinese also showed a deep trust in drugs that the doctors dispensed—sometimes an inordinate amount of trust, judging by this letter from Dr. Bosch written from Sio-khe:

> Faith in drugs [among Chinese patients] is unlimited; prescriptions with [only] one sort of medicine are no good; the sicker a person, the greater variety of drugs he must take. I was called to see a person with malaria. He showed me a prescription from a Chinese physician containing some twenty ingredients, none of them was quinine. I gave him quinine and nothing else and told him so. Coming back to see me, one could hear him say, "I was sick and only one of his drugs made me better, what might not a concoction of 15 drugs of his accomplish!"[33]

Dr. Holleman reported having a similar experience at Leng-na that also involved malaria and quinine:

I remember a patient who had malaria. He was given
sufficient quinine for five days. However, acting on the
assumption that if a little medicine was good, a lot would
be better, he took five days' supply all in one dose. The
next day I asked him how he was feeling. He replied,
"That medicine was wonderful. I took it all at once and
now my ears are ringing and I can hardly stand up!"[34]

The increasing number and size of gifts to the hospitals from
Chinese donors are a further indication that the populace as a
whole was pleased with what was being done. This is further
confirmed by patients who traveled long distances, sometimes as
much as a hundred miles, to see the "foreign doctor." According
to the mission report of 1932, one-third of the patients at
Hope-Wilhelmina came from outside the immediate Amoy area.[35]

Reports of successful cures and operations no doubt supplied
the hospitals with some of their best public relation advertising.
Among the most gratifying to both doctors and patients were
operations that restored a patient's sight. Note, for example, this
letter dated February 15, 1910, by Dr. Otte, one of his last letters
before he died:

I wish you could be with me when the bandages are taken
off the eyes of the blind whose sight has been restored.
One man, whose case was almost hopeless, when for the
first time in years he saw something he held in his hand
(it was a match) was so happy that his face simply beamed.
A woman who had been blind for ten years was given a
needle to thread. When she had succeeded, she simply
screamed with delight.[36]

As another example of how successful operations could promote good will, note the following incident that, as reported by
Dr. Veldman, occurred at the Blauvelt Memorial Hospital in 1926:

One of those [among the 700 in-patients] treated was a girl
living two days' walk north of us. She had a huge tumor on
her back. It bothered her greatly, but the main concern of
her parents was that with such an appendage no one would
buy her for a wife! Dr. Iap removed it and her relief, after
fourteen years of wearing it, gave her a smile that will be a
great advertisement for the hospital in her county.[37]

The fact that the doctor who performed the surgery, Dr. Iap

Kapchum, was a Chinese physician, obviously added to the praise heaped on the hospital. Doctors could, of course, only do so much, and there were always those pensive occasions when patients had to be told they had waited too long and could not be cured.

Beginning in the early 1900s, the doctors started holding clinics on a more or less regular basis at other communities. Dr. Otte, for example, began visiting Tong-an in 1902 at intervals of about once a month, taking with him a selected quantity of medicine and his "ever-ready tooth forceps" for extracting teeth. As explained by Otte, these clinics had a three-fold purpose:

> The most obvious is the relief of the women and children seen. The second is to let them know of the hospital where more serious ills can be treated, and to disarm any prejudice against it. The last and most important is to let these women hear of their Saviour. [38]

As soon as the word spread that the foreign doctor had arrived, he would be overwhelmed by the number of patients coming to see him. Because women with bound feet had difficulty walking, they especially appreciated these visits by the doctor.

Evangelism became an important part of these clinics, especially when the visits were prolonged for a week or two. Thus, in 1905, Dr. Stumpf left one of his better students in charge at Neerbosch while he and two students along with the hospital preacher spent two weeks at Hon-thau-poa. They began each day with a chapel service, after which about forty patients were treated. After that, according to Stumpf, "we went to a village, a clan house, or to a market place with books to sell and a Sunday-school lesson picture roll." He added that they had no trouble finding an audience to listen. [39]

Visits to a clan house could be a major undertaking by itself as is clearly evident from this description of one that Stumpf and his party visited:

> It measures 600 feet in circumference, 60 feet high, the walls are very thick, it has four stories, and in all there are 816 rooms. On the outside there are windows on the top story only. On the inside there is a verandah around the three upper stories and windows and doors open into these. The large circular court with its well in the center is a busy place. The only door to the enormous place is ten

feet high and seven wide.[40]

Sunday clinicals were no different from those of other days, as the doctor would see patients between services. Thus, according to a letter from Sio-khe, dated Christmas Day 1901, the Reverend Hobart Studley, while accompanying Dr. Stumpf on a medical-evangelistic trip, reported that "during the hours between services," the doctor "prescribed for seventy-six patients."[41]

Not to be overlooked in evaluating the work of doctors as they traveled around holding clinicals, are the public meetings that were held in the churches and schools on the subject of personal hygiene and sanitation. Special attention was given to plague prevention. Illustrated lantern slides on these topics were particularly popular with the audiences.[42]

Opium addiction continued to be a problem after 1900 as it had been before. In 1905, Hope Hospital reported that the increase in opium patients was such that a large room had to be set aside for them. A fee of two dollars was charged in order to keep the number within bounds. In 1917, Dr. Bosch introduced at Neerbosch what was known as the "Town-Lambert treatment" with reportedly excellent results. Its success attracted the attention of one of the local officials at Sio-khe who, after visiting the hospital, issued a directive advising addicts to go there and enroll in the program. A report of two years later states that opium patients were arriving at Neerbosch almost weekly and on one occasion fourteen of the unfortunates came in together. Without mentioning what methods were used, Blauvelt Hospital in 1928 gave the following information about its opium patients:

> Among the in-patients of the year we have had 80 cases who came in to be cured of the opium habit. This has been one of the joys of the year to carry these men and women through to overcoming that evil habit. We are happy to have reports from our country preachers that some of those that have been "cured" have become, since their return, constant hearers of the Gospel.[43]

In 1929, Blauvelt reported having "106 opium cures."[44]

As in the period before 1900, hospital work included looking after not only the needs of the body but also those of the soul. The following, written in 1923, is a common refrain found in the missionary literature of the time:

> It is the unfaltering purpose of the Mission, as it is of the Board, that its Medical Institutions, like its Educational, shall contribute unceasingly to the building up of the Kingdom of Christ, and that they shall always represent the spirit of the Great Physician which led him to minister to the souls of men through the ministry of healing.[45]

Evangelistic work in the hospitals differed little from what was practiced before 1900. As a general rule, worship services of about one-half hour were held twice daily in the chapel or dining room. Out-patients were expected to attend the morning sessions before going to the clinics. In looking after the spiritual needs of the in-patients, the hospitals soon began employing full-time preachers for the men's wards and full-time Bible women for the women's and children's wards. The Bible women, in particular, became an indispensable part of the hospital staff. Note, in this respect, Dr. Vandeweg's admiration for the Bible woman at Blauvelt:

> This Biblewoman-matron-lady-preacher is a splendid woman. She has been the matron of the Woman's school here for years. And she has the right spirit. During the forenoon, when the patients come from all directions, she sits in the chapel and talks to all of them that are waiting. She tells them of the gospel and explains the pictures that hang on the wall. By her attractive ways, she gains the confidence of the people in the hospital. In the afternoon she sits at the bedside of the patients and tells them the old, old story, or she teaches them the hymns, and repeats those words over and over again till they know them by heart. Then she starts to sing them with the patients in the wards, and, after a few days, we are so far that we can teach them the tune in the evening before the service. It sounds ever so sweet when, in different corners of the building, we hear these heathen patients sing the best songs we have. One of their favorites is "Jesus Loves Me." We sing that hymn day after day, and the patients repeat it for themselves till it dawns upon their souls that Jesus loves them.[46]

As in the past, considerable personal evangelistic work was carried on in the hospitals through visits from the missionary women and the local Chinese pastors and preachers. Some came on a regularly scheduled basis. Katherine Talmage, for example, made it a point to visit Wilhelmina Hospital twice a week and always on certain days. Students from the seminary also helped out at the Kulangsu and Amoy City hospitals. The distribution of religious tracts likewise continued to be an important part of the hospital evangelization program. For example, at Neerbosch, Dr. Hofstra prepared with the help of the pastor of the Sio-khe church, a special booklet that was sold to the patients for "five coppers" (about one penny). Its contents included the Ten Commandments, the Lord's Prayer, the Apostles' Creed, about a dozen hymns, and several prayers for individual and family use.

In the same manner that political turmoil in China affected other aspects of mission work during this period, it also affected the hospitals. The frequent fighting that broke out, particularly during the 1920s, placed a strain on hospitals because of the care required by wounded and sick soldiers. Thus, at Neerbosch in 1923, about one-half of the 807 in-patients were soldiers. And at Blauvelt, the widow of Dr. Vandeweg, in commenting about the fighting that had been going on ten miles away in the country but was beginning to reach the outskirts of Tong-an, reported the following:

> We thought we had been busy before, but it was nothing in comparison with what started then. Day and night most serious cases were brought in. The chapel had to be transformed into a regular ward, but without beds; the verandas and halls were also crowded, and even on the landing of the stairs there were four soldiers. Some of our missionaries came to help in dressing the wounds. That was very tiresome work as most of the patients were on the floor.[47]

As might be expected, members of the hospital staffs took advantage of the opportunity to bring the Christian message to the soldiers. This was no easy task because many of the hospitalized came from some distance and were thus unacquainted with the Amoy dialect. Note, for example, the special efforts made by the Neerbosch staff in 1925 to reach such patients:

For the soldiers who speak a very different dialect we have bought tracts and Gospels written in their own dialects, and some young preachers have promised to come to speak to them. Once a week we give them lantern slide lectures on Bible stories and the life of Christ.[48]

Although Neerbosch hospital at Sio-khe and Blauvelt at Tong-an managed in the end to survive the political crises, Fagg hospital at Leng-na was less fortunate. Marauding Communist soldiers thoroughly ransacked it in May, 1929, and occupied the town for several months. The damage inflicted on the hospital was complete. As reported by Dr. Holleman: "All furniture, drugs, and equipment were destroyed or taken. Doors, windows, and wooden floors were either broken-down or torn up. What is now left of our property is empty buildings." This took place, Holleman added, despite the high optimism existing before the disaster struck:

Prior to the Communist raids, the Hospital was well on the way to a record year. A total of 5,500 out-patients and nearly 300 in-patients brought our total to more than 1,000 above any previous year at the same date. Good will of the populace was being increasingly obtained and the evangelistic work was bearing more fruit than ever.[49]

When the Communist attack occurred, Dr. Holleman decided that his family and that of the Reverend Henry Poppen, should leave Leng-na. Poppen himself was in Kaulangsu at the time. The families were therefore directed to take refuge in a school on the edge of the city where Holleman planned to meet them later. Unfortunately, he ran into some Communist soldiers and was taken prisoner. It was to be a month before he would see his family again. The two families, dressed in Chinese clothing and assisted by friends, eventually managed to flee the city and after four days of difficult travel reached the safety of Changchow, from where they made their way to Kulangsu.

Meanwhile, some of the Communists, after participating in looting that included the missionary homes, left Leng-na about as quickly as they came, taking Holleman with them. For the next few days, he was obliged to march with his captors, sometimes as much as twenty miles a day, all the time zigzagging to avoid enemy troops. On the fifth day, during the confusion brought on by a sudden order to retreat, Holleman managed to escape. After hiding for two days, he made his way to the home of a Christian family. Because of Communist soldiers in the area, he remained with his friends for almost three weeks. The stay also gave the doctor an opportunity to "mend" his sore feet, which had become bruised and swollen from the marching. Finally, when it was considered safe, Holleman made his way to Swatow and from there to Kulangsu, where he was reunited with his family.[50]

According to Holleman's own account, he was treated kindly by the soldiers during his capture "and suffered no more hardship than they did themselves." He also had many kind remarks about the heart-warming support and concern shown him by old friends during and after his ordeal:

> Even before we left [Leng-na], those few poor people who dared to come out on the street followed me as I marched, and inquired if there was anything they could do. One gave me an umbrella and offered money; another ran for a bowl of macaroni; another for a cup of tea; and nearly all expressed solicitude. We had hardly left [the city] before various organizations, such as the Chamber of Commerce, the Post Office, and the Church, were planning for my ransom. Even before word was received from Amoy, the [Leng-na] people had already prepared $7,000.... Throughout all the South Fukien Church, as soon as the news was known, there were held special prayer meetings for my safe return.... The gates of Heaven were literally bombarded with prayers.[51]

Holleman added that after his return, he was "deluged with letters and visits from my Chinese friends, many of whom I had never met."

Rather than despair about the future of Leng-na, Holleman spoke of the recent happenings there as having simply brought the work "to a sudden and dramatic *pause*" but certainly not to an end. He added that it "may be one year, it may be five years" before the work is resumed but he had no doubt it would happen eventually. Indeed, he was so certain of this that after a brief rest, he spent a short time among the Chinese in Manila raising funds to refurnish Fagg Hospital. He collected nearly $5,000.[52] Following his return to China, he worked in the Kulangsu hospitals but kept himself "free to return to Leng-na at the first opportunity." It is interesting to note in this respect that during his "exile" at Kulangsu, a large number of people from Leng-na came to see him for treatment. As Holleman put it, this "shows that what we did in Leng-na was neither unappreciated nor forgotten." In further noting that what had been accomplished, could not be undone, he wrote:

> During the past ten years a total of about 70,000 treatments have been given, a great deal of instruction has been given in hygiene and public health, many have heard the gospel, about ten have joined the church. These results will be lasting and justify the expenditures.[53]

Despite the setback at Leng-na in 1929, the situation elsewhere seemed to be gradually improving by 1930 relative to threats from the Communists and various bandit groups. The situation at Neerbosch, for example, had frequently appeared so desperate in the past as to make it inadvisable to embark on any new construction projects or even to make repairs. Thus, the new electric light plant that had been given by the Bethany Reformed Church of Chicago in 1927 was still in boxes in Amoy City three years later. This soon changed, however. In November, 1930, work began on an "engine house" and the new plant was expected to be installed within a few months. As Dr. Hofstra described the prevailing optimism, "The skies seem to be clearing. The future looks brighter and we are looking forward to a year of hard and undisturbed work."[54]

Unfortunately, once again the optimism was not soundly based, as political disturbances continued to break out. Twice in 1933, for example, the mission staff had to vacate Neerbosch. Although the disturbances were not as severe as they had been, the resultant "paucity of patients" was sufficient to cut deeply into the budgets of the upcountry hospitals. As a consequence, beginning in July, 1933, the Kulangsu hospitals began shouldering the financial burdens of all the mission's medical work. Notwithstanding this added burden, Hope-Wihelmina still reported a "substantial" financial balance at the end of 1934.[55] But this was not to last. The outbreak of war between China and Japan in 1937 put a severe damper on Kulangsu's contacts with the mainland, contacts that were cut off entirely after Pearl Harbor.

XVI
The War Years, 1937-1945

Two wars broke out between China and Japan during the 1930s. The first of these, the Sino-Japanese War of 1931-1933, was centered in Manchuria. Because of its distance from Amoy and the limited military activity involved, it had little effect on the mission. This was by no means the case, however, with the second conflict that broke out in July, 1937. Starting with some skirmishes in the vicinity of Peking, the fighting spread quickly. No match for Japan's military might, most of China's coastal cities—including Amoy—were occupied by Japanese troops by mid-1938.

It is interesting to note that before the outbreak of the 1937 war (which merged with World War II following the Japanese attack on Pearl Harbor on December 7, 1941), the mission had been optimistic about the future. As stated in the introductory remarks of its annual report for 1937, the year

> opened with the promise of great things. The country was rejoicing over the...progress toward national unity, cleaner politics, economic relief, the eradication of bandits, and the extension of communications.... At this time of phenomenal advance, perhaps no group of folk felt deeper joy or cherished a broader hope than did the Christian Church. With a Christian ruler at the head of the country, they felt that soon they would no longer be the mustard seed, but the tree, and that soon China might know the blessedness of "the nation whose God is the Lord."[1]

This optimism quickly changed in the summer of 1937. As the above report further added, the outbreak of war between Japan and China soon "turned joy to mourning and hope to despair." As fighting began moving down the coast, it was only a matter of time before Amoy became involved. The expected came on May 10, 1938, when, after extensive naval shelling and aerial bombardment, enemy troops moved in. Organized resistance came to an end after two days and Amoy City and the island were in Japanese hands. However, because of its international status, the Japanese left Kulangsu alone for the present.[2]

When Amoy Island fell, the Sin-koe church was occupied for a time and the parsonage ransacked. The pastor was taken prisoner and not released until several months later, when he was permitted to take charge of his congregation once again. Other churches on the island suffered in varying degrees. At one place, ten people were killed and the church building partly burned, and at another place, a church was badly damaged by shelling. Within a year after the fall of the island, about one-half of its church membership had gone to Kulangsu or the mainland or was residing abroad. Some of the refugees later returned to their homes, but many did not. Financially, the island churches were able to continue only because of remittances from members overseas, which totaled a fair amount when converted into Chinese currency. One of the greatest difficulties was the securing of preachers. At the large Tek-chhiu-kha church, the work in 1939 was carried on by two Bible women assisted by members of the consistory.[3]

Tens of thousands of Chinese who fled from Amoy and other nearby islands went initially to Kulangsu. Others went directly to the mainland of China, and still others managed to relocate in Southeast Asia.[4] To bring order out of chaos, an International Relief Committee composed of four foreigners and five Chinese was quickly formed with the Reverend Henry Poppen as chairman. Refugees were housed in factories, churches, temples, and schools, but emergency mat buildings had to be constructed to accommodate most of them. As explained by nurse Jessie Platz, such dwellings were large, with each family spreading out its "quilt or blanket and whatever spot that covered, that was their area. The whole family lived on that spot."[5]

To help feed the refugees, 5,000 bags of rice stored in warehouses in Amoy City were brought to Kulangsu under the protection of American and British gunboats. As to how the rice was cooked and distributed, note Poppen's explanation:

> Two canning factories on the island were immediately made available. The entire staff of each factory was put into service and augmented by volunteer labor from the refugee camps. Steam cookers and boilers were put into use. Camp leaders were quickly appointed; the camps were organized into groups of twenty-five and the rice distributed from the cooking centers carried in empty five gallon kerosene tins supplied by the Standard Vacuum Oil Company and the Asiatic Oil Company. In this way 90,000 meals were provided each day, consisting of soft boiled rice and beans mixed with soy sauce.[6]

The refugees provided their own bowls and chopsticks. A special milk dispensary was established for women with babies.

Appeals for help received a good response. The Chinese in Manila, for example, provided $30,000; and a Chinese businessman in Singapore gave $20,000. Bundles of used clothing arrived from numerous places, including far-off London. As cooler weather set in, $15,000 worth of wool, cloth, and thread were purchased in Shanghai, and twenty women from the camps were put to work making quilts. For its part, the Board of Foreign Missions sent out a national appeal asking for $15,000 to help meet expenses associated with the refugee camps. Nearly $16,000 was raised within a brief period. About one-half of this was used for relief in the Amoy area and for evacuation expenses. The remainder was sent to the National Christian Council for distribution among refugees thoughout China.

Shortage of essentials, not the least of which was firewood for cooking, prompted Poppen and the Relief Committee to move the refugees elsewhere as quickly as possible. Many went to the Tong-an and Sio-khe districts; others went to the North River district, which because of its rugged terrain was less subject to enemy aerial bombing. A number of refugees also left for Chinese settlements in Southeast Asia. Of great importance was the task of looking after the medical needs of the refugees. As superintendent of Hope Hospital, Dr. Holleman was made chairman of the Relief Committee's Medical Department. Thanks in large part to his work and that of his assistants, no serious epidemics occurred. The rapidity with which the refugees were moved out and relocated on the mainland also helped cut down the spread of disease.[7]

As might be expected, opportunities for evangelization among the refugees were not overlooked. In this respect, the following remarks by Leona Vander Linden are notable:

> We invited the women to come three afternoons a week to the High School for religious instruction. More than 160 responded. After reciting and singing hymns and choruses, they listen to a Bible lesson, then they are divided into classes for a period to study the Romanized Colloquial. The last period was left for sewing, for every mother was given a length of cloth for a garment for one of her children, while the unmarried girls got cloth for themselves. At certain stages in their lessons more cloth is given them.[8]

There were more direct ways of evangelization too, as explained by a worker at Sio-khe:

> We try not to give them bread alone. We sing and talk to them and give them a message to carry away. Without Christ in their hearts to give them strength and hope and love and salvation what good will just a little more physical strength do them?[9]

Many of the refugees who relocated in the interior had already accepted Christ and were thereby a unique means for evangelizing new areas. As Ruth Holleman wrote, thanks to them, "Many a little obscure village where no Christian had ever trod is now hearing for the first time the Gospel message."[10]

The need for the missionaries at Kulangsu to keep in touch with the inland stations created a perplexing problem. So too did the relaying of essentials like medicine and food as well as Christian literature and school supplies. By negotiating with the Japanese, the missionaries obtained permission to use two motor launches appropriately called the "Hope" and the "Red Cross." The former belonged to Hope-Wilhelmina Hospital and the latter was owned jointly by the Reformed and London Society missions, having been recently purchased from a local business firm. By observing certain rules and adhering to an approved schedule, they could travel up the river to Changchow or across the bay to Tong-an. The Reverends Veenschoten at Changchow and Eckerson at Tong-an took charge of the boats and their cargo at the inland stations. The Japanese also gave the International Relief Committee permission to operate four junks for bringing much needed supplies of charcoal and firewood from the mainland. All these privileges were revoked in the fall of 1941 in retaliation for the killing of a Japanese official at Kulangsu.

Carrying on mission work in the midst of war and having part of the country occupied by hostile forces naturally created problems for the missionaries. In the words of the Reverend William Angus, written in 1939, work in the various districts was "one of continued adjustment to war conditions."[11] This included not being allowed to leave Kulangsu for the mainland without permission, and having to comply with two sets of differing and sometimes conflicting sets of regulations—those of the Japanese occupiers in some places and those of petty Chinese officials elsewhere.

Travel accommodations, which had been steadily improving in the past, were also adversely affected by the war. In order to interrupt possible Japanese troop movements, the Chinese deliberately tore up many roads and destroyed major bridges. This meant that transportation by motor vehicle was frequently impossible. Therefore, unless a destination could be reached by water, travel was limited to a combination of walking and using a sedan chair. The results of this can be seen in Jeannette Veldman's description of a trip from Kulangsu to Tong-an in the fall of 1941 that took two days, whereas before the war it could have been made in about an hour by motor bus.[12]

Because moving around was taking longer, missionaries at times also had to put up with lodging conditions that were reminiscent of those of a generation or two earlier. This is clearly brought out in Jessie Platz's description of the accommodations provided her and another nurse when they spent the night in a small chapel while traveling in the summer of 1941 from Kulangsu to Changchow:

> By putting two benches together we each had
> beds—such beds! We were far from prepared. All I did

was to borrow a bednet at Kulangsu, so I had nothing soft to temper the hard seats to my unaccustomed back. This nice little chapel was open on four sides—not a bit of privacy, but it was cool.[13]

Everything considered, the mission schools did not fare too badly during the war years. There were at first some serious problems resulting from the initial uncertainties about the war and from using school buildings for housing refugees. According to one report, some schools lost 50 percent and more of their students during the last half of 1937.[14] Declines in enrollment in Free China proved to be temporary in most cases, and significant growth soon became the rule. In 1940, for example, the mission reported: "All Christian schools are crowded, several seriously overcrowded. Their combined enrollment is almost double what it was a few years ago."[15] Most schools retained their high enrollments throughout the rest of the war. Enrollment increased not only in the cities, but also in some of the villages. At the little school of Soa-sia in the Changchow area, for example, it increased from 20 to 140 pupils, and at the small town of Thah-thau, also in the Changchow area, it increased from 20 to 105. Increases in enrollment came about not only by a gradual return to prewar routines, but also by the influx of refugees. Because Japanese air raids generally took place during the mid-hours of the day, it soon became customary in large communities like Changchow to set school hours for early mornings and late afternoons.

The task of accommodating the larger enrollments was met by converting trunks, trunk racks, bed boards, and dining tables into desks and benches. The problem of attracting enough qualified teachers was less easy to solve, particularly since salaries were lower than those paid by government schools. Missionary wives assisted wherever they could, especially among the refugee children. Thus, Ruth Holleman and Alma Vander Meer took charge of music classes at Kulangsu, and Anna Boot taught the Romanized colloquial to beginning classes.

Despite the war, the Chinese government made an effort to increase its number of primary schools while upgrading their standards, thereby offering serious competition to any mission schools whose standards were low. Similarly, to meet the entrance requirements of the government's normal and medical schools, the mission's middle schools (especially those of senior middle grade) had to increase their offerings and keep the standards high. Some schools met the challenge very well. When Luman Shafer, the secretary of the Board of Foreign Missions, visited the mission in the early fall of 1941, he reported that the Yo-tek Middle School for Girls on Kulangsu had an enrollment of 420 students—the largest in its long history—and that a person "would have to go a long way to find a finer school."[16]

The presence of large numbers of refugee children in the schools meant that more pupils than usual were coming from non-Christian homes. Since the restrictions on teaching Bible courses and requiring attendance at the daily worship services had been lifted, the mission schools welcomed the evangelistic challenges that were presented. That the schools had not lost their evangelistic goals is evident in the following remark by Tena Holkeboer respecting the Girls' Middle School in Kulangsu: "While every phase of our educational program is given undue emphasis, the work of evangelism and training for Christian leadership is always our primary aim."[17]

The war brought major changes for the South Fukien Theological Seminary and Talmage College. When Changchow was subjected to increased bombing in early 1938 (over 2,000 bombs were dropped on the city within a few months), the two institutions were moved to villages in the rugged North River district: the seminary to Eng-hok and Talmage to Hoa-an.[18] The moves did not hurt the enrollment of either school. Seminary enrollment was twenty-two in the fall of 1938, only four less than it had been the previous year. Eight were new students. Talmage had 278 students, the highest in the school's history, and, in 1940, its enrollment reached 475.[19] The seminary was very ably served during this period of "exile" by its principal, the Reverend Henry De Pree. Talmage was likewise well-run by its principals, first by William Vander Meer until his return to America in 1944, and then by Lin Yu-lin.

The communities of Eng-hok and Hoa-an were about twenty-five miles apart and located at high altitudes. De Pree described Eng-hok as a "mountain-top village" and rather primitive in appearance. The seminary facilities left something to be desired. The building in which most of the classes were held, for example, was described in 1940 as follows:

> Instead of brick walls and concrete floors we have mud
> walls and earth floors downstairs and rough wooden
> floors upstairs. Last year no glass was procurable locally or
> in Changchow and the cold was trying in the winter
> months. I brought some glass from Hong Kong, so this
> year we have windows that give us light and shut out the
> cold. Mrs. De Pree and I have some rooms in the building
> that serves for classrooms and dormitory.[20]

When Shafer visited the seminary in the fall of 1941, he, like
others before him, was critical of the quality of the students. He
strongly recommended that the school accept only senior Middle
School students, declaring that the "presence of lower grade
students, following a kind of Gresham's law, acts as a deterrent to
men of higher grade. Young men of talent see only the lower
grade aspect of the institution and are not attracted to it." With
respect to the staff, Shafer further declared that "a strengthening
of the faculty on the Chinese side" was particularly needed. The
staff at this time consisted of four men, De Pree (for whom Shafer
had considerable praise), a Reverend Philips who had only
recently been sent out by the London Missionary Society, and two
young Chinese instructors.[21]

Although Hoa-an, like Eng-hok, was also a small village (it had
a population of only 700), Talmage's accommodations were
significantly better than those of the seminary. The community
had once been a major center for growing and exporting tea and
home to a number of wealthy families. When the Japanese took
over Formosa (Taiwan) after the Sino-Japanese War of 1894-1895
and developed a superior grade of tea, the Hoa-an tea trade
collapsed. As a result, several fine vacant houses were available for
the Talmage faculty and students. Moreover, thanks to cooperation
with local officials, a building was constructed providing an
assembly hall (an essential in view of the size of the student body)
and two large classrooms. Because even the Hoa-an area
experienced occasional air raids and they invariably occurred
during the midday period, Talmage followed the example of the
Changchow schools and commenced school classes early in the
morning and resumed them in late afternoon.

Like so many aspects of mission work during the war, medical care also changed. When Amoy Island fell to the Japanese, the staff of Hope-Wilhelmina Hospital was immediately mobilized to meet the increased demand. The following statistics from a report for 1938 clearly indicate the dimensions of the demand:

> About 400 wounded soldiers were taken care of in the first few days. Although equipped to accommodate only 120 the hospital treated over 200 in-patients for several months. The previous yearly average has been 1,500 but this year the total reached 3,588. The attendance of the out-patients rose from a daily average of 60 to 250. The total for the year was 42,511 out-patients, four times that of the year before.[22]

Refugees accounted for much of the later increase, as did the closing of the mission's Tek-chhiu-kha branch hospital in Amoy City.

The Nurses Training School that was carried on in conjunction with Hope-Wilhelmina Hospital was also kept busy. Under the direction of Jeannette Veldman and Jean Nienhuis, it graduated fifteen students in 1939, the largest number to that date. This was none too many, considering that the upcountry hospitals at Sio-khe, Tong-an, and Leng-na (reopened in 1939) were heavily dependent on the school for nurses.

After the American entry into the war, following the attack on Pearl Harbor, Kulangsu became fair game for the Japanese, including Hope-Wilhelmina Hospital. Within a few months after the Japanese occupied Kulangsu, it, for all intensive purposes, no longer functioned as a hospital. Instead, the ground floor was turned into a detention camp for some forty British, Norwegian, and other Allied sailors whose ships were unlucky enough to have been captured by the Japanese. With the help of two or three Chinese nurses, Jeannette Veldman did what she could to make these "non-paying guests," as she called them, as comfortable as possible. As will be described more fully elsewhere,[23] the Japanese invaders eventually appropriated virtually everything from the hospital that was movable and also caused serious structural damage.

Next in importance to Hope-Wilhelmina Hospital was the Changchow Union Hospital, which moved into the buildings of the seminary when it relocated in the North River district. The move resulted in a significantly increased number of in-patients because of the larger accommodations that were available, especially when compared to the old Fahmy buildings described previously.[24] Dormitory rooms were converted into examination rooms, and private rooms and classrooms became wards. The case load also increased because the new location placed the hospital on the perimeter instead of inside the city, as was the case before. Thus it was less subject to bombing raids. The total number of patients cared for in 1939 was 20,903, of whom 2,780 were in-patients and 18,123 were out-patients. These figures more than doubled in 1940.[25]

As the inflation spiral continued to rise, many of the poorer Chinese in Changchow could no longer afford to rent rickshaws to take them to the newly located hospital. As a consequence, some were so ill when they did come in that it took a much longer time to recover—if indeed they recovered at all. To help remedy this problem, more house calls were made. In addition, the government established what was termed a Refugee Hospital in the city. Unfortunately, no provision was made for medicine or for doctors and nurses. As a result, a doctor and nurses from Union Hospital began making regular visits there. According to a report of 1943, nurses made 8,069 city calls and 2,579 calls at the Refugee Hospital.[26]

Dr. Richard Hofstra, who had been serving in China since 1922, was in charge of the Changchow hospital. He was ably assisted by Dr. Douglas Harmon of the London Missionary Society. Harmon arrived in late 1939 as a replacement for Wilfrid Busby who had retired a few months earlier. The hospital also had from two to four Chinese doctors and a large nursing staff. The latter included three foreigners— Jessie Platz, Harriet Boot,[27] and Phyllis Reed, an English woman. In 1943, there were also twenty-nine graduate student nurses. In view of the later closing of the nursing school at Kulangsu, it was fortunate that, thanks especially to Platz, the Changchow hospital eventually developed an excellent nursing school of its own.[28]

With respect to the other upcountry hospitals at Sio-khe, Tong-an, and Leng-na, which were served by Chinese doctors, plans were developed for placing them under the supervision of the Changchow hospital. Also under its supervision was a small

English Presbyterian hospital located southwest of Amoy at Changpu. Because of wartime conditions, oversight of the four hospitals amounted to little more than one or two visits a year by someone from the Changchow institution and occasional correspondence and the filing of reports.

The trend for giving the Chinese a greater role in the supervision of mission institutions was continued during the war years with respect to the hospitals. Thus, the Board of Managers of the Changchow hospital in 1939 was made up of eleven members, eight of whom were Chinese. The three non-Chinese consisted of one representative from each of the three missions making up the South Fukien Synod.

Financial help for the hospitals came from several sources, including the International Relief Committee of China (a relief organization established primarily by the American Red Cross); the China Christian Education Association, which made contributions primarily for nurses' training; Reformed congregations in the United States; the London Missionary Society; local Chinese friends; and hospital patients. With respect to the last mentioned, however, much of the medical work was well below cost or even free of charge.

Salary increases never kept up with the steady rise in the cost of living and because government hospitals paid better than the mission hospitals, it was difficult to retain sufficient Chinese doctors and nurses. This was particularly true of smaller hospitals. In 1942, for example, two Chinese doctors left to go into private practice and a third resigned a short time later. Fortunately, this situation gradually improved late in the war.

Medicine and supplies became increasingly scarce as the war dragged on. As might be expected, inflation hit the cost of medicine particularly hard. In a letter of May, 1942, from Richard Hofstra to his wife in the States, he noted that the year before, a ten-ounce tin of quinine (an essential for combatting malaria) could be purchased for about $2,000, Chinese currency. By the end of the year, the price had jumped to $7,000, and a short time later to $35,000. Similarly, while a pound of aspirin powder in the spring of 1941 was selling for $20, by December it had risen to $80 and, according to Hofstra, was currently costing $800.[29] To help meet the demand for medicine, experiments were made with substitutes and some use was made of native herb medicines.

With respect to hospital needs other than medicinal, it frequently became a matter of making do with what one had, as is brought out in these remarks of 1943 by chief nurse Platz:

> Anyone going through our wards would immediately notice the bed sheets patched with many patches, not always of uniform color, the patients wearing their own clothes instead of hospital clothes. He would notice the lack of paint on beds and furniture, the improvised bed pans etc. of wood and tin, instead of the white enamel. And he would often see dressings although clean yet discolored by frequent salvaging, and kept in place by strings instead of bandages. Shortage of supplies and material has made it difficult to keep up the proper technique in the care of the patients and has destroyed that appearance of neatness and cleanliness that we all like to see in a hospital.[30]

Evangelistic work in the hospitals continued to be carried on as in the past. The 1939 report for Changchow Union Hospital described such work as of the "greatest importance," but added that it was the most difficult to measure of all the hospital's activities. "Except in a small percentages of cases," the report read, "it is impossible to learn definitely whether a patient has accepted Christ as his Saviour. We continue to sow the seed trusting that the Holy Spirit will use and bless our efforts. Much of the harvest must be left for others to gather."[31] Unfortunately, staff shortages and inadequate transportation, combined with other pressing matters, made it difficult for hospitals to send teams of workers into the villages as often as before the war.

Always looking for new ways for "harvesting souls," the South Fukien Church in 1938 gave enthusiastic support to a plan for commemorating, in 1942, the 100th anniversary of the arrival of David Abeel and the beginning of mission work at Amoy. The plan, submitted by a special synodical committee, the Centenary Committee, called for bringing "the gospel at least once to every village and home in South Fukien" before 1942.[32] At a special meeting of the Committee on May 16, 1940, it was agreed that the primary goal of the celebration and campaign should not be on financial matters but on winning converts. Put another way, the emphasis should not be on "bricks and mortar" but on "dedicated lives."[33]

To assist in the project, plans called for sending out groups of Christian volunteers (variously called "Expeditionary Bands" and "Gospel Bands") to proclaim the Good News at open meetings, and for smaller groups of two or three to engage in "house to house" visitation.[34] Getting competent volunteer workers for Kulangsu and the larger communities was not considered a major problem. To deal with the "country" regions, the Centenary Committee recommended that the rural churches assist by holding brief training sessions.

As to the progress made in reaching the centenary goal, the mission's annual report of 1940 declared that "the great evangelistic movement" was going forward and cited as evidence the adding of a number of new members on confession.[35] Evidence of progress was also noted by Secretary Shafer in his report to the Board of Foreign Missions:

> The campaign for visitation in every home in South Fukien before 1942...is being vigorously carried out. The Changchow area has been done thoroughly within a radius of ten miles of each church. In Sio-khe the campaign is 60% complete. The campaign is now being pushed on the island of Kulangsu under the vigorous leadership of Miss Holkeboer. There are 150 volunteer workers engaged in this work.[36]

It should be noted that the work, including that at Kulangsu, was carried on almost entirely by lay persons, with missionaries and Chinese pastors serving as an executive committee and helping plan the work.

When the centennial year 1942 finally arrived, the Amoy churches observed the occasion in fitting style. The celebration of the churches in the Sio-khe district was typical:

> As the Sio-khe church [building] was too small to accommodate the crowd, a huge bamboo tent was erected on the Girls' School playground. Delegates came from every church, more than 200. They arranged for their own keep in church groups. $5000 was raised by the 5 organized churches of the District for expenses. On Friday night the local church histories were given. On Saturday, besides

other addresses, Mr. Angus gave a historical review of the past 100 years. In the afternoon there was a picnic, and in the evening the Girls' School gave a play before an outdoor audience of about 3,000. On Sunday, Mr. Angus baptized and admitted into the church 67 men and women, representing additions to the 5 churches.[37]

The centennial observance at Changchow was an even more prodigious affair.

As a kind of grand finale to the centennial observances, the full South Fukien Synod met in 1942 for the first time since 1936. In view of the mission's being on the threshold of a new century of work, the Reverend Ngaw Peng-au, who preached the opening sermon, appropriately chose as his text Isaiah 54:2, "Enlarge the place of thy tent." Although it was admitted that the centennial campaign had not reached all the goals, and in some cases did not come close, nevertheless, considering the obstacles that had to be overcome, general overall satisfaction was expressed with the results. Indeed, confident of the future, the synod announced a new goal. Known as the "Five Year Resolution," it stated that by 1947, the financial support of the some 350 churches and outstations under the jurisdiction of the synod should come entirely from local sources. Unfortunately, as will be explained in the following chapter, China's worsening inflation made it impossible to achieve that goal.

For its part, the Reformed church in the States was also determined not to let the hundredth anniversary of the mission pass unnoticed. Several articles appeared in the *Church Herald*, and a small booklet, *Miracle of a Century*, was published describing the mission's work.[38] Money was also subscribed, with the churches raising over $14,000 for what was known as the Centenary Fund, and the Women's Board raising another $10,000 for what was called the David Abeel Fund.

Numerous gatherings were held in the churches throughout the country, the most notable of which was at the West End Collegiate Church in New York February 22, 1942. Under the auspices of the Board of Foreign Missions, it was attended by a distinguished body of representatives from various denominational and interdenominational agencies. The opening remarks were given by none other than Mrs. Lin Yu-tang, wife of the famous Chinese author and philosopher. She had long-standing connections with the Chinese church, being the daughter of an Amoy elder and a graduate of the Po Tek girl's school on Kulangsu, where she later taught for a time. Addresses were also given by the Reverend Abbe Livingston Warnshuis, secretary of the International Missionary Council and a former missionary of fifteen years' experience at Amoy, and by Dr. C. L. Hsia, advisor to the minister of foreign affairs of the Chinese government. Hsia spoke as the personal representative of the Chinese ambassador to the United States.

Centenary services were also held elsewhere, including a solemn observance at Abeel's gravesite in Greenwood Cementery, Brooklyn, New York, on February 24, 100 years to the day after Abeel landed in Amoy. About two weeks later on March 10, a special service, preceded by a Chinese dinner, was held at the First Reformed Church in Athens, New York, which was Abeel's first ministerial charge (1826-1828) following his graduation from New Brunswick Seminary. General Synod, at its 1942 session at Albany, New York, also held a special anniversary service June 8. A highlight of the event was the commissioning of four new recruits for the mission: namely, Dr. Donald and Hannah Bosch, the Reverend John P. Muilenburg, and Anne De Young, R.N.[39]

As events turned out, Muilenburg and De Young did not get to China until several months after the war because of difficulty in making travel arrangements. Dr. Bosch never did get there, having been called up to serve in the United States Army, after which he and Mrs. Bosch took service with the Reformed church's mission in Arabia. Several other missionaries were also commissioned later for China, including the Reverend Joseph and Marion Esther, the Reverend Gordon and Bertha Van Wyk, and Gladys Kooy, but they too had to wait to obtain transportation.

New appointees who were unable to leave for the Amoy field as soon as planned were encouraged by the Board of Foreign Missions to use the opportunity to prepare themselves more fully for the time when they could enter China. Several of them did this by studying Mandarin and Chinese culture at a newly estab-lished school in California. This institution, formerly known as the Peking School of Chinese Studies, had been established about 1910 to train foreigners (especially missionaries, businessmen, and diplomatic and military personnel) in Mandarin. When the Japanese occupied Peking, the school was moved to the campus of the University of California at Berkeley.[40] Other new recruits, while awaiting transportation to China, studied elsewhere. Gordon Van Wyk, for example, who had been delegated to teach at Fukien Christian University, with which the Amoy mission had close ties, began work on an M.A. in history at Yale.

From the outbreak of the war in 1937, the Board of Foreign Missions maintained close contact with the missionaries. Telegraph messages were initially received and transmitted through the American and British gunboats in the harbor, and later through the consular office in Kulangsu. In reviewing various options as to what the mission staff should do about the situation, the board advised the evacuation of mothers and children and any persons who had physical ailments. It further suggested that anyone due for a furlough in the near future should also consider leaving. With respect to others, the board advised discretion regarding who and how many should stay, "following out the principle of manning parts where the greatest service could be rendered to our Chinese friends, disregarding entirely considerations of property interests." [41]

As American relations with Japan steadily worsened in 1940 and 1941, the American consulate at Kulangsu strongly urged the missionaries to take caution and seriously consider leaving China. The home board also periodically restated its policy that they should feel free to leave China. By and large, only missionary wives and mothers heeded the advice. Moreover, several missionaries who had taken furloughs returned to China after about a year. Among the returnees were the Angus and Vander Meer families with their five children.[42]

The decision on the part of the Reformed missionaries to remain in China despite difficult wartime conditions was not unique but was practiced throughout China by missionaries of all denominations. It was this dedication and close relationship that developed between the foreign missionaries and the Chinese that later prompted De Pree to write an article appropriately entitled "Are We One?":

> I have been greatly impressed by the unique
> opportunity the war gave missionaries in China to show

their oneness with the people. This has enabled them to make a special contribution and has made a deep impression. Some missionaries refused to desert their posts and were interned. Some who were interned refused opportunities for an exchange of prisoners. They did this because they were devoted to their work but also because of their attachment to their Chinese brethren. Others shared the dangers, difficulties, and hardships of moving institutions into free China. And here again under deprivations and uncertainties they showed the desire to help carry the heavy burdens the Chinese were carrying.[43]

In view of the position taken by the missionaries to stay and help their Chinese brethren, the government of China decided to withdraw all restrictions on the teaching of Christianity in the mission schools.

When the last of the Reformed departees had bidden farewell to China in the summer of 1941, the mission staff still consisted of twenty missionaries. This number was soon increased by two with the return of the Reverends Poppen and Veenschoten who had been in America on furlough. Leaving their families behind, they arrived at Kulangsu November 27, 1941, just ten days before the Japanese attack on Pearl Harbor. It is interesting to note that because of the worsening diplomatic situation, the Board of Foreign Missions had dispatched a letter a few days before Pearl Harbor suggesting that the missionaries on Kulangsu relocate somewhere in Free China. The letter came too late to be of any influence, although some money that the board had sent a short time earlier did arrive in time.

On the same day that Pearl Harbor was attacked on December 7, 1941 (December 8, Chinese time), the Japanese occupied Kulangsu, resulting in the immediate internment of the missionaries. Initially, for about a week, they were housed under guard in a girls' school and a small, seldom used Japanese hospital. During their absence, the Japanese searched their residences and confiscated all radios, photographic equipment, and firearms. Mission schools were closed for a few months and then allowed to reopen after some reorganization by the Japanese. Principals and teachers were shifted around in the hopes of breaking any feeling of solidarity within the school, and westerners, including neutrals, were not allowed to participate as teachers or administrators.

As developments eventually unfolded, the five male missionaries (Koeppe, Oltman, Poppen, Veenschoten, and Voskuil) were billeted together in two adjoining missionary houses. Five of the women (Mrs. Angus and Mrs. Vander Meer and the Misses Beekman, Green, and Smies) were similarly grouped in the missionary home known as Sa-loh. For the present, Jeannette Veldman was housed in the mission hospital.[44]

For safety reasons, Agnes Angus and Alma Vander Meer had been staying at Kulangsu with the children, while their husbands continued to work upcountry. Thus it happened that after Pearl Harbor and the Japanese occupation of Kulangsu, these two families found themselves separated. Little did they realize how long the separation would last. The two mothers with their children were later repatriated in the summer of 1942 to the United States, but William Vander Meer continued to work as head of Talmage College until 1944, when he returned to the United States, and William Angus continued his labors as an itinerant evangelist in Free China until the war ended.

The missionaries at Kulangsu were instructed not to go outside the walls of their compounds without securing prior permission, but there were exceptions to the restriction. Dr. Oltman, as a physician, was given an armband permitting him to move about Kulangsu to make house calls on foreign belligerents and neutrals and to make occasional visits to the mission hospital. Alma Vander Meer, because of her Danish passport, also was not placed under house arrest to the extent that the other missionaries were. To assist her in getting past the Japanese guards and soldiers, she was given an armband with Japanese characters stating she was a "friendly enemy." Her special citizenship status enabled her to carry messages occasionally to and from the men. In describing these visits later, she gave the following rather amusing recollection:

> I remember they had a big picture of President Roosevelt that had come with the *New York Times*. They had that standing on their mantelpiece. Whenever a Japanese officer would come to see them and sit down and talk with

them, he would just quietly go and turn the picture around and after he had gone, the missionaries would turn the picture back.[45]

According to Theodore Oltman, the Japanese treated the missionary internees quite well. When their bank accounts were frozen, he reported that their captors were fairly generous in letting them requisition sums of money from time to time for their needs. Moreover, they were allowed to keep their servants and have them go out and purchase food. Religious services were permitted, and the missionaries could leave their compounds to attend them. Oltman attributed these leniencies to the fact that the missionaries during this period of internment were under the jurisdiction of Japanese navy personnel, who, he declared, "were actually a little more genteel, not quite as coarse as the army."[46]

Geraldine Smies, who was repatriated in June, 1942, also indicated that the missionaries on Kulangsu were being treated well. Upon her return to the States, Smies stated that Edna Beekman and Katherine Green were "comfortable" at Sa-loh and

> have sufficient food and money, and are enjoying their home. Miss Beekman tends her garden, and the chickens and ducks. Miss Green pursues her hobby of studying Chinese character, and writes Chinese fairy stories, which she reads to Miss Beekman for criticism.... Every other day they are given a mimeographed Japanese newspaper published in English by the Japanese, one issue of which paid a tribute to "the missionaries who stick to their posts."[47]

The internees, despite having certain freedoms, were not permitted to have radios, although some missionaries managed to hide theirs from the Japanese for a time. Alma Vander Meer succeeded in this, and when she was repatriated in June, 1942, she gave her radio to Michael Veenschoten. The missionaries also learned some news from their Chinese servants, but they on the whole were hesitant to pass on any information. Because the radios belonging to neutral foreigners in Kulangsu were not confiscated, Oltman, in making house calls among them, was able to get occasional news from the outside and pass it along.[48]

With the entry of the United States into the war, the problem of maintaining contact between the board and the missionaries became a major concern. Limited contact with those working in Free China was possible, as communications could be directed through the Nationalist wartime capital at Chungking, where the United States maintained an embassy. Money could also be sent through the Bank of China and the Missions Bureau. The latter was a cooperative organization that the various missions had established at Chungking. Maintaining communication with the missionaries on Kulangsu in Occupied China was more difficult, but there were some contacts. Jeannette Veldman, for example, received an occasional letter from her father in America, and Geraldine Smies reported sending cards on a regular basis to Ruth Broekema at Tong-an and receiving cards from her in return.[49]

Soon after Pearl Harbor, the American and Japanese governments began discussing the exchange of American personnel in Occupied China and Japanese nationals in the United States. As a result of these talks, application forms for repatriation were distributed in March, 1942, among the Americans at Kulangsu. Except in the case of government officials, the Japanese did not require anyone to leave, although they strongly urged them to do so. Evacuees were allowed to take personal effects and a certain amount of money with them, and before departure were permitted to sell the rest of their property at auction.

The procedure, as finally worked out, provided for a number of Americans to be sent in the spring of 1942 from Kulangsu to Shanghai, which was to be the final port of departure. At Shanghai, they were to board an Italian ship, the 18,765-ton *Conte Verdi*, for passage to the port of Lorenco Marques in Portuguese East Africa.[50] Here they would be exchanged for Japanese nationals being brought there from the United States aboard a Swedish ship, the 18,350-ton *Gripsholm*, which in turn would take the repatriated Americans back to the States.

The missionaries at Kulangsu, knowing there was to be another chance for repatriation later, decided that women with children (Agnes Angus and Alma Vander Meer) should leave this time along with Edwin Koeppe, who was in poor health. Also repatriated with this group were Geraldine Smies, Theodore Oltman, and Henry Voskuil.[51] Left behind were Henry Poppen, Michael

Veenschoten, Edna Beekman, Katherine Green, and Jeannette Veldman. Arrangements were made for a small Japanese coastal steamer to take the evacuees to Shanghai. Because it carried other passengers besides those from Kulangsu, it was crowded with missionaries, newspaper correspondents, business personnel, and consular officials. The food was reported as being "wretched," and the service and treatment poor. Mrs. Angus and Mrs. Vander Meer and their children, for example, had to sleep on mats on the deck in one of the holds of the ship. The evacuation took place in two stages, with the first group leaving Kulangsu on April 16 and the second on May 14. Each trip took about a week because the ship traveled only during the day, anchoring near the coast at night with lights out. The missionaries stayed in Shanghai for some time until the *Conte Verdi* was ready. During this interval, they were treated well, received good food and lodging, and were given considerable freedom to walk around.[52]

The *Conte Verdi* set sail in July. The Italian crew, according to Alma Vander Meer, provided friendly service, even though their country was on the side of the Axis powers. After steaming down the China coast, the ship stopped at Singapore to pick up fresh water, then set out across the Indian Ocean for Lorenco Marques. Outside Singapore, a Japanese ship, carrying evacuees from Japan, joined the *Conte Verdi*. The two ships, readily identifiable with red crosses painted on their sides and kept brightly lighted at night, then set sail across the Indian Ocean within sight of each other. Japanese planes buzzed them occasionally but otherwise left them alone. Vander Meer gives the following colorful account of the *Conte Verdi's* arrival at Lorenco Marques:

> It was really exciting to see the American gunboats there, the crew all on deck waving to us and blowing the whistles, the victory signal. And we saw the big ship, the *Gripsholm*, lying in the harbor there, a beautiful white ship painted in gold and red crosses around in different places. Our ship docked near the *Gripsholm*, and the exchange of prisoners took place. It was interesting to see that the Japanese had been allowed to take crates with what we understand were sewing machines, and typewriters, and bicycles, and all kinds of supplies, and what we had was mostly carried in our hands as we

boarded the *Gripsholm*. The table was set on deck for us and we had a great American feast. Beautiful American food, and we sang "God Bless America" as we stood there around the table of abundance.[53]

The *Gripsholm* arrived in New York August 25, ending, for those who had left from Shanghai, a voyage of over 18,000 miles. Of the approximately 1,500 passengers on board, nearly one-half were persons associated with mission work. All received a joyous welcome and were happy to be back—none more so then the six men and women and five children who had been associated with the Reformed church's Amoy mission. In the midst of their joy, however, their thoughts no doubt also went back to the husbands, fathers, and friends still in China, including the five Reformed missionaries who remained interned in Kulangsu.[54]

Life for those on Kulangsu went on pretty much as before. When Oltman left, Veenschoten was appointed in his place as a representative of the Americans, allowing him to move about quite freely with the usual identifying armband. According to a report of September 4, 1942, concerning the status of the missionaries, "All seem to have somewhat more freedom than they did [before]. They can now visit one another more frequently, and when Jeannette Veldman had the 'flu' she was allowed [to leave her room at the hospital] to go to Sa-loh to rest up." Later, she was permitted to remain there with the other two women on a permanent basis.[55]

That the Kulangsu missionaries were getting along quite well is also shown in a later report, this one from Jessie Platz at Changchow and based on information supplied by two of her friends from Kulangsu. Concerning the women at Sa-loh, she wrote:

They are all well. Since their former servants all came inland, Miss Veldman makes the breakfast, Miss Green the supper, and Miss Beekman washes the dishes. They have one helper who comes in at noon.... Beekman is teaching three little Danish children in order to get money for food for the three crippled children in the Pity the Little Children's Home. [They] still have canned goods and jam, get vegetables from gardens and are very economical, not buying much. Friends give them things—a chicken for Christmas and a duck for New

Year's.[56]

To quote from another report, this one written after the last of the Kulangsu missionaries had been repatriated:

> Life on Kulangsu was quite comfortable, the main difficulty being to find occupation for mind and hands....
> As time went on, [Veenschoten] and Mr. Poppen were permitted to go from their home to visit the women missionaries at Sa-loh. Twice a week they "painted the town red"—playing dominoes! Sundays they gathered for coffee, and held a devotional service. The sacrament of communion refreshed and strengthened them.[57]

Although it was thought that the five Reformed missionaries who had remained behind at Kulangsu would also soon be repatriated, it was more than a year before they finally left. The procedure for their leaving was quite similar to that of the first exchange. They, too, were first brought to Shanghai and had to wait several weeks before continuing on the next leg to freedom. The ship they boarded at Shanghai, however, was not the Italian *Conte Verdi* but a Japanese liner, the *Teia Maru*. To prevent the *Conte Verdi* from falling into Japanese hands when Italy surrendered to the Allies in Europe, the Italian crew had scuttled it in Shanghai harbor.

The location where the exchange took place was also different, namely, the port of Mormugao in Portuguese India. It was the *Gripsholm*, however, that picked up the evacuees at Mormugao and brought them to the United States. After stops at Port Elizabeth, South Africa, and Rio de Janeiro, Brazil, it arrived at Jersey City on December 1, 1943. For its 1,440 passengers, this meant the end of a seventy-four-day sea voyage of 16,000 miles. Of the 1,200 American passengers, about 1,000 came from Occupied China, eighty from Japan, and the rest from the Philippines and French Indo-China.

Missionaries made up the largest group of repatriates, with Protestants numbering 504 (representing thirty-five denominations) and Catholics 162. A few days after their arrival, the five Reformed missionaries received a "joyous, thankful welcome" at the denominational board rooms in New York from some eighty relatives, furloughed missionaries, and board members. On the following day, they joined more than 350 other missionary repatriates for a "Service of Thanksgiving and Intercession" in the Collegiate Reformed Church of St Nicholas on 5th Avenue and 48th Street. The gathering was sponsored by the Greater New York Federation of Churches and the Foreign Missions Conference of North America.[58]

The missionaries who had been repatriated and planned to return to China after the war kept themselves occupied in several useful ways. Dr. Hofstra spent some time studying the treatment of tuberculosis at a sanitarium in New York state, nurse Veldman studied public health at Columbia University, and nurse Nienhuis pursued similar work in Denver. Two missionaries, De Velder and Veenschoten, took the opportunity to enroll in short courses in Mandarin at Yale, and Poppen taught the Amoy dialect to a group of Navy men at the University of Colorado at Boulder. A few missionaries also joined for brief periods the new appointees who were studying Chinese language and culture at the Berkeley school in California.

Some of the repatriated missionaries kept themselves active by traveling around the country visiting churches and mission fests, describing the work the Reformed church was doing in China. Thus, the Reverend Edwin Koeppe, who was among the first group of repatriates to leave Occupied China in 1942, reported in 1945 that he had visited over 200 churches from the East Coast to Kansas, had spoken over 500 times, and had traveled more than 45,000 miles.[59]

One Reformed missionary managed to obtain travel booking *in the direction* of China after the United States became involved in the conflict. This was the indomitable veteran Tena Holkeboer, and she did not quite make it all the way to China until after the war—although she gave it a good try! She was in the United States on her third furlough at the time of Pearl Harbor. After months of trying to get back to China, she finally managed to make her way to Lisbon as a passenger on a Portuguese freighter. At Lisbon, she boarded a small vessel for Portuguese East Africa, which she reached twenty-eight days later. After being stranded there for three months, she took a train to Durban in Natal, South Africa, from where, after another wait, she took passage on a ship that was part of an Allied convoy enroute to Columbo, Ceylon (now Sri Lanka). Delayed there for a time by food poisoning, she finally managed to reach Calcutta, from which she hoped to catch an Army plane into China. When this was denied her, she waited out the war by working the next year and a half at the Reformd church's Arcot mission in South India. Although Tena Holkeboer was pleased with her work in India, it was not like Amoy, and she set out for it as soon as transportation became available after the war.

With all the Kulangsu missionaries safely back in America, eleven Reformed missionaries were still left in China, but with an important difference—they were in Free China. The eleven were distributed as follows: Dr. Richard Hofstra and Jessie Platz and Elizabeth Bruce at Changchow; the Reverend Henry and Kate De Pree and William Vander Meer in the North River district; Ruth Broekema and the Reverend Frank Eckerson at Tong-an; and the Reverend Walter and Harriet De Velder and the Reverend William Angus, who moved around among several stations.

At Changchow, Hofstra and Platz continued their usual labors at the Union Hospital. They also engaged in nurses' training and made occasional visits to the other upcountry hospitals to confer with their resident Chinese physicians. Bruce kept herself occupied teaching in the boys' and girls' schools and the women's Bible school. She also did evangelistic work throughout the city, and once a month met with the city pastors, Bible Women, school teachers, and consistory members for fellowship and Bible study.

When the Japanese began bombing Changchow after the fall of Amoy City in 1938, large American flags and signs were displayed around the mission buildings. Flags were also painted on the roof tiles of the buildings. Later, after Pearl Harbor and America's entrance into the war, one of the first things that had to be done involved turning the tiles so as to cover the flags. Some years later, Bruce, in writing about her wartime experiences, posed an interesting question: "I wonder today, 1971, as I write this, if the Communists have discovered them?" Because of the blackout at night, she also reminisced that her evenings at Changchow were frequently quite boring. "So," as she explained, "night after night I played the piano. It was my hobby. I loved to do creative writing. I wrote the music and lyrics to 'I love America,' and many hymns."[60]

In the North River district, the seminary and Talmage College continued under the able direction of the De Prees and Vander Meer respectively. In both situations, the students, in addition to their studies, made their presence felt in several ways. Seminary students, for example, looked after about a half dozen preaching stations as well as a number of Sunday schools. Contributions by Talmage students were somewhat different. They took over management of the local primary school, an act that soon doubled its enrollment, and, in cooperation with a local physician, opened a dispensary which treated an average of fifty patients a day. They also assisted in giving thousands of inoculations for plague, cholera, typhoid, and small pox to the residents of Hoa-an and nearby villages. Like the students at the seminary, those at Talmage conducted Sunday schools in several villages and held Sabbath services at three neighboring chapels. In cooperation with the local government, Talmage students also assisted farmers in planting 100,000 seedling tung trees on the neighboring hillsides for tung oil production.[61]

The Reverends Angus, De Velder, and Eckerson engaged themselves primarily in the traditional kinds of evangelism. All three men had to take on extra duties because Poppen and Veenschoten, who normally would have helped with the upcountry work, were interned at Kulangsu and later repatriated. Responsibilities included attending classis meetings, preachers' conferences, and conferences of elders and deacons; ordaining Chinese preachers and dedicating new mission buildings; performing the sacraments at places that had no ordained pastor; opening new stations and installing new pastors; and smoothing over any frictions that might develop among the congregations.

In view of the poor transportation facilities resulting from wartime conditions, missionary travels were generally of an itinerant nature, involving a circular course with the terminal point near the place where the tour started. The travels could be very lengthy and time consuming. Thus, in May and June, 1941, the Reverend and Mrs. De Velder spent two months in the North River district. During that time, they walked some 200 miles and visited six mother churches and seventeen outstations. Harriet De Velder, a nurse, supplemented her husband's work by giving medical attention to those who sought it. Similarly, in early 1943, the Reverends Angus and De Velder took trips together totaling 700 miles, 450 of which were covered on foot. In many respects, modes of travel were not too different from those followed by the late nineteenth century misssionaries. But, as one of the reports put it, "All was done joyfully to help build the South Fukien Church." Because of failing health, Eckerson did not carry on as much itinerant work as the others.[62]

In addition to engaging in the more traditional approaches to evangelism, the three men had special assignments. Thus Eckerson, as chairman of the synod's Centenary Committee, was charged with making sure that the mission's centennial would be properly observed. Similarly, Angus played a major role in organizing training institutes for lay workers, and De Velder, as executive director of youth work for the South Fukien Church, had special responsibility in that field of endeavor.

A novel development in reference to De Velder's work was the introduction of youth fellowship conferences, the first of which were held in the summer of 1942. Modeled as much as possible after those in America, each lasted about a week, during which time efforts were made to give young Chinese a well-rounded program mixing evangelism with play and recreation. The conferences were so well received that they henceforth became a regular summer feature.[63]

Ruth Broekema's work undoubtedly changed the most in wartime. Since first arriving in China in 1924, her work had been confined almost entirely to the Tong-an district and devoted especially to education; however, the war years found her visiting churches not only in the Tong-an district but elsewhere as well, including an adjoining London Missionary district that was short-handed. She also worked closely with Angus in organizing worker retreats, and with De Velder in convening youth conferences.[64]

One of the major problems facing the mission during the last years of the war was inflation, as prices went up almost daily. For example, in January, 1943, rice was selling for $3 per pound Chinese currency; by April, it had risen to $21. The inflation rate eventually became so serious that, as described here by De Velder, drastic action had to be taken:

> Our salaries could not keep pace with inflation because we were getting unfavorable exchange and [so] in the

summer of 1943 the Board allowed the Mission to set its
own salaries as needs arose because the communications
between America and China were so slow that by the time
the Board granted a salary, further inflation had overtaken
us.[65]

Inflation fell particularly hard on Chinese clergy laboring
among small congregations, despite efforts by the South Fukien
Synod to rectify the problem. As explained by Angus:

Because of the continued rise in prices, Synod fixed the
basic salaries of church workers in terms of commodities.
Each worker must receive wood for fuel and oil for light,
not kerosene oil which is about $2,000 a gallon. Families
of three or less receive thirty catties of rice per member
per month, and families of more than three, twenty-five
catties per month. A catty is half a kilogram. The rest of
the salary is paid in money, a part according to the number
in the family, and a smaller part according to the
qualifications of the worker. Unfortunately, Synod's
committee fixes the minimum money salary at the
beginning of the year and it soon becomes obsolete. It is
one of my perennial tasks as I visit the churches to try and
get the congregations to pay their pastors and preachers at
least Synod's minimum, and more if possible.[66]

It is thus not surprising that, as Angus further explained, some of
the younger clergy left the ministry to take up teaching. Others
tried to combine it with other types of work, which invariably
resulted in a lowering of the minister's efficiency in carrying on
pastoral duties. By the close of the war in 1945, increasing costs
were also forcing the cancelation of some training institutes for
lay people and even classis meetings.

As the war went on, it became increasingly difficult to purchase
certain articles, including some food items. Elizabeth Bruce, in
reminiscing in 1971 about food shortages during the war years,
wrote: "We had no bread, no white potatoes, no milk, next to no
meat and rice was rationed. I lost 40 pounds. Good old
peanuts...kept us alive. Did you ever make a meatloaf of peanuts
and sweet potatoes? Try it sometime."[67] As kerosene became
scarce, peanuts were put to another use. Their oil was used for
lamps, including those in the churches, despite its giving off a

foul smell and furnishing poor light. Unfortunately, like almost everything else, peanut oil prices eventually also soared.

The missionaries received a pleasant surprise in the summer of 1944 when a group of American sailors arrived in the Amoy area and rented various buildings from the mission for housing. The men were sent there to observe Japanese shipping in Amoy harbor and along the coast and to take soundings. They also established a weather station near Changchow, provided a means for rescuing downed pilots, and trained Chinese guerrillas at a camp near Hoa-an. As Angus reported in 1945, "These servicemen provided a pleasant link with America." The De Prees welcomed them to their home at Eng-hok, as did Ruth Broekema at Tong-an. The visitors in return gave the missionaries razor blades and shaving cream along with books and magazines, and occasionally even candy bars and coffee.[68]

An exchange of views among the missionaries in early 1944 indicated that they should be giving some attention to furloughs. The Board of Foreign Missions also discussed the matter occasionally, including the proposition that because of the strain under which the missionaries were working, the usual seven-year rule should not apply. The end result of the discussions was the drawing up of a potential furlough slate. Elizabeth Bruce, who already had seven years of service since her last furlough, was placed at the top of the list, followed by William Vander Meer. Both of them left in the spring of 1944. The next to leave were the De Velders, Richard Hofstra, and Jessie Platz. Their unexpected departure in June, 1944, was prompted by warnings that the Japanese were planning a major offensive that might place Leng-na and Changchow in danger of being cut off. Concern for the De Velders was especially heightened because of their two small children.

As the Japanese had control of the coastline, the missionaries had only one practical avenue of departure from China, namely, by air from the American base at Kunming to Calcutta, India. Getting from South Fukien to Kunming, which was located in Yunan province in southwestern China, was not easily done, however. For starters, it involved a zig-zag route of more than 1,000 miles, using whatever travel means available, to Kwelin in the northeast corner of Kwangsi province. (For this leg of the journey, the De

Velders traveled by truck, bus, and plane, in that order.) At Kwelin, the site of another major air base, the travelers boarded a DC 47, provided by General Chennault's Fourteenth Air Force, for Kunming. Walter De Velder described the Kunming base as a "beehive of activity" with thousands of American GIs present.

Getting caught in enemy air raids at any of these stops proved to be more than distinct possibilities, but the travelers also had at least two pleasant encounters on the trip. The first was at Kwelin, where they had an opportunity to meet Colonel Frank Otte, who was born in Amoy and was a son of the famous Dr. Abraham Otte who served the Amoy mission from 1887 to 1910.[69] The second was at Kunming, where they could meet an old friend and former colleague, Major Theodore Oltman, who had served the mission hospitals for several years as a doctor but was now one of the base's medical officers.

At Kunming, the missionaries, after obtaining the necessary visas for entering British India, boarded another DC 47 for the nine-hour flight over the Himalaya Mountains to Calcutta. Then came a wait for transportation to America. In the case of the De Velders, they spent four months serving the Reformed church's Arcot mission in South India before taking passage to the States aboard an American troopship that left Bombay December 15, 1944. It arrived at San Pedro, California, February 2, 1945, via Australia, New Zealand, New Caledonia, and the Fiji Islands.[70]

The departure of Bruce, Vander Meer, the De Velders, Hofstra, and Platz, all in 1944, left only five Reformed missionaries to continue on, namely, Angus, Broekema, the De Prees, and Eckerson. It should be noted that by this time, the foreign staff of the two sister missions in South Fukien had also been reduced, with the English Presbyterians retaining only three in the field and the London Missionary Society only four. In his customary keen-witted way of explaining situations, Angus, in the mission's year-end report for 1944, described the reduced status of the staff thus: "Since the beginning of Japan's war on China, the Mission has been on a skeleton staff basis. Each year it became more and more evident that the skeleton was being reduced to a mere bag of bones and this year in June we find there were only five bones left."[71] To their credit, the "five bones" remained for the duration, carrying on as best they could.

XVII
The Post-War Years,
1945-1949

When the war with Japan ended in August, 1945, there were only five Reformed missionaries serving in China. These were the Reverends Frank Eckerson and William Angus, the Reverend Henry and Kate De Pree, and Ruth Broekema. All were veterans, having served a combined total of 159 years in China. Lack of accommodations made it difficult to get them home as quickly as was hoped after the war ended, and one never returned. Although Frank Eckerson had not been back to the States since 1934 and was fully entitled to a furlough, this tireless worker chose to remain in China. As events turned out, he died there on November 8, 1949, at age seventy-three after forty-six years of service.[1]

The return of missionaries to China took place gradually after the war because of transportation problems. Initially, they returned singly or in small groups. The first of the "Old China Hands" to return were the Reverend Michael Veenschoten December 19, 1945, Tena Holkeboer January 9, 1946, and the Reverend Henry Poppen January 18, 1946. They were soon followed by the Reverend John Muilenburg and Katherine Green, and then by Drs. Clarence Holleman and Richard Hofstra, the Reverend Edwin Koepe, and Jessie Platz.

Transportation facilities had improved sufficiently by September of 1946 to allow about a dozen Reformed missionaries to leave San Francisco aboard the *Marine Lynx* of the American President Lines. All the returnees had served in China before and were part of a passenger list that included nearly 400 missionaries destined for fields in East Asia. This was one of the largest peacetime movements of missionaries in history. Henry Luce, the son of missionary parents and editor-in-chief of *Life* magazine, addressed the group. Passage aboard the vessel was arranged by the Foreign Missions Conference of North America with three ports of call on its itinerary: Manila, Shanghai, and Hong Kong. Accommodations were those of a troop transport with passengers assigned to small cabins and tiers of bunks. Not everyone was satisfied with these arrangements, and some dubbed the ship the "Marine Stinks." A few months later another group of Reformed missionaries left San Francisco, again with a few hundred other missionaries destined for East Asia and all having to put up with troopship accommodations. Several passengers among the second group were missionary wives, including Dorothy Poppen, Stella Veenschoten, and Virginia Muilenburg, on their way to join husbands who had left earlier.[2]

Despite difficulties in obtaining transportation, there were thirty-six Reformed missionaries in the Amoy field by the end of 1946. These included ten ordained men, four unordained men, and twenty-two women—of whom ten were single. A few additional Reformed missionaries arrived after 1946, bringing the total number to nearly fifty. With few exceptions, all were still serving in China when the Communists occupied the Amoy region in late 1949. About a dozen and a half of the post-war missionaries were new to the field. The last to arrive was the Reverend Wilbur Brandli, who came in 1949.

It is interesting to note that although conditions in China had changed considerably over the years, the new recruits, especially those who located in the upcountry places, had some of the same reactions to their surroundings as did the missionaries who arrived in the nineteenth century. Newcomers, for example, continued to be struck by the curiosity the Chinese had about foreigners. Thus, the Reverend Joseph and Marion Esther, who arrived in 1946 and labored in the Tong-an region, reported in 1947:

> Our children are to the Chinese what a hippo would be to any United States village. They are wonders to behold and are stared at frankly.... As a private excursion, our family planned an ascent of a mountain near our house, a

fifteen minute hike rewarding us with a grand view of the valley. At the top we counted our family and found that we had thirty children and some grown up ones. Privacy![3]

Similarly, Dr. Jack Hill, who, with his wife, Joan, arrived in 1947 and was also scheduled to serve at Tong-an, showed surprise at some of the street scenes. Describing his experiences the day after he first set foot in China he wrote:

The next day my indoctrination began. As I arose and looked out over the housetops of Kulangsu across the harbor at Amoy, and gazed over the distant landscape, I saw the "Stern and rockbound coast" and beyond, low mountains rising perhaps 500-2,000 feet. Once on the street I became acquainted with new scenes—narrow unpaved streets and open shops displaying carcasses of fresh meat, fish, bolts of bright-colored cloth.... Pigs of all sizes, but always black, shift for themselves, along with the chickens, ducks, dogs, and cats, most of which present gaunt undernourished appearances as they scurry about dodging the pedestrians. Once reclining on the street, however, these animals acquire an air of complete indifference to what goes on about them and sleep soundly though passers-by must detour around them continually.

Haggling over prices of articles bought in the shops was another new experience to witness and endure. The shopkeeper sets some absurdly high price and the buyer offers a mere half the sum. Then follows a mutual guffaw at each other's ridiculous statements. Once that formality is past, faces darken and haggling is begun in earnest; both parties at timely intervals threaten to walk away in disgust. Inchwise and with verbose reasoning an agreement is reached, then faces immediately drop their surly, clouded expressions for benign complacency.[4]

Upon the request of the mission and the Church of South Fukien, the Board of Foreign Missions sent a small deputation to Amoy in the autumn of 1946. Made up of the Reverend Luman Shafer, secretary of the board, and the Reverend Anthony Van Westenburg, the primary purpose of the visit was to examine at first hand and carefully evaluate the conditions at the mission.

For six weeks, the two men labored at their task virtually from dawn to dusk. For example, after spending a week at Kulangsu and Changchow, they were whisked off on a 250-mile, ten-day trip to the Leng-na district—the first of three trips made into the interior. All in all, as Shafer later reported, he and Van Westenburg

> visited every station of the Mission, attended the meetings of two Classes, one ordination service, preached in several of the churches, and shared in Mission conferences and conferences with representatives of the other two Missions and the Executive Committee of Synod.[5]

According to the deputation's report, "The most serious factor in the present situation and one that most directly affects the Mission, is that of inflation." It noted that the present exchange rate was $3,350 CNC (Chinese National Currency) to one American dollar, as compared to a ratio of two to one before the war.[6] Prices were soon of the runaway kind. For example, a letter from Poppen to the Board of Foreign Missions dated May 6, 1946, stated that in a single ten-day period the price of rice had increased from $3,000 CNC to $7,000 CNC per peck, and that the end was not in sight.[7] A serious crop failure in the spring of 1946 added to the difficulties facing the churches, especially since the Chinese ministers and teachers received a large part of their salary in rice rather than money.

Skyrocketing prices brought about some strange situations as is clearly evident in this excerpt from the mission's annual report for 1946: "We are [involved in] eleven grammar and high schools in the area and the reported income in fees from these schools runs into the hundreds of millions, whereas it represents only a few thousands in actual value."[8] As another example of how inflation sometimes bordered on the bizarre, Alma Vander Meer later recalled an occasion in which a letter to one of her sons required twenty-eight stamps with an inflated combined value of $8,540 but in real value, only twenty cents. It is not surprising that the postmaster informed her that she might be unable to send any more such letters because there was not enough room on the envelope for more stamps.[9] Because of spiraling inflation (by late 1947 it took 100,000 Chinese dollars to equal one American dollar), the missionaries were eventually authorized to fix their own salaries to meet the ever changing situation.

In other ways, too, the situation facing the missionaries after the war was not an enviable one. Eight years of conflict had left much of the country devastated and many churches, schools, hospitals, and missionary residences in poor condition. In some cases it was a matter of repairing buildings that were already deteriorating before the war. In other instances, it involved rebuilding what had been damaged as a result of aerial bombing or because of deliberate dismantling. With respect to the latter, when American warplanes from the Philippines began flying over Amoy City, the Japanese removed the roofs of buildings to get at beams that could be used for fortifications and air-raid shelters. The removal of girders and other supports frequently left the walls in a weakened condition. The Chinese also did their share of dismantling because of the fuel shortage. It was not uncommon, for example, for window and door frames, and even furniture, to be broken up and used as fuel or sold as such by the bundle. It is thus not surprising that returning missionaries sometimes had to put up with inadequate housing. At the end of 1946, for example, the missionary residences on Flag Staff Hill on Kulangsu Island were still without roofs and with virtually "hollowed out" interiors. At Leng-na, the De Velder family was housed in what at best were semi-repaired quarters, and Katherine Green had to be satisfied with little more than a dry roof.[10]

In view of the considerable amount of rehabilitation of old buildings and new construction that was needed, the Board of Foreign Missions sent out an appeal for "someone with the requisite knowledge and skill to help reconstruct damaged Mission properties." The board was overjoyed in late 1946 when a person with such qualifications offered himself as a candidate for the job. His name was Demarest Romaine, Jr., a young man of Reformed church background and a graduate of Stevens Institute of Technology. It is interesting to note that he had some firsthand acquaintance with China's reconstruction needs, having served in the U.S. Navy in Chinese coastal waters during the closing months of the war.

Because young Romaine's appointment was for a "short term" (that is, three years) and because of the nature of his work, he was not obligated to spend the usual one or two years learning Chinese. His responsibility involved planning and designing construction projects and serving as the "number one" overseer for most of them. Major new construction included a combination classroom and chapel building for Talmage College and a 150-bed Union Hospital at Changchow; classroom buildings for the girls' primary and secondary schools at Kulangsu; missionary residences at Kulangsu, Sio-khe, and elsewhere; and several places of worship. In the way of rehabilitation, there were buildings of all types that needed repair. Because Romaine could not be present at the construction sites at all times, others helped in the supervision, including Veenschoten at Sio-khe, Koepe and Holleman at Kulangsu, and Hofstra at Changchow.

Funding for these projects came from several sources. The improved financial situation in the United States prompted the Board of Foreign Missions to anticipate what the mission's needs might be when peace returned to China. To that end, $20,000 in emergency funds was set aside for construction purposes in 1944, and nearly double that amount in 1945. A newly introduced program known as the United Advance Fund, ending in 1948, was also instrumental in raising money. Help likewise came from individual congregations in the States, various philanthropic organizations, and the Chinese people.[11]

To illustrate more specifically the various sources of help that became available, the construction and furnishing of the new classroom building for the Yoh-tek Girl's Primary School at Kulangsu can be taken as a case in point, particularly since very few of the expenses were borne by the mission itself. A large part of the costs were met by gifts from the women of the Reformed church and the David Abeel Memorial Fund (described in the previous chapter), while 6,000 pounds of flour donated by UNRRA (United Nations Relief and Rehabilitation Administration) helped pay the wages of the workmen.

Particularly remarkable was the support and loyalty shown by Yoh-tek's graduates, especially those who were living abroad. Gifts were primarily in the form of furnishings and included ten teachers' desks, 290 double desks and benches for the pupils, and a piano from the Manila Alumnae Association, and fifty small chairs and a slide and swing set for kindergartners from the

Penang Alumnae Association. Similarly, an iron fence to be placed around the school yard and iron bars for the first floor windows were furnished by graduates residing at Singapore, while graduates on the Philippine island of Cebu paid the expenses for beautifying the U-shaped central court used for flag-raising ceremonies and physical exercises. Graduates acting individually also contributed furnishings. Thus, one gave thirty metal beds and another contributed fifteen double wardrobes for storing clothing.

Later, a two-story building with two small and eight large classrooms was constructed for the Yoh-tek Girls' High School. It was made possible from funds raised on the occasion of the Jubilee of the Women's Board of Foreign Missions. Sometimes it happened that a single, wealthy Chinese individual bore the brunt of the construction costs. Thanks to funds donated by Mr. Yu Khe-thai, a wealthy Manila business executive, for example, a chapel was also constructed on Yo-tek's campus. It was built as a memorial to Yu's wife, an alumnae of Yok-tek's primary department.

New construction was sometimes stretched out over long periods of time because of the lack of heavy equipment and the unsatisfactory nature of the soil. This is clearly shown in Dr. Hofstra's account of the "hard struggle" (Hofstra's words) involved in preparing the foundations for Changchow's Union Hospital:

> First the high mounds of rubble and dirt had to be cleared away and the plot levelled off. Then trenches had to be dug for strong foundations. We had to dig deep to find solid ground. More than one thousand piles had to be driven down into spots where there seemed to be no bottom. Although the plans were drawn by a good architect, the actual work was done by local people who had no experience in the construction of large buildings. There were no bulldozers, no cranes, no pile drivers, no cement mixers, no trucks to ease and speed up the work. Everything had to be done by hand. A long, dreary, rainy season of five months duration made it impossible to work for more than a few days at a time. Financial instability, rapid rise in prices and difficulty in obtaining stone and other materials brought many a discouraging halt in the

progress. Altogether about 150,000 cubic feet of rubble had to be cleared off the plot, about 100,000 cubic feet of ground dug out for foundation trenches, about 1,500 piles driven in, about 60,000 cubic feet of stone laid down. It took almost eighteen months to get the foundation in.[12]

As noted in an earlier chapter, the ability of the missionaries to carry on evangelistic work was gradually becoming easier before the war because of the road building programs of the Nationalist government and various local authorities. Unfortunately, as Shafer and Van Westenburg discovered during their visit to China in 1946, many of these programs had been "placed on hold" after 1937. Moreover, to restrict possible Japanese troop movements, bridges and culverts had often been destroyed and deep trenches dug across the main roads for a distance of about sixty-five miles inland. Until these roads became passable again, returning missionaries often found travel conditions less convenient than they had been when they left China.

For places where satisfactory roads were available, missionary groups after the war found it useful to have their own motor vehicles. The advantage in this is clearly shown in these remarks written by Walter De Velder when Leng-na received a new 1946 Ford station wagon as a gift from several Reformed churches in Michigan and New Jersey:

> The car should prove to be a great time saver. One spends endless time waiting for buses. It will be of great use in the transporting of medicines, literature, etc. It will provide transportation also for our workers. The day after [it] arrived I took a team of five to a small village seven miles from town where we went to preach. The entire time spent was less than four hours. Ordinarily it would have taken an entire day and it would have been a very tiring one at that. The Ford is a pioneer in the Amoy Mission. It is a great asset in our work and its wheels will have a share in building the Kingdom of God in this important part of the earth.[13]

The disadvantage cited by De Velder of spending "endless time" waiting for a bus was not the only inconvenience associated with that form of travel, as is brought out in a letter by Jack Hill, written soon after his arrival in China in 1947:

Schedules are followed more or less, and the wise
traveler gets to the bus at least half an hour early, buys his
ticket and climbs aboard. He settles himself as comfortably
as possible on the narrow wooden benches along the walls
and waits. If he knows anything about cars he will
recognize after a time that the "motor bus" is a one and a
half ton truck of one of the three popular American makes
and anywhere from seven to seventeen years old. Over his
head is a homemade wooden cab with glassless windows
lining both sides. These square apertures can be
obliterated by wooden boards raised from slots below, and
held in place quite often until the end of the ride.
Finally, when it appears perfectly obvious that not another
passenger can possibly squeeze himself into the bus, even
to stand around the heap of belongings in the center of the
floor, then at least five more are admitted to insinuate
themselves and their luggage slowly and persistently on
the seated passengers. The journey then is made in
comparative comfort, dependent of course on minor
matters such as road surface, dust, or cold air.[14]

Improved roads, however, never became universally available,
with the result that walking remained a common means of travel
in rugged areas. Note in this regard the comments by Joseph
Esther who, in the company of Clarence Holleman and two local
Chinese ministers, made an eight-day tour in late 1947 of the
An-hoe region (north of Tong-an) where the mission had labored
for many years:

The roads are so poor that I doubt if we walked one
mile that week where a bicycle could have been used.
Even walking sometimes more resembled crawling,
climbing, or sliding. We walked across creaking board
bridges, over stepping stones in rapids, and even in one
place waded through the icy spring waters nearly up to
our waist.[15]

Walking had its compensations, however, and Esther, as a
recent arrival, was no different from past new recruits as he
described some of the "marvelously beautiful views" in what he
called "one of earth's grand beauty areas":

Towering granite mountains beyond wide and deep

chasms, grass covered hills, wooded valleys, picturesque villages (picturesque from a distance only), dashing waterfalls, tumbling rills, limpid pools, terraced rice paddies on every hand; mountain flowers in profusion at our feet! Blue skies overhead and sometimes clouds below us![16]

The extensive postwar construction activity was, of course, a prologue to the long-standing objective of the mission, namely, evangelization. As noted in the previous chapter, the churches during the war strenuously sought to realize the hundredth anniversary goals of bringing the gospel to every household in South Fukien by 1942 and making all the churches self-supporting within five years. Significant progress continued to be made in both these areas during the early years of the war, but the infrequent meetings of synod and classes and the preoccupation of the Chinese with the problem of simply surviving, offset some of the gains. As expressed by De Pree, the enthusiasm shown by Chinese preachers, teachers, and hospital workers early in the war was gradually replaced by a feeling of weariness: "For years it kept many near the point of starvation. When peace came they expected a better day would dawn. Instead, things have grown worse. Churches that were independent and took care of their own budget, now have difficulties."[17]

Angus, who like De Pree remained in China throughout the war, was in full agreement with De Pree's analysis of the situation:

> Many pastors and preachers did not receive enough money to support them and their families. If they wished to live, they were forced to engage in buying and selling commodities, farm, or teach. The younger preachers could usually qualify as primary school teachers.
>
> Thus the Church and its workers were preoccupied with financial problems and membership decreased. Some churches reported one, two or even no accessions during the year. The churches and church workers put up a brave fight but the struggle has been a long one and they are tired.[18]

Angus noted, however, that this flagging of the spirit was less true in areas occupied by the Japanese where the people "in their danger and suffering...had drawn closer to God."

Adjustment to the situation was obviously going to take time. The convening of the first post-war synod in February, 1946, and the reappearance of the Little Northfield retreats for ministers and church leaders gradually helped get things back on track. It is interesting to note that the synod expected the South Fukien Church to be more independently Chinese after the war. Missionaries were to serve on committees as before, but always under the direction of Chinese chairmen. Another step in this direction was taken with the decision to place every area of work, including the location and assignment of missionaries, directly under the Chinese church itself. The latter matter was fully discussed and agreed to by the visiting deputation from the board.[19]

The shortage of young Chinese ministers became a major problem for the mission's evangelistic program. Remedying this problem was primarily the responsibility of the seminary, which after an absence of seven years, returned to Changchow after the war. Both faculty and students were happy to get back. As Henry De Pree stated, paraphrasing Moses (Deut. 1:6) addressing the Israelites about moving on, "We have dwelt long enough on the mountain."

The seminary had only twenty students when it reopened at Changchow—two less than when it moved to Eng-hok in 1938. This was far too few a number to meet the future demands of the churches. In explaining the shortage of recruits for the ministry, De Pree wrote:

> It is easy to find causes for this. The materialistic spirit increased by the war, the very evident deprivation and worry preachers had to undergo because of the inadequate salaries under the high cost of living, the allurement of well-paid government positions for young people—all these things tend to keep young men out of the ministry. War conditions made synod meetings or large conferences difficult and each little church struggled on by itself. So there was no united aggressive program of the church to appeal to young people in contrast with the wide organization and manifold propaganda in the political sphere.[20]

Six of the twenty seminary students were women, which, as also explained by De Pree, created something of a dilemma:

> In South Fukien as in other parts of China a characteristic of the times seems to be that an increasing number of women wish to come to the seminaries. In one classis a pastor said, "You can't give us too many women graduates." But in most classes the churches are not quite so sure that a woman preacher would meet their needs. This is a question that the Church will have to work out. We are most thankful for the devotion and consecration of "the devout women not a few." Some graduates are doing very fine work in religious education in schools and we long to see some of the larger churches use them as assistants. If God has called them He will find a place for them in His church. But in many parts of China, leaders feel that in proportion the men offering themselves are far too few.[21]

The fact that several women were enrolled in the seminary was in keeping with the larger trend of women playing a more active role in the churches. In 1942, for example, three times as many women as men were baptized, and over one-third of the deacons were women.[22]

In late 1946, De Pree returned to America where, after a highly deserved vacation, he was appointed head of the newly-inaugurated Department of Religious Education at Hope College in Holland, Michigan. Before leaving China, where he had been associated with the seminary since 1925 (usually as president), De Pree strongly urged, as others had done before him, that only graduates of senior middle schools be admitted and that the seminary program be broadened to four years. The deputation from the Board of Foreign Missions that visited China in 1946 was equally adamant in stressing the need for upgrading the school, declaring the matter to be one of the most critical problems facing the South Fukien Church:

> If we were to express an opinion, it would call for the immediate reorganization of the curriculum so that the course leading to ordination would be based on middle school graduation. If that cannot be done, the Seminary should either combine with some other institution or

institutions in the general area, or arrange for students for the pastoral ministry to go to Nanking Theological Seminary or some other high grade institution. The South Fukien Seminary would, in that case, confine itself to the training of pastors' assistants and lay workers.[23]

Suggestions such as the above proved difficult to carry out because of the urgent need for preachers. In 1948, of the twenty students enrolled in the seminary, only four were graduates of senior middle schools.[24]

Fortunately, the steady increase in the missionary staff helped meet post-war commitments. This was especially true with respect to the return of those missionaries who had served in China before the war. Several of these were veterans of long standing whose work dated back to the early 1920s and even before. The Chinese churches, in asking for missionary help after the war, tended to be quite precise in their requests, by asking for specialists (teachers of science, persons trained in religious education, nurses, and so forth) rather than, as explained by Poppen, "the general type of missionary."[25]

The practice that started during the war of having new appointees take language classes before leaving for China was continued after the war. Everett and Edith Kleinjans, for example, upon being appointed in May, 1947, spent time at the University of Michigan studying Chinese and methods of teaching English to Chinese. Similarly, Wilbur Brandli, who arrived at Amoy in 1949, the last Reformed recruit to be sent to China, studied Chinese at Yale before departing.

The language training post-war appointees engaged in at home was, of course, Mandarin. Although some veteran missionaries questioned this training, the recruits seemed to agree that it was helpful. They also agreed, however, that they still had much to learn upon reaching China. Typical of their experience was that of Anne De Young, who served the Amoy mission as a registered nurse from 1946 to 1951:

> I have been steadily working away at the Amoy dialect, having two hours a day with my teacher and studying the rest of the time by myself. It is a slow process but I can see some progress. By putting forth a little extra energy in April I think I can cover my first year's requirements and

be ready for my first examination in May. The study of Chinese character and Mandarin which I had in Berkeley, California makes it possible for me to do this in about half the time it normally takes, so again I am very grateful for that year in California.[26]

Further light on this matter is shed by the Reverend Gordon Van Wyk who, with his wife Bertha, also served in China from 1946 to 1951. In a letter of 1947 to the *Church Herald*, he wrote that thanks to their preliminary language study in the States, they were "from the first...able to fend for [themselves] in shopping trips to town and in carrying on an ordinary conversation with students."[27] But this by no means meant they were accomplished linguists. In Van Wyk's letter, which was written after he and his wife had already been in China for several months, he further informed his readers that "language study continues to be our main concern here in the field, as I imagine it will be for some time to come."

As was true with new recruits in the past, proper pronunciation remained the biggest hurdle. According to Jack Hill this was due in large part to tone changes, with some Chinese words having as many as seven tone changes and thereby having seven unrelated meanings.[28] It is therefore not surprising that newcomers, even after having had preliminary training in the States, were frequently embarrassed. Joseph Esther described a few such incidents in an article appropriately entitled, "Language Growing Pains":

> When the preacher spoke of needing more sin, the foreigners were amazed and the Chinese nodded approval. Sin means faith. When at a feast I called a lady Kau, the good natured people smiled and explained to me that I had called her a monkey. I meant gau, pronounced almost the same way but meaning "clever". In Amoy I wanted to tell a friend that we had a great wind and found him suppressing a smile. He told me that I had said, "We have a great grandfather today."[29]

Some new approaches to evangelization were introduced during the post-war period and many of the old ways were refined. One of the latter was the joint medical-evangelistic arrangement, and nowhere did it become more highly developed that in the Sio-khe district. As explained by Alma Vander Meer, a registered nurse, most of the medical work being done there was hospital centered. To be of greater service, she proposed that a team of workers go out among the villages on a regular basis and do a combination of preaching, preventive medicine, and evangelism. Other staff members agreed, including Vander Meer's foreign co-worker, Elizabeth Bruce, and the two Chinese staff persons, the Reverend Pan and Dr. Saw.

In order to win a favorable reception at a village, the original plan called for a visit by the team to former hospital patients. It was soon discovered, however, that greater success could be achieved by courting the good will of the village elders and the principals of the schools. It was also found helpful if some of the church people from Sio-khe accompanied the team. As explained by Vander Meer in the summer of 1948, "We have thus far made thirty trips to villages altogether, walking seventy-three miles. Many villages have been visited two or three times, to follow up the work started. We have visited twelve schools with an enrollment of sixty to one hundred students."[30]

Villages were informed in advance of an impending visit, and when the day came, the visiting team invariably found the villagers and school children eagerly awaiting their arrival. As explained by Vander Meer, the procedure was as follows:

> Our program starts with a sing. We teach them short religious songs and health choruses. Dr. Saw, our vivacious young doctor, then takes the lead and, using health charts, he tells about germs and bugs, and he not only gets his ideas across but wins his way into the hearts of the people. His subjects are: methods of prevention of disease, the curse of malaria, the danger of hookworm, and whatever message fits the particular need.
>
> After we have played the Victrola and done some more singing, the evangelistic team takes over. Dr. Saw goes to see the sick in the village and then returns to the school, where many are waiting to be examined. We find that malaria, hookworm, malnutrition and tuberculosis undermine the health of many people. Scabies is so common that we are surprised to find a family without it. Dr. Saw has treated more than five hundred people in

three village clinics. Because of poverty and fear, most of
these patients would never come to the hospital. Now that
they know us and feel that we are their friends, many
have come to the hospital for follow-up treatments. We
have found an unexpected response to our offer to give
plague inoculations, in spite of the fact that this was
something altogether new to them. All told, more than
three thousand people were inoculated against plagues....
After the program, the people are eager to have us visit in
their homes. We have words of praise for those who keep
their homes clean and neat and constructive suggestions
where improvements could be made.[31]

In evaluating reasons for the ready acceptance of the Sio-khe
program by the villagers, several factors can be noted. First, the
missionary participants were both veterans, Elizabeth Bruce
having served in China since 1921 and Alma Vander Meer since
1923. Secondly, the two women had a way that endeared them to
the people they were serving. Note, for example, the following
excerpt from an article of 1947 that Bruce sent to the *Church
Herald*:

We have happy fellowship here with our Chinese
Christians. All work together on these different projects.
Friends come to see us by ones and twos, tens and
twenties, and some Sundays after church we have as many
as sixty visitors. All love to see our home, the pictures,
the dolls, the Victrola, the jigsaw puzzles, and the little
weather forecaster. In the street, people call out to us,
"Are the children out today?" meaning, "Will it be good
weather?" The women like to see the handiwork and the
beds; the young men are interested in the star chart, and
the farmers want to see the thermometer and barometer.[32]

In view of the above, there can be little wonder why, when the
two women returned to Sio-khe after the war, Bruce was able to
write in her memoirs: "What a reception we received in Sio-khe.
Half the town walked out to meet us. What a welcome!"[33]

In further evaluating the program's success at Sio-khe, note
must be taken of the competence of the two main Chinese
participants, Dr. Saw and the Reverend Pan. Saw was a man of
experience and dedication who, against difficult odds, had

faithfully managed to keep the Sio-khe hospital open throughout the war years. And Pan was a young pastor of considerable zeal who had graduated from Talmage College and the Nanking Theological Seminary and served a Baptist church in Shanghai during the war.[34]

Encouraged by the success of the "teach, preach, and heal" program at Sio-khe, other mission stations were inspired to do likewise. The Tong-an station, for example, did so with a major innovation, namely, the use of a mobile unit. Upon hearing that Joseph Esther and Jack Hill at Tong-an were considering buying a station wagon for their work, CNRRA (the Chinese organization for handling UNRRA contributions) presented them with a nearly new two-ton Ford truck.[35] With money from friends in Michigan, a suitable top was built for it and a variety of visual aids were purchased, including a slide projector and screen, a collection of Bible slides, a movie camera, a record player with records, and several flannel boards. A loudspeaker and portable electric generator were also acquired. Finally, two special trunks were made for holding small surgical instruments and a variety of medicines.

Thus equipped, the truck, which became known as the "Happy News Healing Truck," would venture out with its joint evangelistic medical team to visit the churches and chapels in the Tong-an district. Upon arrival at one of these places, the record player, amplified by the loud-speaker apparatus, would peal out its music. What then followed is explained in this communication by Esther:

> As farmers from the rice paddies came streaming in and villagers came on the run, Dr. Hill and the nurse prepared the doctor's room while a pastor and I hastily placed dark cloth over the church windows so we could show pictures. We were off to a very busy morning. While the doctor examined patients, we held meetings, showing pictures and preaching Christ for the whole morning to a room packed tight with wondering villagers. Then, with everyone still wanting more, we hastily ate our simple meal of rice and vegetables, and hurried on to another village, where we put on the same program. For a year and a half the red-letter day each month was the day when our

Good-News-Healing car pulled in. The more often we
came, the bigger the crowd.[36]

Requests for the mobile unit soon began coming in from villages
throughout the district, and, at the time the Communists
occupied the Tong-an station, plans were in the offing for making
long treks into previously untouched rural areas.

Another important avenue for evangelism involved giving
greater attention to working among students. A breakthrough
developed in this field when John Muilenburg was invited in
1947 to meet with a group of Amoy University students on a
regular basis on Sunday afternoons. In the summer of 1947 he
reported that 180 students had been organized into fifteen small
circles which met once or twice a week "for devotions and
inspiration." He further related that "quite a few professors and
associates are interested in Christianity and several now desire
baptism."[37] Because some of the students and a few faculty
members of Amoy City's middle schools and normal school were
also wanting to learn more about Christianity, he began holding
occasional meetings with them. As a result of this step-by-step
process, working among students became virtually a full time job
for Muilenburg and thus a new avenue of evangelism emerged.

While Muilenburg was becoming thus occupied in and around
Amoy City, the Van Wyks became similarly engaged at Fukien
Christian University. As has been mentioned, this school, located
at Foochow, was one of about a dozen Christian colleges and
universities in China. As an interdenominational institution, it
attracted students from several different missions, including
those who were members of the Synod of South Fukien. From an
early date, the Reformed mission made annual appropriations to
the school, and one of its missionaries served on the University's
Board of Directors. Later, shortly before the Communist takeover
of the area, the Board of Foreign Missions appropriated $7,000
(USC) for the construction of a faculty residence on the campus.
The Van Wyks became the first representatives of the Reformed
church to serve on the faculty. Gordon Van Wyk was primarily
responsible for teaching courses in history, but he also organized a
college band and, more significantly, directed fifteen Christian
fellowships on the campus involving about 200 students. Bertha
Van Wyk became actively involved at the school by tutoring

students in English and assisting in teaching vocal music.

The Van Wyks' work in music was in keeping with the mission's effort to give greater attention to music as a form of worship. As noted previously, church choirs in the past generally left something to be desired, and congregational singing was even worse. The improvements that took place can be seen in the following comparison made by Elizabeth Bruce between the music she heard in the Sio-khe church when she first served there in the early 1920s versus what she heard upon her return after the war:

> The choir of fifteen, composed of high school teachers and students, sang a well-known anthem and sang it well. How different all was from twenty-five years ago when we came to this church! Then...the singing was quite poor, but now the choir sings in four parts and there is good congregational singing.[38]

Fortunately, too, some of the new post-war recruits had special talents in music. John Muilenburg, for example, who had great success in working with young people, played a variety of musical instruments and had studied a year at the Westminister Choir School. Another new recruit, nurse Anne De Young, also was helpful in this field. Already during her first year in China while still studying the language, she devoted much of her free time to working with church choirs and directing a glee club at the Girls' High School at Kulangsu. She also met once a week with a group of freshman from Amoy University who were interested in Western music. Similarly, Helen Oltman, also a registered nurse and the wife of Dr. Theodore Oltman (but not a new recruit, having served in China before the war), became active in training a forty-voice choir in 1948 for the Leng-na Church in the North River district. In most cases, however, good music remained a new experience among the churches, and directors had to work with what they had. In one instance, for example, De Young, in preparing special music for an Easter service, had to work with a group made up of four sopranos, three altos, five basses and ten tenors!

One of the major areas to experience congregational growth during and after the war was Leng-na and the North River district. As has been mentioned, the London Missionary Society transferred that area (encompassing about 2,000 square miles) to the Reformed mission in 1919. Developments under the new "management" proceeded quite well until 1929 when an onslaught by Communist soldiers and a long period of political unrest brought the mission's influence to a virtual standstill, although Chinese Christian leaders managed to keep Christianity alive in some areas.

The movement of large numbers of refugees into the North River district following the Japanese invasion in 1937, and the relocation there of the seminary and Talmage College in 1938, prompted the mission to assume a more active role in that region once again. Fagg Hospital was rehabilitated somewhat and reopened in 1939 on a limited basis under the direction of a Chinese doctor. Construction of a new church began in 1940.

Mission activity in the North River district was pursued with even greater vigor after the war ended. Walter De Velder and his family returned to Leng-na in 1946, and Theodore and Helen Oltman were assigned to Fagg Hospital in 1947. All mission buildings were renovated and the church was finally completed. Construction of the latter had been sporadic because of the war and lack of funding. With the exception of $500 raised by De Velder in the States, all financial costs for the church were met by money raised among Chinese in South Fukien and Chinese living abroad. A small book room was opened in the basement of the church and later moved to a shop on Leng-na's main street. As to its use, Helen Oltman reported in a letter to the *Church Herald*:

> Every time I have been in or have passed by, there are from four to ten men reading at the tables. It is quite attractive, with whitewashed walls and maps and Bible pictures and posters hung thereon. The young preacher in charge gives his mornings to the hospital and his afternoons and evenings to the Reading Room.[39]

Under the able direction of Helen Oltman, a registered nurse, and with the untiring assistance of the Chinese preacher, combined meetings dealing with health matters and the Christian message were held on a regular basis at designated places in the North River district. They followed the same plan that proved so successful in the Sio-khe district. Because many of those attending were war refugees who had located in the Leng-na area on a permanent basis, the meetings were held in both the local dialect and Mandarin.

After the war and especially in the late 1940s, the mission documents reflect a growing interest in extending evangelistic work to areas currently receiving only limited attention or none at all. In most instances, such work was planned in cooperation with the other missions. Thus, there were discussions in 1948 with the London Missionary Society about pursuing a cooperative endeavor in the Ting-chow district. Discussions of a similar kind also got underway with the English Presbyterians in what was called the Shanghang Mid-Hakka region. The appearance and eventual triumph of the Communists in these areas prevented much from being accomplished.[40]

Beginning in early 1946, discussions also went on between the Board of Foreign Missions and the Church of Christ in China regarding requests by the latter for a Reformed missionary family to locate in Yunnan province in southwestern China. The board responded by sending some financial aid for the new enterprise and announced on at least three occasions that it would look for an "evangelistic family" to send to Yunnan. No one was sent, however. In October, 1948, the board informed the Church of Christ that "in view of increased obligations in South Fukien and other countries where the Reformed Church is at work," no appointment would be made "in the foreseeable future." Although not specifically mentioned, the changing political situation vis-a-vis the Nationalists and Communists no doubt figured prominently in the board's decision.[41]

As in the past, education after the war was given considerable attention, with both religious training and the academics being stressed as before. Schools that had been closed were reopened, and buildings that had become dilapidated were repaired. In some instances, they were replaced by new structures as was the case, described earlier, with the Yok-tek girls' primary and secondary schools at Kulangsu.

The mission schools improved during this period with respect to curricular offerings and academic standards. This can no doubt be attributed in part to continuing the reforms introduced before the war, but two special reasons can also be noted. First, as the board's deputation pointed out in 1946, government schools at both the elementary and secondary levels were of better quality than in the past, and the mission schools therefore had to improve because of stronger competition.[42] Secondly, there were new standards that schools had to meet to acquire government registration, without which it was difficult for graduates to transfer elsewhere for advanced studies. The impact upgrading had on enrollment can be seen in what took place at Tong-an's Livingstone-Easter School. When this school acquired registration after several failed attempts, its enrollment increased "from a mere handful to more than sixty."[43]

While laying greater stress on a broader curriculum and on higher standards, the mission schools never lost sight of their primary goal, namely, the winning and retaining of souls for Christ. The deputation report of 1946 gives some rather surprising statistics on the opportunities for evangelism that were present among the student bodies. According to the report, less than half the students in the mission schools came from Christian homes. Even at the Yok-tek girls' primary school at Kulangsu only two-fifths of its 491 pupils in the fall of 1946 came from Christian homes. At Livingstone-Easter they made up one-third. The deputation report also points out significant variations existing among the schools regarding the number of Christian versus non-Christian teachers. At Yok-tek primary, for example, fifteen of the sixteen teachers were Christian, and at Livingstone-Easter all nine were Christian, whereas at Sio-khe, it was four out of seven and at Changping it was six out of ten.[44]

In view of China's special post-war needs, it is not surprising that considerable attention was focused on Talmage College. As might be expected, the faculty and student body, upon returning to Changchow from Hwan-an, found the scene quite different from what it had been when they left. Virtually all the buildings showed scars of war and the campus as a whole needed a "facelift," as is explained by Henry Poppen in the mission's report of 1946:

It has taken more than a term to bring about a state of pre-war normalcy but progress is being made. The campus has been beautified, trenches and tank traps dug by the Chinese military forces have been filled, pillboxes have been removed, and a small herd of cows and calves are again grazing peacefully on the grounds, giving the pastoral touch which is so delightful.[45]

Prospects for Talmage's future looked bright. In 1947, the principal, Mr. Lin Yu-lin, returned from a year's study in America, and the Board of Foreign Missions appointed two new foreign teachers to serve on the faculty, namely, Everett and Edith Kleinjans, both of whom had degrees in English. In the way of new construction, a combination classroom and chapel was built. The two-story structure, financed in part by the Reformed church's United Advance Fund and private donations, had four large classrooms on the first floor and a 500-seat chapel on the second. Nor were other essentials for a first-class school overlooked. New scientific equipment was placed in the biology, chemistry, and physics laboratories, and the library was enlarged by several thousand books. In view of these improvements, it is not surprising that the 1949 spring term opened with a record enrollment of 564 students, and plans were in the offing for building another dormitory.[46]

The attention given Talmage College did not mean that the mission was neglecting education for girls. Quite the contrary, as is demonstrated by the fact that both Yok-tek girls' schools at Kulangsu—the primary (which had been closed during the war) and the secondary—had enrollments near 500 in the fall of 1946. Interest in female education is also shown in the founding of a girls' secondary school at Leng-na. Known as the Poe-tek Middle School for Girls (the word "poe" meaning to nourish or strengthen and "tek" indicating virtue or moral excellence), the new school opened in September, 1948, with seventy-eight pupils. They met in rented rooms near the church, but a new building was soon under construction. Funding came from several sources, including a $3,000 gift from the Immanuel Reformed Church of Grand Rapids. Enrollment for the 1949 fall term was 134 and in the following spring it stood at 195. These figures would have been higher, but the victory of the Communists at Leng-na in late August, 1949, discouraged many parents from enrolling their daughters.[47]

Along with renewed interest in secondary education for girls, greater attention was given after the war to "short term" school sessions for girls and young women. These lasted about a month and were intended to be followed by additional sessions spread out over a three- or four-year period. As explained by Ruth Broekema, one of the chief supporters of the program, it took some adjustment on the part of many students "to come to a clean, airy building, to apply their minds in learning to read and write, and not think merely of cooking rice, washing clothes, and cutting grass for fuel."[48]

Because, as was further explained by Broekema, home living had to be "built upon Christ," a large part of the program centered on Bible study. Similarly, much discussion was devoted to relationships in the family—"living with in-laws, really being a big sister, being polite and respectful to all, and trying to show the neighbors by one's deeds that we are Christian." Cooking was taught, as were such special skills as hemstitching, embroidering, and knitting. For those who did not know how to read or needed improvement, classes in Romanized colloquial were available. Considerable attention was also given to cleanliness and hygiene. Lessons on these were put into practice every day—especially on Saturdays when the floors were thoroughly scrubbed. Nurses taught hygiene and either the missionary or a Chinese doctor gave each student a physical examination upon enrollment.

Among the more novel post-war plans in education was the idea of sending Chinese Christian leaders to America for study. Thus, in the winter of 1946, provision was made for the Reverend C. T. Tsai, one of the commissioners of the Church of Christ in China, to spend several months at Princeton. Tsai was a graduate of Talmage College, studied theology at South Fukien Seminary, and had a B.A. degree from Fukien Christian University. Ordained in 1934, he served as pastor of some of South Fukien's largest churches, including those at Chioh-be, Changchow, and Amoy City. While studying in America, Tsai received an honorary doctorate from Hope College.

Two of the mission's finest school principals—Mr. Lin Yu-lin and Miss Carol Chen—were also given the opportunity to do post-graduate work in America after the war. In 1947, Lin, who succeeded Vander Meer as principal of Talmage College (a position he had held for sixteen years), was given a leave of absence by Talmage's Board of Managers to study high school administration at Columbia University. Like the Reverend Tsai,

Lin was a product of the Amoy mission schools and Fukien Christian University. Carol Chen was principal of the girls' middle school at Kulangsu, of which she was a graduate, and had a M.A. degree from Yenching University. She spent the 1947-1948 academic year at Columbia University and Union Theological Seminary.

Some attention was also given to vocational education after the war. Thus, when Principal Lin of Talmage College was sent abroad to study in 1947, he was asked to pay careful attention to what was being done in that field in America. In early 1949, Demarest Romaine, the mission's construction engineer, noted that "ways" were being explored "by which the living standards of the Chinese can be bettered by industrial and agricultural" training. A few agricultural seminars were held in rural areas as were some industrial and trade institutes in the cities. In 1949, the mission and the Board of Managers of Talmage College requested the Board of Foreign Missions to send an agriculturalist to the South Fukien field. The board at home gave its approval and asked its search committee to place the request on the "priority list." Unfortunately, the rapidly deteriorating political situation in 1949 cast a pall over most of these endeavors. In the way of some practical application of scientific farming, the enterprising Joseph Esther embarked on a small rural improvement program of his own by having high-grade roosters sent from America to correct the poor fertilization quality of eggs which local Chinese farmers were using for reproduction purposes. Esther, along with his colleague Jack Hill, also ordered a variety of garden seedlings from the States for distribution among the villages.[49]

Medical work at the hospitals got back on track a little more slowly than education. Rehabilitating Hope-Wihelmina Hospital, for example, proved to be a major undertaking. Few buildings experienced as much damage at the hands of the occupying Japanese as did this venerable institution that had done so much for the Chinese people. It received not only structural damage but had been stripped of almost everything that was movable, including medical equipment and supplies, furniture, electrical wiring, and plumbing fixtures as well as windows and doors.

In keeping with Clarence Holleman's past practice (a result

perhaps of his Calvinist and small-town rural upbringing in South Dakota), he was determined that the hospital's restoration take place without financial help from the Board of Foreign Missions. It was primarily through his efforts that $100,000 (U.S. currency) was collected from local Chinese and those living abroad. Another $75,000 worth of equipment and supplies were acquired from various relief organizations, including UNRRA and several Red Cross groups.

But progress was slow—even for what would normally be minor matters. As reported by Jeannette Veldman, the hospital's supervisor of nurses, "Every cupboard, every chair or bookcase had to be made by local carpenters on the premises and we had to draw an accurate diagram of each before they could begin."[50] Similarly, the hundred beds that had been ordered from Manila in the summer of 1946 did not arrive until the following May and were in such a rusty condition that they had to be sandpapered and entirely repainted—all by hand. Not until the early summer of 1947, about five years after the Japanese had closed it down, was the hospital finally opened. New construction and other improvements continued, however, with the result that Holleman could report in early 1949 that the building and its equipment were superior to the hospital's previous condition.

On May 12, 1949, the institution celebrated its 50th anniversary by holding an open house with directed tours—*directed* because, as explained by Ruth Holleman, it was easy to lose oneself "in the labyrinth of rooms, stairs, halls, and passageways."[51] As to how far the hospital had progressed during those fifty years can be seen in Dr. Holleman's account of the services given during the previous year. These included:

> lectures on hygiene in several churches and schools; x-ray examinations of nearly two thousand students and other individuals; 40,500 visits to our out-patients, of whom over 25 per cent were seen free; over 10,000 free vaccinations for smallpox, typhoid and diptheria, as well as many other activities.[52]

Concomitant with the rehabilitation of the Hope-Wihelmina Hospital was the construction of the new Changchow Union Hospital. Because the old hospital had been located in a part of Changchow subject to frequent air-raids, medical services were transferred to the seminary buildings on the edge of the city when the seminary moved to the North River district for the duration. With the end of the war and the seminary wanting the return of its buildings, a site for the new hospital was obtained nearby. Construction was slow, however. As was noted previously, it took eighteen months just to lay the foundations, and the opening did not take place until late 1947. A small leper clinic was added to the institution in 1948. That a new hospital was very much needed is demonstrated by the fact that in its first full year of operation it treated nearly 2,250 in-patients and 21,000 out-patients, and its nursing school enrolled thirty students. The arrival of Jeanne Walvoord in 1948 made a welcome addition to the Changchow staff. She served as director of nursing and director of the School of Nursing until her expulsion by the Communists in 1951.

Although Fagg Memorial Hospital at Leng-na was a much smaller institution than any of the above hospitals, its needs were just as demanding in view of its being the only major hospital in an area involving a population of a half million Chinese. Fagg had been closed for about ten years after 1929 because of various political disturbances. Through Holleman's efforts, some repairs were made and it was reopened in the late 1930s under the direction of a Chinese doctor. Unfortunately, because of wartime and other difficulties, it ran at a "low ebb" until the return of Theodore Oltman in early 1947.

As explained by Oltman, a four-point program was immediately set up involving the following: first, making all the necessary repairs and embarking on some new construction; second, restocking the hospital with the necessary supplies; third, setting up an electric lighting system and an x-ray plant; and fourth, building up the staff. A large part of the expenses associated with the renovation were met with funds from the Reformed church's Advance Program, but there were other sources of help. The electric light plant and x-ray machine, for example, were furnished by UNRRA. Similarly, the construction of a new building for the isolation of patients with contagious diseases was made possible by a special gift from the Sunday schools of the Reformed churches in Orange City, Iowa, while friends of the First Presbyterian Church in Newton, Kansas (where Oltman once practiced) provided funds for new surgical instruments and supplies.[53]

The changed status that occurred at Fagg Hospital after Oltman had been there about a year can be seen in this excerpt from a letter he wrote in January, 1948:

> On our arrival the hospital staff, exclusive of the servant workers, consisted of one doctor, one evangelist, two nurses and one office worker. We now have three doctors, including myself, four Chinese graduate nurses and a fifth in prospect, the evangelist, a woman preacher, a pharmacist, and the office worker, and we are training a laboratory and x-ray technician. There were seven patients in the hospital when we first arrived. We now vary from thirty-five to forty in-patients. When we can secure more nurses to care for patients, the hospital capacity can be increased to sixty beds. The hospital cares for about two hundred clinic or out-patients weekly.[54]

As was the case with the other mission hospitals, many of the services rendered at Fagg were gratis or nearly so. This is clearly brought out in another excerpt from the above letter:

> Over fifty per cent of our work is charity. Even the patients who are supposed to pay the full charges in private rooms do not meet the expense of their care and treatment. A patient in a strictly private room pays, if he can, the interesting sum of fifteen cents, figuring in American money, for room rent and ten cents for his daily medicines and dressings. Operations are figured at from one fourth to one sixth the ordinary cost of such in the United States, but few people are able to pay the full amount, and deductions from fifty per cent to totally free treatment are usual. We are able to run things this way because of donations in money or in the form of supplies that come to us from various sources.[55]

Oltman remained at Leng-na until his expulsion by the Communists in October, 1951, making him the last of the Reformed missionaries to leave China.

Like Fagg Hospital at Leng-na, Blauvelt Hospital at Tong-an also suffered during the war years. When Jean Nienhuis, a nurse of more than twenty years' experience at Hope-Wihelmina, returned to China in January 1947, she was overjoyed at being assigned to Blauvelt. She had visited it several times before the war and remembered it as "a neat little hospital" and was looking forward to "life and work in a country station" instead of the bustling hospital where she had worked in the past. Nienhuis's reaction to seeing Blauvelt for the first time upon her return to China was obviously one of dismay:

> What a shock awaited me! The war years had been hard on everyone and everything, and the Tong-an hospital was no exception. I found only a discouraged skeleton staff hanging on in a state of despair. Empty cupboards, empty drug bottles, no supplies to work with—small wonder that hope and courage and the will to go on were well nigh gone.[56]

Although discouraged, Nienhuis rose to the challenge. The thirty-room brick hospital underwent a thorough cleaning, rooms were painted, new bedding was brought in (mostly through help from UNRRA), and the kitchen was remodeled. To top it off, a young doctor, Jack Warren Hill, a recent graduate of Wayne University Medical School, arrived in the autumn to take over as resident physician. Accompanying him was his wife, Joan Veenschoten Hill, the daughter of the Reverend and Mrs. Veenschoten whose missionary service in China went back to 1917.

Neerbosch Hospital at Sio-khe, too, was not without problems in 1945. Although from the outside it appeared very much like it had before the war, having suffered no serious structural damage, a closer look showed it lacked many necessities. As explained by one of the missionaries in 1947: "The electric light plant is no more; the water pump is broken; the sterilizer is useless; the rooms and the furniture need paint; and we are short many supplies, such as sewing machine, washing machine, linens, and blankets."[57] Unlike the other mission hospitals that have been discussed, Sio-khe did not get a resident foreign doctor after the war, although Richard Hofstra from Changchow visited it from time to time. The Sio-khe station did, however, have a competent Chinese doctor in the person of Dr. Saw.

In trying to bring the various hospitals back to normalcy as quickly as possible after nearly a decade of war, the medical staff never lost sight of Dr. Otte's old dictum that hospitals be concerned about "the diseases of the spirit as well as the diseases of the body." Thus, Oltman, in outlining the objectives of Leng-na's Fagg Hospital in 1947, declared that he and his staff would "strive to keep the hospital atmosphere truly Christian." To that end, as further described by Oltman:

> Our professional staff meets together in short devotional services three mornings a week. One of these meetings is a general one for all the hospital employees. Almost all of our workers are church members. Our hospital evangelist is a part-time worker. He heads up the religious program of the institution. Each morning he spends in personal contacts with the clinic patients and in-patients, talking with them, praying with them, and presenting Christian literature. We have recently engaged the half time services of a deaconess in the local church; she supplements the work of the man evangelist, especially in contacts with women patients. The city church is about two blocks away from the hospital. All of our workers attend regularly. Patients are invited each week to attend the services.[58]

Similar concerns for the Christian witness of healing were present at the other mission hospitals. Note, for example, the attention given this matter at Hope-Wilhelmina Hospital as described by nurse Anne De Young:

> Now you will want to know what evangelistic efforts are being made. We have a full-time hospital pastor who visits the patients each day, conducts a Sunday morning service in the chapel, teaches a Bible class for the coolies and another for the students and nurses, and occasionally holds special evening meetings when he explains the Bible story as illustrated by Veldman's beautiful colored slides.[59]

XVIII
Closing the Mission,
1949-1951

By 1948, missionary life was beginning to take on its old complexion. Most of the "old China hands" had returned, and a few new missionaries had been added. Decrepit looking missionary buildings had been renovated and several new ones constructed. Attendance at religious gatherings, especially revival meetings, was on the increase, and enrollments in the schools were up. The so-called "three-self movement" of self-governing, self-financing, and self-propagating was taking firmer root, and travel around the mission field was becoming easier, thanks to improved roads and motor vehicles. Home life for the missionaries and their families was likewise getting better. Residences were no longer described as merely livable but comfortable as well. For relaxation, the missionaries could garden or play tennis and volleyball. Keeping in touch with the outside world was also easier through radio, the New York *Times*, and *Time* magazine. Telegrams could reach America in a day, and regular air mail service was being established.

Although the situation was gradually returning to normal and progress was being made, mission work in South Fukien province, after three years of peace, was not without problems. Among the major difficulties was the shortage of pastors and preachers. As a result, there continued to be places within the Reformed mission's area of responsibility that were being inadequately cared for. Similarly, schools were often overcrowded and had to make do with limited equipment.

Inflation was another problem, with the Chinese currency

continuing to depreciate almost daily. As Jeane Walvoord, director of nurses at Changchow Union Hospital, remarked in an interview in 1976:

> It just was wild. People who had charge of finances found it very difficult to pay the teachers in the school or the hospital workers. Because inflation was so great [and rising almost daily], they had to find something that was stable. So they took rice, which was quite stable. You paid them in so many pounds of rice for their salary. Sometimes instead of giving them money, you would give them so much rice: bartering.[1]

How absurd the inflation situation had become is clearly shown in this remark by Joann Hill describing some ordinary shopping at Tong-an: "I can remember taking wads of Nationalist money in a suitcase down to the grocery store to get canned goods, and getting rid of the whole case of money —millions of dollars."[2]

If the mission had been given sufficient time, it perhaps could have worked out these problems, but time was a luxury it did not have. The dislocations brought on by eight years of war with Japan were soon compounded by civil strife between the Nationalists and the Communists. By late 1947, the struggle was broadening, with more troops being engaged and with the tide of battle gradually swinging in favor of the Communists. Major fighting, however, at first was confined primarily to the northern part of China, with only scattered pockets of Communists in the south. As a consequence, mission work in the Amoy area went on with little interruption, but only for a short time. The annual report from Amoy describing the events of 1948 contained the startling observation that it was "fairly certain" the Amoy area would "come under the control of a new Communist-dominated government some time within the next year or so."[3] The Board of Foreign Missions was kept fully informed of all new developments. Between January 3 and February 7, 1949, for example—a little more than a month's time—secretary Shafer received nine letters from the missionaries, two from Poppen and one from each of the following: Hofstra, Van Wyk, Vander Meer, Angus, De Velder, Bruce, and Esther.

Excerpts from a letter by the Esthers at Tongan, dated April 27, 1949, bring into sharp focus why the missionaries saw little hope for a Nationalist victory at this time. After first pointing out the "chaotic times as exemplified in the money situation," the letter turns to a description of the Nationalist soldiers:

Thousands of soldiers have arrived and are going around without orders trying to force people out of their houses so they can take over.... On their pitifully small salaries, these men must shift for themselves. They are destitute, ill-clad, disliked, unable to talk the local language, lonesome, hopeless, [and] completely demoralized. On them is the government pinning its hope. In these two situations, that of money and of the soldier, you see mirrored China's plight.[4]

Although anticipating an eventual Communist victory, the missionaries were nevertheless surprised at the rapid progress the Communist armies made as they began moving southward. As one of the missionaries remarked:

After all, there had been rumors so often about Communist activity, so we didn't really think that it would come that fast. At times it was hard to sift the news because the news really came by the grapevine. It was hard to sift the truth from the exaggerated or the false news that we got.[5]

The sympathies of the missionaries were clearly with the Nationalists. Although a mission report of 1947 recognized that there was "ineptitude and corruption" in the Nationalist government, it nevertheless declared that China's greatest hope for the future lay with the Nationalists. As the report expressed it:

The central government of China has at the top probably the best leadership of any Chinese government of recent times. Though its practice often denies it, it is dedicated to democratic principles and there is more hope in the long run for true democracy and freedom under this leadership than under that of the Communists in the North.[6]

Ruth Broekema, a veteran missionary who served in China from 1924-1951 and one of five who stayed throughout the war, later made this comment about the Nationalist leadership: "Chiang [Kai-shek] with all his faults—he had his faults—was the best

China had."[7]

As Communist armies continued victorious in the north and began pushing into central China with equal success, the American Department of State issued warnings to American citizens that the situation was becoming critical. The reaction of the Amoy missionaries to this news was similar to what it had been when war broke out with Japan in 1937, namely, one of "sitting it out" for the present and evacuating only if it became absolutely necessary. Indeed, judging from the view expressed in a letter of late 1948 by the mission's secretary, the Reverend Henry Poppen, to the Board of Foreign Missions, the missionaries might even stay if the government changed hands:

> I think we are all aware of the danger of leaving the field entirely to the hands of those who do not think as we do, and we are also fully aware of the fact that once we leave [and] a new government takes over, it is not going to be easy to get back on the field. I think some of us are rather intrigued with the prospects of working under new conditions and philosophies of government. As we look back over the years under the present Kuo Min Tang [sic] we are reminded that they have not been years without difficulties and unpleasant experiences. We shall expect some of this under a new regime, but I am sure we shall manage to survive. In spite of all that has happened since the Revolution of 1911, I think we can safely say that the Christian Movement has emerged from each period stronger and more confident. The war years have been hard years but the Church has come through with a clearer vision of her task.[8]

It was typical of mission spokesmen like Poppen to put the current crisis in perspective by comparing it with past crises and noting how the mission managed to survive on previous occasions—a fact that gave encouragement to the missionaries as they viewed the present situation. Past crises often cited included the Taiping Rebellion of the 1850s, the Boxer uprising of 1900, the political disturbances of 1927-1929, and the dark years following the outbreak of war with Japan in 1937. In another letter to the board, dated June 21, 1949, Poppen continued to look at the bright side of things but also stressed the need to be realistic. "All the schools," he wrote, "including the Seminary and Fukien Christian University, had a very successful year." He further noted that although the "liberators" were expected at any time, the mission was "proceeding with plans for another year's work, while not ignoring the ever-present 'if' in China."9

As reports of more Communist victories began coming in, Reformed church members in the States began raising questions about the effect Amoy's fall might have on the missionaries. In responding to their questions, Secretary Shafer, as the board's chief spokesman, discussed the crisis in an article published in the January 7, 1949, issue of the *Church Herald*. He pointed out that support for the Nationalist government was indeed crumbling and that its days were apparently numbered. He declared optimistically, however, that this did not mean the situation was hopeless. As to what should be done if and when Amoy fell to the Communists, Shafer added:

The first thing to be said is that the new government in China would still be a Chinese government and there would still be 450,000,000 people in China who need the Gospel. Our missionaries would not face the same situation as they did in the war with Japan. It is not a question between internment by a foreign government and evacuation. It is a question of living and working in the new regime which would be predominantly Communist.10

Three months later, at the suggestion of the board, Shafer wrote another letter to the *Church Herald*, this one based on the board's deliberations at its February meeting. In it, he reiterated that "it was only a question of time when Mao Tse-tung and his Communist government [would] take over control of all China." In anticipation of that event, Shafer listed three things that Reformed church members should keep in mind:

1. Missions in China from the beginning in 1807 have operated under various sorts of governments; some liberal, some repressive, and through it all the church has continued to grow.

2. Our primary concern is with the people of China, not with the particular government under which they live. Missionaries have learned through the years, as guests of the countries and peoples of mission lands, how to be neutral in matters of politics

and government.

3. In this present crisis our missionaries do not propose to leave until they are forced out or until it should become clear that to stay longer would endanger life.[11]

The hope of the board in early 1949 was that the change from the existing government to a new one would occur gradually and thereby give the mission an opportunity to adjust. Schafer urged his readers "not to yield to hysteria or a spirit of defeatism" but to "look confidently to God for His guidance and protection, remembering that in His good providence He rules and overrules."

In all its decisions and recommendations, the board repeatedly stated that the missionaries knew the Chinese situation best and that it had great confidence in their judgment. Therefore, as was the case about a decade earlier in 1937, the board informed the missionaries that they should feel free to leave at any time if, in their opinion, circumstances made it advisable to do so. They were also told that any who left China should consider "whether it would be possible to evacuate to the Philippines, the Dutch Indies, Penang, Rangoon, Formosa [i.e., Taiwan], where Chinese communities live, or even to India or Japan, rather than the United States."[12]

In mid-August, 1949, the missionaries spent three days together at Kulangsu "in prayer and worship, discourses and decisions" to determine what plans to follow if the "bamboo curtain" fell. Each person was encouraged to state his or her reasons for leaving or staying, after which anyone who wished could offer "advice, warning, [or] encouragement." As described later by one of the participants, even the prayers appeared to be specific and precise: "Our discussions began with prayer and ended with prayer, not empty, stilted stereotyped prayers heavy with 'glittering generalities,' but simple, earnest prayers which made plain to each of us the need for decision."[13]

All the missionaries decided to remain in the field, except two families whose "circumstances made it imperative" they return to the States. These included Harriet De Velder with five children and the Reverend Joseph and Marion Esther with three small children. Mrs. De Velder and children left in August aboard the *President Cleveland*, and the Esthers left in September by plane.

As to why the other missionaries decided to remain in China, nurse Jeane Walvoord, when asked that question a number of years later, gave this answer:

> Well, there are many things that go into a decision like that. I think, mainly, it was because I felt definitely that I could still contribute to the medical work. Another thing was that I was single. I had no dependents to be responsible for. I was just responsible for myself. I felt that as long as the Chinese—all of my nurses in the hospital and the church people had asked that we stay—I felt that I should try it. I had been led and called to do that work.[14]

What the mission had been anticipating for some time finally occurred. Within a few weeks after the meeting at Kulangsu, the upcountry stations of Leng-na, Changchow, Sio-khe, and Tong-an were in Communist hands. By this time, Foochow, the site of Fukien Christian University, had also fallen. The transition at these places was brought about without fighting, except at Tong-an and Changchow where it was of short duration.[15]

In explaining why the upcountry stations fell so quickly, the missionaries pointed to the rather languid views the Chinese held about the strife between the Nationalists and Communists. The Reverend Gordon Van Wyk, for example, said his Chinese friends at Foochow would respond with something like the following whenever the subject of their country's future came up for discussion:

> Well, we're Chinese. We're much more resilient than you folks are. We bend like the bamboo. We've had revolutions. China [has] had revolutions all through its history. But the revolution comes today and it's gone tomorrow. And we'll be back to the same; we'll be back to the old ways very soon. And therefore, there will be an upset in our life for a while, but China will continue on.[16]

Another general reaction, according to Van Wyk, was "We'll weather this storm, so don't worry too much."[17] Similarly, Alma Vander Meer reported that the Chinese at Sio-khe would often say: "It won't last forever, and maybe conditions will get better. It couldn't be much worse than it is now."[18]

When the Communists occupied the upcountry stations, all the interior missionaries remained at their posts except Alma Vander Meer and Elizabeth Bruce, who happened to be vacationing at Kulangsu at the time the Communists took Sio-khe. On the advice of friends that it would be unsafe to return and their presence might make Chinese Christians suspect in the minds of the Communists, the two women decided to remain at Kulangsu. The admonition was not unfounded as is demonstrated by the fact that six Christian friends of the missionaries were executed at Sio-khe. Included among the victims were the pastor and the head of the government school. Later, Communist troops also took over the missionary residences and, except for a few rooms, converted Neerbosch Hospital into a military prison.[19]

The other missionaries at this time were distributed as follows: at Foochow—the Gordon Van Wyks; at Leng-na—the Oltmans and Anguses, De Velder and Frances Eenennaam; at Tong-an—the Hills, Broekema, Kooy, and Nienhuis; at Changchow—the Hofstras, Kleinjans, Koeppes, Poppens, Veenstra, Romaine, and Walvoord; and at Kulangsu—the Hollemans and Muilenburgs, Brandli, Eckerson (who was hospitalized), Beekman, De Young, and Veldman. The Hollemans left China few months after the meeting. In leaving, Dr. Holleman made it clear they were not leaving under pressure but because they were due for furloughs. He also noted he had attained his goals with respect to renovating Hope-Wilhelmina Hospital and indicated he would like to return later and start some new work wherever the South Fukien Synod would appoint him.[20]

Although the upcountry stations had all fallen by early September, 1949, and Foochow already in mid-August, the Communists held off for a time in taking Amoy City and Kulangsu. When the fall of these places finally came, it was preceded by several weeks of sporadic cannon fire. Finally, as described by Wilbur Brandli, on the night of October 16, a night "long to be remembered," there came "a pre-invasion barrage, and the next day, October 17, found us under a new flag."[21]

Fortunately, no harm befell any of the missionaries or their families during the bombing and shelling of Kulangsu, although some residences and the Yok-tek girls' high school were damaged. Initially, there also was some difficulty in maintaining communication with the upcountry stations, but this proved temporary. The fall of Amoy City and Kulangsu did not bring an end to military activity, however, as Nationalists continued to hold some of the strategic offshore islands, such as Quemoy, which were only a few miles off the coast. It is thus not surprising that Kulangsu was often caught in the crossfire between the Communists on Amoy Island and the Nationalist warships in the outer harbor. Bombs from Nationalist planes also sometimes fell unintentionally on Kulangsu.

Despite the victory of the Communists at the upcountry stations and Kulangsu, the board tended to be optimistic about the future. The report for 1949 noted, for example, that the Chinese on the whole were not philosophers or ideologues but practical farmers and businessmen and thus pragmatists when it came to making adjustments. To quote from the board's analysis of the situation:

> If any country should be able to reshape Communism to serve its own practical good, that country should be China. Although apparently ruled by monarchs, the people's inherent freedom of thought and action has been axiomatic. Rulers held sway as long as they respected this inherent right of the people. [22]

The board further noted that the Chinese Christian church in general, and the church of South Fukien in particular, had survived major problems in the past and would likely do so again:

> In Fukien and Kwantung provinces, this Church is more united and more self-governing than in any other section of China. The Communists recognize this strength. If any Christian community be able to continue in its own way of life, that community should be the Church of South Fukien, where the ideals of Christianity have permeated the entire social structure. The history of the Christian Church in China has proved that she can survive opposition and that adversity has brought to the surface the Divine power within her. [23]

The board's optimism seemed to have some basis in fact during the first several months after the "liberation"—a term used by the Communists to describe their victories. With a few exceptions, the new regime left the missionaries and their Chinese colleagues unmolested: churches continued to hold services as before; the 1949 Christmas season was properly observed (including caroling); there was little or no interference with the work of the theological seminary or the hospitals; Christian students were allowed to gather for fellowship on the Amoy University campus; a series of revival meetings with thousands in attendance was permitted to take place at Kulangsu; and classis meetings were allowed to convene at their regularly scheduled times.

Even in the early months of 1950, several developments seemed to indicate that the mission might be able to survive under the new regime. For example, the Reverend Edwin Koeppe, who replaced Henry De Pree as head of the seminary, reported in a letter from Changchow dated January 15, 1950, that the new political authorities were leaving the staff alone and that work at the school was going on the same as before. "Instead of having fewer students, or as some feared, no school at all," wrote Koeppe, "we have the largest enrollment in the history of the school." Twenty new students were enrolled in the current term, bringing the total to forty-five. Similarly, in a letter written the same day as Koeppe's, John Muilenburg wrote that he was carrying on his "Christian work" on the campus of Amoy University, despite its being under Communist control, and was holding regular church services. In the latter case, however, he added that only "convinced Christians" were attending—about thirty-five in all. And in February, Secretary Shafer reported that the salary checks for the missionaries were being received regularly as were letters, which he pointed out, should continue to be sent to the usual addresses.[24]

There also were some favorable portents coming out of Leng-na, where Walter De Velder reported in the fall of 1950 that despite "many restrictions and pressures" from the new government, "a vigorous program in Christian life, teaching, and fellowship" was being maintained. Although Bible classes and worship on the school grounds of the new Poe-tek high school for girls were prohibited except on Sundays, more than 90 percent of the girls attended daily Bible classes and chapel at the church, located near the school. De Velder further added that the school had an enrollment of 195 pupils, compared to 134 in 1949, and 65 when the school opened in 1948. All of this occurred despite the girls being "subjected to a great deal of ridicule and scorn from the various government propaganda agencies." With respect to Fagg Memorial Hospital, De Velder noted that it was carrying "on a vigorous program of evangelism, not only in the hospital itself but in follow-up work among the patients who have left the hospital."[25] In view of the above development, it is not surprising that these early months after the Communist takeover were sometimes referred to as the "honeymoon period."

But there were exceptions to the new government's forbearance. A major difficulty in adhering to Communist regulations was the manner in which the country was divided into military zones, with local authorities sometimes making their own rules. As a result, the degree of leniency varied from place to place, as indicated by the troubles at Sio-khe. It was soon demonstrated elsewhere, too, that although the so-called New Democracy in China permitted churches to exist and recognized the right of Christians to worship, it was in theory opposed to religion and would try to make it subservient to the state.

It is thus not surprising that more restrictions were gradually placed on the missionaries and their work. New limitations applied especially to travel and to what the missionaries said and wrote. With respect to the latter, the Board of Foreign Missions reminded its members that they, too, should be careful about criticizing the new government, lest their remarks find their way to China and add to the burdens of the missionaries and their Chinese friends. The editor of the *Church Herald* was also alerted to the need for such precautions.[26]

Interrogations of the missionaries were also stepped up. The questions concerned such matters as the length of their stay in China, the exact nature of their work, and how much they paid their servants and how well they treated them. (There seems to have been no criticism at this time about their having servants.) The missionaries were also asked who their friends were. According to Alma Vander Meer the pat, and very safe answer to a question like that was, "Well, everybody is our friend."[27] Missionaries were likewise often asked during these interrogations what they thought of the Communist movement. Many years later, when William Angus was asked how he handled such questions, he replied, "Oh, I just gave them some non-committal answers."[28]

Rules regarding the work and conduct of Chinese churches and pastors were laid down from time to time. As explained by Jeane Walvoord concerning the situation at Changchow:

> The pastors all received a certain amount of indoctrination. They were told they had to have a fifteen minute talk on the Communist viewpoint and principles at the beginning of the service, also, there were certain things they were not to speak on or mention in sermons.[29]

Some churches, especially in the villages, were closed with a promise they would reopen later, but this did not always happen. In many cases, the church was the largest building in a village and it was too much of a temptation not to use it as a Communist meeting hall or a place for storing grain. When churches were closed, the government allowed people to meet in private homes, but limitations were placed on the number that could congregate together.[30]

With the passage of time, the missionaries began having fewer illusions about being able to remain in China. They also became increasingly aware that their presence as foreigners was becoming a handicap for Chinese Christians in their dealings with the new government. To understand this development and the stronger stand the Communists were taking toward the missionaries, note must be taken of several factors that were widening the rift between Communist China and the United States. These include the outbreak of the Korean War in June, 1950; the United States' increasing its economic and military aid to Chiang Kai-shek's government; President Truman's deploying the United States Seventh Fleet between mainland China and Taiwan to prevent a Communist invasion of that island; and the United States' opposing the entry of the People's Republic of China into the United Nations.

The effect that the Korean War had on the presence of the missionaries is clearly brought out in some remarks made by Gordon Van Wyk regarding the situation at Fukien Christian University. The war, he delared,

> had made us enemy aliens and that put us in a new category. Up to this point [our Chinese friends] had always said, "We don't like America, but we like you

Americans." But now we had become enemy aliens, and it was about this time, June of 1950, that the Fukien Christian University told us that now we are an embarrassment. Up to this point they had said there was no need for us to leave. But from June on they said, "You'd better consider leaving."[31]

The Van Wyks did no more teaching after June, 1950, and soon requested exit permits to return to the United States.

Similar situations existed elsewhere. Jack Hill reported that when the Korean War broke out "there was [at Tong-an] a big rash of anti-American propaganda. We had parades against Americans and everything else."[32] And at Kulangsu, as Alma Vander Meer later recalled, "There were posters all over town showing Chiang Kai-shek and the United States president committing atrocities."[33]

Some conception of how missionary life gradually changed under Communist rule can be gathered by looking at the experiences of Ruth Broekema, who spent nineteen months under the Communists at Tong-an. When the Communists arrived in September, 1949, the mission station was under the care of five missionaries, including Jack and Joann Hill, Gladys Kooy, Jean Nienhuis, and Broekema. The compound in which they resided was located just outside the city walls and consisted of three residences, the Blauvelt Hospital, a girls' school, a conference building, and a tennis court. The Communists appropriated the girls' school and the empty residence that formerly housed the Esther family. The empty residence was used to house the top Communist officials—called the "up and ups" by Broekema.[34]

When the Communists arrived at Tong-an, the missionaries were placed under virtual house arrest, although they were permitted to leave the compound occasionally to take walks and go into the city for errands. Guards were stationed in the compound, but this was done not so much to keep an eye on the missionaries as to protect the Communist officials. Even on their walks, the missionaries were never accompanied by guards. The soldiers enjoyed standing around for what seemed hours on end observing the missionaries. This was done more out of curiosity than anything else, and occurred frequently because the rotation system was constantly bringing new soldiers into the compound. Most of the soldiers came from northern China and spoke only Mandarin, thus creating a communication problem.

One of the most uneasy and annoying aspects of life under the Communists was the specious manner in which the missionaries were interrogated. An aim of the interrogations was, of course, to find out something about the missionaries or their Chinese friends that could be used for leveling charges against them. Unfortunately, as explained by Broekema, the Communists in their questioning would endlessly "go around and round about this and that" before finally getting to the point. There also were petty chores that the missionaries were occasionally ordered to do. For example, Broekema and Nienhuis were told in one instance to make a detailed list of everything in their homes—"even to the last pin, a straight pin or anything. Every single tack. Everything." After working on the inventory for many days and getting someone to help write it in Chinese character (as demanded by the Communists), the missionaries were told after a couple of weeks to forget the whole thing!

A tennis court, located near the residence of the single missionary women, gave them an opportunity to witness firsthand some of the indoctrination procedures used by the Communists. These included movies that some of the townspeople, as well as the soldiers, were expected to attend. As described by Broekema, the films were "total propaganda." The opening scenes generally depicted a miserable, careworn group of villages or small farms that, after the arrival of communism, were quickly transformed into "a happy, happy, wonderful utopia"—to use Broekema's description. The tennis court also became a showcase for demonstrating how the Communists conducted their indoctrination sessions. A small platform would be set up from which an "instructor" would talk to a group of townspeople or soldiers who were required to attend, and after a time would be encouraged to participate in the discussion. As explained by Dr. Hill:

> They would sit and discuss and discuss and discuss, until such time as the people all came to agree that this was the way that it ought to be, and of course that was the Communist way. The Communist was very patient and he

would just keep on discussing it, and working it around.
He didn't actually coerce anybody, but they just sat there
until eventually they agreed.[35]

Hill added that those "who weren't thinking as the Communists
wanted them to think...were sent to Foochow or somewhere up
the line to other indoctrination stations. There they got further
education."

Early in 1951, members of the Tong-an Church consistory were
summoned to a meeting at Foochow designed as a brainwashing
session. Soon after their return, the pastor in late February sent
word to Broekema and Nienhuis (the Hill family and Gladys
Kooy had already left for the United States in December, 1950)
that it would be better if they no longer attended church services
lest their presence cast suspicions on some of the Chinese church
members. From this time forward, the situation became more
difficult. As explained by Broekema:

> We carried on our work as best we could. We were
> curtailed here and there. The Communists spread it
> around that they didn't come to kill the Christians. "We
> know the blood of the martyrs is the seed of the church.
> We aren't going to kill you, we're going to freeze you out."
> And that's just what they did. This and that was curtailed.
> You couldn't have this meeting. You couldn't have that
> meeting. One day they called me up to the office and they
> said, "Now, you can't go out to visit any of those churches
> in the villages. You have to get a permit from the security
> police." Well, when I asked for a permit, they wouldn't
> give me one, and that's the way they did it.[36]

Worried about their Chinese friends, the two women soon made
it a point to get rid of all their notes and burned any books and
papers that might be used to incriminate them. If the missionaries
met anyone they knew while going into town or taking walks, they
would turn their heads the other way so that their friends would
not have to acknowledge them. This was done for the safety of the
Chinese in the event they were being watched. It was not an easy
thing to do when meeting small children who could not
understand why their old friends did not respond when being
called.

Broekema and Nienhuis waited until late December, 1950,

before applying for permits to return to the United States. They delayed making applications out of consideration for the Hill family, who they thought should have the first opportunity to leave. As events turned out, the two women did not receive their exit permits until April 19, 1951—four months after making their applications.

Other missionaries also had their trying moments under the Communists after the "honeymoon period" came to an end. A review of what took place at some of the mission hospitals can serve as an example. Particularly annoying was the uncertainty as to what the Communists had in mind. Instead of talking directly with the mission doctors and nurses, the Communists frequently called in members of the Chinese medical staff and asked them what was being done or said in the hospitals. Communist spies were sometimes planted among the patients in order to secure information. As Jeane Walvoord later reported regarding the situation at the Changchow hospital, this "round about method" of trying to find out something caused considerable suspense and tension. She also noted that care had to be taken in respect to visiting with the Chinese except in an official way and only at the hospital. This situation became increasingly worse and eventually reached the point, as it did with Broekema at Tong-an, in which Walvoord stopped going to church.

Also annoying was the requirement that a certain percentage of the Chinese staff had to attend periodic indoctrination and self-criticism meetings, making it difficult at times to take adequate care of patient needs. The Changchow meetings were held on Talmage College's athletic field, which adjoined the hospital grounds. Chinese staff members were also expected to attend the public accusation trials and to witness executions when such punishment was meted out. [37]

During most of the first year after the Communists arrived, the foreign staffs continued to have a significant voice in running the hospitals. But this arrangement ended suddenly when, as Theodore Oltman later described in reminiscing about events at Fagg Hospital at Leng-na, the Communists "really took over the running and administration" of the institution. [38] Everything had to be inventoried, even down to the last pin, and then seals were placed on the doors to the operating room, drug room, and all storerooms. Because staff members would not dare break these seals when use of one of these rooms was needed, someone had to be sent to police headquarters with a request to open the door. This was especially annoying with reference to the operating room, as is clearly brought out in this description by Walvoord of what occurred at Changchow:

> [The authorities would] send up two or three police [who] would go into the operating room, and the operating nurse would be so scared because they would make a list of all the articles taken. They would go into the instrument room with her, and they'd make a list of all the instruments. They didn't know one instrument from another, but anyway, they'd make a list. She reeled off the name of the instruments, and then, they'd make a list of all the things that we would use in that operation down to the last little safety pin. At the close of the operation, we had to call them back again, and then, they'd check to see that everything they'd taken out was really replaced.... And then, if anything was missing like a safety pin, oh! the fuss. Oh! Such a storm would come up.[39]

When the Communists finally took over the complete direction of Changchow Union Hospital in December, 1950, Walvoord seldom returned there except when called. Dr. Hofstra went more often, but did little more than sit at his desk. As Walvoord explained, "As long as it was our hospital and under our control, that was one thing. But when...it became *their* hospital, so to speak, that was a totally different situation."[40] Edwin Koeppe experienced the same frustration as head of Talmage College. He, too, found little to do after the Communists took over the school.

Similar developments took place at Fagg Hospital but with a difference. In addition to commandeering the hospital, the Oltman and Angus houses were taken over. The Communists claimed they were needed for housing some of the faculty and students of Amoy University, part of which had been relocated at Leng-na in order to escape Nationalist shelling at Amoy City. Dr. Oltman (his family had been given permission in June, 1950, to leave China) and the Anguses were then housed in the hospital.

In late December, 1950, the People's Republic of China seized American property and froze American public and private bank funds in retaliation for similar action taken a few weeks earlier by the American government vis-a-vis Chinese assets in the United States.[41] The seizure on the part of the Communist government included mission property and funds, and meant one more set of inconveniences with which the missionaries had to contend. In anticipation that the Communists would resort to such action, the missionaries had taken special precautions beforehand and had stocked up on supplies. As the problem continued, however, the missionaries eventually had to seek solutions to their shortage of money, which often involved selling some of their personal possessions. Because the Communist authorities frowned on this practice at Changchow, it had to be done with care so as not to get prospective buyers in trouble. Fortunately for the missionaries, a local businessman secretly supplied some of them with money from time to time. At Leng-na, where Communist control was less strict, the selling was done quite openly by Oltman and Angus, with the latter even using one of the church deacons as a middleman.

In view of the increasing anti-American feeling in China, and the growing conviction that the presence of the missionaries was bringing suspicion on Chinese Christians with whom they associated, it is not surprising that departure plans increased sharply in the summer of 1950. In July of that year, for example, the Board of Foreign Missions received cablegrams informing it that the Hill, Kleinjans, and Muilenburg families, Helen Oltman and her children, Gladys Kooy, Wilbur Brandli, and Demarest Romaine had all applied for exit permits. Other applications followed, with the result that in December, 1950, the board received another cablegram, this one stating that nearly all the missionaries had applied for exit permits, and that the three or four who had not done so would be doing so soon. The departure of the Reformed church missionaries was, of course, part of a general exodus of missionaries taking place throughout China after the Communist takeover. By spring of 1952, there were fewer than 100 foreign Protestant missionaries still in the People's Republic of China, compared to more than 3,000 in 1949.[42]

When applying for exit permits, the missionaries had to respond to a variety of questions, such as why they wanted to leave; were they leaving of their own free will; had they been treated fairly by the authorities; what did they think about life in China before the Communists took over; and what did they think of current conditions in China. Responses usually had to be written in both English and Chinese. In the latter case, the Communists provided assistance. The missionaries had to be diplomatic in their answers and were expected, of course, to state pretty much what the Communists wanted to hear. In this respect, Alma Vander Meer later reported she could state without lying that the cities and streets were cleaner, that the schools were open, and that the hospitals were carrying on. Naturally, it would have been unwise to point out the bad effects of the administrative changes that had taken place in the hospitals and foolhardy to describe the brainwashing that was going on.[43]

Almost without exception, there was a long waiting period before an exit permit was approved. The Hills and Gladys Kooy at Tong-an, for example, applied on July 3, 1950, and went to the police station about twice a week to see if there was any word. The usual response, according to Hill, was, "Nothing from up above," or, "No word from up top."[44] Not until late December did their permits finally come through—almost a half year after they applied and fifteen months after the Communist takeover.

Even after receiving exit permits, however, unforeseen obstacles and delays could arise, as the missionary group at Changchow discovered in a very frightening way. By late 1950, all the missionaries there—the Hofstras, Koeppes, Veenstras, Poppens, and Jeane Walvoord—had made requests to leave China and return to the United States. Weeks passed and nothing happened until suddenly they were informed they should do their packing and be ready to leave on a certain day. When that day came, however, their exit permits had not yet arrived. Unfortunately, when they finally put in an appearance, the missionaries were told that Henry Poppen would have to stay. Once again there was a delay, as the missionaries refused to leave without him. A few days later, the police informed them there would be a public trial of Poppen on the next day.

It was not uncommon for a missionary group the size and caliber of the one at Changchow to have one of its members stand trial before being allowed to leave China. If for no other reason, the proceedings made good propaganda among the Chinese people. As to why Poppen was singled out for trial, it undoubtedly was due to his having served in so many capacities during his more than thirty years in China. The positions he held at one time or another included: trustee or board member of Talmage College, Fukien Christian University, Hope-Wilhelmina Hospital, and Changchow Union Hospital; executive secretary of the Y.M.C.A. at Amoy City; principal of Tung Wen Institute (also in Amoy City); director of the International Relief Commission when the Japanese occupied Kulangsu; member of the Kulangsu Municipal Council; director of the South Fukien Religious Tract and Bible Society; and instructor at Talmage College and the seminary.[45] It is likely that while serving in these capacities, Poppen occasionally rankled some Chinese, especially if Walvoord's observation is correct that Poppen was always one to speak his mind.[46]

Poppen's trial was held on the athletic field of the Talmage College campus directly across from the hospital and was attended by about 10,000 Chinese. Although the other missionaries were refused permission to attend, they were allowed to wait in one of the hospital rooms from which they could hear the proceedings via loudspeakers. The trial lasted about three hours, during which time various accusations were made against the plaintiff. Paradoxically, two of his chief accusers were people Poppen had befriended—the one, a teacher he had helped financially in getting an education; the other, a student he had visited frequently in the hospital and whose medical expenses he had paid. The essence of the charge against him was that he was an agent of the United States Government. Accusations were also made against Richard Hofstra and Walvoord, although neither of them was on public trial. Poppen was allowed to speak briefly in his own defense, although the loudspeakers were turned off for that part of the trial.

After the trial, the missionaries went to the Veenschoten house, about a ten minute walk from the Talmage campus, and a few hours later the police delivered Poppen. Everyone was thereupon informed they could leave China and that a bus would pick them up at 5:30 next morning to start them on their way. The departure took place under guard, as Poppen was considered a common criminal and was being deported as such.

The trip took about a week, with a layover at Swatow where the missionaries, except Poppen, were billeted in a hotel. Here they waited about a week for transportation to Hong Kong. Up to this point, Poppen had enjoyed considerable freedom to mix with the other members of the group, but this changed when they reached Swatow. Here Poppen, with his hands tied behind him, was separated from the others and placed in jail. Inquiries about his fate were of no avail. Not until the other missionaries were ready to board a ship for Hong Kong were they informed that Poppen had already sailed two days earlier.[47]

Except for the Koeppes, the Changchow missionaries began leaving Hong Kong for the United States in the latter part of March, 1951. At the request of the Board of Foreign Missions, the Koeppes stayed behind to "act as a liaison" to assist future "freed" missionaries with their financial and lodging needs and to advise them on travel arrangements. By interviewing Chinese refugees from the mainland, the Koeppes could also keep the board informed of what was taking place relative to the South Fukien Church, and could advise the board on what course to follow in the future, especially with respect to a long range policy.

Missionaries who received exit permits early generally did not have too much trouble leaving China. Indeed, it was even possible at first to board a ship at Amoy and go directly to Hong Kong and from there obtain transportation to the States. In doing this, however, the missionaries ran the risk of having their ship fired upon by Nationalist warships that were blockading Amoy's outer harbor. Missionaries who left later generally had to travel by whatever means available. This frequently meant a combination of bus or truck, river boat, and coastal steamer. In cases in which Canton was on the exit itinerary, travel by train was also included. In most instances, the missionaries were provided with what was termed a "travel man" to advise them during their trip.

No matter what form of travel was involved, accommodations were usually poor. Lodging enroute could vary from a relatively fancy hotel to a warehouse, or even a run-down inn with a mud floor. The time elapsing between actually leaving their stations and their arrival at Hong Kong varied from a few days to two weeks. The time lapse in the case of the Gordon Van Wyks with their two small daughters was thirteen days and involved living in the same clothes during much of that time. They spent the first three days in a crowded truck having saw horses and planks for seats and a canvas covering overhead to keep out the sun and rain. Following that came three days and two nights aboard a train, sitting up the entire time. [48]

Petty annoyances and insults on the trip were commonplace. Baggage checks, of which there were many, were a particular nuisance. The first baggage checks took place just prior to leaving their mission stations and were repeated several times enroute—always once each morning and again at night, not infrequently at about one or two a.m. After each check, the trunks were sealed, usually with strips of thin rice paper, and strict orders given for the missionaries not to break the seals. When Elizabeth Bruce, Edna Beekman, and Anne De Young went overland from Kulangsu to Canton (a five-day trip), and were placed on a train to Hong Kong, their baggage was examined no less than thirteen times. [49]

Baggage checks were anything but cursory. For example, when Jack Hill and his family were preparing to leave Tong-an, the examiners went through their luggage in a "very regimented way"—feeling along the seams of the sheets, running a finger between the slices of bread to be sure nothing was being hidden in the sandwiches, and opening the seam of a small stuffed elephant to determine if anything was concealed inside. Later, during one of the midnight baggage checks enroute to Hong Kong, the examiner, on finding a bottle containing aspirins, asked what they were. When the doctor explained they were a form of medicine, he was told to "chew one." This was repeated when the examiner came across a box of Chiclets. In recalling the incident later, Hill said he was glad he had not been asked to eat some of the pancake flour the family had taken along! [50]

Some of the incidents that occurred as the missionaries made their departure from China seem to justify their comments that baggage examiners and other lesser officials were not only deliberately bothersome but at times could be scornful and even threatening as well. The experiences of Ruth Broekema and Jean Nienhuis at Ko-tin can serve as examples. Ko-tin was a seacoast town where missionaries often waited for a small steamer to take them to Swatow, where they would board a larger vessel for Hong-Kong. In the case of Broekema and Nienhuis, who had left Tong-an two days earlier, this involved living in a warehouse room at Ko-tin for a few days.

Early in the evening on their last day at Ko-tin, several Chinese in their late teens, claiming to be local militia, accosted the women and asked to see their luggage. After some parting scornful remarks, they left, only to return later declaring they had been insulted and demanding an apology. The women were surprised at the charge but said they were sorry if they had offended them. To show their disdain for the women, one of the young men spit on his hands and wiped them on Nienhuis's face. When she took a handkerchief to wipe her mouth, he grabbed it, threw it on the floor, and stamped on it.

After another round of insults, such as asking Nienhuis if she, as a nurse, typically took care only of the rich and let the poor die, the group walked to one side of the room to discuss the next move. After a few minutes, one of the members came to Broekema and asked if she were a preacher? As described by Broekema, what happened next was undoubtedly one of the most harrowing incidents experienced by any of the departing missionaries:

> I didn't say anything. He said, "You tell people that when they die they go to Heaven. Well, you can go right now." And he took his gun and put it to my head. It was a big long one and he held it to my head. I didn't say anything. "Well, you do," he said, "you do want to go to Heaven, don't you? You can go right now." Pretty soon he stopped. Then they went back a ways and talked together, then another one came up to me and tried the same thing on me. Then our travel man came in and he called them off.[51]

But they did not leave immediately. The women first had to write an apology, which they did with the help of the travel man because it had to be written in Chinese character.[52]

The missionaries still remaining in China at this time included Broekema and Nienhuis at Tong-an, and the Anguses and Dr. Oltman at Leng-na. Their departure, except for Dr. Oltman's, came about a month later. Oltman's being retained at Leng-na after the other missionaries had left apparently had nothing to do with him personally, but with indecision among the Communist authorities over who should ultimately take over the directorship of Fagg Hospital—the current military unit or a local citizens' group.[53] During the extra months that Oltman stayed, he continued to reside in the hospital but did virtually no work. He went to the police station about every three or four days to inquire about his exit permit, and in the meantime sold his furniture and other items to get money for living expenses. In commenting later about his prolonged stay, he declared: "I was beat. Not beaten, but I mean, I was in poor health. I think I weighed 119 pounds. My clothes hung like rags on me."[54] But finally, Oltman's exit permit also came through, thus ending the 109-year history of the Reformed church mission at Amoy. On August 18, 1951, the Board of Foreign Missions in New York received the following cablegram from Koeppe: "Oltman Arrived 18th Hong Kong Our Liberation Complete Hallelujah."[55]

Conclusion

In reviewing the more than 100 years of history of the Amoy mission, several observations come to mind. One of the most striking is the increasing complexity of the work. Although evangelism always received primary emphasis, it was never given a narrow interpretation. From an early date the missionaries established not only churches and preaching stations, they also founded an array of schools and hospitals and later orphanages and refuges for opium addicts. Similarly, along with preaching the gospel, the missionaries moralized on a variety of subjects, especially the emancipation of women. Finally, the missionaries responded positively to the growing demand for more Western learning in the schools, promoted literacy among adults, and published a vast amount of material in the Romanized vernacular.

Throughout its history, the work of the mission was frustrated by inadequate staffing, both foreign and Chinese. When the comity of missions was agreed upon with the English Presbyterians and London Missionary Society, the Reformed mission accepted responsibility for about 3 million Chinese, a figure that rose to 4 million with the addition of the North River district in 1919. The number of Reformed missionaries was highest in 1923 when the total was fifty-one—twenty men and thirty-one women. This breaks down to a ratio of one missionary for every 78,000 Chinese. If the sixteen missionaries who were on furlough at the time were excluded, the disparity would be even greater. Statistics regarding the availability of clergymen are equally startling. In 1923, the mission reported having twelve ordained missionaries in the field along with fourteen ordained Chinese pastors and fifty-two Chinese preachers—for a total of seventy-eight clergymen, which gave a ratio of about one for every 50,000 Chinese.[1]

Among the most notable achievements of the mission was the success it had in two closely related endeavors, namely, founding an indigenous Chinese church and promoting interdenominational cooperation. With respect to the former, the mission from an early date gave the Chinese a voice (eventually it became almost a dominant voice) in making decisions affecting the mission. Indeed, by the 1930s the missionaries in their annual reports to the Board of Foreign Missions in New York tended to describe their work as church-centered rather than mission-centered. With respect to promoting interdenominational cooperation, the mission did pioneer work in founding joint conferences on a variety of matters and helped establish a cooperative Religious Tract Society. Looming high above its ecumenical efforts, however, was the mission's allying itself with the English Presbyterians and London Missionary Society in organizing the Church of South Fukien. This organization served as an inspiration for other missions throughout China and became a model for the later Church of Christ in China.

In comparing reports and letters coming out of Amoy during the first few decades with those of later years, the reader cannot help but note a gradual change of mood regarding the celerity at which conversions were taking place. Early missionary literature speaks of "increasing numbers," "filled chapels," "large classes of inquirers," and the like. In reflecting on the large mass of Chinese who remained untouched by the gospel message, it was not long, however, before the missionaries were becoming patently aware that the day of salvation was still a long way off for most Chinese. It is thus not surprising that later reports out of Amoy contain comments like these: the present age is one of "seed sowing" rather than "seed harvesting"; "a nation as large and as old as China cannot be remade in a day"; and "seed planted and taking root in a soil rank with superstition and idolatry...cannot expect to become a thrifty tree in one generation, but it must go on growing consecutively...and from one generation to another, i.e., from parents to children and to children's children."[2] In support of comments like the above, references to Christ's parables about the leaven and mustard seed were not uncommon.

Missionaries in China became one of the most important sources of information by which Americans learned about the Chinese people. Such information was transmitted by letters and reports missionaries sent home and by speeches and sermons they delivered when they were in the States on furlough or as retirees. By such means, as one historian has pointed out, comments from missionaries helped formulate views about China that could be "scholarly, dispassionate, and compassionate," or could be "self-righteous, narrow, condescending, and culturally insensitive."[3]

Comments by Reformed missionaries fit into both of the above categories but were tempered toward the milder side during the second half of their stay in China. In the early decades, descriptions such as the following were not uncommon: "A waste howling wilderness" (1846); "Satan's throne in the Chinese heart is guarded by a rampart of superstition and error, the accretion of thousands of years" (1876); "As Africa is the Dark Continent, China is the Dark Empire" (1889); and "Upon them was the blindness of generations; ignorance enveloped them like a solid wall" (1907). Among the more positive later remarks were those indicating that the Chinese were slow to act because of their cautious nature regarding sudden change: "How fast [they move] none can tell. There are no frog-like movements in the Chinese way of doing things. When they jump they know where they will land, and when landed they generally stay landed" (1903); "The slow-moving Orient may still have much to teach the Occident that goes at break-neck speed" (1926); and "When preachers are giving the Gospel message to Chinese villagers, a common taunt is, 'Show it to me.' These people may not have heard of the man from Missouri but they speak his language. They are illiterate and limited in their knowledge of the world, but they have their own traditions and culture; and their ignorance of the modern world does not preclude shrewdness and intelligence" (1938).[4]

In evaluating the 100 years of mission work at Amoy, one cannot help noting that it is a story of noble deeds performed by men and women of determination and unbounded faith. Despite innumerable burdens—learning a difficult language, enduring the hardships of evangelistic touring, experiencing the deaths of loved ones and separation from families, living in fear of bandits and unruly soldiers—the faith of these workers never wavered. The labors of the missionary women must especially not pass unnoticed. Like the men—whom they generally outnumbered by a significant margin—the women occupied stations and went on evangelistic tours, but were particularly noteworthy as pioneers in teaching, nursing, and visiting Chinese women in their homes.

What happened to the missionaries after they left Amoy was in most cases a kind of continuum of their previous activity. Even before the last of the Reformed missionaries, Dr. Theodore Oltman, left China in August, 1951, the Board of Foreign Missions had delegated the veteran Tena Holkeboer to make a survey of mission opportunities among the many millions of Chinese scattered throughout Southeast Asia, including the Philippine Islands, Taiwan, Indonesia, and Malaysia. As a result of her findings, the board resolved to establish an "Amoy Mission in the Philippines." The plan called for sending former Amoy missionaries to work among the tens of thousands of Amoy-speaking Chinese residing in Manila, Cebu City, Legaspi, and other parts of the Philippines. By 1954, sixteen of the "old China hands" who had served in Amoy were laboring in the Philippines as pastors, educators, doctors, and nurses—all working in much the same manner as they had in China.

In due time, the work was expanded to include Taiwan, where the Amoy dialect was commonly spoken, and still later, Hong Kong as well. In the mission literature of the time, this was called the "Triangle Plan," and later as "Work with Overseas Chinese." As examples of former Amoy missionaries moving into these new areas, Jeane Walvoord and Ruth Broekema were assigned to Taiwan in July, 1954, followed soon after by Dr. Richard and Johanna Hofstra. Similarly, Elizabeth Bruce and the Reverend Walter and Harriet De Velder were assigned to work with two Amoy-speaking congregations in Hong Kong. For a brief period in the mid-1950s, two former members of the Amoy mission staff, the Reverend Henry and Dorothy Poppen, were even dispatched to Singapore, which is 85 percent Chinese, and to Malaysia, which is 40 percent Chinese. It is interesting to note that during the first few years after 1951 the board tended to look upon these various assignments as a kind of "lend-lease" arrangement, always holding out the possibility that these missionaries might someday return to the Chinese mainland should the bamboo curtain ever be sufficiently raised to allow such a return.

The closing of the mission in 1951 did not mean that the work the missionaries had started in the Amoy area also came to a close. By no means. Preaching and Christian worship continued under Chinese direction, although some changes had to be made in accordance with the demands of the Communist party and the State. This is not to say there were no problems. The most serious challenge occurred when Chairman Mao launched the so-called "great proletarian cultural revolution" of 1966-1976 with its assault on what were termed the "four olds"—old ideology, old culture, old customs, old habits. As a consequence, churches were closed, accusation trials were held, religious leaders were arrested, and atrocities were committed. Despite intense persecution, however, Christianity survived as "house gatherings" replaced formal worship services. In the end, the Red Guards who had led the assault were curbed, and there was a gradual return to post-liberation conditions, that is, freedom of religion with limitations. It is important to note that it was the Chinese themselves, acting on their own volition, who weathered the storm. There were no missionaries present to advise them. The Reverend John Talmage and his colleagues who had challenged the General Synod a century earlier on the matter of establishing an independent indigenous Chinese church would have been pleased to see how deeply their views had taken root.

Bibliographical Note

The denominational journals published by the Reformed Church in America provide some of the best primary source material on the history of the Amoy mission. The *Mission Field*, published monthly from 1887 to 1922, contains numerous letters written by the missionaries as well as other documentary material. In 1922, it merged with the *Christian Intelligencer*, a weekly that began publication in 1830. Already carrying information on Reformed church mission work before the merger, the *Christian Intelligencer* now increased such coverage. In 1934, it merged with the *Leader* and became known as the *Intelligencer-Leader*. The name was changed to the *Church Herald* in 1944, but the publication remained a weekly magazine until 1973, when it became a bi-weekly, and in 1989, a monthly. Many of the original letters and other documents bearing on the Amoy mission that are found in the denominational archives were printed in these journals.

Next in importance to the denominational journals are the annually published *Reports* of the Board of Foreign Missions. In these are found detailed accounts of the board's reaction to what was happening in Amoy based on information, often quoted verbatim, furnished by the missionaries.

For the period covering the last few decades of the mission, an invaluable source is the "Old China Hands Oral History Project" of the mid-1970s. This is a collection of interviews with sixteen Amoy missionaries carried out under the supervision of two professors at Hope College, Michigan. The interviews are excellently done and contain considerable information not found elsewhere. The original tapes are in the archives at Hope College, but printed transcripts have been made—some of eighty or more pages in length.

The *Chinese Recorder* covers all the missions in China, including that at Amoy. This monthly journal was published in English by the Methodist Press of Foochow from 1867 to 1872 and by the Presbyterian Press of Shanghai from 1874 to 1941. It contains general information about mission work in China as well as articles about individual missions and missionaries. All aspects of mission work—evangelical, educational, medical, and social—are covered. It is available on microfilm. In 1986, a very careful, two-volume index was compiled by Kathleen L. Lodwick (Wilmington, Del: Scholarly Resources, Inc., 1986). The major part of the *Index* comprises indexes to persons, missions, organizations, and subjects.

There are two major repositories for archival material on the Amoy mission, the Reformed Church Archives, located in Sage Library at New Brunswick Theological Seminary in New Brunswick, New Jersey, and the Van Wylen Library at Hope College in Holland, Michigan. The general contents of these two archives as they pertain to the Amoy mission are described in *Christianity in China: A Scholar's Guide to Resources in the Libraries and Archives of the United States*, edited by Archie R. Crouch, e.a. (Armonk, N.Y.: M. E.Sharpe, Inc., 1989).

A few books written by Amoy missionaries were published about 1900. These include two by Philip Pitcher, *Fifty Years in Amoy* (New York: Reformed Church in America, 1893) and *In and About Amoy* (Shanghai: Methodist Publishing House, 1909) and one by John G. Fagg, *Forty Years in China: A Biography of the Reverend John Van Nest Talmage* (New York: Reformed Church in America, 1894). There have also been a few brief commemorative pamphlets, but these contain little solid information of use to the historian. Typical is "The Story of the Amoy Mission after One Hundred Years 1842-1942" which contains some thirty small pictures and the equivalent of about ten pages of text. On about the same order is "Miracle of a Century" by Henry Poppen, which also appeared as a commemorative for 1942.

For a study that covers the entire history of Christian missions in China, the best work is still Kenneth S. Latourette's *A History of Christian Missions in China* (New York: Paragon Book Gallery, 1975; reprint of the 1929 edition). There are, of course, numerous excellent monographs on various aspects of mission work in China such as, to mention a few, Jessie G. Lutz, *China and the Christian Colleges 1851-1864* (Ithaca: Cornell University Press, 1971), Eugene P. Boardman, *Christian Influence on the Ideology of the Taiping Rebellion,* (Madison: University of Wisconsin Press, 1952), and Jessie G. Lutz, ed., *Christian Missions in China: Evangelists of What?* (Boston: D. C. Heath, 1965). For the titles of other monographs, the reader need only check the bibliographies found in such general histories as Immanuel C. Y. Hsu's *The Rise of Modern China* (New York: Oxford University Press, 3rd ed., 1983) or Ranbir Vohra's *China's Path to Modernization: A Historical Review from 1800 to the Present* (Englewood Cliffs, N.J.: Prentice Hall, 1987).

Appendix

Missionaries who served in China in chronological order with dates of their service

David Abeel	1842-1845
Elihu Doty	1844-1865
Eleanor (Ackley) Doty ..	1844-1845
William J. Pohlman	1844-1849
Theodosia R. (Scudder) Pohlman	1844-1845
John Van Nest Talmage .	1847-1892
Mary (Smith) Doty	1847-1858
Abby F. (Woodruff) Talmage	1850-1862
John Samson Joralmon ..	1855-1860
Martha (Condit) Joralmon	1855-1860
Daniel Rapalje	1858-1901
Alvin Ostrom	1858-1864
Susan (Webster) Ostrom	1858-1864
Caroline E. Adriance ...	1859-1864
John E. Watkins	1860-1860
Sara (Hewston) Watkins	1860-1860
Leonard W. Kip	1861-1901
Augustus Blauvelt	1861-1864
Jennie (Zabriskie) Blauvelt	1861-1864
J. Howard Van Doren ...	1864-1873
Mary E. (Van Deventer) Talmage	1865-1912
Helen (Culbertson) Kip	1865-1918
John A. Davis	1868-1871
Emma C. (Wyckoff) Davis	1868-1871

Helen M. Van Doren ...	1870-1877
Katherine M. Talmage ..	1874-1927
Mary Elizabeth Talmage	1874-1927
David M. Talmage	1877-1880
Alice (Ostrom) Rapalje	1878-1901
Alexander S. Van Dyck	1882-1896
Phillip W. Pitcher	1885-1915
Anna F. (Merritt) Pitcher	1885-1916
Alice (Kip) Van Dyck ...	1886-1896
Y. May King	1887-1888
John A. Otte	1887-1910
Frances (Phelps) Otte ..	1887-1911
John G. Fagg	1887-1894
Margaret (Gillespie) Fagg	1889-1894
Elizabeth M. Cappon ...	1891-1909
Nellie Zwemer	1891-1930
Margaret C. Morrison ..	1892-1931
Lilly N. Duryee	1894-1937
Isaac Spencer Finney Dodd	1894-1895
Mary (Carpenter) Dodd	1894-1895
Alexander D. D. Fraser	1895-1898
Francis Theo. B. Fest ..	1896-1898
Emmy M. (Hartwig) Fest	1896-1898
Hobart E. Studley	1896-1903
M. Van B. Calkoen	1896-1899
Edith J. (Holbrow) Studley	1898-1903

C. Otto Stumpf 1899-1906
Eleanor (Barwood)
Stumpf 1899-1906
Angie M. Myers 1899-1904
Louise Brink 1899-1902
A. Livingston Warnshuis 1900-1921
Anna (De Vries)
Warnshuis 1900-1921
Douwe Cornelius Ruigh 1902-1905
Harry P. Boot 1903-1940
Nettie (Kleinheksel) Boot 1903-1908
Frank Eckerson 1903-1949
Sarah R. Duryee 1903-1905
Alice Duryee 1903-1911
Christine (Carst) Ruigh 1904-1905
Elizabeth H. Blauvelt ... 1905-1908
Gertrude Wonnink 1906-1908
Henry J. Voskuil 1907-1944
Henry P. DePree 1907-1948
Kate (Everhard) DePree 1907-1948
Katherine R. Green 1907-1950
Mary W. (Shepard)
Voskuil 1908-1944
Anna H. (Meengs) Boot 1908-1940
Steward Day 1908-1914; 1916-1930
Rachel M. (Smith)
Day 1908-1914; 1916-1930
John H. Snoke 1908-1918
Mary E. (Shelton) Snoke 1908-1918
Leona Vander Linden .. 1909-1947
Andrew Benthuis 1909-1914
William H. Giebel 1909-1913
Herman Renskers 1910-1933
Bessie M. (Ogsbury)
Renskers 1910-1933
Edward Strick 1911-1924
Edith (Walker) Strick .. 1911-1924
Maude Norling 1912-1922
Edna Beekman 1914-1951
George W. Dunlap 1915-1917
Taeke Bosch 1915-1931
Margaret (Brown) Bosch 1915-1931
Frederick J. Weersing .. 1915-1922
Bata (Bemis) Weersing .. 1915-1922

Edith C. Boynton 1915-1923
Lyman A. Talman 1916-1931
Rose E. (Hiller) Talman 1916-1931
H. Michael Veenschoten 1917-1951
Stella E. (Girard)
Veenschoten 1917-1951
Henry Poppen 1918-1951
Dorothy C. (Trompen)
Poppen 1918-1951
Harvey I. Todd 1918-1923
Edwin W. Koeppe 1919-1951
Elizabeth M. (Renskers)
Koeppe 1919-1951
Clarence H. Holleman 1919-1950
Ruth (Vanden Berg)
Holleman 1919-1950
Matthijs Vandeweg 1919-1926
Maria A. (Stempels)
Vandeweg 1919-1926
Petra Johnsen 1920-1922
Henry Beltman 1920-1928
Sara (Trompen) Beltman 1920-1928
Tena Holkeboer 1920-1948
Jean Nienhuis 1920-1951
William Vander
Meer 1920-1923; 1926-1951
Ethel M. (Langwith)
Todd 1921-1923
Elizabeth G. Bruce 1921-1951
Richard Hofstra 1922-1951
Johanna (Jansma) Hofstra 1922-1951
Clara C. Borgman 1923-1925
Alma L. (Mathiesen) Vander
Meer 1923-1951
Adam J. Westmaas 1923-1930
Nellie K. Westmaas 1923-1930
George T. Kots 1923-1926
Ruth Broekema 1924-1951
William R. Angus 1925-1951
Agnes J. (Buikema) Angus 1925-1951
Harold Eugene Veldman 1926-1930
Pearl P. Veldman 1926-1930
Helen Joldersma 1926-1928
Hazel M. Luben 1928-1931

Walter de
Velder 1929-1932; 1936-1950
Theodore V.
Oltman ... 1930-1943; 1947-1950
Helen (McGuish)
Oltman ... 1930-1943; 1947-1950
Jeanette Veldman 1930-1951
Jessie M. Platz 1930-1947
Jeane W. Walvoord 1931-1951
Catharine Bleakney 1931-1934
A. Ethel Boot 1935-1938
Margaret (Otte) de Velder 1936-1940
Harriet (Boot) de Velder 1938-1950
Geraldine Cornelia Smies 1939-1945
Anna R. De Young 1945-1951
John P. Muilenburg 1946-1950

Virginia (Turpin)
Muilenburg 1946-1950
Joseph R. Esther 1946-1949
Marion (Boot) Esther .. 1946-1949
Gladys M. Kooy 1946-1951
Gordon J. Van Wyk 1946-1951
Bertha (Vis) Van Wyk .. 1946-1951
Frances E. Van
Eenennaam 1946-1951
Demarest Romaine Jr. . 1946-1950
Jack W. Hill 1947-1951
Joann (Veenschoten) Hill 1947-1951
Everett Kleinjans 1948-1950
Edith (Klaaren) Kleinjans 1948-1950
Wilbur R. Brandli 1949-1950

Endnotes

Abbreviations used in the notes (For descriptions of these see the Bibliographical Note)

AR – *Annual Report of the Board of Foreign Missions*

CI — *Christian Intelligencer*

CH – *Church Herald*

IL – *Intelligencer-Leader*

JAH – Joint Archives of Holland

RCA – Reformed Church Archives

OI – Oral Interviews

Chapter I

1. Immanuel C. Y. Hsu, *The Rise of Modern China*, 3rd ed. (New York: Oxford University Press, 1983), p. 7.
2. Ranbir Vohra, *China's Path to Modernization: An Historical Review from 1800 to the Present* (Englewood Cliffs, N.J.: Prentice Hall, 1987), pp. 33-34.
3. The terms are discussed in Hsu, *Rise of Modern China*, pp. 400-401.
4. The Reverend C. G. Sparham of the London Missionary Society said it well when he stated the warlords "may be compared to the medieval barons of England. For selfish ends they keep up armies,

and to support these armies they make war on their neighbors or on the central government." "Cooperation in China," *Chronicles of the London Missionary Society*, March 1921, p. 62.
5. Akira Iriye, e.a., *The World of Asia* (St. Louis: Forum Press, 1979), p. 71.

Chapter II

1. Founded in 1826, the society's charter stated its purpose to be the improvement of "the social and moral conditions of Seamen, by uniting the efforts of the wise and

good, in their behalf, by promoting in every port, boarding-houses of good character, saving banks, registers offices, libraries, reading rooms and schools, and also the ministrations of the Gospel and other religious blessings." General Synod, the highest legislative body of the Reformed church, frequently commended the society to its churches as being worthy of financial support.

2. For an account of the early history of the American Board see Clifton Jackson Phillips, *Protestant America and the Pagan World: The First Half Century of the American Board of Commissioners for Foreign Missions*, No. 32 of the Harvard East Asian Monographs (Cambridge: Harvard University Press, 1969).

3. For a discussion of the separation from the American Board, see *Acts and Proceedings of General Synod* (New York: Board of Publication, 1857), pp. 227-236. Henceforth cited as *Acts and Proceedings*.

4. For a detailed history of this mission see Gerald De Jong, *Mission to Borneo* (New Brunswick, N.J.: Reformed Church Historical Society, n. d.).

5. Abeel took passage aboard the *Morrison*, which was owned by David W. C. Olyphant, as was the *Roman* on which he made his first voyage in 1829. Olyphant was a New York merchant whose firm was engaged in the China trade. A devout Christian, he gave free passage to missionaries and refused to participate in the opium trade, two practices that gained for the firm's office in Canton the nickname of "Zion's Corner." *Dictionary of American Biography*, VII, Part 2 (New York: Scribners), p. 34.

6. Abeel to the *Christian Intelligencer. CI*, December 31, 1842, p. 94.

7. Pohlman to the First Reformed Church of Albany from Amoy, September 17, 1845, *CI*, April 2, 1846, p. 150 and April 9, 1846, p.154. See also "Missionary Operations at Amoy for the Year 1846," *CI*, May 27, 1847, p. 182.

8. For a list of diseases and afflictions that were treated, see reports by Hepburn, *Chinese Repository*, XV, No.4 (April 1846), pp. 181-184 and Cumming, ibid., XVII, No. 5, (May 1848), pp. 250-254. Hepburn states that nearly one-third of the cases treated were afflictions of the eyes.

9. For the life of Abeel see G. R. Williamson, *Memoirs of the Reverend David Abeel, Late Missionary to China* (New York: R. Carter, 1845). Williamson was a nephew of Abeel. For a lengthy synopsis of the book, see the *Chinese Repository*, XVIII, No. 5 (May 1849), pp. 260-275.

10. As quoted in "David Abeel, Pioneer Missionary to China," by the Reverend John G. Fagg, *Chinese Recorder*, XXV, April 1894.

11. Abeel to De Witt from Kolongsu, March 4, 1842, *CI*, August 27, 1842, p. 22. See also *Acts and Proceedings*, June 1843, p. 255.

12. Pohlman from Amoy to the American Board, July 3, 1844,

Missionary Herald, February 1845, p. 52. See also *CI*, April 2, 1846, p. 150. In many other places in the Dutch East Indies, however, including Batavia, the seat of the colonial government, the Amoy dialect was in common use among the Chinese.

13. *CI*, July 10, 1845, p. 206. See also ibid., June 12, 1845, pp. 190-191 and Pohlman and Doty's letter to the *Chinese Repository*, XV, No. 7, p. 356.

14. *CI*, March 4, 1847, p. 134.

15. Pohlman from Amoy to the First Reformed Church of Albany, September 17, 1846, *CI*, May 6, 1847, p. 170.

16. Pohlman from Amoy to the First Reformed Church of Albany, October 20, 1845, *CI*, April 9, 1846, p. 154. See also his letters to De Witt of November 6, 1845, *CI*, April 2, 1846, p. 150 and to the First Reformed Church of Albany, September 17, 1846, *CI*, May 6, 1847, p. 170.

17. As examples of these addresses, see the descriptions of those given by Talmage as reported in *CI*, November 1, 1849, p. 66 for a talk he gave on October 22 in the First Reformed Church at Pough-keepsie, New York, and in *CI*, November 15, 1849, p. 74 for an address given about a week later in the Second Reformed Church at Coxsackie, New York.

18. For a brief account of the coming and going of other missionary groups during the early period, see the *Chinese Recorder*, VII (March-April), 1876, pp. 106-107.

19. Richard Lovett, *The History of the London Missionary Society 1795-1895*, 2 vols. (London: Oxford University Press, 1899), II, p. 483.

20. Edward Band, *Working His Purpose Out: The History of the English Presbyterian Mission* (London: Presbyterian Church of England Publishing Office, 1947), p. 13.

21. "Semi-Annual Report of the Mission at Amoy, China," prepared by Pohlman at Amoy, dated December 13, 1847, and addressed to Anderson and De Witt, *CI*, April 20, 1848, p. 162 and April 27, 1848, p. 166. See also "Missionary Operations at Amoy for the Year 1846," *CI*, May 27, 1847, p. 182.

22. The local magistrates had earlier given permission to build, but in the event there might be some opposition from some of the people, Pohlman and Doty considered it wise to reinforce the consent of the local authorities by obtaining permission from the provincial governing head as well. Doty to Anderson from Amoy, March 16, 1848, *CI*, July 27, 1848, p. 10.

23. "Semi-Annual Report," *CI*, April 27, 1848, p. 166.

24. With the gradual liberation of Chinese women, a development in which the missionaries played an important role, screens were eventually removed from the churches. As late as the Second World War, however, it was not uncommon for Chinese men and women, especially those who were older, to sit on opposite sides of

the church. OI, Broekema, pp. 91-92.

25. For an eyewitness account of the wreck of the *Omega* and the cruel treatment of the survivors who made it to shore, see the *Chinese Repository*, XVIII, No. 1 (January 1849), pp. 51-53.

26. For an account of the Sin-koe-a church see "The History of the First Protestant Church in China after One Hundred Years." The thirty-one page booklet was written by the Reverend Lin Jin-gi in 1948 on the one hundredth anniversary of the church. Lin, who became pastor of the church in 1943, based his account primarily on the church records except for the years 1910-1931, some of which were destroyed in a fire. A copy of Lin's work is found in JAH, box W88-055.

27. Ibid., pp. 25, 29-30. See also *CH,* April 2, 1948, pp. 7, 19.

28. When this church burned down in 1909, it was replaced by a massive brick structure.

29. For accounts of these contacts and others involving the upper classes see "Semi-Annual Report, 1847," *CI,* April 27, 1848, p. 166; Pohlman to the First Church of Albany from Amoy, September 14, 1845, *CI,* April 9, 1846, p. 154; and Doty to the secretary of the American Board from Amoy, March 16, 1848, *CI,* July 20, 1848, p. 6.

30. "Semi-Annual Report, 1847," *CI,* April 27, 1848, p. 166. See also Pohlman to the First Reformed Church of Albany, September 17,

1846, from Amoy, *CI,* May 6, 1847, p. 170.

31. Pohlman to Anderson and De Witt, May 1, 1847 from Amoy, *CI,* December 2, 1847, p. 82.

32. Ibid.

33. Ibid.

Chapter III

1. Pohlman to Anderson and De Witt, May 1, 1847, *CI,* December 2, 1847, p. 82. For some changes introduced later see *AR,* 1913, pp. 8-9.

2. *Mission Field,* XIII, No. 10 (February 1901), p. 341.

3. For a first-hand account of the Monthly Concert and other religious gatherings see the letter of Pohlman to the First Reformed Church of Albany, September 17, 1845, *CI,* April 2, 1846, p. 150 and April 9, 1846, p. 154.

4. Pohlman to Anderson and De Witt, May 1, 1847, *CI,* December 2, 1847, p. 82.

5. *CI,* October 12, 1854, 57. See also the letter of June 25, 1855, from Doty to the American Board, *CI,* November 25, 1855, p. 86.

6. *CI,* April 27, 1848, p. 166.

7. *CI,* May 29, 1856, p. 189.

8. There are many thousands of characters, although not nearly all have to be learned to become an informed reader. For a discussion of the Chinese language see Yu-kuang Chu, "The Chinese Language," in John Meskill, ed., *An Introduction to Chinese Civilization* (Lexington, Mass.: D.C. Heath, 1973), pp. 587-615.

9. Talmage to Anderson and De Witt, July 14, 1851, *CI*, January 1, 1852, p. 101. For a general discussion of the orthography and pronunciation of the Amoy Romanization in use at this time with respect to vowels, dipthongs, nasals, consonants, aspirants, and all the important tones, see Philip W. Pitcher, *In and About Amoy* (Shanghai: Methodist Publishing House, 1909), pp. 201-207.

10. Ibid, p. 210

11. *Chinese Repository* XX, No.7 (July 1851), pp. 472, 474.

12. *Dictionary of American Biography*, *III* (*New* York: Scribners, 1930), pp. 389-390.

13. Already in his college days Talmage had shown a unique aptitude for languages, as is shown in the following information supplied by his biographer, who also was his colleague in China for many years: "John Talmage had made such substantial attainments in Hebrew and Greek, that when some years afterward the distinguished Dr. McClelland [in 1881] resigned as professor of these languages in the Theological Seminary at New Brunswick, [Talmage] was talked of as Dr. McClelland's successor, and but for the conviction that he ought not to be removed from the Amoy Mission, his appointment would have been earnestly advocated in the General Synod." J. G. Fagg, *Forty Years in South China: The Life of Rev. John Van Nest Talmage* (New York: Reformed Church in America, 1894), p. 45.

14. For an account of the life of Carstairs Douglas see "Memorial Sketch of Carstairs Douglas," *Chinese Recorder*, June 1890, pp. 266-271.

15. For a discussion of this cooperative effort see Pohlman to the First Reformed Church of Albany, September 17, 1845, *CI*, April 2, 1846, p. 150.

16. *AR*, 1863, p. 14.

17. Pitcher, *In and About Amoy*, p. 209.

18. For a detailed account of the two services, see *Chinese Repository*, XV, No. 7 (July 1846), pp. 357-361. See also the letter from Pohlman to the American Board, May 1, 1846, *Missionary Herald*, September 1846, p. 321. The names of the two converts are also given as Hok-kui-peyh and Un-sia-peyh.

19. See pages 79-80, 83-84, 90.

20. As quoted in Band, *History of the English Presbyterian Mission*, p. 17.

21. The letter is found without date in Islay Burns, *Memoir of the Rev. Wm. C. Burns* (New York: Robert Carter and Brothers, 1879), pp. 415-417.

22. James Johnston, *China and Formosa: The Story of the Mission of the Presbyterian Church of England* (New York: Fleming H. Revell, n.d.), p. 123.

23. *CI*, September 21, 1854, p. 45.

24. *CI*, November 25, 1855, p. 86.

25. Joralmon to the *Christian Intelligencer*, *CI*, December 18, 1856, p. 98.

26. For discussion of this subject see Lin, "History of the First

Reformed Church in China," pp. 15-17 and *AR*, 1859, pp. 9-10.

27. Addressed to the Middle Dutch Reformed Church, Brooklyn, September 12, 1848, *CI*, January 18, 1849, p. 109.

28. *CI*, May 29, 1856, p. 189.

29. See, for example, "Induction of a Native Pastor at Chiang-chiu, China," *Chronicle of the London Missionary Society*, July 1891, pp. 210-213.

Chapter IV

1. *CI*, April 2, 1846, p. 150.
2. Ibid.
3 Pohlman to the First Reformed Church of Albany, September 17, 1846, in *CI*, May 6, 1847, p. 170. See also *Missionary Herald*, September 1846, p. 321.
4. The Greenwich Church, organized in 1803, was dissolved in 1866.
5. Kip to the Reverend Philip Pelts, secretary of the Board of Foreign Mission, *CI*, November 26, 1863, p. 189.
6. Isaiah 54:2-3.
7. For descriptions of these visits to Changchow and Tong-an see "Semi-Annual Report of the Mission at Amoy," 1847, *CI*, April 20, 1848, p. 162 and April 27, 1848, p. 166.
8. Joralmon to his former minister, the Reverend James Scott of Newark, New Jersey, April 16, 1857, *CI*, July 30, 1857, p. 17.
9. Ibid.
10. *CI*, April 9, 1846, p. 154.
11. "Semi-Annual Report, 1847," *CI*, April 20, 1848, p. 162.

12. Joralmon to the Reverend Scott, April 16, 1857, *CI*, July 30, 1857, p. 17.
13. See page 31.
14. Pohlman to the First Reformed Church of Albany, September 17, 1846, *CI*, May 6, 1847, p. 170.
15. Pohlman to Anderson and De Witt, May 1, 1847, *CI*, December 2, 1847, p. 82.
16. Stronach to Doty, April 8, 1846, *CI*, October 15, 1846, p. 54. Doty was still in the United States at this time as a result of bringing his and Pohlman's children there following the deaths of their wives.
17. *CI*, September 13, 1849, p. 38.
18. Ibid. In his remarks, Talmage noted that General Synod had reported in 1848 that there currently were sixty ordained ministers without charge. For other comments about the need for more missionaries, see Pohlman's letter to De Witt, June 22, 1846, *CI*, October 15, 1846, p. 54 and Pohlman to Anderson and De Witt, May 25, 1847, *CI*, December 16, 1847, p. 90.
19. *CI*, December 25, 1856, p. 101.
20. A description of Amoy in 1866 describes its streets as "rather more dirty than those of most Chinese towns." Donald Matheson, *Narrative of the Mission to China of the English Presbyterian Church* (London: James Nisbet & Co., 1866), p. 3.
21. There are several pamphlets on this cemetery in RCA, 724 China Mission, Box 1, "Papers, 1856-1951."

22. Rapalje to Peltz from Amoy, November 5, 1863, in mss, ibid.
23. Johnson, *China and Formosa*, p. 68. See also Matheson, *Narrative of the Mission to China*, p. 5.
24. On Burns's use of Chinese converts from the Reformed mission see Burns, *Memoir*, pp. 388-393, 404, 406.
25. For a description of the Taiping Rebellion, see Hsu, *Rise of Modern China*, pp. 221-253. For the religious views of Hung and the Taipings, see Eugene P. Boardman, *Christian Influence on the Ideology of the Taiping Rebellion* (Madison, Wisc.: University of Wisconsin Press, 1952).
26. Burns to Matheson of the English Presbyterian Board in England January 16, 1854, as quoted in Johnston, *China and Formosa*, p. 88. See also Talmage's letter of August 18, 1854, to the American Board in *CI*, January 18, 1855, p. 113.
27. As quoted in Johnston, *China and Formosa*, pp. 91-92.
28. As quoted in Burns, *Memoir*, p. 404. The successes were accompanied, however, with occasional interruptions from some of the local people. In a few instances these were serious enough to require the meetings to be moved to the second floor.
29. The letter is found in Burns, *Memoir*, pp. 423-425.
30. *CI*, November 29, 1855, p. 85.

Chapter V

1. Fagg, *Forty Years*, p. 171.

2. The division of territory is described in the *Chronicle of the London Missionary Society*, February 1899, pp. 53, 54.
3. Johnston, *China and Formosa*, pp. 85-86.
4. John Van Nest Talmage, *History and Ecclesiastical Relations of the Churches of the Presbyterian Order at Amoy, China* (New York: Wynkoop, Hallenbeck & Thomas, Printers, 1863), p. 13.
5. As quoted in Band, *History of the English Presbyterian Mission*, p. 48.
6. Talmage in a letter to *CI* from Amoy dated May 30, 1856, *CI*, September 25, 1856, p. 50.
7. The rules, with explanations, are found in Lin, "History of the First Protestant Church," pp. 13-14.
8. Talmage, *History and Ecclesiastical Relations*, p. 14. See also *CI*, November 5, 1857, p. 4.
9. The letter is found in Fagg, *Forty Years*, pp. 173-184.
10. Ibid., p. 181.
11. Ibid.
12. The letter, dated October 1, 1856, is found in ibid, pp. 184-185. It is addressed to Thomas De Witt of the Board of Foreign Missions.
13. The committee's report is found in *Acts and Proceedings*, 1857, pp. 225-227.
14. Talmage, *History and Ecclesiastical Relations*, p. 24.
15. *Acts and Proceedings*, 1852, pp. 279-280; 1857, pp. 225-227.
16. The procedure for the division into two churches is discussed in Lin, "History of the First Protestant Church," pp. 17-18.

17. *AR*, 1864, p. 14. The spellings of these two names varies.
18. The committee's report is in ibid., June 1862, pp. 195-198.
19. This portion of the report from the English committee is quoted in Fagg, *Forty Years*, pp. 207-208. A more lengthy excerpt is in Talmage, *History and Ecclesiastical Relations*, pp. 32-35.
20. *AR*, 1863, p. 16.
21. The lengthy report is found in *Acts and Proceedings*, 1863, pp. 333-340.
22. Talmage's remarks are found in *CI*, June 25, 1863, pp. 2-3.
23. Ibid., p. 2. To understand the use of the term Dutch in these remarks, it must be noted that this term was a part of the official corporate name of the Reformed Church in America until 1867.
24. The comments by Schieffelin and Porter are found in *CI*, June 25, 1863, p. 3.
25. Chambers's remarks are found in ibid., p. 3. In view of Chambers's presidency of General Synod, one would have thought he would have been more neutral. His firm stand is also surprising in view of his long friendship with Doty, a friendship that dated back to the early 1830s when he and Doty had been roommates at Rutgers. Chambers had also been Talmage's pastor at Somerville, New Jersey, and had preached one of the farewell sermons when the latter left for China in 1850.
26. Talmage, *History and Ecclesiastical Relations*, pp. 49-53.
27. Ibid., p. 66.

28. *CI*, November 12, 1863, p. 2.
29. The letter is in Fagg, *Forty Years*, pp. 219-220.
30. *Acts and Proceedings*, June 1864, pp. 490-491. For additional information on synod's discussion of the majority and minority reports see *CI*, June 16, 1864, p. 2.

Chapter VI

1. Following the retirement of the Reverend Talmage in 1889 and his death in 1892, Mrs. Talmage returned to China where she died in 1912. When the Reverend Kip retired in 1898 and died in 1901, Mrs. Kip returned to China where she labored until 1918, when she returned to the States.
2. These are the kind of thoughts still being expressed a half century later. See Jack Hill, "China," *CH*, February 27, 1948, pp. 14-15.
3. *Mission Field*, XIV, No. 11 (March 1901), p. 398.
4. A study of the sixty-four Reformed men and women who went out to Amoy between 1842 and 1906 indicates that twenty-six, or nearly 40 percent, resigned for reasons of health. Philip Pitcher, "The American Reformed Church Mission," p. 9. RCA, 724 China Mission, Box 2, "Papers, 1856-1951."
5. *Mission Field*, X, No 1 (May 1897), p. 21.
6. *AR*, 1891, p. 34.
7. Ibid., 1898, p. 11.
8. Ibid., 1871, p. 20.
9. Letter of March 7, 1865, to the

Reverend Philip Peltz of the Board of Foreign Mission. RCA, 724 China Mission, Box 2, "Papers, 1856-1951."

10. *Chinese Records*, XVI (October 1885), p. 396. Vacations, of course, even extended ones, did not always prove to be a cure-all for illness or despondency. The Reverend John Howard Van Doren, for example, who was absent on a health trip for three months in 1873 and returned feeling much better, discovered the improvement to be temporary and was compelled to return to the United States in that same year.

11. *Chinese Recorder*, October, 1896, p. 511. In the late summer of 1902, Dr. C. Otto Stumpf, the Reformed medical doctor at Sio-khe, reported, "There is a community of over two hundred foreigners on the hill top [at Kuliang], seventy-five percent of whom are missionaries." "A Summer Resort in the Summer," *Mission Field*, XV, No. 8 (December 1902), p. 276.

12. Olive Miller, "The Amoy Missionary Society Sanitarium," *Chronicle of the London Missionary Society*, September 1897, p. 211. See also John Macgowan, *Pictures of Southern China*, (London: The Religious Tract Society, 1897), pp. 92-95 and *Mission Field*, X, No 1, May 1897, p. 21.

13. *CI*, December 12, 1894, pp. 5-6.

14. Ibid., September 3, 1902, p. 576. See also ibid., August 7, 1901, p. 508 and December 4, 1901, p. 788.

15. The letter is found in *Acts and Proceedings*, June 1887, pp.

330-332. See also the letter from a Chinese pastor of Second Amoy to Secretary Cobb in *Mission Field*, XIII, No. 11 (March 1901), p. 384. In 1900, an elder of one of Amoy's churches donated $600 to the Board of Foreign Missions toward the expense of sending another missionary.

16. This was based on the findings of a special three-man committee of Reformed church leaders in America acting in behalf of the Board of Foreign Missions, *CI*, December 2, 1880, p. 3-4.

17. *Mission Field*, X, No. 5 (September 1897-8), p. 149.

18. Henry Cobb, *Far Hence:A Budget of Letters from Our Mission Fields in Asia* (New York: Woman's Board of Foreign Missions, 1893), p. 149. For an account of the life and work of the Reverend Iap see that by his friend and colleague, the Reverend Philip Pitcher, in *CI*, July 1 and July 8, pp. 418, 432-433.

19. *Mission Field*, IX, No.10 (February 1897), p. 326.

20. *AR*, 1873, p. 10.

21. *Missionary Review of the World*, III, No. 1 (January 1890), pp. 50-51.

22. Band, *History of the English Presbyterian Mission*, p. 233.

23. For a discussion of missionary visits into new areas see chapter 8.

24. *AR*, 1894, p. 4.

25. See pages 182-183.

26. *AR*, 1886, p. 27.

27. *Mission Field*, III, No. 6 (June 1890), p. 184. See also Rapalje's observation in *AR*, 1897, p. 3.

28. *AR*, 1898, p. 7.

Chapter VII

1. *AR*, 1900, p. viii.
2. For the founding of schools and a hospital at Sio-khe see pages 121-123 and 152-153.
3. These observations were made by Cobb in a letter written from Amoy, June 3, 1892. *Mission Field*, V, No. 8 (August 1892), p. 249.
4. The Reverend Pitcher, who visited Tong-an frequently in the early years, reported that at one time few "enterprises" met with more bitter opposition than Chang-chow. Philip Pitcher, *Fifty Years in Amoy* (New York: Reformed Church in America, 1893), p. 122.
5. It is important that this factor be kept in mind in evaluating the membership rolls of a church for specific years. Membership figures of a particular church include those of its outstations. Thus, when an outstation was raised to the status of a church, the membership of that church that had been sponsoring it was automatically reduced.
6. For an explanation of the naming of some of these union churches, see Pitcher's explanation in the *Mission Field*, II, No. 5 (May 1889), pp. 23-24.
7. *Mission Field*, III, No. 12 (December 1890), p. 373.
8. Ibid., XIII, No. 10 (February 1901), p. 341.
9. *Mission Field*, V, No. 1 (January 1892), p. 25. The letter is found on pp. 23-25.
10. Ibid., VII, No. 1 (March 1894), p. 6. See also ibid., V, No. 3 (March 18,

1892, p. 89.
11. *AR*, 1880, p. 9.
12. *Mission Field*, IV, No. 5 (May 1891), p. 162.
13. *AR*, 1868, p. 9.
14. Mimeographed pamphlet, "The Amoy Mission of the Reformed Church in America," p. 9. RCA, 724 China Mission, Box 1, "Papers, 1856-1951."
15. *AR*, 1872, p. 14. See also ibid., 1873, p. 9.
16. Ibid., 1888, p. 28; 1898, pp. 4-5.
17. Ibid., 1901, p. 3.
18. *Mission Field*, II, No. 4 (April 1889), pp. 24-25. See also ibid., II, No. 6 (June 1889), p. 20.
19. *AR*, 1892, p. 20.
20. The two classes went by other names, too, including Chin-chiu and Chiang-chiu.
21. Band, *History of the English Presbyterian Mission*, p. 289.
22. For accounts of some of the synods see *CI*, May 29, 1901, p. 349; June 3, 1903, p. 351; and June 22, 1904, pp. 397-398.
    The questions that were discussed were not too different from those being discussed in gatherings of the London Missionary Society. See Richard Lovett, *The History of the London Missionary Society 1795-1895*, 2 vols. (London: Oxford University Press, 1899), pp. 505-506.
23. The committee's report, entitled "Paper on the Amoy Mission," is found in *CI*, December 2, 1880, pp. 3-4.
24. Cobb, *Far Hence*, pp. 145-147.
25. *AR*, 1889, p. 34.
26. Ibid., 1899, p. 4.

Chapter VIII

1. *Mission Field*, IV, No. 7 (July 1891), p. 226.
2. Ibid., IV, No. 11 (November 1891), p. 355.
3. *Far Hence*, p. 177.
4. *Mission Field*, VI, No. 8 (August 1893), p. 2.
5. Ibid., IV, No. 7 (July 1891), p. 226. For more details on the ins and outs of travel by sedan chair, see M. E. Talamage "A Day in China," *Mission Gleaner*, IV, No. 3 (March-April), 1887, pp. 9-12.
6. *Mission Field*, IV, No. 6 (June 1891), pp. 195-196.
7. Ibid., VI, No. 8 (August 1893), p. 2.
8. *Far Hence*, pp. 140-141.
9. Ibid., pp. 143-144. For another account of traveling aboard a cumbersome houseboat, see the letter by Otte of January 25, 1889, *Mission Field*, II, No. 5 (May 1889), pp. 22-23.
10. *Far Hence*, pp. 135-136.
11. The two excerpts are from a letter written April 30, 1892, ibid., pp. 138-142.
12. *Mission Field*, IV, No. 7 (July 1891), p. 22.
13. Ibid., IV, No. 8 (August 1891), p. 257.
14. *Mission Field*, III, No. 12 (December 1890), p. 373.
15. Written from Sio-khe March 6, 1891, ibid., IV, No. 6 (June 1891), pp. 195-196.
16. *AR* 1873. p. 9.
17. Studley's account of the journey is found in *CI*, May 19, 1897, pp. 4-6.
18. *Mission Field*, II, No. 6 (June 1889), p. 19.
19. For an account of one of these travels involving the Kips, see ibid., XI, No. 5 (September 1898), p. 148.
20. Ibid., II, No. 1, (January 1888), p. 23.
21. Ibid., II, No. 3 (March 1889), p. 25.
22. Ibid., IX, No. 10 (February 1897), p. 321.
23. Ibid., II, No. 4 (April 1889), p. 25. See also ibid., V, No. 8 (August 1892), p. 250 and *CI*, May 19, 1897, pp. 4-6.
24. *AR*, 1896, p. 7.

Chapter IX

1. *AR*, 1872, p. 15.
2. Ibid., 1889, p. 38. For similar reports in which Pitcher stressed the importance of education as an arm of evangelization see *Chinese Recorder*, XXIII (April 1892), pp. 164-166 and XXVI (February 1895), pp. 74-78. Pitcher's remarks take on special meaning when it is realized that during his thirty years in China (1885-1915) no one among the Reformed missionaries was a stronger advocate of education than he.
3. *Acts and Proceedings*, 1870, p. 119.
4. *Chinese Recorder*, XXI (February 1890), p. 72.
5. *Mission Field*, XXXIV, No. 9 (January 1922), p. 227.
6. The Women's Board of Foreign Missions was organized in 1875 as auxiliary to the Board of Foreign Missions.
7. "Chinese Education a Factor in Evangelization" *Chinese Recorder*, XXI (February 1890), p. 74.

8. *AR,* 1875, p. 9.
9. From a letter written by Cobb, from Kulangsu, May 5, 1892, and published in *Far Hence,* p. 148.
10. *Mission Field,* XVII, No. 4 (August 1904), pp. 145-146; XVIII, No. 3 (July 1905), p. 98; and XXIX, No. 3 (July 1916), p. 135.
11. *AR,* 1880, p. 14.
12. Ibid., 1883, p. 23. See also Pitcher, *Fifty Years in Amoy,* p. 75.
13. Although the missionaries were critical of the emphasis placed on memorization in the traditional Chinese schools, teachers today would be surprised at the large amount of rote learning that the missionaries themselves expected from Chinese children with respect to the study of the Scriptures.
14. *AR,* 1890, p. 30. See also ibid., 1888, p. 37.
15. Ibid., 1889, p. 40.
16. *AR,* 1888, p. 36.
17. The Reverend James Sadler in the *Chronicle of the London Missionary Society,* March 1882, p. 88.
18. Pitcher, *Fifty Years in Amoy,* p. 52.
19. *Chronicle of the London Missionary Society,* March 1882, p. 87. For a full discussion of the status of Chinese women in the late nineteenth century see the several articles that appeared under the title "The Women of China" in the March, April, July, August, October, and December issues of the *Chronicle of the London Missionary Society for 1882.* See also Margaret E. Burton, *The Education of Women in China*

(London and New York: Fleming H. Revell Co., 1911).
20. There is considerable uncertainty as to why the custom of foot-binding was introduced but it lasted about a thousand years. The process involved tightly binding the feet of young girls at about age six with short strips of cloth, with only the big toe remaining free. The other four gradually folded beneath the sole. The feet remained bound for several years, leaving the bones or arches misshapen and the instep forced into a high arch. The feet thus formed, often called "lily feet" or "golden lilies," were supposed to be a mark of respectability and make a woman more attractive. It was a painful process and made walking difficult for the rest of a woman's life.
21. *AR,* 1869, p. 16.
22. For a description of the school's curriculum, see Olive Miller, "Training Christian Women in Amoy," *Chronicle of the London Missionary Society* (April 1897), pp. 84-86.
23. "Greetings from Amoy," a mimeographed pamphlet issued in 1907 in remembrance of the 75th anniversary of the founding of the Board of Foreign Missions, pp. 6-7.
24. P. 19. See also Rapalje's "Womans' Work for Women." *Mission Field,* I, No. 3 (March 1888), p. 26.

Chapter X

1. *AR,* 1881, p. 12.
2. Ibid., 1879, p. 10. See also ibid.,

1871, p. 16; 1874, p. 9; and 1878, p. 10.

3. Ibid., 1888, p. 4.

4. Ibid., 1890, p. 29.

5. Pitcher, *Fifty Years in Amoy*, p. 185; *AR*, 1892, p. 22.

6. *AR*, 1893, p.33.

7. Band, *History of the English Presbyterian Mission*, p. 235.

8. For a discussion of this see *AR*, 1894, pp. 7-8. For a chronology of events, including dates when certain courses were added to the curriculum, see the *Talmage College Handbook*, 1935, pp. 4-6.

9. *Chinese Recorder*, XXI (February 1890), p. 76.

10. For a lengthy discussion of the English question see ibid., pp. 76-78 and *AR*, 1884, pp. 26-27 and 1901, p. 11. No doubt the competition arising from the founding of several so-called Anglo-Chinese schools helped bring the Middle School around on the English question. For a discussion of such a school at Changchow, one that had definite Christian underpinnings, see an article by the Reverend Hobard Studley in *Mission Field*, X, No. 9 (January 1898), pp. 269-271,

11. *AR*, 1890, pp. 29-30.

12. *Catalogue and Special Report of the Boys Academy*, 1895, p. 11.

13. Ibid., p. 13. See also *Chinese Recorder*, XXVI (July 1895), p. 332.

14. *AR*, 1901, p.11. See also "Where the Reformed Church is Working in China," p. 10, a mimeographed pamphlet published in 1906. RCA, 724 China Mission, Box 1 "Papers, 1856-1951."

15. *Mission Field*, X, No. 7 (November 1897), p. 203.

16. *AR*, 1887, p. 13.

17. *Mission Field*, X, No. 7 (November 1897), p. 203.

18. *AR*, 1896, pp. 4-5. See also Philip Pitcher's article "Country Schools," *Chinese Recorder*, XXVI (February 1895), pp. 74-78.

19. *AR*, 1893, p. 33.

20. Ibid., 1889, p. 38.

21. Ibid., 1890, p. 28. See also ibid., 1888, p. 39.

22. *Mission Field*, I, No. 11 (November 1888), pp. 26-27.

23. *AR*, 1892, p. 23.

24. For a more complete description of the building, see *Mission Field*, VIII, No. 4 (October 1895), pp. 89-91.

Chapter XI

1. *Chinese Recorder*, XXI (February 1890), p. 72. See also the comments by Dr. John Otte in *Mission Field*, I, No. 3 (March 1888), p. 25.

2. Pitcher, *Fifty Years in Amoy*, p. 254.

3. Despite her being of Chinese birth, Miss King apparently had not spent much time in China. A report of March 1888 describes her as being busy "studying the language and maturing her plans for work among the women." *Mission Field*, I, No. 3 (March 1888), p. 270.

4. Several booklets have been written on the life of Dr. Otte, including A. L. Warnshuis, *A Brief Sketch of the Life and Work of John A. Otte* (New York: Board of Foreign

Missions, 1911); H. M. Van Nes, *Dr. J. A. Otte, Zendeling, Arts in China* (Zeist: Drukkerij van de Stichting Hoenderloo, 1936); and Frances Phelps Otte, *Pioneering in Medical Missions* (Holland, Mich.: Old News Printers, 1939).

5. *Mission Field*, II, No. 1 (October 1889), p. 25.
6. Ibid., p. 26.
7. Ibid., p. 25.
8. Ibid.
9. Secretary Cobb of the Board of Foreign Missions commented in 1892, following a visit to the Sio-khe hospital: "The difficulties of medical practice are immense, owing to the ignorance of the people of the simplest laws of health, their foolish and superstitious notions in regard to the body, disease, and its remedies, their unwillingness or inability to comprehend or comply with the directions given them, and the universal addictedness to dirt." Letter from Cobb dated May 5, 1892, *Far Hence*, p. 146.
10. *Mission Field*, VI, No. 1 (January 1893).
11. *AR*, 1893, p. 39.
12. "Report of the Neerbosch Hospital, July 1893-July 1894," pp. 13-14. The writer is grateful to Russell Gasero, Reformed church archivist, for locating this and similar material on the mission hospitals.
13. *AR*, 1895, p. 14.
14. Ibid., 1894, pp. 16-17.
15. Ibid., p. 15. See also the "Report of the Neerbosch Hospital, July 1893-July 1894," p. 12.

16. *AR*, 1891, pp. 33-34.
17. "Report of the Neerbosch Hospital," July 1893-July 1894, p. 11.
18. Two-page promotional folder issued by Otte in 1896.
19. *AR*, 1899, p. 13.
20. "Hope Hospital and Netherlands Woman's Hospital," Report for 1898, p. 7.
21. *Mission Field*, XI, No. 10 (February 1899), p. 325; reprinted from the *Missionary Gleaner*.)
22. "Hope Hospital and Netherlands Woman's Hospital," Report for 1899, p. 4.
23. *Mission Field*, XI, No. 1 (April 1899), p. 17.
24. Ibid.
25. *Mission Field*, XIII, No. 10 (February 1899-1900), pp. 343-346.
26. Ibid.
27. "Hope Hospital and Netherlands Woman's Hospital," Report for 1899, p. 9.
28. *AR*, for 1900, p. 13.

Chapter XII

1. These statistics are taken from the *AR* for the years indicated.
2. *AR*, 1918, p. 22.
3. Ibid., 1909, p. iv.
4. *Mission Field*, XXXIV, No. 9 (January 1922), pp. 218-219. See also ibid., XXXIX, No. 11 (March 1917), p. 492.
5. RCA, 723 China Mission, Box 5, "Correspondence, 1900-1905."
6. Ibid.
7. *Mission Field*, XXIV, No. 3 (July 1911), p. 117.
8. *AR*, 1901, pp. 12-13.

9. Henry De Pree, "Need for Women Workers in the Amoy Mission," *CI,* July 1930, p. 452. See also "A Call from the Far East," *CI,* March 25, 1908, p. 200. The latter was an appeal by the Womans' Board of Foreign Missions for three young women for the China field, whose need, it stated, "is urgent, indeed it is imperative."

10. *AR,* 1917, p. xv.

11. For the names of these see the appendix.

12. The statistics for these years are taken from *AR.* Unfortunately, beginning in 1933, the reports do not break down the native workers by categories. For brief accounts of some of the major Chinese pastors of this period see: John G. Fagg, "How Pastor Iap Became a Christian," *Mission Field,* No. 2 (June 1917), pp. 52-55; Philip Pitcher, "In Memoriam: The Rev. Ti Pheng-theng," *CI,* January 1, 1908, pp. 9-10; H. A. Poppen, "Out of the Lives of Men: Ang Kheh-chiong," *IL,* October 21, 1936, p. 12; and "Death of Amoy's Oldest Pastor, Rev. Tan Khe-hong," *IL,* April 16, 1937, p. 15.

13. "Greetings from Amoy: 1842-1907," p. 24. The pamphlet was published on orders of the General Synod as part of the centenary that various missions were observing in 1907 commemorating the hundredth anniversary of the arrival of the Reverend Robert Morrison, the first Protestant missionary to serve in China.

14. *AR,* 1921, p. 6.

15. Ibid., 1904, p. 10. See also ibid., 1917, p. 23.

16. Ibid., 1913, p. 10.

17. Ibid., 1923, p. 15.

18. Ibid., 1915, p. 4. See also ibid., 1917, p. 28 and 1929, pp. 3-4.

19. For an account of the type of work performed by the Bible women at this time see Leona Vander Linden, "An Afternoon with the Bible Woman," *CI,* October 20, 1926, p. 673. This is an account of Vander Linden's observations as she accompanied a Bible woman on one of her daily rounds.

20. *AR,* 1900, p. 5. *Mission Field,* XXIV, No. 9 (June 1922), p. 219. It should be noted that these budget crunches at home affected not only the Reformed church's mission in China but also its mission in India, Arabia, and elsewhere. This is clearly brought out in an excerpt from a report issued by the denominational Board of Foreign Missions in 1922: "Appropriations...have just been made and the news is on its way to [all] the fields that for the third consecutive year only very slight increases have been made for a work which is growing by leaps and bounds. For the third year we have had practically to disregard the pages upon pages of careful estimates of needs sent in by the fields, and to grant only what has been given in previous years, which, in the case of at least one mission, is 50 percent below the figures of their estimated needs."

21. *AR,* 1933, p. 14.

22. Ibid., 1912, p. 43.
23. John G. Fagg, " A Pavilion from the Heat and Home Sweet Home," *CI*, June 1, 1910, p. 343. To further justify this request, Fagg noted that Eckerson had been living in two rooms that the secretary ironically described as "More than adequately ventilated through numerous cracks in the board walls."
24. *CI*, March 24, 1909, p. 187. The churches were those at Alton and Sioux Center.
25. *AR*, 1914, pp. 18-19.
26. Ibid., 1912, p. 16.
27. F.M. Potter, "Reflections of a Layman," *CI*, June 11, 1930, p. 394. See also H. P. De Pree, "Amoy Classis Dedicates a Church," *CI*, September 5, 1928, p. 570.
28. *Mission Field*, XIX, No. 11 (March 1907), p. 393.
29. Ibid., XXIII, No. 2 (June 1910), pp. 54-55.
30. Ibid., XXIV, No. 4 (August 1911), p. 146.
31. For an account of the fire see Philip Pitcher, "The Loss of the Tek-chhiu-kha Church Property by Fire," *CI*, December 16, 1903, pp. 824-825.
32. F. M. Potter, "Reflections of a Layman," *CI*, June 11, 1930, p. 394. It is interesting to note that when Potter preached at Second Amoy during his visit, his interpreter was a Mr. Chiu, a young Chinese who graduated from Hope College in Holland, Michigan, a few years earlier and was currently serving as principal at Talmage College.
33. *Mission Field*, XXII, No. 3 (July

1909), pp. 95-97; ibid., XXXIII, No. 8 (December 1920), p. 197.
34. *AR*, 1921, p. x.
35. Ibid., 1927, pp. 5-7.
36. Ibid.
37. In describing the broader ecumenical movements that took place in China as they affected the Reformed mission, the writer relied on Kenneth Scott Latourette, *A History of Christian Missions in China* (New York: Paragon Book Gallery, 1975, reprint of 1929 edition), pp. 669-672, 794-801 and *A History of the Ecumenical Movement 1517-1948* edited by Ruth Rouse and Stephen C. Neill, 2nd ed. (Philadelphia: Westminister Press, 1968), pp. 358-360, 377-387.
38. For a discussion of the Centenary Conference from the perspective of the Reformed mission see Philip W. Pitcher, "The China Centenary Conference," in *Mission Field*, XX, No. 4 (August 1907), pp. 126-129. See also the remarks by A. L. Warnshuis in *CI*, July 10, 1907, p. 490.
39. For a rather detailed account of the conference see A. L. Warnshuis, "Edinburgh in China," *CI*, July 9, 1913, pp. 444-445.
40. Stephen Neill, *A History of Christian Missions* (Grand Rapids, Mich.: William B. Eerdmans, 1964), p. 546.
41. For more information on the Continuation Conference and Continuation Committee and Warnshuis's new duties see *CI*, July 21, 1915, p. 475; April 19, 1916, pp. 252-253; and August 2,

1916, p. 498. For a biography of Warnshuis and the distinguished administrative role he played in world missions after leaving China see Norman Goodall, *Christian Ambassador: A Life of A. Livingston Warnshuis* (Manhasset, N.Y.: Channel Press, 1963.)

42. For a careful account of the first General Assembly see Henry P. De Pree, "The First General Assembly of the Church of Christ in China," *CI,* January 4, 1928, p. 9. See also by the same writer a letter to William Chamberlain, secretary of the Board of Foreign Missions, *CI,* December 7, 1927, p. 780.

43. *Mission Field*, XXII No. 4 (August 1919), p. 118; ibid., XXXIV, No. 5 (September 1921), p. 118; *AR*, 1927, p. 3; ibid., 1930, p. 4.

44. *Christian Missions in China*, pp. 800, 801.

45. E. Shilston Box, "The Church in China," *Chronicles of the London Missionary Society*, March 1934, p. 58.

Chapter XIII

1. "A Plea for Amoy," *Mission Field*, XIV, No. 11 (March 1901), p. 398.

2. *AR*, for 1921, p. 3.

3. For a discussion of the aims of the Sunday schools and how they were organized see William Vander Meer, "First Birthday of a Chinese Sunday School," *CI,* August 28, 1929, p. 550 and Chhoa Chi-teng, "A Model Chinese Sunday School," ibid., September 10, 1930, p. 599.

4. *AR*, 1913, p. 22.

5. Ibid., 1918, p. 10.

6. "Social Rooms at the Tek-cchiu-kha Church, Amoy," *CI,* August 14, 1929, pp. 514-515.

7. *AR,* 1925, p. 3. See also Lyman A. Talman, "The South Fukien Religious Tract Society," *CI,* May 8, 1929, p. 292.

8. *AR,* 1919, p. 29.

9. "Ordination of Pastor Saw The-liu," *CI,* August 21, 1929, p. 533.

10. For accounts of Sung's revival meetings see Edna Beekman, "Remarkable Revival in China," *IL,* March 20, 1935, p. 13 and Tena Holkeboer, "Something Happened," ibid., December 23, 1936, p. 127.

11. "The Amoy Church Awakened," *CI,* February 28, 1923, p. 133. See also H. P. De Pree, "Evangelistic Campaign in China," ibid., April 10, 1918, pp. 351-352 and Edna Beekman, "Revival Meetings in Amoy," ibid., September 5, 1928, p. 571.

12. *Mission Field*, XXVII, No. 10 (February 1915), p. 406. See also pp. 407-409. Page 408 has a picture of the Chinese officials as well as many Chinese businessmen and missionaries who attended the luncheon. Most of those present are identified.

13. Henry J. Voskuil, "The Five Year Movement in the Sio-khe District," *CI,* February 4, 1931, p. 67; Katherine Green, "Forward Movements in China," Ibid., pp. 68-69; Lau Hiong-eng, "Plans for Church Work in Changchow City," *IL,* July 24, 1935, p. 13; and

Leona Vander Linden, "Lay Workers' Bible Training Institute, Changchow, China," ibid., July 22, 1936, p. 12.

14. Henry A. Poppen, "Amoy Again Pioneers," *IL*, December 2, 1936, p. 12.

15. Ibid.

16. *Mission Field*, XV, No. 11 (March 1902), pp. 391-192.

17. Ibid., XXX, No. 4 (August 1917), pp. 143-144. See also ibid., XXX, No. 11 (March 1918), pp. 518-519.

18. Nellie Zwemer writing in the *Mission Field*, XXXI, No. 12 (April 1919), p. 648. Zwemer was accompanied by Leona Vander Linden. See also ibid., XXXI, No 1 (May 1918), pp. 37-39; XXXII, No. 2 (June 1919), pp. 70-71; and XXXIII, No. 5 (September 1920), p. 121.

19. *AR*, 1914, p. 18.

20. Ibid.

21. *AR*, 1908, p. 14.

22. Katherine Green, "An Appreciation of Miss Nellie Zwemer," *CH*, June 15, 1945, p. 2.

23. *Mission Field*, XXX, No. 4 (August 1917), pp. 143-144. See also ibid., XXX, No. 11 (March 1918), pp. 518-519.

24. *AR*, 1929, p. 9.

25. *Mission Field*, XVII, No. 11 (March 1905), p. 403.

26. See pages 108-109.

27. J. S. Snoke, "Motor Boats in China," *Mission Field*, XXVI, No. 10 (February 1914), pp. 371-372.

28. *AR*, 1923, p. 3.

29. Ibid., 1929, p. 14.

30. Ibid., 1930, p. 9.

31. Ibid., 1928, p. 17.

32. Ibid., 1929, p. 15.

33. *Mission Field*, XXIII, No. 3 (July 1910), pp. 113-114.

34. Ibid., XVII, No. 1 (May 1904), p. 21.

35. Ibid., XXIX, No. 7 (November 1916), p. 303.

36. Ibid., XXII, No. 11 (March 1910), pp. 434-435.

37. Ibid., XXX, No. 6 (October 1917), pp. 225-227. For an another account describing some of the discomforts of travel see "First Impressions of Tong-an," ibid., XXIX, No. 12 (April 1917), pp. 542-543.

38. Taeke Bosch, "Worship in a Chinese Church," *Mission Field*, XXIX, No. 2 (June 1916), pp. 72-73. The article was written a few months after his arrival in China where he served from 1915 to 1931.

39. "Presiding over a Consistory Meeting in a Chinese Church," *Mission Field*, XXXIII, No. 7 (November 1920), pp. 178-179.

40. The figures were generally taken from the statistics found in the "General Summary Table" near the end of each annual report of the Board of Foreign Missions and occasionally from the beginning of the particular report dealing specifically with the Amoy mission.

41. See pages 42-44, 52-53, 83-85, and 90.

42. *AR*, 1934, p. 5. See also H. A. Poppen, "And Made a Daily Study of the Scriptures," *IL*, September 25, 1935, p. 12.

43. *AR*, 1925, p. 4.

44. Ibid., 1909, p. 11.
45. "Emancipation of Chinese Womanhood," *CI*, September 1, 1926, p. 561.
46. *AR*, 1916, p. 5.
47. *Chronicles of the London Missionary Society*, February 1881, pp. 40-41 and August 1912, p. 176.
48. H. A. Poppen, "Amoy Again Pioneers," *IL*, December 2, 1936, p. 12.

Chapter XIV

1. *Mission Field*, XXI, No. 9 (January 1909), p. 351.
2. Ibid., XXIV, No. 9 (January 1922), p. 220. See also the comments by Miss Mary Talmage, who at the time had served as a teacher in China for over 30 years. Ibid., XXXIV, No. 9 (January 1922), p. 227. Weersing's being sent to China as the mission's first trained educationist came about only after numerous requests to the Board of Foreign Missions. The choice was a good one. Educated at Hope College in Holland, Michigan, and the University of Minnesota in studies that would fit him for the work of superintendent of schools, he came to China determined to raise the standards and efficiency of the mission's educational program.
3. See pages 35-36, 118-119.
4. "Parochial Schools in the Amoy Mission," *Mission Field*, XIX, No. 5 (September 1906), pp. 178-180.
5. Ibid.
6. *Mission Field*, XIX, No. 5

(September 1906), pp. 178-180.
7. *AR*, 1920, p. 11.
8. Ibid., pp. 10-13.
9. Ibid.
10. *Mission Field*, XVII, No. 4 (August 1904), pp. 145-146.
11. Ibid., XXV, No. 10 (February 1913), p. 399.
12. *AR*, 1912, p. 36. See also ibid., 1910, p. 25.
13. *Mission Field*, XXXIII, No. 8 (December 1920), pp. 200-203.
14. *AR*, 1918, p. 27.
15. Ibid., 1913, p. 32.
16. Ibid., 1903, p. 11.
17. See pages 122-123, 137-139.
18. Abbe Warnshuis, "Opportunities in China," *Mission Field*, XX, No. 8 (December 1907), p. 294. Italics are by Warnshuis. Pitcher also stressed the need for a college. See ibid., XX, No. 3 (July 1907), pp. 96-97 and XIII, No. 11 (March 1910), pp. 446-450.
19. *AR*, 1919, p. 18.
20. "Talmage College Catalogue," 1935, p. 8.
21. Descriptions of his work in China are found in Henry Beltman, *90 Years with Uncle Henry*, (Garden Grove, Calif.: Robert Schuller Ministries, 1984).
22. "Talmage College Catalogue," 1935, p. 10.
23. Henry Beltman, "Emancipation of Chinese Womanhood," *CI*, September 1, 1926, p. 561. See also Edna K. Beekman, "A Chinese Athletic Event," ibid., October 5, 1932, p. 630.
24. *AR*, 1921, p. 18.
25. *AR*, 1906, p. 13.
26. *Mission Field*, XXI, No. 5

(September 1908), p. 182.

27. *AR*, 1915, pp. 20-21. See also ibid., 1918, p. xii.

28. *Mission Field*, XXXIV, No. 9 (January 1922), pp. 219-221.

29. *AR*, 1926, p. 2. See also Band, *History of the English Presbyterian Mission*, p. 440.

30. *AR*, 1920, p. 11.

31. H. P. De Pree, "Special Meeting of the Amoy Mission," *CI*, July 24, 1929, p. 474.

32. "The Chinese Educational Situation," *CI*, September 3, 1930, pp. 582-583 contains the main points of the petition and a translation of the ministry's reply. See also *AR*, 1931, p. 21.

33. See pp 7-9 regarding why Sun enjoyed such high respect among the Chinese.

34. *AR*, 1930, p. 16. See also "Opening New Pathways for God in China," *CI*, March 30, 1932, p. 195.

35. In 1936, for example, out of 240 pupils at the Changchow Boy's Primary School, nearly 80 came from Christian homes. At the Kulangsu school, the ratio was slightly lower (50 out of 200), but at Tong-an, the Livingstone Easter School had an enrollment of 137 of whom 70 percent were from Christian homes. *AR*, 1936, pp. 15-17.

36. *AR*, 1930, p. 19.

37. For the early history of the seminary see pages 134-135, 143-144.

38. *AR*, 1907, p. 36. For additional information on the failure of the seminary to attract more good students see the anniversary pamphlet of 1907, pp. 19-20.

39. Band, *History of the English Presbyterian Mission*, p. 294.

40. As quoted in ibid., p. 295.

41. *AR*, 1918, p. 29.

42. Ibid., 1922, p. 14. See also ibid., 1923, p. 6.

43. E. W. Koeppe, "A Class of Four Hundred in the Seminary," *CI*, June 24, 1925, p. 395.

44. For accounts of what took place as the three missions attempted to combine their seminary work during these years, see the various annual reports in *CI*, April 19, 1911, p. 250; January 7, 1925, p. 8; and April 4, 1926, p. 227.

45. "News Notes from Amoy," *CI*, January 7, 1925, p. 8.

46. *AR*, 1929, p. 5.

47. Henry P. De Pree, "Can the Chinese Preacher Preach?" *Mission Field*, XXIX, No. 7 (November 1916), pp. 294-295.

Chapter XV

1. *Mission Field*, XIV, No. 6 (October 1901), p. 195; *AR*, 1900, p. 19.

2. *Mission Field*, XIX, No. 2 (June 1906), p. 61.

3. *AR*, 1916, p. 16.

4. Ibid., 1915, pp. 13-14.

5. *Mission Field*, XVIII, No. 10 (February 1906), p. 347.

6. *AR*, 1911, p. 29.

7. See pp 160-163.

8. *Mission Field*, XXIII, No. 10 (February 1911), p. 382. Cf. ibid., XVIII, No. 11 (March 1906), p. 393.

9. *AR*, 1911, p. 32.

10. Ibid., 1940, p. 50.

11. For a description of the new

facility see "The New Tek-chhiu-khe Hospital in Amoy City" by the Reverend William Angus based on an interview with Dr. Bosch. *CI*, January 25, 1928, pp. 50-51.

12. Letter of September 13, 1930, written at Kulangsu by Dr. Clarence Holleman to friends in Cleveland, Ohio. *CI*, December 3, 1930, p. 795.

13. *AR*, 1928, p. 7. See also *CI*, August 1, 1933, p. 443. The term "Mex" refers to a unit of value that generally was about one-half the value of an American dollar.

14. *CI*, January 22, 1908, p. 55. It is interesting to note that Dr. Harold Veldman reported raising the hospital fee slightly in 1928 "on the basis that a more ready appreciation of the hospital services is gained on the payment of just fees." Veldman added, however, that the "needy" would not be turned away. *AR*, 1928, p. 23.

15. Ibid., 1921, p. 23.

16. Ibid., 1923, p. 12.

17. *Mission Field*, No. 8 (December 1920), p. 194. For additional discussion of the construction of Blauvelt Hospital see *CI*, August 20, 1920, p. 503; April 26, 1922, p. 268.

18. Ibid., April 4, 1923, p. 216.

19. Fahmy was accompanied by his wife, the former Susan Duryee, who with her sister Lily had arrived in China from New Jersey in 1903 to serve the Reformed mission.

20. For a lengthy tribute to Dr. Otte by his good and long-time friend, the Reverend Philip Pitcher, see "In Memorium—Dr. Otte," *CI*, June 22, 1910, p. 396.

21. For a lengthy tribute to this saintly man by one of his colleagues, Dr. Taeke Bosch, see "An Appreciation of Matthijs Vandeweg," *CI*, November 22, 1922, p. 743.

22. *AR*, 1911, p. 31.

23. Ibid., 1925, p. 5 and 1928, p. 22.

24. Ibid., p. 7.

25. Ibid., 1926, p. 14.

26. For accounts of the experiences of some of the foreign nurses who served the mission hospitals during these years see the taped interviews in the "Old China Hands Oral History Project" with the following women: Helen McGuish Oltman, Jessie Platz, Jeanette Veldman, Jeane Walvoord, and Alma Mathiesen Vander Meer. The last mentioned was born and educated in Copenhagen. In 1922 she went to New York for a year's nursing internship. While there she became acquainted with Margaret Fagg, widow of the Reverend John Fagg who had served in China in the late 1800s. On Mrs. Fagg's suggestion, she went to Amoy in 1923. There she met and married William Vander Meer. Mr. Vander Meer died in 1945 shortly after his return from Free China. Mrs. Vander Meer returned to China after the war and remained until 1951. She died in 1991 at age ninety-seven.

27. *AR*, 1923, p. 27.

28. Ibid., 1914, p. 14. Being called upon to do dental work was not

uncommon. In 1908, Otte reported pulling 189 teeth. *CI*, April 15, 1908, p. 249.

29. For a discussion of doctors being called on to give vaccinations as a preventive measure when plagues broke out, see the *Mission Field*, XXXII, No. 5 (September 1919), pp. 145-147; ibid., XXXII, No. 9 (January 1920), pp. 317-319.

30. *Mission Field*, XX, No. 5 (September 1907), p. 169.

31. *AR*, 1908, pp. 27-28.

32. Ibid., 1914, pp. 14-15.

33. *Mission Field*, XXX, No. 2 (June 1917), pp. 60-61.

34. *CI*, June 1960, p. 13.

35. *AR*, 1932, p. 15.

36. *CI*, May 4, 1910, p. 277.

37. *AR*, 1926, p. 20. For more illustrations of interesting cases and patients handled during this period see these accounts in the *Mission Field*, XIX, No. 9 (January 1907), pp. 326-328; XXVI, No. 8 (December 1913), pp. 275-278; XXIX No. 6 (October 1916), pp. 248-251; and XXXII, No. 9 (January 1920), pp. 342-344.

38. *AR*, 1902, p. 9. See also p. 16.

39. *Mission Field*, XVIII, No. 6 (October 1905), p. 210.

40. Ibid. See also ibid., XXI, No. 4 (August 1908), p. 140 describing a visit by the Reverend Dennis Voskuil to what probably was this same clan house.

41. *CI*, February 19, 1902, p. 115.

42. For descriptions of medical evangelistic journeys during this period see these accounts in the *Mission Field*, XV, No 4 (August 1902), pp. 138-141; XXXI, No. 5 (September 1918), pp. 255-258; and XXXII, No. 5 (September 1919), pp. 145-147.

43. *AR*, 1928, p. 22.

44. Ibid., 1929, p. 16. See also ibid., 1904, p. 15; 1917, p. 26; and 1919, p. 27.

45. Ibid., 1923.

46. Dr. M. Vandeweg, "Medicine and the Gospel in the New Tong-an Hospital," *CI*, April 26, 1922, p. 268.

47. *AR*, 1924, pp. 20-21.

48. Ibid., 1925, p. 15. See also ibid., 1918, pp. 32-33.

49. Ibid., 1929, p. 25.

50. For description of Holleman's capture and escape see *CI*, June 5, 1929, p. 353; July 3, 1929, p. 418; August 7, 1929, pp. 498-499; and the *Chinese Recorder*, Vol. 60, No. 7 (July 1929), pp. 473-474.

51. *CI*, August 7, 1929, p. 499. See also the *Chinese Recorder*, Vol. 60, No. 8 (August 1929), pp. 539-540.

52. *CI*, December 3, 1930, p. 795.

53. *AR*, 1929, p. 25.

54. Ibid., 1930, p. 15.

55. Ibid., 1933, p. 17 and 1934, p. 15.

Chapter XVI

1. *AR*, 1937, p. 14.

2. For an account of the fighting, see Poppen's letters of May 12 and May 25, 1938, to the Board of Foreign Missions (RCA,. 723 China Mission, Box 10, "Correspondence, 1931-1943").

3. *AR*, 1938, p. 16 and 1939, p. 12.

4. Statistics on the number who located at Kulangsu vary from 40,000 to 60,000. When the

secretary of the Board of Foreign Missions visited the mission in the early fall of 1941, he made the following entry in his notes: "One morning Dr. Holleman took me across to the island of Amoy. The island had a population of about 300,000, which has now dwindled to about 110,000 under Japanese occupation." Luman Shafer, "From the Traveler," *IL,* October 10, 1941, p. 12.

5. OI, Platz, pp. 17-18.

6. *IL,* July 7, 1939, p. 5.

7. For accounts of the refugee problem, see OI, Platz, pp. 17-22 and Poppen's letter of June 6, 1938, to the Board of Foreign Missions (RCA, 723 China Mission, Box 10, "Correspondence, 1931-1943").

8. *IL,* May 12, 1939, p. 12.

9. *Annual Report of the Women's Board for Foreign Missions for 1938*, p. 19.

10. *CH,* May 23, 1947, pp. 4-5. See also OI, Bruce, pp. 28-29.

11. *AR,* 1939, p. 11. See also ibid., 1940, p. 9.

12. "More Modern Methods," *CH,* December 26, 1941, p. 12. The title was obviously intended to be facetious.

13. "Word from China," *CH,* October 24, 1941, p. 13.

14. *AR,* 1937, p. 15.

15. Ibid., 1940, p. 10.

16. "Report of the Board of Foreign Missions on the Deputation to Japan and China, 1941," p. 14.

17. *AR,* 1939, p. 24. For a general discussion of Christian education throughout China during the early

part of the war see E. H. Cressy, "Effect of the War on Christian Education," *Chinese Recorder,* January 1941, pp. 5-9.

18. The seminary moved back to Changchow for a brief period in early 1944, locating in some recently repaired buildings on property that had been purchased before the war for the construction of a new union hospital. This property adjoined that of the seminary property. Because of uncertainty about Japanese war aims in the area, the seminary moved back to Eng-hok after a few months.

19. Students in good standing were able to avoid being drafted into the Chinese army, which probably explains in part the record enrollment.

20. Henry De Pree, "Back on the Job," *CH,* February 23, 1940, p. 10.

21. "Report on the Deputation to . . . China, 1941," pp. 16-17. For a general discussion of the Christian ministry throughout south China during this period see Carleton Lacy, "The Ministry in War Times," *Chinese Recorder,* May 1941, pp. 244-251.

22. *AR,* 1938, p. 19.

23. See pp. 309-310.

24. See pp. 241-242.

25. "Annual Report of the Changchow Union Hospital for 1939," p. 4 (RCA, 724 China Mission, Box 2, "Papers, 1856-1951"). For a general discussion of the wartime work at Changchow Union Hospital, see OI, Platz, pp. 24-29.

26. "Annual Report of the Changchow

Union Hospital for 1943," p. 3 (RCA, 724 China Mission, Box 2, "Papers, 1856-1951").

27. Harriet Boot, RN, was the daughter of the Reverend and Mrs. Harry Boot, missionaries in China from 1903 to 1940. Harriet later became the wife of the Reverend Walter De Velder.

28. For more information on the role played by the nurses, see Jessie Platz, "Nursing in Wartime," *CH*, February 23, 1945, pp. 12-13.

29. *IL*, September 18, 1942, p. 2.

30. Comments by Jessie Platz in "Report on the Changchow Hospital for 1943," p. 2 (RCA, 724 China Mission, Box 2, Papers, 1856-1951).

31. Ibid., for 1939, p. 5.

32. Letter from Poppen to Shafer, January 29, 1938 (RCA, 723 China Mission, Box 10, "Correspondence, 1931-1943").

33. Minutes of the Amoy Mission for May 16, 1940, p. 3 (RCA, 721 China Mission, Minutes of the Amoy Mission, 1918-1951).

34. "Report on the Deputation to...China, 1941," p. 18. For a discussion of the campaign on Kulangsu Island, see Edna Beekman, "The Centenary on Kulangsu," *IL*, November 7, 1941, pp. 12-13.

35. *AR*, 1940, p. 27.

36. *CH*, September 4, 1942, p. 7.

37. "1942 Mission Report," p. 4 (RCA, 720 China Mission, Mission Reports, 1936-1948). For another description of the centennial observance at Sio-khe see Angus's letter to his wife written October 14,

1942, *IL*, February 5, 1943, p. 17.

38. In making suggestions to the home board, the missionaries recommended the publication of a centennial history of the mission, which Angus agreed to write. The board unfortunately had other plans. "Our position," Angus was informed, "is that these long histories are not read by the people in the Church and that we have to get out something of a little more popular character. We are therefore issuing a pictorial history booklet which will be ready for distribution at the coming meeting of General Synod." Shafer to Angus, May 15, 1941, pp. 3-4 (RCA, 721 China Mission, "Minutes of the Amoy Mission, 1918-1951").

39. It is interesting to note that among these four young people, there were three—Mrs. Bosch, the Reverend Muilenburg, and Miss De Young—whose fathers were ministers, while the fourth, Dr. Bosch, was a son of former missionaries to Amoy.

40. For a discussion of the kind of training received at Berkeley, see John Muilenburg, "The California College in China," *IL*, February 26, 1943, pp. 7-8, and Joseph Esther, "We Prepare for China," *CH*, February 25, 1944, pp. 9-10. Some of the veteran missionaries had misgivings about new recruits learning Mandarin before coming to China, thinking it might prove a handicap to their later studying the Amoy dialect. For a discussion of this question see the letter by

Angus to Shafer, July 29, 1941 (RCA, 723 China Mission, Box 10, "Correspondence, 1928-1943") and by Poppen to Shafer, March 29, 1948 (RCA, 723 China Mission, Box 11, "Correspondence, 1944-1949").

41. *AR*, 1937, p. 6.

42. The return to Amoy of two families with five children would seem to indicate that the home board was not overly concerned about the Chinese situation at this time. On the other hand, when Elizabeth Bruce and Jeanette Veldman were returning from furloughs a short time later, they were advised to disembark at Columbo, Ceylon (present-day Sri Lanka), and proceed instead to the Reformed church's Arcot mission in southern India. Their stay at Arcot proved to be only temporary, however, and they soon resumed their work in China.

43. *CH*, February 21, 1947, p. 9.

44. An excellent account of what transpired at Kulangsu after the Japanese takeover is a 12-page report by Dr. Oltman. It apparently was written at the request of the American government. A copy is found in RCA, 724 China Mission, Box 2, "Papers, 1865-1951". See also *IL*, September 11, 1942, p. 4.

45. OI, Vander Meer, p. 18.

46. OI, Oltman, p. 20.

47. *IL*, September 11, 1942, p. 10. See also ibid., October 30, 1942, p. 13.

48. Pages 24-35 of "Narrative," a manuscript compiled by Alma Vander Meer in 1977 about her life in China, provides an excellent account of missionary life under Japanese rule at Kulangsu. A copy is found in the "Oral Interviews" collection under Vander Meer. See also OI, Vander Meer, pp. 13-23.

49. *IL*, September 11, 1942, p. 10.

50. Lorenco Marques goes by various spellings. It is today called Maputo and is the capital of Mozambique.

51. Dr. Oltman was not notified that he was to be one of the evacuees until a few hours before departure time. He had requested permission to stay and help look after the medical needs of the internees left behind. The Japanese had him classified as "Government Personnel" because of work he occasionally did for the United States Immigration Service in inspecting and vaccinating Chinese immigrants going to the Philippines. The exchange agreement between the United States and Japan was quite specific about the repatriation of government personnel. OI, Oltman, p. 21.

52. For an account of the trip to Shanghai and their stay there, see Vander Meer's "Narrative," pp. 33-34, and OI, Oltman, pp. 21-22.

53. Vander Meer, "Narrative," pp. 34-35.

54. For more information on the experiences of the evacuees see the following 1942 issues of *IL*: April 24, p. 11; June 12, p. 2; and September 11, p. 3. The following 1942 issues of the *New York Times* also contain general information: June 5, p. 6; June 25, p. 6; June 28, p. 9; July 30, p. 1; August 26, pp. 7,

18; August 27, p. 4; and August 28, p. 8.

55. *IL,* September 4, 1942, p. 5.
56. Ibid., June 11, 1943, pp. 8-9.
57. Ibid., December 17, 1943, p. 3.
58. For information on the arrival and reception of the missionaries see *IL,* December 17, 1943, pp. 3-4 and the following 1943 issues of the *New York Times:* October 14, p. 16; November 12, p. 10; November 27, p. 5; December 1, p. 5; December 2, pp. 1, 18, 24; December 3, p. 25; December 4, p. 14.
59. *CH,* February 28, 1945, p. 8.
60. Elizabeth Bruce, "Such as I Have." (JAH, Mss. 1971, W88-315, China Mission, Box 1).
61. For accounts of the work at Talmage during this period see "War Times Advance near Amoy," *IL,* March 28, 1941, p. 13, and "Christian Institutions in China," *CH,* May 11, 1945, pp. 13, 20, both written by William Vander Meer.
62. For accounts of these and other evangelistic tours see Angus's letters to the Board of Foreign Missions of October 3, 1944, and May 3, 1945 (RCA, 723 China Mission, Box 11, 'Correspondence, 1944-1949"), and short descriptions in the following issues of *IL:* September 4, 1942, p. 4; October 23, 1942, p. 12; and August 13, 1943, p. 5.
63. For a description of the first Youth Fellowship Conference see Harriet De Velder, "Youth Finds a Way," *IL,* December 25, 1942, pp. 16-17, 21.
64. For more information on the wartime evangelistic work of the missionaries in Free China see the files of Angus and Broekema in the "Old China Hands Project;" De Velder, *Across Three Continents,* pp. 20-34; and Angus, "Out of China," *CH,* August 16, 1946, p. 8. Broekema's file also contains interesting information on visits by American GIs who stopped at Tong-an to rest while traveling along the coast on secret missions aimed at finding information about what the Japanese military was doing.

65. De Velder, *Across Three Continents,* p. 29. See also *AR,* 1939, p. 9.
66. Angus to the Board of Foreign Missions written at Sio-khe, October 10, 1944 (RCA, 723 China Mission, Box 11, "Correspondence, 1944-1949").
67. Bruce, "Such as I Have," p. 24.
68. Pp. 3-4 of a 25-page mission report for 1945 written by Angus (RCA, China Mission 720, "Mission Reports, 1936-1948").
69. Colonel Otte was known to the missionaries for another reason too. He regularly sent American magazines and newspapers to Walter De Velder, many of which ended up being avidly read by other members of the mission as they were passed around.
70. For accounts of the departures of these missionaries see Bruce, "Such as I Have," pp. 24-28; *CH,* September 1, 1944, pp. 3-4; and De Velder, *Across Three Continents,* pp. 34-36. As events turned out, the rumors about a large Japanese offensive were not without

foundation. In late 1944, they undertook a major campaign that resulted in the capture of Kwelin and the driving of a wedge from Hankow in the north to Canton in the south, thereby cutting that area of China in two. The threat from the Japanese was serious enough at Changchow so that many members of the Chinese hospital staff as well as medical supplies were relocated in the North River district for a time.

71. "Report of the Amoy Mission 1944," p. 2 (RCA, 720 China Mission, Mission Reports, 1934-1948).

Chapter XVII

1. For a brief summary of Eckerson's life, see Luman J. Shafer, "The Man Behind the China Centenary," *CH,* September 4, 1942, pp. 7-8.
2. For the names of the Reformed missionaries aboard these ships, see *CH,* August 16, 1946, p. 7, and January 1947, p. 14.
3. "Tong-an Journal," *CH,* September 26, 1947, p. 4.
4. "China," *CH,* February 27, 1948, pp. 14-15. Hill also was struck by the unique form of river travel.
5. Letter from Shafer to Benes, editor of the *Church Herald, CH,* February 21, 1947, p. 21. Before going to Amoy, Shafer and Van Westenberg spent about four weeks visiting with Chinese religious leaders and attending interdenominational meetings at Shanghai and Nanking. A report of their

visit was later published under the title "Report to the Board of Foreign Missions of the Deputation to China September-December 1946," henceforth referred to as "Deputation Report, 1946."

6. Deputation Report, 1946," p. 9.
7. "Minutes of the Executive Committee of the Board of Foreign Missions" for 6/13/46, p. 2379. Henceforth referred to as "Executive Committee Minutes."
8. *AR,* 1946, p. 7.
9. "Narrative," p. 3. See also "China," *CH,* February 27, 1948, p. 14.
10. For a general discussion of the reconstruction problems see the "Deputation Report, 1946," pp. 24-29.
11. For a discussion of some of these sources of help see Angus's remarks in the mission's report for 1945 (RCA, 720 China Mission, "Mission Reports, 1936-1948").
12. *CH,* March 14, 1949, p. 12. It is interesting to note that the 60,000 cubic feet of stone came from the old city wall. Following a visit to Yamen (the local civil authorities) by Dr. Hofstra, the Reverend Poppen, and several members of the Hospital's Board of Managers, permission was granted for their use. *CH,* December 12, 1947, p. 5.
13. "The Ford and Us," *CH,* April 18, 1947, p. 23.
14. "China," *CH,* February 27, 1948, p. 15.
15. *CH,* February 27, 1948, p. 4.
16. Ibid.
17. "Are We One." *CH,* February 21, 1947, pp. 9, 28.
18. "Out of China," *CH,* August 16,

1946, p. 8.
19. Ibid.
20. *AR* for 1946, p. 7.
21. "Do We Face a Famine," *CH*, October 11, 1946, p. 6.
22. "Mission Report for 1942," p. 2 (RCA, 720 China Mission, "Mission Reports, 1936-1948").
23. "Deputation Report, 1946," p. 67. See also p. 46.
24. *AR*, 1948, pp. 6-7.
25. Letter from Poppen to Shafer, March 30, 1946 (RCA, 723 China Mission, Box 11, "Correspondence, 1944-1949"). Poppen was the mission's secretary at the time.
26. "Christian Opportunities in China," *CH*, June 13, 1947, p. 8.
27. "Life at Fukien University," *CH*, November 2, 1947, p. 14.
28. "China," *CH*, February 27, 1948, p. 15.
29. *CH*, September 26, 1947, p. 4.
30. "Sio-khe Branches Out," *CH*, September 24, 1948, p. 4.
31. Ibid., p. 45.
32. *CH*, May 23, 1947, p. 5.
33. Bruce, "Such as I Have," p. 30.
34 *CH*, May 23, 1947, p. 5. It is also noteworthy that Pan's being able to preach in Mandarin as well as in the Amoy dialect proved to be a boon because of the large number of soldiers (sometimes as many as 200) who were stationed nearby and attended worship services on Sundays. The number that could be reached in this way over a period of time was greatly enlarged because the soldiers were rotated every six months.
35. At the same time that CNRRA furnished the Tong-an district

with the truck, it presented the Changchow district with a Chevrolet staff car. "Executive Committee Minutes," 10\14\48, p. 2587.
36. Joseph Esther, "The Gospel Car on Four Wheels," *CH*, February 7, 1950, pp. 9, 29. See also Joseph Esther, "The Happy News Healing Truck in Action," *CH*, July 29, 1949, p. 9.
37. "Executive Committee Minutes," 6/30/47, p. 2470. See also ibid., for 10/13/48, p. 2587.
38. *CH*, May 23, 1947, p. 4.
39. "Opportunities for Service at Lengna," *CH*, February 18, 1949, p. 13.
40. There are several references to these endeavors in the "Executive Committee Minutes" for 1948.
41. Ibid., 10/14/48, p. 2590.
42. "Deputation Report for 1946, " p. 29. See also pp. 40-41.
43. "Mission Report for 1946," (RCA, 720 China Mission, "Mission Reports, 1936-1948").
44. "Deputation Report for 1946," pp. 38-41.
45. "Mission Report for 1946" (RCA, 720 China Mission, "Mission Reports, 1936-1948").
46. Demarest Romaine, "Building Operations in South Fukien," *CH*, February 18, 1949. See also Dorothy Poppen, "Recent Events in Changchow," *CH*, April 1, 1949, p. 4.
47. Walter De Velder, "Poe-tek Girls School," *CH*, March 24, 1950, pp. 4, 8-9.
48. "Short Term Schools in Home and Family Life," *CH*, May 5, 1950, p. 5.

49. *CH,* February 18, 1949, p. 14. See also "Executive Committee Minutes," 4/8/48, p. 2543 and 11/13/49, p. 2676.
50. *CH,* October 10, 1947, p. 4. See also *AR,* 1948, p. 8.
51. *CH,* September 9, 1949, p. 4.
52. Ibid.
53. Oltman's goals are explained in OI, Oltman, pp. 28-29.
54. T. V. Oltman, "One Hospital for Half a Million People," *CH,* February 18, 1948, pp. 16-17.
55. Ibid.
56. *CH,* September 30, 1949, p. 5.
57. Elizabeth Bruce "A New Post in Old China," Ibid., May 23, 1947, p. 4.
58. "One Hospital for Half a Million People," *CH,* February 18, 1948, pp. 16-17. See also Helen Oltman, "Opportunities for Service at Leng-na, ibid., p. 13.
59. "The Daily Witness of the Missionary Nurse," *CH,* February 18, 1949, p. 15.

Chapter XVIII

1. OI, Walvoord, pp. 44-45.
2. OI, Joann Hill, p. 22.
3. *AR,* 1948, p. 4.
4. The letter is addressed simply to "Dear Friends" (RCA, 723 China Mission, Box 11, "Correspondence, 1944-1949"). See also OI, Joann Hill, p. 22.
5. OI, Walvoord, pp. 39-40.
6. *AR,* 1947, p. 4. See also *CH,* January 7, 1949, p. 5.
7. OI, Broekema, p. 88. See also a letter of December 8, 1946, from Secretary Shafer to editor of the *Church Herald, CH,* January 10, 1947, p. 8.
8. RCA, 723 China Mission, Box 11, "Correspondence, 1944-1949."
9. "Executive Committee Minutes," September 15, 1949, p. 266.
10. "The China Situation and Our Amoy Mission," *CI,* January 7, 1949, p. 4.
11. "A Statement on the Situation in China," *CH,* March 18, 1949, pp. 12, 16.
12. *AR,* 1948, p. 3. See also n. 11 above.
13. Dr. Jack Hill, "A Letter from China," *CH,* September 30, 1949, pp. 4-5. The letter was written at Kulangsu on August 21, 1949, and gives a good account of the pros and cons for staying and leaving. See also a letter from Poppen to the board written at Changchow, September 7, 1949 (RCA, 723 China Mission, Box 11, "Correspondence, 1944-1949").
14. OI, Walvoord, p. 43.
15. The fighting between the Nationalists and Communists at Tong-an lasted only a few hours. Some of it occurred within a half-mile of the mission compound. The 35-bed hospital had about 200 casualties to look after. All were Nationalists, as the Communists looked after their own wounded. At Changchow, the fighting also lasted only about a half day.
16. OI, Van Wyk, p. 38.
17. Ibid.
18. OI, Vander Meer, p. 29. See also OI, Walvoord, p. 43; OI, Oltman, p. 32, and OI, Angus, p. 39.
19. OI, Bruce, p. 16; "Such as I Have," p. 34.

20. "Latest News from China," *CH*, November 11, 1949. It is worth noting that upon Holleman's resignation, the hospital was turned over to its first Chinese superintendent, Dr. C. T. Huang, son of Dr. David Huang, who was trained by and worked with Dr. Otte for many years. The new superintendent was well qualified to take Holleman's place, having graduated from St. John's Medical College and having already given sixteen years of service to the hospital.

21. "My First Days in China," *CH*, May 19, 1950, p. 5.

22. *AR*, 1949, p. 4.

23. Ibid.

24. *CH*, February 17, 1950, p. 7; February 24, 1950, p. 18; May 19, 1950, p. 5.

25. "Word from Leng-na," *CH*, January 12, 1951, pp. 4-5.

26. Shafer in a letter addressed to "Dear Friends," April 30, 1951 (RCA, 723 China Mission, Box 2, "Papers, 1856-1951").

27. Vander Meer, "Narrative." p. 45.

28. OI, Angus, p. 33.

29. OI, Walvoord, p. 54.

30. Ibid., pp. 55-56.

31. OI, Van Wyk, p. 43. See also Shafer, "Our Missionaries in China," *CH*, July 21, 1950, p. 19.

32. OI, Dr. Hill, p. 32.

33. Vander Meer, "Narrative," p. 46.

34. For a detailed account of the experiences that the Tong-an missionaries had under the Communists see OI, Broekema, pp. 53-56; a letter of April 6, 1951, from Broekema to secretary Shafer

(RCA, 724 China Mission, Box 2, "Papers, 1856-1951"); and OI, Dr. Hill, pp. 23-34.

35. OI, Dr. Hill, p. 30.

36. OI, Broekema, p. 59.

37. For accounts of what took place at Changchow Union Hospital after the Communists occupied the city, see OI, Walvoord, pp. 45-69.

38. OI, Oltman, p. 33.

39. OI, Walvoord, pp. 67-68.

40. Ibid., p. 60. See also pp. 66-67.

41. *New York Times*, December 17, 1950, p. 1, c. 2 and December 29, 1950, p. 1, c. 7.

42. Ibid., March 24, 1952, p. 2, c. 4.

43. OI, Vander Meer, pp. 28-29; Vander Meer, "Narrative," p. 47.

44. OI, Hill, p. 33.

45. The 1954 edition of *Who's Who in America* carries a 4-inch column in fine print listing the various positions held by Poppen.

46. OI, Walvoord, p. 73. According to Walvoord, Poppen had a "fiery disposition. He could flare up, but after his flare up, as far as he was concerned, it was done and forgotten, and everybody forgot about it."

47. For an account of Poppen's trial and the accusations brought against him, as listened to by one of the missionaries, see OI, Walvoord, pp. 73-83. See also Henry Poppen, "My Trial in China," *Presbyterian Life*, February 20, 1954, pp. 8-9, 37-38.

48. For an account of the travel experiences of the Van Wyks see OI, Van Wyk, pp. 45-55.

49. Bruce, "Such as I Have," p. 35. Alma Vander Meer and Jeanette

Veldman were planning to accompany this group, but Vander Meer's being hospitalized prevented this. As a result, she, with Veldman as her accompanying nurse, were allowed to go directly by ship from Amoy to Hong Kong.
50. OI, Hill, pp. 34-35, 38-39.
51. OI, Broekema, p. 70. The account of the departure of Broekema and Nienhuis is found in ibid., pp. 65-71.
52. The writing of an apology could also be an experience not soon to be forgotten. The Hills, for example, in writing an apology for "offending the People's Democracy of China" had to have theirs rewritten four times by three different individuals before the officer in charge finally found it acceptable. The experiences of the Hills in leaving China are found in OI, Dr. Hill, pp. 34-41.
53. Letter from Koeppe to Secretary Shafer from Hong Kong, May 18, 1951 (RCA, 724 China Mission, Box 2, "Papers, 1856-1951").

54. OI, Oltman, p. 22.
55. "Executive Committee Minutes," September 20, 1951, Volume 13, p. 2848.

Conclusion

1. The statistics are based on *AR*, 1923.
2. Abbe Warnshuis, "Where the Reformed Church is working in China" (RCA, 724 China Mission, Box 1, "Papers, 1856-1951"); *AR*, 1931, pp. vii-viii; *Chinese Recorder*, XXVIII, August 1897, 362-363.
3. James Thomson, e.a., *Sentimental Imperialists: The American Experiences in East Asia* (New York: Harper & Row, 1981), pp. 45-46.
4. *CI*, May 6, 1847, p. 170: *AR*, 1876, p. 7; *Mission Field*, II, No. 6 (June 1889), p. 20; *AR*, 1907, p. 3; Philip Pitcher, *Fifty Years in Amoy*, pp. 194-195; *CI*, September 1, 1926, p. 561; *IL*, August 12, 1938, p. 7.

Index

DATE DUE

☐